Red Sox Roll Call

ALSO BY WILLIAM F. MCNEIL AND FROM MCFARLAND

*All-Stars for All Time: A Sabermetric Ranking
of the Major League Best, 1876–2007* (2009)

Miracle in Chavez Ravine: The Los Angeles Dodgers in 1988 (2008)

*Black Baseball Out of Season: Pay for Play Outside of
the Negro Leagues* (2007; paperback 2012)

The Evolution of Pitching in Major League Baseball (2006)

*Backstop: A History of the Catcher and a Sabermetric Ranking
of 50 All-Time Greats* (2006)

*Visitors to Ancient America: The Evidence for European and Asian Presence
in America Prior to Columbus* (2005)

Gabby Hartnett: The Life and Times of the Cubs' Greatest Catcher (2004)

*The Single-Season Home Run Kings:
Ruth, Maris, McGwire, Sosa, and Bonds,* 2d ed. (2003)

*The California Winter League: America's First Integrated
Professional Baseball League* (2002; paperback 2008)

*Cool Papas and Double Duties: The All-Time Greats
of the Negro Leagues* (2001; paperback 2005)

*Baseball's Other All-Stars: The Greatest Players from the Negro Leagues,
the Japanese Leagues, the Mexican League, and the Pre–1960 Winter Leagues
in Cuba, Puerto Rico and the Dominican Republic* (2000)

*The King of Swat: An Analysis of Baseball's Home Run Hitters from
the Major, Minor, Negro and Japanese Leagues* (1997)

Red Sox Roll Call

200 Memorable Players, 1901–2011

William F. McNeil

McFarland & Company, Inc., Publishers
Jefferson, North Carolina, and London

All photographs courtesy Boston Red Sox unless otherwise noted.

LIBRARY OF CONGRESS CATALOGUING-IN-PUBLICATION DATA

McNeil, William.
Red Sox roll call : 200 memorable players,
1901–2011 / William F. McNeil.
p.   cm.

ISBN 978-0-7864-6471-5
softcover : acid free paper ∞

1. Boston Red Sox (Baseball team)—Biography.
2. Boston Red Sox (Baseball team)—History.
3. Baseball Players—Rating of—United States.   I. Title.
GV875.B62M324   2012   796.357092'274461—dc23   2011046534

BRITISH LIBRARY CATALOGUING DATA ARE AVAILABLE

© 2012 William F. McNeil. All rights reserved

*No part of this book may be reproduced or transmitted in any form
or by any means, electronic or mechanical, including photocopying
or recording, or by any information storage and retrieval system,
without permission in writing from the publisher.*

On the cover: *clockwise from top left* Joe Wood, Jimmy Collins, Babe Ruth, Dennis Ray, "Oil Can" Boyd, Ted Williams, Harry Hooper, Cy Young, Tris Speaker (center); background © 2012 Shutterstock

Manufactured in the United States of America

*McFarland & Company, Inc., Publishers
Box 611, Jefferson, North Carolina 28640
www.mcfarlandpub.com*

This book is dedicated to my great-grandchildren, Anthony James Kruger, Jamie Eileen Riley, Keira Addison Riley, Liam Thomas Riley, and Jianna Lee Kruger. May they all grow up to be loyal members of Red Sox Nation. And if Anthony happens to play for the Red Sox in about twenty years, and Liam plays for the Sox in twenty-five years, I will be there to cheer them on, in spirit, if not in body.

ACKNOWLEDGMENTS

Debbie Matson, Director of Publications for the Boston Red Sox, has been my saving grace many times during the past several years, providing me with numerous photographs of Red Sox players that added immeasurably to the overall presentation of my work. And she came to my rescue once again with photographs for *Red Sox Roll Call*. Mike Ivins, Manager of Photography for the Boston Red Sox, was also been very responsive to my needs, supplying me with additional photographs of Red Sox players, both active and retired.

I am also indebted to John Zajc, former Executive Director of the Society for American Baseball Research (SABR) and Nicholas Frankovich, former Publications Director, for their permission to quote from the SABR Baseball Biography Project. The authors whose works were quoted in this book include Doug Skipper, Bill Nowlin, Tom Simon, Dennis Auger, Andrew Blume, Mark Armour, Mike Richard, Hugh Poland, Ray Birch, Jeff Angus, Don Jensen, Mike Foster, Joanne Hulbert, Herb Crehan, David Southwick, Maurice Bouchard, and Frank Vaccaro.

Other authors whose works were referred to in the text include Hugh Wyatt, David Nevard, Mike Shatzkin, Editor of *The Ballplayers*, Jon Goode, Jeff Horrigan, Bill James, Rob Neyer, Sean Cunningham, Jeff Pearlman, David Jones, James Costello, Michael Santa Maria, Danny Peary, Bill Werber, C. Paul Rogers III, Mark Feeney, W. Harrison Daniel, Leigh Grossman, Stanley Frank, Hugh McGovern, Larry Claflin, Lawrence S. Ritter, Paul J. Zingg, Ty Waterman, Mel Springer, Shelby Peace, John F. Steadman, Victor Debs, Jr., Rich Coberly, Chaz Coggins, Tim Daloisio, Bill Mahoney, Albert Chen, David Halberstam, Ron Marshall, George Sullivan, Gary Gillette, Pete Palmer, Ed Rumill, Harold Kaese, Terry Householder, John Sayles, Dick Stuart, Mark Morgan, Gordon Edes, Cormac Eklof, John Thomase, Iris Webb Glebe, Robert W. Creamer, Donald Honig, Maury Allen, Ron Anderson, Craig Carter, Richard M. Cohen, David S. Neft, Milton Cole, Larry Edmundson, Ray Fitzgerald, Brother Gilbert, Harry Rothgerber, Joe Hoppel, Lloyd Johnson, Miles Wolff, Jim Kaplan, Daniel R. Levitt, Terry McDonell, Mike Miliard, Michael M. Oleksak, Mary Adams Oleksak, Jimmy Powers, Robert S. Redmount, Joseph L. Reichler, John Thorn, Nick Tsiotis, and Andy Dibilis.

CONTENTS

Acknowledgments vi
Introduction 1

The Players 3

Appendix 211
Notes 217
Bibliography 223
Index 227

INTRODUCTION

The Boston entry in the newly formed American League in 1901 was known as the Americans, but the team was also referred to as the Somersets after their owner, Charles W. Somers. When Somers sold the team following the 1902 season, they became known as the Pilgrims, a nickname they held until 1907 when they adopted their current nickname, the Red Sox. Over the ensuing 111 years, the Red Sox have been blessed with some of the greatest players ever to grace major league fields. Starting with Cy Young, the parade of legendary players continued with Tris Speaker, Babe Ruth, Jimmie Foxx, Ted Williams, Carl Yastrzemski, Carlton Fisk, Roger Clemens, Pedro Martinez, Manny Ramirez, and David Ortiz, among others.

This book presents the biographies of 200 of the greatest players, the most idolized players, and the most memorable players ever to don Boston red, white, and blue. The above named players are joined by such Red Sox heroes as Lefty Grove, Dwight Evans, Curt Schilling, Dustin Pedroia, and Smoky Joe Wood. They are all here, the legends, the World Series heroes, and the stars of the great pennant races of the last 111 years. Some of them, like Ted Williams, enjoyed long, illustrious careers with the Red Sox. Some of them streaked across the heavens for a brief period of time and then were gone, like Smoky Joe Wood, and others became legends as a result of one glorious World Series game, like Bernie Carbo, or even just one postseason time at bat, like Dave Roberts. But they all share one thing in common. They left an indelible impression on the minds and hearts of the members of Red Sox Nation, and they will always be remembered fondly and with reverence. The book also contains the biographies of two local heroes, Harry Agganis and Tony Conigliaro, whose major league baseball careers were tragically ended before they could realize their full potential.

THE PLAYERS

Agganis, Harry

Aristotle George "Harry" Agganis, also known as "The Golden Greek," was born in Lynn, Massachusetts, on April 20, 1929. He grew to become a legendary high school and college athlete in the Boston area, excelling in baseball, football, and basketball. After graduating from Boston University, he was drafted by the Cleveland Browns as the successor to the aging Otto Graham, but he disappointed coach Paul Brown by opting for a baseball career, saying, "I've already proven myself in football. I don't know if I can make good in baseball — but I have the confidence I can."[1] Harry Agganis was now a six-foot, two-inch, 200-pound sweet-swinging left-handed hitter, who had posted a .352 batting average in his senior year at Lynn Classical High School, and a .322 average for BU in 1952. His statistics, his all-around athleticism, and his popularity around Boston all convinced the Boston Red Sox to get his name on a contract. His first stop on the professional baseball ladder was a high rung, Boston's top minor league team, the Louisville Colonels of the Triple-A American Association. Playing under former Red Sox third baseman Pinky Higgins, Agganis played every game for the Colonels and hit a brisk .281 with 23 home runs and 111 runs batted in. Louisville finished in third place with a record of 84–70, but Agganis' contributions were recognized when he finished second by one vote to Don Zimmer of St. Paul in the MVP race.

It was obvious, from his achievements in Louisville, that Harry Agganis' minor league career was over, and he would have to prove himself at the major league level in 1954. His chief competition in Boston was Dick Gernert, a 210-pound right-handed slugger who had put 21 balls into orbit and driven in 71 runs in 139 games at first base in 1953. Agganis and Gernert battled head to head for the first base job during the early part of the season, but the competition ended when Gernert contracted hepatitis and was sidelined for the season after playing just 14 games. One of the most memorable days in Agganis' rookie season came on June 6 when he slammed a game-winning two-run homer in the fifth inning of an afternoon game at Fenway Park, hurriedly changed into his cap and gown in the clubhouse, and then drove up Commonwealth Avenue to Braves Field to accept his degree during Boston University's graduation ceremonies. The Golden Greek played in 132 games in 1954, stroking the ball at a .251 clip with 11 homers and 57 RBI in 434 at-bats. He also posted an excellent .990 fielding average and led the league with 89 assists.

Harry Agganis arrived at spring training in 1955, confident that he would begin to realize his potential with the bat. He fully expected to hit better than .300, launch 20 or more home runs, and drive in more than 100 runs. His competition in 1955 was a big, six-foot, four-and-a-half-inch, 200-pound right-handed bomber named Norm Zauchin. The new kid on the block actually won the first base job from Agganis, but after going 0-for-12 in the early going, he yielded his spot to the handsome idol of the female set. Agganis was hitting a cool .313 in 25 games with a .458 slugging percentage through mid–May when his world suddenly came crashing down. The pride of Lynn, Massachusetts, was hospitalized with pneumonia on May 16 and spent ten days in the hospital. He returned to the team in late May and left on a road trip with them. He went 2-for-4, including a double, in Chicago, on June 2, but later that evening, on the train to Kansas City, he started coughing and developed a high fever. He was ordered back to Boston for tests, and was met at the airport by general manager Joe Cronin, who rushed him to Sancta Maria Hospital. He was again diagnosed with pneumonia in the left lung, as well as phlebitis in his right leg. Based on the doctor's reports that he would be out of action for at least two months, the Red Sox put him on the voluntary retired list, meaning he could not play for Boston again that season. As reported by Tsiotis and Dabilis, "On the morning of Monday June 27, the doctors had decided to sit him up in a chair for the first time. As the doctors and nurses were lifting him up, he clutched his chest. "Oh, I've got a terrific pain in my chest," he said. A blood clot had traveled to his lung — a pulmonary embolism. Harry Agganis was dead twenty minutes later."[2]

Harry Agganis

The career statistics of Harry Agganis were modest, a .261 batting average in 157 games played, but in the case of Agganis, it was not about statistics. It was about unlimited potential unrealized, the tragic death of a young man who had just turned 26, and the loss of a revered local legend. Harry Agganis left this world in 1955 and entered the realm of myth where he will live forever in the hearts and souls of Red Sox Nation.

Almada, Mel

Baldomero (Mel) Almada became the first native-born Mexican to play major league baseball when he stepped on the green grass at Fenway Park on September 8, 1933, to face the Detroit Tigers. The 20-year-old center fielder batted leadoff, going 1-for-4 with a base on balls and a run scored, but the Sox lost to Detroit, 4–3. Almada, who was born in the coastal town of Huatabampo, Sonora, Mexico, on February 7, 1913, moved to California at the age of two when his father was appointed to the post of Mexican Consul in Los Angeles. The six-foot-tall, 170-pound athlete played baseball at Los Angeles High School, as well as with several local amateur teams, before entering professional baseball at the age of 19 with the Seattle Indians in the Double-A Pacific Coast League. Almada proved he was not overmatched in the rarefied air of the PCL by tattooing the ball at a healthy .311 clip with the Indians in 1932. The following year, he banged out 204 base hits while batting .323 and was called up to the Red Sox at the end of the season. He appeared in 14 games for the Red Sox in September 1933, batting .341 in 44 at-bats, with one home run. He split the following season between Boston and Kansas City of the American Association, batting .328 for Kansas City but just .233 for Boston.

Mel Almada became Boston's regular center fielder in 1934 and proved to be a fine defensive outfielder with above-average range and a strong throwing arm. Basically a line-drive hitter with outstanding speed, he was a respected leadoff hitter for his ability to see a significant number of pitches.[3] He possessed good baseball fundamentals, striking out only 33 times for every 550 at-bats while drawing 47 bases on balls. He was also an excellent bunter, a good baserunner and seldom hit into a double play. The left-handed hitter had a career year with Boston in 1935, playing in 151 games with 607 at-bats. He stung the ball a .290 clip with a .350 on-base-percentage, 59 RBI, 85 runs scored, and 20 stolen bases. His batting average slipped to .253 the next year, and he played in just 96 games. In 1937, after appearing in 32 games for Boston with a .236 batting average, he was traded to the Washington Senators along with Rick and Wes Ferrell, for Ben Chapman and Bobo Newsom.

Andrews, Mike

Michael Jay Andrews, a native of Los Angeles, California, attended El Camino College before entering professional baseball in 1962 at the age of 19. He began his career modestly enough at the bottom of the professional ladder, with the Olean Red Sox of the Class-D New York–Pennsylvania League, where he handled the shortstop position like a veteran and batted .299 in 114 games with 12 home runs, 12 stolen bases, and 62 runs batted in. His next stop, Winston-Salem in the Single-A Carolina League, was a little tougher, and he struggled to a .255 batting average in 39 games before moving to Waterloo in the Midwest League, where he found his batting stroke, producing a cool .323 average in 75 games. His subsequent way-stops on his trek to the majors included Reading in the Double-A Eastern League where he hit .295 in 139 games, and two years with Toronto in the Triple-A International League, where he hit .246 and .267 in 1965 and 1966 respectively. He played shortstop for the Blue Jays in 1965, but was converted to second baseman the following year, prior to being called up to Boston at the end of the season where he appeared in five games at second base, with three base hits in 18 at-bats.

Mike Andrews became Boston's regular second baseman in 1967, replacing George Smith, whose only full major league season produced a .213 batting average in 128 games. The six-foot, three-inch, 195-pound right-handed hitter was an immediate upgrade as he stroked the ball at a decent .263 clip in 142 games and showed outstanding range and a dependable glove in the field, finishing with a .976 fielding average. In the World Series that year against the St. Louis Cardinals, Andrews batted .308 and handled eight chances in the field without an error. He hit a pinch-hit single in the sixth inning of Game 3 of the Series and carried home the first run of the game for the Red Sox, in a losing effort. He went 2-for-5 with an RBI and a run scored in Boston's 8–4 victory in Game 6 but, like most of the Sox, he was shut down in the Game 7 finale. He had his two best years with the bat in 1968, when he hit .271, and 1969, when he hit .293 with 26 doubles and 15 home runs, but his erratic defense proved his downfall. He led the American League in errors three times, leading to his trade to the Chicago White Sox in 1971 for shortstop Luis Aparicio. Doug Griffin, a Gold Glove second baseman, took his spot in the field. Andrews played three more years in the major leagues, with Chicago and Oakland, before retiring.

During the 1973 World Series between his Oakland Athletics and the New York Mets, he made two errors in the 12th inning of Game 2, leading to three unearned runs in the Mets' 10–7 win, sending Athletics owner Charlie Finley into a frenzy. Finley tried to get Andrews replaced with a fake injury report, but Commissioner Bowie Kuhn saw through the ruse and had Andrews reinstated for Game 4. Andrews appeared as a pinch-hitter in that game, but that was the end of his major league career. He played baseball in Japan in 1975 and then retired. Manager Dick Williams was so disgusted with Finley's behavior that he resigned when the Series was over.

Aparicio, Luis

Venezuela has produced four of the game's greatest shortstops in the modern era, Chico Carrasquel, David Concepcion, Omar Vizquel — and Luis Aparicio. Aparicio was born in Maracaibo, Venezuela, on April 29, 1934. His father, Luis Sr., was his country's greatest shortstop during the 1930s and 1940s. "Little Looie" joined his father's team, the Maracaibo Gavilanes, in 1953 and, in November of that year, as reported by the Oleksaks, "The elder Aparicio gave way to Luis at shortstop, handing his glove over in a special presentation before the game. Aparicio Sr. gave his son a warm hug, sent him out to short and moved over to first base for a few games before retiring."[4] The 19-year-old defensive wizard quickly came to the attention of major league scouts, and he was signed by the Chicago White Sox the following year, beginning a 20-year romance with the major leagues. Little Looie spent two years in the minor leagues, at Waterloo and Memphis, honing his skills and learning a new culture. With the Memphis Chicks of the Southern Association, he batted .273 and led the league with 48 stolen bases, a sign of things to come.

Luis Aparicio didn't waste any time when he became the Chicago White Sox shortstop in 1956. He showed the American League what a world-class shortstop could do in the field, dazzling opponents with his exceptional range and strong throwing arm. According to *The Ballplayers*, White Sox manager Marty Marion, noting the cannon Aparicio was wearing on his arm, told him to play deeper to give him even wider range.[5] In addition to his fielding skills, the five-foot, nine-inch, 155-pound Venezuelan sparked the team on offense as well, hitting a pesky .266 and leading the league in stolen bases with 21, the first of nine consecutive stolen base titles he would win. He capped off his fine rookie season by winning the American League Rookie of the Year Award. White Sox owner Bill Veeck said, "He's the best I've ever seen. He makes plays that I know can't possibly be made, yet he makes them almost every day."[6]

Aparicio turned a good team in a great team known as the "Go-Go" Chicago White Sox. He and his fellow bandits stole 100 or more bases every year between 1957 and 1963, and they ran their way to the American League pennant in 1959 with Aparicio leading the league in stolen bases with 56 and shortstops in fielding percentage with .970. Aparicio played ten years with the White Sox during two tours of duty, five years with Baltimore, and his final three years with the Red Sox. Boston acquired him from Chicago for Mike Andrews in 1971 and he gave the Sox three stellar years in the field although his bat was growing cold and he was no longer the base-stealing threat of his youth.[7] He was a step slower by the time he played out the string in Boston, but he was still in a class by himself in the field with a dependable glove and above-average range.

Armas, Tony

Another Venezuelan appeared on the major league scene in the late 1970s and became one of the top sluggers in the Junior Circuit during the following decade. Antonio Rafael Armas was born in Anzoategui, Venezuela, on July 2, 1953, and began his professional odyssey with the Monroe Pirates in the Single-A Western Carolinas League in 1971, batting .227 with one home run in 31 games. He spent the next five years in the Pittsburgh Pirates farm system before being called up to the big club in September, 1976. The following spring he was traded to the Oakland Athletics, where his career blossomed. In 1980, the six-foot, one-inch, 200-pound right-handed slugger batted .279 with 35 circuit blows and 109 RBI. He tied for the league lead with 22 homers in the strike-shortened 1981 season, and was named the American League Player of the Year. The following year he hit 28 dingers.

Tony Armas was traded to the Boston Red Sox in a five-player deal on December 6, 1982, and took over the center field duties for Ralph Houk's club. The third-place Red Sox immediately self-destructed in 1983, falling to seventh place with a 78–84 record, but it wasn't Armas's fault. In spite of a mediocre .213 batting average, he made his 125 base hits count, slamming 36 home runs and driving in 109 runs, losing the home run title to teammate Jim Rice by three homers. The next year he had a monster season, batting .268 and leading the American League with 43 homers, 123 RBI, and 339 total bases. Boston finished fifth in 1985 with an 81–81 record and Armas had 23 homers and 64 RBI in an injury-plagued season that limited his playing time to just 103 games.

John McNamara led his team to the promised land in 1986, winning 95 games and leaving the New York Yankees sucking dust, five-and-a-half games behind. Armas, who continued to be hampered by leg injuries, was a non-factor in the American League Championship Series, going 2-for-16 for a .125 average as the Sox downed the California Angels in seven games. He had just one pinch-hit at-bat in the World Series, and was released on October 31.[8]

Barrett, Marty

Marty Barrett was, according to boston.com. "the sparkplug for the Boston Red Sox during the 1980s." "The thing I liked most about playing for Boston was that the fans appreciated baseball so much," said Barrett. "There is such a rich tradition there. They understood the game probably better than any city in the country on how it should be played. That's how I made my living, trying to play the game smart. It was nice to know they appreciated it so much."[9] The native of Arcadia, California attended the Arizona State University baseball factory before signing a contract with the Boston Red Sox in 1979. His spent his first year in professional baseball with the pennant-winning Winter Haven Red Sox in the Single-A Florida State League, where he hit .298 in 57 games. He continued to contribute with his bat as well as his glove at way-stops along the trail to the big leagues. In 1981, Barrett scored the winning run in the longest game in organized baseball history, a 33-inning, 3–2 victory for Boston's Triple-A affiliate, the Pawtucket Red Sox, over the Rochester Red Wings.[10] He split 1983 between the big team and Pawtucket, struggling with a .227 average in 28 games with the Red Sox, but hammering the ball at a .345 clip for the PawSox. He became the regular second baseman for Boston in 1984, a position he held for the next five years. He hit a strong .303 in 475 at-bats in his rookie season while leading the American League in fielding with a .987 average. The five-foot, ten-inch, 170-pound right-handed hitter developed into an excellent number two hitter, capable of moving a runner along with a neatly placed bunt or executing a hit-and-run. And his forte was making contact with the ball, striking out only 34 times for every 550 at-bats while drawing 50 bases on balls.

In 1986, manager John McNamara led his team to the Eastern Division title and Marty Barrett was a major factor in the team's success. He batted .286 with 39 doubles, 94 runs scored, 60 RBI, 15 stolen bases, 65 bases on balls, and just 31 strikeouts in 625 at-bats. He was sensational in post-season play, ripping the ball at a .367 clip with 11 base hits and five runs batted in in Boston's seven-game victory over the California Angels in the American League Championship Series. He also took home the Most Valuable Player trophy in recognition of his strong effort. "In the World Series, a losing effort against the New York Mets, Barrett tortured Met pitching to the tune of .433, rapping a World Series record 13 base hits in 30 at-bats, with two doubles and four RBI's. His 24 base hits in the post season is still the major league record."[11]

The following year, he once again produced both offensively and defensively, batting .293 with 15 stolen bases, and leading American League second basemen with a .988 fielding average. He hit .283 in 1988 and had a career-best .990 fielding average with just seven errors in 150 games. But that was beginning of the end for Boston's sparkplug as knee injuries proved his downfall. He played two more years with the Red Sox, appearing in 86 games in 1989 and 62 games in 1990, and then spent one year with the San Diego Padres before retiring. During his major league career, Marty Barrett was known as a tough out at the plate and a smart, slick-fielding second baseman with an above-average arm. He led the American League in fielding average twice, and in putouts, assists, and double plays once each. He also led the league in sacrifice hits three times.

Baylor, Don

Don Baylor was known as a money player, a clutch hitter who rose to the occasion when the chips were on the line. The big, powerful, six-foot, one-inch, 210-pound right-handed slugger joined the Baltimore Orioles full-time in 1972 as their fourth outfielder, taking over the left field position the following year. He played for six teams, including the Boston Red Sox, over the next 17 years, playing on seven first-place teams, three of which made the World Series, and one of which captured the World Series Championship. His greatest year was his MVP season of 1979, when he hit .296 for the California Angels, with 33 doubles, 36 home runs, and league-leading totals in both runs scored (120) and RBI (139).

Baylor's tenure with the Red Sox included all of 1986 and most of 1987. He served as the team's designated hitter, and he played a big part in Boston's march to the American League Championship in 1986. Although his batting average was just .238, he was tough in the clutch, hammering 31 home runs with 93 runs scored and 94 RBI in 160 games. In the ALCS, he stung the ball at a .346 clip with three doubles and a home run in 26 at-bats. One of Baylor's claims to fame was his propensity for being hit by a pitched ball. He led the league in that category eight times in 19 years, including an American League record 35 shots to the ribs in 1986. He also set the American League career mark with 267 hit-by-pitches.

Beckett, Josh

As reported in JockBio.com, "They don't grow power pitchers on trees in Texas — they raise them like cattle. The latest Lone Star stud is Josh Beckett. Strong as a bull, Josh has everything you could want in a hurler: deadly stuff, pinpoint control and a decided mean streak when he toes the rubber."[12] True to the report, Beckett was a powerful young man at 19 years of age, standing six-foot, four-inches tall and weighing near 200 pounds. He was blessed with a blazing fastball that topped out at 96–98 miles per hour, an outstanding curve ball, and a devastating changeup. He had major league scouts drooling.

Josh Beckett

He starred in Little League and he starred in high school. He was rated as the nation's number one high school prospect after going 10–1 with a 0.46 ERA and 155 strikeouts in 75 innings for Spring High.[13] Some scouts were turned off by Beckett's cocky attitude and arrogance, but that didn't deter the Florida Marlins, who signed him to a contract in 1999. Two years later he made his major league debut against the Chicago Cubs on September 4 in Pro Players Stadium in Miami before a houseful of screaming Marlins fans, and he thrilled the mob by pitching six innings of one-hit ball. Overall, his introduction to the major leagues amounted to 24 innings pitched in four games, with a 2–2 record, a 1.50 ERA and 24 strikeouts.

Josh Beckett was now a bona fide major league pitcher. But 2002 was a painful learning experience for the 22-year-old fireballer. He went on the disabled list three times during the season with blisters on his pitching hand, an injury that would torment him for years. In all, he spent 76 days on the DL. When he was healthy, he went 6–7 on the mound in 23 games, with 113 strikeouts in 107⅔ innings, while posting a so-so 4.10 earned run average. The following year, the injury bug struck again, but this time it was not blisters that did him in. It was a sprained elbow that put him on the shelf from May 8 to July 1. He returned to the fray in time to help Jack McKeon's club shock the baseball world with their brilliant play. With Atlanta well on its way to a 12th division title in 13 years and 10th in a row, McKeon, who had replaced Jeff Torborg with the Marlins floundering in fourth place with a 17–22 record, told his team just to go out and have fun. They did that, winning 74 of their last 123 games, and finishing second to the Braves in the National League Eastern Division. Beckett's contribution was a 9–8 mark in 142 innings covering 24 games, with 152 strikeouts and a 3.04 ERA. The wild-card Marlins defeated the Western Division champion San Francisco Giants in the first round of the post-season playoffs, knocking them off in four games. Next they took the measure of the Chicago Cubs, four games to three, in the National League Championship Series. In the World Series against the New York Yankees, the underdog

Marlins upset Joe Torre's mighty Bronx Bombers in six games, and it was the 23-year-old Beckett who put the last nail in the Yankees coffin with a sensational performance, "mixing his fastball, change, and curve with devastating effectiveness"[14] and defeating 21-game winner Andy Pettitte, 2–0, with a complete-game shutout that earned him the World Series MVP.

Josh Beckett was on top of the world, as were the Florida Marlins, but rough times lay ahead. After winning the 2004 league opener against the Montreal Expos, he ran into the blister bugaboo again and spent 60 days on the DL, finishing the season with a disappointing 9–9 record and a 3.79 ERA. In 2005, he was sidelined once again with a blister problem and later with an oblique strain, and he ended his season one week early with a sore shoulder. Still, he managed to start 29 games and pitch 178⅔ innings, good enough to rack up a 15–8 won-loss record with 166 strikeouts and a 3.38 ERA. Even though he now had nearly five years of major league experience, he still showed signs that he had not matured, occasionally trying to throw the ball through a brick wall in an attempt to strike out the batter instead of mixing up his pitches and keeping the batter off-balance. He also had concentration lapses, and problems with his location, that hurt him at crucial times.

The Marlins began to break up their team after the 2005 season in an attempt to control their payroll, and Beckett, along with third baseman Mike Lowell, was shipped off to the Boston Red Sox for prospects shortstop Hanley Ramirez and pitcher Anibal Sanchez. Both players were welcomed with open arms by the Red Sox, who were almost desperate to corral another championship. The cocky right-hander got off to a good start with the Red Sox, winning his debut, a 2–1 decision at Texas on April 5. Trot Nixon crushed a two-run homer in the top of the seventh inning to wipe out a 1–0 Rangers lead and give Beckett his first win. It was a historic day for the Red Sox for another reason — Jonathan Papelbon recorded the first save of his major league career. Beckett won his next two starts, but overall it was an up-and-down season for the big Texan. On July 24, he had a 13–5 record, but from then to the end of the season, covering 12 starts, he won just three games and lost six. He showed flashes of brilliance, but he was also hammered from time to time, once again trying to overpower batters with just his fastball, neglecting his other pitches, and suffering occasional streaks of wildness. The good news was that he did not spend any time on the DL, hopefully leaving his blister problems behind him. And when he was on his game, he was almost unbeatable. The bad news was that when he fell back into his old ways, he took a drubbing.

As 2007 got under way, the Boston Red Sox appeared ready to make a run for the brass ring. They had added a quality starter in Japanese ace Daisuke Matsuzaka, they had found a world-class closer in Jonathan Papelbon and a sensational set-up man in Hideki Okajima, they had a new keystone combination in shortstop Julio Lugo and rookie second baseman Dustin Pedroia, and they had a new slugging right fielder in J.D. Drew. With Beckett and Schilling and Manny and Big Papi and Mike Lowell, they looked like the team to beat in the American League East. Beckett was Terry Francona's choice for Boston's home opener, and the Florida transplant was up to the task. He took on a new maturity in 2007, using all his pitches instead of just relying on his fastball, and became a pitcher instead of a thrower, a strategy that allowed him to locate his pitches better. Beckett opened the season in Kansas City on April 4 and defeated the Royals by a count of 7–1. Three runs in the first inning, including a home run by budding star Kevin Youkilis, gave the Boston right-hander an early cushion. Beckett continued to overpower the opposition during the first month of the season, going 5–0 in April as Boston raced out to a big lead over the New Yorkers. He ran his record to 8–0 in late May, holding the Cleveland Indians to one hit in the first six innings, winning 4–2, increasing Boston's league-best record to 36–15 and widening their lead over the last-place Yankees to 14½ games. That was their high-water mark, however, as the team nearly collapsed in June, going 13–14 for the month. Beckett ran his record to 9–0 on June 8 with a 10–3 victory over Arizona, but then he went into hibernation for two long months from June 9 to August 4, posting a 4–5 record with a 4.05 ERA.

After the All-Star break, the Red Sox went

on a tear, winning 15 of their next 24 games, but by August 21 the lead was down to five games, and they were feeling heat from the Bronx on their necks. They lost three straight to the Yankees from August 28 to 30, with Beckett saddled with a 4–3 loss on the 29th. On September 14, Boston hosted Torre's New York club in another crucial series, and the Yankees took the opener in a slugfest, 8–7, as both Okajima and Papelbon were hammered. The Red Sox starter, Daisuke Matsuzaka, left in the sixth inning with a 5–2 lead but the bullpen let it get away. Beckett was Francona's choice to end Boston's five-game losing streak to the Yankees, and again he came through. Raising his record to 19–6, he stymied the suddenly woeful Bronx Bombers with one run over seven innings, and his teammates routed Chien-Ming Wang in a 10–1 laugher. New York took the getaway game by a 4–3 score, but Boston's lead was still a comfortable four-and-a-half games. They ran hot and cold over the final two weeks of the season, but finally clinched the American League East title on September 28 and celebrated their victory while awaiting their post-season opponent.

In 2007, Josh Beckett exchanged his mantle of a potential star for one that identified him as the ace of the Boston Red Sox staff. He finished the regular season with a 20–7 record and a 3.27 ERA. He also reduced his bases on balls from 74 in 205 innings in 2006 down to 40 walks in 200⅔ innings in 2007, while increasing his strikeouts from 158 to 194. Now, he was "the man" as far as Francona was concerned, and he was designated to start the American League Division Series against the California Angels in Fenway Park on October 3. It was no contest as Beckett held the Western Division champions to four hits en route to a 4–0 victory. The shutout ran his post-season scoreless streak to 19 innings, following his 4–0 shutout win against the New York Yankees in Game 6 of the 2003 World Series. The Red Sox starter fanned eight Angels and didn't issue a single base on balls in his dominating performance. "Beckett was as good as we've ever seen him," Angels manager Mike Scioscia said. "I don't think you can pitch better than that."[15] Terry Francona's charges went on to close out the Angels in three games.

The American League Championship Series against the Cleveland Indians opened in Fenway Park on October 12 with the magnificent Josh Beckett matched against Cleveland's ace, 19-game-winner C.C. Sabathia, and Beckett came away the winner in a 10–3 rout. The Indians roared back to take the next three games by scores of 13–6, 4–2, and 7–3, but Beckett came to Boston's rescue once again in Game 5, stopping Cleveland, 7–1, pitching eight innings and fanning 11. The Red Sox went on from there to win the series in seven games, routing the Tribe by scores of 12–2 and 11–2. Josh Beckett was voted the ALCS MVP after posting two victories in the series.

The World Series pitted the Red Sox against the National League champion Colorado Rockies. The opener in Boston matched that Beckett man against Jeff Francis. The Colorado southpaw had defeated Beckett, 7–1, on June 14, but this was a different day. Terry Francona's warriors jumped on Francis for three runs in the bottom of the first inning, sparked by a leadoff home run into the Monster Seats by rookie second baseman Dustin Pedroia. Beckett struck out the first four batters he faced, joining Mort Cooper and Sandy Koufax as the only pitchers to strike out at least four batters to start a World Series game. Cooper and Koufax each fanned five. The Boston ace pitched seven innings, fanning nine men against one walk, while holding Colorado to one run on six hits, and the Red Sox won another laugher by a 13–1 count. Schilling, Matsuzaka, and Jon Lester followed Beckett to the mound, and they all came away victorious as the Red Sox swept the Rockies four straight to win their second World Championship in four years.

Beckett had another injury-plagued year in 2008, finishing the season with a 12–10 record, pitching 174⅓ innings in 27 starts with a 4.03 ERA. Terry Francona's club captured the wild card spot in the post-season, yielding first place in the American League East to the surprising Tampa Bay Rays. In the ALDS, Boston topped the Anaheim Angels in four games, but Beckett's contribution was a five-inning, four-run, no-decision in Boston's 12-inning loss in Game 3. In the ALCS against the Rays, Boston's ace was raked for eight runs in 4⅓ innings as Tampa Bay defeated the Red Sox, 9–8, in 11 innings, in Game 2. He rebounded in Game 6, holding the Rays to two runs in five innings in a 4–2 Boston victory.

The hard-throwing Texan posted a fine 17–9 record in 2009 with four complete games in 32 starts, and 199 strikeouts in 212⅓ innings pitched, but he faltered in the ALDS, starting and losing Game 2 to the Anaheim Angels by a 4–1 score as the Sox fell in three. And just when he appeared ready to reclaim his spot as the ace of the Boston staff, injuries once again proved his downfall. He struggled through the first two months of the 2010 season with a 1–1 record in eight starts and a dreadful 7.29 ERA after yielding 29 runs over his last 27 innings. He was removed from the game of May 18 in New York after 4⅔ innings with what was diagnosed as a lower back strain and spent 65 days on the disabled list before returning to action on July 23 to face the Seattle Mariners at Safeco Field. He limited the west coast contingent to one run in 5⅔ innings with a no-decision in an eventual 2–1 Boston victory. The big right-hander ran hot and cold down the stretch, finishing the season with a 6–6 record in 21 starts with a 5.78 earned-run-average.

Josh Beckett bounced back in 2011 to record a 13-7 mark with a fine 2.89 ERA, bringing his eleven-year major league career record to 125 victories against 81 losses. Now the 30-year-old flamethrower is looking forward to an injury-free season in 2012. One he hopes will help to bring new Red Sox manager Bobby Valentine a coveted World Championship.

Bellhorn, Mark

The six-foot, one-inch, 195-pound second baseman enjoyed a ten-year major league career through 2007, and he achieved reasonable success with a modicum of talent. The right-handed hitter spent seven years bouncing back and forth between the minor leagues and the major leagues, but he couldn't seem to find his batting stroke in the big-time, his average ranging from .135 to .228. After hitting a combined .221 with the Chicago Cubs and Colorado Rockies in 2003, he was traded to the Boston Red Sox, who were desperate for a second baseman after Todd Walker, who had given them excellent second base play in 2003, left as a free agent.

Bellhorn played 138 games at second base for the Red Sox in 2004, and although he was erratic, both in the field and at the plate, he had some big moments in Boston's pennant drive. Overall, he batted .264 in 138 games with 17 homers and 82 RBI. Boston finished behind the Yankees once again, their 98–64 record leaving them three games out of first place, but they did qualify for the post-season as the wild-card entry.

In the ALDS Bellhorn batted just .091 with one hit in eleven at-bats, but in the ALCS against the Yankees his bat came to life in the clutch. He batted just .192 but four of his five hits were for extra bases. His three-run home run with two men out in the fourth inning of Game 6 paced the Red Sox to a 4–2 victory, and his home run in the eighth inning of Game 7 put the icing on the cake as Boston routed Joe Torre's charges by a 10–3 score. In the World Series against the St. Louis Cardinals, Bellhorn came up big again, batting .300 with a double, a home run, and four RBI in four games. In Game 1, he took a slider from Julian Tavarez and hit it off the Pesky Pole in right field for a game-winning two-run homer in the eighth inning, thus becoming the first second baseman in history to hit home runs in three consecutive post-season games.

Bellhorn played 84 games for Boston in 2005, but was released on August 26, subsequently signing with the New York Yankees. His Boston tenure was characterized by his erratic offense that included a .247 batting average and 286 strikeouts in 806 at-bats.

Berry, Charlie

Charles Francis Berry, a rugged 185-pounder, was signed by Connie Mack as a catcher in 1925 and played ten games for the Philadelphia Athletics that summer, batting .214 with one double in 14 at-bats. During the fall, he played professional football, playing end for the Pottsville Maroons of the National Football League and leading the league in scoring with 74 points. Charlie Berry concentrated on his baseball career after 1925, and he played in the Big Show for 11 years. Following his ten-game exposure with the A's, he spent the next two years in the minor leagues before being purchased by the Boston Red Sox in 1928. He spent four-plus years with the Red Sox when they were the perennial cellar-dwellers of the American League, finishing last three times and sixth in 1931. Berry shared the catching duties from 1928–30, and then became the main catcher in 1931. The six foot tall, right-handed hitter was a decent catcher both offensively and defensively. He had a strong throwing arm that cut down 47.5 percent of potential base stealers, more than five percentage points above the league average, and at the plate he put together seasons of .260, .242, .289, and .283, with decent power and run production. "Berry is also remembered for a collision with Babe Ruth that sent the slugger flying into the air. In 1931, during a game between the New York Yankees and the Red Sox, Ruth collided with Berry at home plate while trying to score on a sacrifice fly. Ruth was carried off the field at Fenway Park and taken to a hospital, and missed two weeks of play."[16]

Boggs, Wade

Wade Anthony Boggs is the greatest third baseman in Boston Red Sox history, and was one of the top major league hitters over the past 60 years. The six-foot, two-inch, 190-pound left-handed hitter was born in Omaha, Nebraska, on June 15, 1958, and was raised in Tampa, Florida, attending Plant High School and Hillsborough Community College. He was drafted by the Boston Red Sox in the seventh round of the 1976 amateur draft, and was assigned to their Elmira farm club in the Single-A New York–Pennsylvania League. Over the next six years, Boggs played with four teams in the Red Sox farm system, usually stinging the ball at a better-than-.300 average, but earning negative marks for his fielding. He was tried at every infield and outfield position in the minors without finding a comfortable fit. According to one scouting report, he had difficulty making the throw from third base to first base. Another report noted that he "cannot field. He has trouble both to his right and left. His throws are sometimes aimed."[17]

In spite of the concern about his defense, Wade Boggs earned a shot at a position on the Red Sox after leading the International League in hitting in 1981, batting .335 with Pawtucket. During his first year in Boston, he split his time between first base and third base, earning high marks for his fielding at third base where he had a good .967 fielding average with outstanding range. Thereafter, he was Boston's regular third baseman and worked hard at that aspect of his game until he eventually became a Gold Glove third baseman. In the early years, however, his bat did the talking. He hit .349 as a rookie, and followed that with a league-leading .361 average in 1983. He also chipped in with 44 doubles and 100 runs scored that year. Boggs went on to win four more batting titles over the next five years, with averages of .368, .357, .363, and .366. After he won his fifth batting title in 1998, it was noted that "With an easy left-handed stroke that sprays line drives to all fields, an outstanding eye for the strike zone, and a litany of routines that borders on the fanatical, Wade Boggs, the American League's perennial batting champion, has become a baseball anomaly, a player whose statistics are so staggering as to defy contemporary comparison. In the post–World War II era of declining batting averages, Boggs' .356 career mark through 1988 is the fourth highest in major league history, behind Ty Cobb, Rogers Hornsby, and Joe Jackson."[18] Reportedly, Ted Williams watched a film of the 18-month-old Boggs swinging a bat, and said his swing was perfect.

Wade Boggs was a meticulous batter who followed the same routine day after day, season

Wade Boggs

after season. He was known as one of the game's most superstitious players. He awoke at the same time every day, ate chicken before every game, thus earning the nickname "Chicken Man," took batting practice and ran wind sprints at precisely the same time before every night home game, took exactly 150 ground balls in infield practice, and drew a Hebrew word in the dirt before every at-bat. Boggs hit .330 in 1989, not enough to win the batting title, but it did give him one record. With his 205 base hits, he became the only player in the twentieth century to have seven consecutive 200-hit seasons. He did lead the league with 51 doubles and 113 runs scored. Boggs' 18-year major league career included 11 years with the Boston Red Sox, five years with the New York Yankees, and two years with his hometown Tampa Bay Devil Rays. He hit .338 during his Red Sox tenure, with 2,098 base hits in 6,213 at-bats, plus 1,004 bases on balls and just 470 strikeouts. He appeared in three American League Championship Series and one World Series with Boston, batting .322 in the ALCS and .290 in the World Series. He was a member of the New York Yankees World Championship team in 1996, and he led the victory lap around Yankee Stadium, riding horseback behind a New York City police officer, with his fist held high. Boggs reached a personal milestone on August 7, 1999, when he hit a home run off Chris Haney of the Cleveland Indians. It was his 3,000th base hit, making him the only player in baseball history to homer for his 3,000th hit. He knelt down and kissed home plate after completing his home run trot.

When Boggs retired after the 1999 season, he left a .328 career batting average plus many honors. He appeared in 12 All-Star games, batting .321. He led the league in batting average five times, runs scored twice, base hits once, doubles twice, bases on balls twice, and on-base percentage six times. On defense, he led the league in fielding average twice, putouts three times, and double plays four times. He won two Gold Gloves, the first one when he was 36 years old, and his fielding average differential to the league fielding average and his range factor differential compare favorably with the differentials of the great third basemen of the twentieth century: Brooks Robinson, Graig Nettles, and Billy Cox. Over his 18-year major league career, his fielding average of .962 was 11 points higher than the league average and his 2.62 range factor was 29 points above the league average. He was elected to the National Baseball Hall of Fame in Cooperstown, New York in 2005.

Boone, Ike

Isaac Morgan "Ike" Boone was one of the great hitters in baseball history, but his weak defense and his lack of speed relegated him to the minor leagues for most of his career. The six-foot, 195-pound left-handed hitter entered professional baseball in 1920 with Cedartown in the Class-D Georgia State League, the bottom rung of the baseball ladder, and he tore that league apart, leading the league in batting average (.403), base hits (117), runs scored (63), and home runs (10). He moved all the way up to New Orleans of the Single-A Southern Association the next year and led the league in both batting (.389) and triples (27). He hit .329 for Little Rock in 1922 and then destroyed Texas League pitching in 1923, leading the league in just about every offensive category, including batting (.402), base hits (241), doubles (53), triples (26), and runs scored (134).

Ike Boone played two games with the New York Giants in 1922, and five games with the Boston Red Sox the next year, before becoming the Red Sox regular right fielder in 1924. He out-hit and out-slugged most major leaguers, but once again his defense let him down. He batted .337 with Boston in 487 at-bats in his rookie season, with 31 doubles, 13 homers, and 98 RBI, while striking out only 32 times. The next year he hit .330 in 476 at-bats with 34 doubles, nine homers, 68 RBI, and 19 strikeouts. Unfortunately, he was a liability both in the field and on the base-paths. Over the two-year period, he stole just three bases and was thrown out six times. He was a poor fielder with limited range, and many balls that would have been caught by a decent outfielder sailed past Boone for extra bases. The big outfielder was up and down, between the majors and the minors four more times over the next seven years, but his Boston Red Sox career was over. He went on to have a distinguished minor league career for several years, primarily in the

Pacific Coast League. In 1929, he had a season for the ages, batting .407 for Mission in the PCL in 198 games with 323 base hits, 55 home runs, 218 runs batted in, and a professional baseball record 553 total bases. Boone led the International League in batting in 1931 (.356) and 1934 (.372). When he finally put the bats away for good, he left behind an all-time organized baseball career batting average of .370. If the American League had had a designated hitter when Ike Boone played, he might have compiled one of the highest career batting averages in major league history.

Boyd, Dennis "Oil Can"

The Boston Red Sox have had their share of characters over the years, including Steve Lyons and Bill "Spaceman" Lee, but none of them were more flamboyant and at times more irritating than Dennis "Oil Can" Boyd. The Meridian, Mississippi, native, who earned his nickname in his hometown where beer was called oil, was drafted by the Boston Red Sox in the 16th round of the 1980 amateur draft out of Jackson State University. Sent to Elmira in the Single-A New York–Pennsylvania League at the age of 20, he won seven and lost one with a 2.48 ERA. The next year he won 14 games with Winter Haven in the Florida State League, and in 1982 he won another 14 games with Bristol in the Eastern League, earning him a late-season call-up to Boston, where he pitched in three games, losing his only decision.

Oil Can split the 1983 season between Pawtucket in the International League and Boston, where he pitched in 15 games with a 4–8 record in spite of a decent 3.28 ERA. At first the Boston fans were amused by Boyd's appearance. He stood six-foot, one-inch tall and weighed a wispy 155 pounds, looking like someone in the throes of starvation. But he was cocky to the point of arrogance and he threw bullets. The fans loved the colorful right-hander but opponents were irritated by his antics on the mound, like pointing fingers and pumping his fist. He annoyed his managers, and his teammates were alternately entertained and irritated by his tantrums. In 1986, after he was left off the All-Star team in spite of an 11–6 record, he caused such a rumpus that he was suspended for three weeks by his team and ended up in the psychiatric ward at the University of Massachusetts Medical Center. In the 1986 World Series, Oil Can was supposed to start Game 7 but, when the game was rained out, manager John McNamara scratched him and went with his ace, Bruce Hurst. Oil Can sat down and cried.

On the mound, Boyd could be overpowering. He went 12–12 with the Red Sox in 1984, 15–13 the following year, and 16–10 in the pennant year of 1986. That year, he started 30 games, threw 10 complete games, and pitched 214⅓ innings with a 3.78 earned run average. He split two decisions with the California Angels in the ALCS, losing Game 3 but bouncing back with a strong effort in Game 6, winning 10–4. He was hammered by the New York Mets, 7–1, in Game 3 of the World Series.

Oil Can Boyd's career went into decline after 1986. He missed most of the 1987 season with a blood clot in his right shoulder, an injury that required surgery on August 21 and would plague him the rest of his career, sending him to the DL numerous times and eventually into early retirement. In 1988, he won nine games against eight losses for Boston, pitching in 23 games and, after being limited to just ten games the following year, he left Boston and signed with the Montreal Expos.

Dennis "Oil Can" Boyd

Bragg, Darren

Darren Bragg, a native of Waterbury, Connecticut, played four years of baseball at Georgia Tech University and was subsequently elected to their Hall of Fame, Class of 2002. The five-foot, nine-inch, 180-pound left-handed hitter was drafted by the Seattle Mariners in 1991 and sent to their Peninsula Pilots farm team in the Single-A Carolina League, where he hit .224 in 69 games. After two more years of seasoning, he finally delivered on his potential with the Calgary Cannons of the Triple-A Pacific Coast League, stinging the ball at a .350 clip in 500 at-bats, with 33 doubles, 17 home runs, 85 RBI, 112 runs scored, and 28 stolen bases. His performance in Calgary earned him a cup of coffee with Seattle at the end of the PCL season.

Bragg spent the next year and a half with the Mariners before he was traded to the Boston Red Sox for Jamie Moyer on July 30, 1996. He played all outfield positions in his two and a half years in Boston, playing primarily center field in 1997 and right field in 1998. He led the league with a .996 fielding percentage in 1998 and was a better-than-average defensive outfielder with average range. At the plate he batted .257 for Boston in 1997 with 35 doubles, 57 RBI and ten stolen bases. The following year he hit .279 in 409 at-bats with 29 doubles and 57 RBI. Overall, he cracked 302 base hits in 1,144 at-bats for a .264 batting average during his Boston tenure. He went on to spend another six years in the major leagues, playing for seven teams, before retiring in 2004.

Bressoud, Eddie

Eddie Bressoud was a dependable major league shortstop for 12 years, spending time with the New York Giants, San Francisco Giants, Boston Red Sox, New York Mets and St. Louis Cardinals. The 30-year-old shortstop, who first joined the Giants in 1956, came to the Red Sox in 1962 replacing Don Buddin. He was an immediate upgrade from the erratic Buddin, giving Boston some decent defense. The Los Angeles native had good range and a reliable glove. He also gave Pinky Higgins' team some pop with the bat. A six-foot, one-inch, 180-pound right-handed hitter, he learned how to hit fly balls in the direction of the famous Green Monster that hovered over the left fielder just 315 feet from home plate. Prior to joining Boston, Bressoud had averaged .237 in 1,242 major league at-bats, with just 23 doubles, 12 home runs, and 47 RBI for every 550 at-bats. His four years in Boston, however, produced a .270 batting average in 1,958 at-bats, with 115 doubles, 57 home runs, and 208 RBI. In 1962, he had his first strong year. His defense was as good as any of the top major league shortstops. He produced a .965 fielding percentage, higher than Dick Groat and Maury Wills, and he had better range than Wills. He also had 482 assists and participated in 107 double plays. With the bat, Bressoud whacked 40 doubles and 14 homers with 68 RBI. The next year he hit 23 doubles and 20 homers with 60 RBI, and in 1964 he continued his offensive contributions with 41 doubles and 15 home runs with 55 RBI. He also had a 20-game hit streak that year, en route to a career-high .293 batting average. Unfortunately for Eddie Bressoud, Rico Petrocelli's arrival in 1965 spelled finis to his Red Sox career. The 34-year-old shortstop went to the Mets in 1966 and closed out his major league career the following year with the Cardinals.

Brewer, Tom

The ace of the Red Sox pitching staff in the late 1950's was a six-foot, one-inch, 175-pound curveball artist from Wadesboro, North Carolina. After attending Elon College for one year in 1951 he was drafted by the Boston Red Sox and left school to join their farm team in High Point-Thomasville in the Class-D North Carolina State League, where he set the league on its heels, going 19–3 in 23 games covering 198 innings pitched with a 2.55 ERA. Brewer's rise to the top of the baseball world was interrupted by two years of military service during the Korean War, but he was back and ready to go in 1954. The 22-year-old rookie right-hander made his major league debut with Boston in Fenway Park on Sunday afternoon, April 24, 1954, and he was shown no respect by Eddie Joost's Philadelphia Athletics, who drove him from the box with one out in the fourth inning after he had been touched up for four runs on seven base hits. He bounced back from that outing to post a respectable 10–9 record in 33 games pitched, with 23 starts and seven complete games while pitching 162⅔ innings for Lou Boudreau's fourth-place club.

In 1955, Brewer picked up the pace, throwing 192⅔ innings in 33 games pitched with 28 starts, nine complete games and two shutouts. He lowered his ERA to 4.20 serving as the number three man on the Boston pitching staff, but even with the likes of Ted Williams, Jackie Jensen, Billy Goodman, and Jimmy Piersall on the team, they could not compete against the pitching-rich staffs of the Yankees, Indians, and White Sox. The Red Sox finished a distant fourth, 12 games behind the pennant-winning Yankees and a full seven games behind the third-place White Sox.

Tom Brewer had his best season in the major leagues in 1956, assuming the leadership role on the pitching staff and posting a career-high 19 victories against just nine losses. He was now strictly a starting pitcher, with 32 games pitched, 15 complete games, 244⅓ innings, four shutouts, and a 3.50 ERA. He was not just a one-dimensional player. Brewer was also an excellent fielder and a decent hitter. He led the league's pitchers in putouts while finishing with a .988 fielding average. And his 2.95 range factor per nine innings (RF/9) was miles above the 1.92 league average for pitchers. In 1956, Brewer was particularly dangerous at the plate, scorching the ball at a .298 clip with a triple, a home run, 14 runs scored, and 13 RBI in 94 at-bats. The next year, he went 16–13 on the mound, again with 15 complete games in 32 starts, with two shutouts in 238⅓ innings. He hit .202 with 15 runs scored and fielded .966 while leading the league in putouts and assists. And again his 3.21 range factor per nine innings far outdistanced the league average for pitchers, which was 1.99.

Brewer's career peaked in 1956 and 1957, and began to decline over the next three years, with his won-lost records slipping to 12–12, 10–12, and 10–15 respectively. But in fairness to Brewer, he pitched for a team that finished third, fifth, and seventh from 1958 to 1960, and he had decent ERAs the first two years. As 1961 arrived, Tom Brewer became disenchanted, and he retired after pitching just ten games, leaving with a 3–2 record and a 3.43 ERA in 42 innings. He was just 29 years old. His career marks, all with Boston, showed a 91–82 won-lost mark, a 4.00 ERA, a .207 lifetime batting average and a .967 fielding percentage. The handsome right-hander went on to enjoy a long career as the pitching coach for the Cheraw Braves High School baseball team. The popular Brewer was honored when the South Carolina school renamed their baseball field Tom Brewer Field and the town declared March 21, 2009, Tom Brewer Day.

Brunansky, Tom

The big, strong right-handed hitter from Covina, California, fashioned a 14-year big league career by his ability to hit the ball out of the park. Tom Brunansky began his climb to the top of the baseball scene in 1978, signing with the California Angels after former president Richard M. Nixon helped Angel's owner Gene Autry convince the 17-year-old high school graduate that his future was with the Angels. Brunansky was farmed out to Idaho Falls in the Rookie Pioneer League that summer, where he hit .332 with six homers in 190 at bats. He hit 23 homers with Salinas in the California League in 1979, 24 homers for the El Paso Diablos in the Double-A Texas League the following year, and 22 homers in 343 at-bats for Salt Lake City in the Pacific Coast League in 1981. The six-foot, four-inch, 205-pound outfielder received a late-season call-up by the California Angels, and he responded by sending three balls out of the park in 33 at-bats.

The following May, Bruno, as he was called, was traded to the Minnesota Twins. He went on to enjoy a successful six-year sojourn in Minnesota, helping Tom Kelly's team capture a World Championship in 1987 by putting 32 balls into orbit during the regular season and driving in 85 runs. He starred in the ALCS, batting .412 with four doubles, two homers, and nine RBI in the Twins' five-game demolition of the Detroit Tigers, but he was less of a factor in the World Series against the St. Louis Cardinals, hitting just .200 in Minnesota's seven-game triumph.

The Twins traded Bruno to the Cardinals the following year, and he hit 22 and 20 home runs respectively for the Cardinals, before being traded to the Boston Red Sox in 1990. He played the better part of three seasons with Boston, leaving as a free agent after the 1992 season. He eventually signed with Milwaukee, and was traded back to Boston on June 16, 1994. In 1990, he helped the Red Sox capture the American League East title by two games over the Toronto Blue Jays, hitting 15 home runs and driving in 71 runs in 129 games. He went just 1-for-12 in the ALCS as the Sox fell to the Oakland A's in four games. Bruno slammed 16 homers and drove in 70 runs in 1991, and hit another 15 homers with 74 RBI the following year. On his return to Boston in 1994, he hit .237 in 48 games with 10 homers and 34 RBI. His statistics with Boston over three-and-a-half years included 457 games played with a .252 batting average. Even though he had a low .245 career batting average, he also coaxed 770 bases on balls out of opposing pitchers, giving him a .327 on-base-percentage. Like most of today's sluggers, he went down swinging frequently, 321 times in 1,555 at-bats in Boston. Brunansky also contributed to his team in the field. He was a good defensive right fielder with better than average range and a strong throwing arm. For his career, he hit more than 20 home runs in a season eight times and more than 30 home runs in a season twice. He was selected for the American League All-Star team in 1985 en route to hitting 27 home runs and driving in 90 teammates.

Buckner, Bill

Bill Buckner was the type of player any manager would like to have on his team. He was a hard-nosed scrapper who gave 100 percent every time he stepped on a ball field. He asked no quarter and he gave none. Another Californian, he was drafted by the Los Angeles Dodgers in June 1968 and assigned to Ogden in the Pioneer League where he tattooed the ball at a .344 clip in 64 games while holding down first base. Three years later, at the age of 21, he joined the Los Angeles Dodgers on a full-time basis, playing in LA until the fall of 1976 when he was traded to the Chicago Cubs for Rick Monday. He played a little over seven years with the Cubs before he was traded to the Boston Red Sox for Dennis Eckersley on May 25, 1984. The six-foot, one-inch, 182-pound left-handed swinger put together three outstanding seasons in Boston beginning in 1984, when he hit 21 doubles and 11 home runs, with 67 RBI in 439 at bats. He passed a personal milestone during the season, collecting his 2,000th major league hit on June 27 in Baltimore. The next year, he stung the ball at a .299 clip with 201 base hits, 46 doubles, 16 homers, 110 RBI, and 18 stolen bases. During the 1986 pennant drive, hitting out of the third slot in the batting order, he hit a hard .267 with 39 doubles, 16 homers, and 102 RBI, to help John McNamara's team capture the pennant. In the ALCS against the California Angels, Buckner hit .214 with three RBI as the Sox prevailed in seven games, but he aggravated an ankle injury in Game 5, and was taken out of the game in favor of Dave Stapleton. The gutsy first baseman started Games 6 and 7, but was replaced by Stapleton in the late innings for defensive purposes if the Sox had the lead. In the World Series against the New York Mets, Buckner was replaced by Stapleton in the late innings of Games 1, 2, and 5, all won by Boston. He played all of Games 3 and 4, won by New York. It was only in Game 6 where manager John McNamara fell asleep at the switch, leaving the gimpy Buckner in the game in the bottom of the tenth inning with the Red Sox nursing a 5–3 lead. The rest is history, and Buckner was unfairly crucified when he should have been awarded a medal for playing on two bad ankles. There were other more deserving scapegoats than Buckner, notably Roger Clemens, who could pitch only 11⅓ innings in two games after winning 24 games with ten complete games during the regular season, and who asked to come out of Game 6 because he had a blister on his pitching hand, just six outs away from a World Championship, Bob Stanley, who wild-pitched the tying run home and put the winning run in scoring position in the fateful tenth inning, and Calvin Schiraldi, who was the losing pitcher in both Games 6 and 7, being hammered for seven runs in three innings.

Buckner was traded to California midway through the 1987 season, but he returned to Boston in 1990 to finish out his 22-year major league career. He played 526 games for the Red Sox over five years, with a .279 batting average. "Billy Buck" had 2,715 base hits in 9,397 at bats for a .289 batting average during his major league career. He hit over .300 seven times, and he led the league in batting once and in doubles twice. On defense, he led the league's first basemen in putouts once and in assists four times. In 1985 he set a major league record for assists by a first baseman with 184.

Buddin, Don

Don Buddin was born in Turbeville, South Carolina on May 5, 1934, and 18 years later he was drafted by the Boston Red Sox, who sent him to the Greenville Patriots in the Class-B Pioneer League. There he had what would turn out to be his best season as a professional, batting .300 with 25 home runs and a league-leading 123 runs batted in. Three years later, at the age of 22, Buddin was the regular shortstop for the Boston Red Sox. He was called the "cocky rookie" by some people, but his cockiness didn't help him on the field. He batted just .239 with 62 strikeouts in 377 at bats and, on defense, he made 29 errors in 114 games for a .953 fielding average though he did lead the league with 98 double plays. He spent the 1957 season in the minors, returning to the Red Sox the following year, but he didn't fare much better the second time around. Batting mainly in the leadoff position, he hit .237 with 74 runs scored in 497 at-bats, and no stolen bases. He led the league in double plays again, this time with 102, but he also led the league in errors with 31. The Fenway Park fans began to heckle the erratic shortstop about this time, calling him "Bootsie" Buddin. The five-foot, 11-inch, 178-pound shortstop could go to his right or left satisfactorily, but he seemed to be mesmerized by balls hit directly at him, and the fans would groan because they knew what was about to happen.

Things didn't get any better for Buddin over his last three years with the team. His batting average went from .241 to .263, his fielding average ranged from .949 to .956, and his errors ranged from 23 to 35, the last figure leading the league in 1959. The Red Sox management finally traded their erratic shortstop to the Houston Colt 45s for Eddie Bressoud on November 26, 1961.

Burks, Ellis

He was an outstanding high school athlete that Minnesota Twins manager Tom Kelly once referred to as a future MVP. Ellis Burks may never have been selected as an MVP but he had a notable major league career that covered 18 years with five teams. He was drafted by the Boston Red Sox after graduating from high school in 1983, and was sent to Elmira in the Single-A New York–Pennsylvania League for

Ellis Burks

seasoning. The six-foot, two-inch, 188-pound right-handed hitter struggled at the plate in Elmira, batting .241 in 53 games, but the next year, with Winter Haven in the Florida State League, he increased his batting average 15 points to .256 and stole 29 bases in 112 games. He spent the 1985 and '86 seasons with New Britain in the Double-A Eastern League, batting .254 and .273 respectively. He showed some signs of power in his bat with New Britain, slamming 10 homers in 1985 and 14 the following year. He also flashed his speed on the bases, stealing 17 bases in '85 and 31 bases in '86.

In 1987, Ellis Burks was installed as the Boston Red Sox's regular center fielder, and the 22-year-old greyhound immediately became a fan favorite. He stroked the ball at a surprising .272 clip in 133 games and 558 at bats, with 94 runs scored, 30 doubles, 20 home runs, 59 RBI, and 27 stolen bases. He was just the third player in Boston Red Sox history to hit 20 home runs and steal 20 bases in the same year, the others being Carl Yastrzemski and Jackie Jensen. He also proved to be one of the best center fielders in the American League, with outstanding range, a reliable glove, and a strong but erratic throwing arm. He led the American League in assists with 15 that year and was named to the All-Rookie team. The next year, he ignored the sophomore jinx, batting .294 with 37 doubles, 18 homers, 92 RBI, and 25 stolen bases.

The chink in Burks' armor reared its ugly head in 1989. Boston's star center fielder was injury-prone. He got off the mark quickly and was hitting .280 on June 15 when he was shut down with a bad shoulder that required surgery. The injury kept him on the shelf for 47 days while the Red Sox struggled to stay in the pennant race. When he returned on August 1, they were in second place, just three games behind division leader Baltimore. Burks stung the ball at a .337 clip over the next five weeks before another injury ended his season and Boston couldn't grab the brass ring, finishing the season in third place with 83 wins against 79 losses, six games behind the Toronto Blue Jays. Burks finished the season with a .303 batting average in 399 at bats with 12 homers and 21 stolen bases. Over the years, Burks would lose time on the DL with back problems, bad knees, and other miscellaneous ailments.

Burks bounced back to play 150 games in 1990, but over his last 14 years, he would play over 150 games just once more, 140 or more games three times, and 120 or more games eight times. He had the perfect blend of speed and power and he gave 100 percent every time he stepped on a ball field, but his aggressive attitude led to his many injuries. Those injuries maddened teammates, fans, and managers alike, but to Burks it was just a product of playing good, hard baseball. "They're all baseball injuries, it's not like I got hurt falling out of the damn bed," he told newspaper reporters in 1999."[19]

Ellis Burks had a big season with the Red Sox in 1990, batting .296 with 33 doubles, 21 homers, and 89 RBI but, hobbled by injuries, he stole just nine bases in 20 attempts. His playing time declined over his last two years in Boston, to 130 games in 1991 and 66 games the following year. The Red Sox released him after the 1992 season and he went on to play 12 more years in the majors, five with the Colorado Rockies, before returning to Boston to close out his active playing career in 2004. The rarefied air in Denver worked wonders on Burks' offensive productivity. He had a career year in 1996, playing in 156 games with 613 at bats and 211 base hits, good for a .344 batting average. He led the league in runs scored with 142, ripped 45 doubles and 40 home runs, drove in 128 runs, and stole 32 bases. He returned to Boston in 2004, playing in just 11 games with 33 at-bats. He did not play in the post-season, but he was still a member of the miracle team that ended "The Curse of the Bambino," and he won his World Series ring, a fitting end to an outstanding career.

Burleson, Rick

He was called aggressive, scrappy, hard working, and intense, and his nickname, "Rooster," says it all. Rick Burleson was a hustler who was considered one of the best defensive shortstops in Boston Red Sox history. He had outstanding range, a strong throwing arm, and a sure glove. He led the league in fielding in 1979 with an average of .980, earning a Gold Glove. He led the league in putouts three times, assists and double plays twice each, and triple plays once. He set a major league record for the most double plays by a shortstop in a season, 147 in 1980, and he set a major league record for most assists in a game, with 15 in a 20-inning game with California in 1982. He also holds the Red

Rick Burleson

Sox record for the most double plays by a shortstop in a career with 827. Rooster was named to four American League All-Star teams and played in three games.

Richard Paul Burleson was born in Lynwood, California, on April 29, 1951. The Boston Red Sox signed the 19-year-old to a contract in 1970 and sent him to their farm team in Winter Haven, Florida, where he played 118 games at shortstop and batted .220. The five-foot, ten-inch, 165-pound right-handed hitter played his way up the minor league ladder over the next three years, refining his skills and continuing to dazzle the fans with his defensive play.

After playing ten games with Pawtucket in 1974 and spanking the ball at a .341 clip, Rick Burleson was called up to the big club. His debut, on May 4, was a day Burleson would rather forget. Playing in front of the home crowd, he went hitless in two at-bats and committed three errors. Once he settled in, however, he showed the Red Sox faithful how shortstop should be played. He played with enthusiasm, ranged far and wide for balls that had gone through for base hits in other seasons, and gunned down surprised batters with boring regularity. More than that, he showed unexpected power and consistency at the plate, hitting a robust .284 with 22 doubles in 384 at-bats. The next year, with more confidence, and with a year's experience in the majors under his belt, he quickly became a fan favorite with his quickness and his aggressiveness. He helped stabilize the Boston defense and was a major factor in their successful pennant run. In the American League Championship Series against the Oakland Athletics, Burleson ripped A's pitching for a .444 average with two doubles, an RBI, and two runs scored in Boston's three-game sweep. Against the Cincinnati Reds in the World Series, he hit .292 with seven hits in seven games, including a double and two RBI. In the opening game of the Series, Rooster went three-for-three with an RBI as Boston coasted, 6–0. In Game 4, won by Boston 5–4, he had a double and an RBI in four at-bats.

Burleson gave Boston five more years of sterling shortstop play, hitting between .273 and .291, except for 1978 when his average slipped to .248. He was an All-Star from 1977 to 1979 and again in 1981. Yet Boston management shocked Red Sox Nation by trading their popular shortstop to the California Angels for Carney Lansford. "I was disappointed to be traded from Boston after being there for seven years and basically in my prime," said Burleson. "I turned 30 that year and they traded (Fred) Lynn, myself and let Fisk go."[20] Burleson's time with California was less than satisfactory. His five years with the Angels were interrupted by frequent rotator cuff injuries and he was released after the 1986 season. He played one more year, with the Baltimore Orioles, batting .208, and then retired. He was selected for the Boston Red Sox Hall of Fame in 2002.

Burns, George

George Burns was a hard-hitting first baseman whose bat kept him in the major leagues. He had good range in the field, but his glove was questionable as he led American League first basemen in errors four times during his 16-year career. The six-foot, one-half-inch, 180-pound right-handed hitter came out of Niles, Ohio, in 1913 at the age of 20 to rap the ball at a .338 clip for Burlington and Ottumwa in the Class-D Central Association. His batting performance brought about his sale to the Detroit Tigers, who sent him to their farm club in Sioux City of the Single-A Western League where he continued to scorch the ball, leading to his recall by the Tigers near the end of the season, although he didn't get into any games in Detroit.

He played for the Tigers for four years, batting between .226 and .291, and then was traded to the Philadelphia Athletics where he exploded at the plate, hammering the ball at a .352 clip in 1918, finishing second in the league to Ty Cobb's .382, and he led the league with 178 base hits, 236 total bases, and eight hit-by-pitches. He sparkled on defense as well, leading all first basemen with 104 assists and 109 double plays. He moved on to Cleveland in 1919 and helped Tris Speaker's team win the World Championship the following year. The year 1922 found him wearing a Boston Red Sox uniform after a trade for Stuffy McInnis, and he gave the Red Sox two good years with the bat, rattling the Fenway fences to the tune of .306 in 1922 and .328 the following year. The line-drive hitter quickly found the gaps in the outfield, as well as the short left field wall, during his stay in Boston and hit 79 doubles in his two season with the Red Sox. In 1923, he got the first hit ever in the newly constructed Yankee Stadium, and later in the year he turned in an unassisted triple play, the first by a first baseman in major league history.[21] Boston traded him back to Cleveland in 1924 and he played another six years before age caught up with him. George Burns ended his career with the Philadelphia Athletics in 1929, having accumulated 2,018 base hits, good for a .307 career batting average. While with Philadelphia, he participated in the famous ten-run rally in the seventh inning of Game 4 of the 1929 World Series that brought the A's back from an 8–0 deficit to a 10–8 victory. Burns pinch-hit in the inning and batted twice, going 0 for 2.

Carbo, Bernie

He was originally drafted by the Cincinnati Reds in the 1965 amateur draft ahead of Johnny Bench, but he never realized his full potential. He spent 12 years in the major leagues as a journeyman outfielder, playing more than 100 games in only half of them, and only once playing more than 118 games in a season. Bernardo "Bernie"

Bernie Carbo

Carbo, who was born in Detroit, Michigan, on August 5, 1947, was farmed out to Tampa in the Florida State League after he was drafted, hitting a barely visible .218 in 71 games. He bounced around in the minors for another four years before he got his chance with the big club, and he earned that chance by leading the American Association in doubles (37) and batting (.359) with the Indianapolis Indians. When he finally broke through in 1970, he made Cincinnati management sit up and take notice. Playing in 125 games, he was named the Rookie of the Year by *The Sporting News* ripping the ball at a .310 clip with 21 homers and 63 RBI. Unfortunately, the sophomore jinx jumped up and bit him the next year, his average tumbled to .219, and his home run output fell to five. Sparky Anderson, who had Bobby Tolan sitting in the wings, quickly shipped Carbo off to St. Louis where he spent the next two years in relative obscurity.

He was rescued by the Boston Red Sox in 1974 when he was acquired in exchange for Reggie Smith. He played a total of five years with Boston in two tours of duty. His first tenure with Boston, from 1974 to early 1976, included the 1975 World Series that made him a Red Sox legend. He played 117 games with the Red Sox in 1974, including 94 games as part of a four-man outfield rotation that included Juan Beniquez, Dwight Evans, and Tommy Harper. Carbo hit a modest .249 for the year but he put 12 balls into orbit and drove in 61 runs in 338 at bats. The next year was a pennant year in Boston as the Red Sox won the Eastern Division title by four-and-a-half games over Baltimore, and Carbo was an important cog in the championship machinery by hitting .257 with 15 homers and 50 RBI in 319 at-bats. He didn't play in the three-game sweep of the Oakland Athletics in the ALCS, but he was one of the more famous players to emerge from the World Series against the Cincinnati Reds. He appeared in four games in the Series, batting .429 with three hits, two of them pinch-hit home runs. He came off the bench in the seventh inning of Game 3, an eventual ten-inning loss, and drove a pitch by right-hander Clay Carroll into the lower left field seats at Crosley Field. One week later, in Game 6, Bernie Carbo became an instant legend. Batting in the bottom of the eighth inning, with Sparky Anderson's team holding a comfortable 6–3 lead, he stepped to the plate with two men on base, two outs, and Cincinnati's fireman, Rawley Eastwick, on the mound. He looked hopelessly overmatched against Eastwick while waving feebly at a 2–2 pitch and barely fouling it off. But on the next pitch, he got his revenge, jumping on an Eastwick fastball and drilling it into the center field bleachers for a game-tying home run. As he rounded third base, he yelled to former teammate Pete Rose, "Hey Pete, don't you wish you were that strong?" to which Rose replied, "This is fun." Carlton Fisk's dramatic foul-pole homer eventually won the game four innings later.

A Boston favorite, he was traded to Milwaukee 18 games into the 1976 season, but returned to Boston the following year. He batted .289 with 15 homers and 34 RBI in 228 at-bats for the Red Sox in 1977, and in June 1978 was discarded again, this time in a sale to Cleveland. Carbo's pal Bill Lee sounded off about the deal, claiming that Carbo was "the best tenth man in baseball."[22] Lee himself was gone a year later. Bernie Carbo retired from the game in 1980 after an interesting 12-year career.

Carrigan, Bill

A native of Maine and a baseball star at Holy Cross, Bill Carrigan was nicknamed "Rough" for obvious reasons. He was a stocky five-foot, ten-inch, 185-pound backstop in the mold of give no quarter and ask none. He joined the Red Sox in 1906 at the age of 22, but after hitting just .211 he was loaned to Toronto of the Eastern League to refine his skills. He not only developed as a defensive catcher in Toronto, he also stung the ball at a .319 clip, and returned to Boston the following year. Catchers in the early days of the game were coveted for their defensive prowess, such as handling a pitching staff, calling a game, blocking the plate, minimizing passed balls and wild pitches, and gunning down prospective base stealers. The top catchers of the day had a caught-stealing percentage in the 45 percent range, and Carrigan nailed his 45 percent.

He played with the Red Sox from 1906 through 1916 and was the regular catcher from 1909 through 1914, serving as the team's backup catcher the other five years. He batted .235, .296, .249, .289, and .263 between 1908 and 1912. He batted only seven times in the 1912 World Series, going hitless in as Hick Cady handled the catching chores in Boston's eight-game World Championship triumph. The 29-year-old catcher was promoted to player-manager midway through the 1913 season, replacing Jake Stahl who was fired when the team was floundering in fifth place with a 39–41 won-lost record. Carrigan did a fine job turning the team around, winning 40 of the remaining 70 games and going 91–62 the following year to finish in second place, eight-and-a-half games behind the pennant-winning Philadelphia Athletics. The Down-Easter batted .242 in 87 games in 1913 and .253 in 82 games the following year, in addition to guiding the team from the bench.

Bill Carrigan worked his managing magic in 1915 and 1916, winning the World Series both years. In 1915, he played in just 46 games, batting .200, but he brought the team home first with a 101–50 record, and in the World Series he took the measure of the Philadelphia Phillies in five games. The following year he played in 33 games with a .270 average, and his team won the American League pennant again with a 91–63 record and defeated the Brooklyn Robins in the World Series, also in five games. He had just five at-bats total in the two Series, with two hits and one RBI.

Bill "Rough" Carrigan retired from baseball after the 1916 season to become a banker in Maine, but his separation from the game he loved was more than he could handle, and he returned to manage one more time, from 1927 through 1929. He should have stayed in Maine as the Red Sox finished last every year. Carrigan's career totals with Boston were 709 games played with 1,970 at-bats and 506 base hits for a .257 batting average. He was one of the best defensive catchers of his day, leading the league in fielding average twice and in putouts once. He also had a seven-year managerial record of 489–500.

Chapman, Ben

As noted in *Red Sox Nation Guide to the Players*, "The man from Tennessee is best remembered for the vicious racial slurs he directed at Jackie Robinson when he was the manager of the Philadelphia Phillies in 1947."[23] He is also remembered for the racial epithets he directed toward Buddy Myer in 1933, igniting one of the most vicious brawls ever seen on a major league field. That dark side of Ben Chapman was unfortunate, because he was an outstanding baseball player who had exceptional speed, a strong throwing arm, and a consistent bat. He signed his first professional baseball contract with the New York Yankees in 1928 at the age of 22, and they optioned him to Asheville in the Class-B South Atlantic League, where he showed Yankees management that he belonged in fast company by smoking the ball at a .336 clip with 105 runs scored and 30 stolen bases in 147 games. Asheville won the pennant by a whopping 18 games, and Chapman hit the ball hard, ran the bases aggressively, and played a solid third base. The next year, he duplicated his .336 batting average with St. Paul in the highly rated American Association. He also led the league in runs scored with 162 in 168 games and stole 26 bases.

That was the end of Ben Chapman's minor league seasoning. He played in the major leagues for the next 15 years. The six-foot, 190-pound speedster was an immediate hit along the Great White Way as he put together seasons of .316, .315, .299, .312, .308, and .289, and he led the league in stolen bases three times with a high of 61 stolen bases in 1931. His numbers were in decline in 1936 and his temper cooled New York management's love affair with him, leading to a trade to the Washington Senators where he played parts of two years before he was shuffled off to the Boston Red Sox. He covered right field for Boston for 113 games in 1937, batting .307 with 23 doubles, 11 triples, seven home runs, 57 RBI and a league-leading 35 stolen bases, 27 with Boston. The next year, he rattled the Fenway Park fences with a .340 batting average, 40 doubles, 92 runs scored, 80 RBI, and 13 stolen bases in 127 games. Despite his offensive pyrotechnics, the 29-year-old outfielder was traded to Cleveland in 1938.

Cicotte, Eddie

Eddie Cicotte was one of the infamous "Black Sox" players who threw the 1919 World Series to the Cincinnati Reds and were subsequently banned from organized baseball for life by baseball commissioner Kenesaw Mountain Landis. Cicotte, like many of Charles Comiskey's players, was grossly underpaid and, after pleading guilty to the conspiracy, he confessed, "I did it for the wife and kiddies."

Before Cicotte became involved in the evil deed, however, he was one of the best right-handed pitchers in the major leagues. He had come out of Detroit, Michigan, in 1904, entering organized baseball with Calumet in the Class-D Copper Country Soo League. The following year, as a member of the Detroit Tiger's organization, he went 15–9 with Augusta in the Class-C South Atlantic League and 1–1 in a three-game trial with the Tigers. He won 18 games against 9 losses for Des Moines in the Single-A Western League in 1906, and he followed that with a 21–14 year with Lincoln in the same league. Unfortunately for Detroit, they had sold the rights to Cicotte to Lincoln and he was claimed by the Boston Red Sox after the 1907 season.

Eddie Cicotte became a regular starter for the Red Sox in 1908, compiling an 11–12 record for the fifth-place Red Sox in spite of an outstanding 2.43 ERA. Cicotte pitched for Boston for four-and-a-half years, with won-lost records of 14–5, 15–11, 11–15, and 1–3. He was waived to Chicago on July 22, 1912, and spent the rest of his career in the Windy City. The five-foot, nine-inch, 175-pound right-hander was primarily a junk ball pitcher who relied on the shine ball and the knuckleball for his success, but he also threw a fastball and a curve to confuse batters. Cicotte was quoted in "Baseball Magazine" in 1917 as saying, "The knuckle ball has been of great value to me. I confess that I depend upon it a good deal in my work. I think it is no exaggeration to say that out of 100 average balls that I throw, 75 are knuckle balls."[24]

Clemens, Roger

On April 29, 1986, in a Fenway Park night game against the Seattle Mariners, Roger "Rocket" Clemens set a major league record by striking out 20 batters in a regulation nine-inning game. Tom Cheney of the Washington Senators had fanned 21 batters in a 1962 game, but that was a 16-inning affair. The 23-year-old fireballer, in his third major league season after compiling records on 9–4 and 7–5 for the

Red Sox during his first two years, got off to a fast start in 1986, defeating the Chicago White Sox, 7–2, on April 11, beating the Kansas City Royals, 6–2, with a complete game effort on April 17, and taking the measure of the Detroit Tigers, 6–4, with ten strikeouts in 6⅔ innings, on April 22.

The April 29 game was Clemens' 39th career start, and he faced a team that was destined to finish the season in the West Division cellar. The Rocket mowed down the first three Mariners batters on strikes. He fanned two more in the second, one in the third, and then eight in a row between the fourth and sixth innings, tying an American League record. In the top of the seventh, he struck out Phil Bradley and Ken Phelps, for numbers 15 and 16, but then Gorman Thomas upset the applecart. He took an 0–2 fastball downtown, driving it into the left field screen and giving right-hander Mike Moore, a 17-game winner in 1985, a 1–0 lead. But Clemens' teammates were not about to see his magnificent effort go for naught. After the first two batters were retired in the bottom of the inning, Steve Lyons singled to right field and Glenn Hoffman walked to bring up Dwight Evans. Boston's all-time right fielder jumped on a 2–2 sinker from Moore and sent it screaming into the screen over the Green Monster, and suddenly the Sox were back in control, 3–1. Clemens didn't waste any pitches in the eighth and ninth innings, fanning two men in each inning and inducing Phelps to ground out short to first to end the game. Manager John McNamara said, "I watched perfect games by Catfish Hunter and Mike Witt, but this was the most awesome pitching performance I've ever seen."[25]

The Rocket went on from there to pace the Red Sox to the American League pennant, compiling a 24–4 record, leading the league in victories, won-lost percentage (.857), and earned run average (2.48). Along the way, he completed ten of 33 starts and fanned 238 batters in 254 innings pitched. His efforts were rewarded with his league's Cy Young Award and its Most Valuable Player award. In the American League Championship Series against the California Angels, he posted a 1–1 record, defeating the AL west representative, 8–1, in the game 7 finale. But in the World Series, it was a different story. He failed to complete either of his starts in the seven-game loss to the New York Mets, pitching 4⅓ innings in Game 2 and seven innings in Game 6, both no-decisions. He had, in fact, the World Championship in the palm of his sturdy right hand in game six, holding a 3–2 lead and just six outs from glory, an opportunity to bring the title back to Boston after a drought of 68 years, but he couldn't pull the trigger. According to Sean Cunningham, "Clemens gave himself the hook in the game, telling manager John McNamara, 'That's all I can pitch.' Clemens later informed the press, 'My blister was at the point where I couldn't finish off my slider. I didn't want to hang my slider and jeopardize my team. But I thought I did my job.'"[26] Roger Clemens put together six more solid years in Boston, winning two more Cy Young Awards, and leading the Red Sox to two Eastern Division titles, but after experiencing four sub-par years, he opted for free agency and joined the Toronto Blue Jays in 1997.

During his 13-year Boston tenure, the intimidating, arrogant, six-foot, four-inch, 235-pound power pitcher appeared in 383 games, including 382 starts, with 100 complete games

Roger Clemens

and 38 shutouts. He compiled a 192–111 won-lost record with 2,590 strikeouts in 2,776 innings pitched, and a 3.06 ERA. Using a 96 mph, four-seam fastball, a 91 mph, two-seam fastball, a curveball, a change of pace, and pinpoint control to perfection, the big Ohioan dominated the American League from 1986 to 1992. Then, beginning in 1993, his career went into decline. His won-lost records from 1993 through 1996 were 11–14, 9–7, 10–5, and 10–13, and his innings pitched plummeted from about 260 innings a year to as few as 140 innings a year. It looked like his career was about over at the age of 34, but suddenly he went on to revitalize his career in Toronto, New York, and Houston over the next 11 years, winning another 162 games against 73 losses, winning 20 or more games three times, and capturing four more Cy Young Awards. His resurgence was credited to the development of a split-fingered fastball in Toronto, where the 35-year-old Clemens went 21–7 in 1997 and 20–6 the following year, bringing him his fourth and fifth Cy Young awards, and restoring him to the prominence he had enjoyed during his prime in Boston.

He won two World Championships as a member of the New York Yankees, winning the title in 1999 and again in 2000. Moving on to Houston in 2004, Rocket earned another Cy Young Award by fashioning a brilliant 18–4 season with a 2.98 earned run average The next year, at the age of 43, he won 13 games against eight losses with a league-leading 1.87 ERA. His 24-year career included 354 wins, 184 losses, 4,672 strikeouts in 4916⅔ innings pitched, 46 shutouts, and a 3.12 ERA. His post–season record showed 12 victories against eight losses, including a 3–0 mark in the World Series.

On the dark side, his sudden resurgence in Toronto and New York may not have been as miraculous as first seen. "Roger Clemens worked hard. But over the course of the 1995 and '96 seasons, his fastball was topping out at 91, 92 mph, and his torso was slowly morphing into that of a beer-league bowler. 'Roger wasn't throwing the ball quite like he used to,' says Mike Greenwell, a Red Sox outfielder. 'He still had great stuff but the velocity was off.' Now, less than a year later, the 34-year-old Clemens was built like a sculptured heavyweight and throwing as hard as he had in the mid–1980's."[27] His world began to fall apart in 2007 when the Mitchell Committee, which was investigating the steroid problem in baseball, reportedly uncovered Clemens' name during their interviews. Roger's trainer, Brian McNamee, told the committee he had injected Clemens with anabolic steroids and Human Growth Hormone (HGH). Evidence against Clemens emerged from other witnesses, including Andy Pettitte. Clemens subsequently testified before a Congressional Committee and denied ever using steroids, but based on the evidence, Congress requested that the Justice Department investigate Clemens to determine if he had lied under oath during his deposition to the Congressional Committee. The case remains ongoing.

Clinton, Lou

Luciean Louis Clinton began his five-year relationship with the Red Sox with the reputation for being a capable defensive outfielder with a strong, accurate throwing arm, as well as a decent hitter with power. He split the 1960 season between Minneapolis and Boston, but his .228 average in The Hub earned him a quick trip to Seattle in the Pacific Coast League in hopes of refining his batting skills. The six-foot, one-inch, 185-pound right-handed slugger had a breakout season in the PCL in 1961, hammering the ball at a .295 clip with 27 doubles, 21 home runs, and 102 runs batted in, in 127 games. Boston recalled him at the end of the season and in 1962 he became the Red Sox regular right fielder. In his first full season in Boston, he looked like the real deal, hitting a solid .294 with 18 homers and 75 RBI in 398 at-bats on a team that finished in eighth place in the American League, their 76–84 record leaving them a full 19 games behind the high-flying New York Yankees. The next year was worse, both for the Sox and for Clinton. Boston had replaced manager Pinky Higgins with Johnny Pesky, but that didn't help. The club finished seventh with a 76–85 record, 28 games behind New York. Clinton tailed off to .232 with the bat although he did slam 22 homers and drive in 77 runs in 560 at-bats. That performance didn't cut it with Red Sox management who were gearing up for a run at the pennant. They had Carl Yastrzemski and Tony Conigliaro standing in the wings, making Lou Clinton expendable, and he was subsequently shuttled off to the Angels in exchange for outfielder Lee Thomas on June 4, 1964.

Collins, Jimmy

At five-feet, nine-inches tall and 178 pounds, he was the greatest third baseman of the first decade of the twentieth century, and a Hall Of Fame inductee of the class of 1945. James Joseph Collins was born in Buffalo, New York, on January 16, 1870, and joined the professional ranks with the hometown Buffalo Bisons of the highly rated Eastern League in 1893. He was sold to the Boston Beaneaters of the National League in 1895, but after hitting just .211 in 38 at-bats he was loaned to the Louisville Colonels of the same league. He had initially played third base for Buffalo but was moved to right field because, according to Stanton Hamlet in *Deadball Stars*, he was "afraid of bunts." He played right field during his 11-game tenure in Boston, but was stationed at third base in Louisville where he "had come to the conclusion that there was only one solution to the bunting game. A third baseman simply had to play in on the edge of the grass to give himself a chance against the 'tap tactics of those fast guys.'"[28] He quickly proved the soundness of his theory against the famed Baltimore Orioles, gunning down John McGraw and Willie Keeler when they tried to intimidate him with bunts.

Returning to the Beaneaters in 1896, Jimmy Collins established himself as the king of the hot corner. He hit a solid .296 for Frank Selee's fourth-place Beaneaters in 1896, and then had a career year in '97 as Boston captured the National League pennant by two games over the Baltimore Orioles. The quiet, businesslike third baseman led the league in putouts, assists, and double plays, while scorching the ball at a .346 clip with 28 doubles, 13 triples, six home runs, 103 runs scored, and 132 runs batted in. He batted .328 the following year with 35 doubles, 107 runs scored, 111 RBI, and a league-leading 15 home runs. He also led the league in putouts. After two more sterling years with the Beaneaters, Collins moved over to the Boston Somersets of the new American League as player-manager.

In the American League's inaugural season of 1901, he brought the team home in second place, four games behind the Chicago White Sox. He was also one of the team's offensive guns, slamming a career-high 42 doubles along with 16 triples, while scoring 108 runs and driving in 94 teammates. After a third-place finish in 1902, Jimmy Collins grabbed the brass ring in 1903, capturing the American League pennant by a whopping 14_ games over Connie Mack's Philadelphia Athletics. Buck Freeman and Patsy Dougherty paced the team's offense, but Collins chipped in with a .296 average, 88 runs scored, and 72 RBI. The slick-fielding third baseman also led the league in putouts, double plays, and fielding average. In the World Series that followed, the first World Series in modern major league baseball history, the team, now known as the Pilgrims, took the measure of the National League champion Pittsburgh Pirates, five games to three, with Bill Dinneen winning three games. The offense was spread out over the entire Pilgrims lineup with six players knocking in four or more runs. Jimmy Collins hit .250 with two triples.

Jimmy Collins

Boston repeated as pennant winners in 1904 but no World Series was played due to a disagreement between the two leagues. Collins, who was now 34 years old, was beginning to slow down at the plate, with his average dropping to the .270's, but he remained at the top of his game in the field, leading the league in putouts in 1904 and consistently showing exceptional glove-work and outstanding range. The year 1905 was the last year he played in more than 100 games for Boston, batting .276 in 131 games, but the Pilgrims slipped to fourth place, 16 games from the top. The following year was an embarrassment as Collins' cohorts fell all the way to the American League cellar, their 49–105 won-lost record leaving them a distant 45½ games behind the pennant-winning Chicago White Sox. The handsome Irishman was replaced as manager by Chick Stahl during the season, after watching his team lose 79 of its first 114 games. He was traded to the Philadelphia Athletics 41 games into the 1907 season, and played with the A's through 1908 when he called it a day and returned to his home in Buffalo.

During his Pilgrims career, Jimmy Collins tattooed the ball to the tune of .296 in 2,972 at-bats. He led the league in putouts five times, assists four times, double plays three times, and fielding average twice during his major league career, and his 601 chances accepted with the Beaneaters in 1899 is still the National League record. The stalwart third baseman was in a league of his own defensively with exceptional range and a .929 fielding average that was 22 points higher than the league average at third base. And, as noted earlier, he was death on bunts, with his aggressive positioning revolutionizing third base play.

Collins, Ray

A native of Colchester, Vermont, the crafty southpaw baffled American League batters for five years with a confusing delivery that was all arms and legs, and propelled the ball toward the plate from a variety of angles, keeping the batter off balance while his curveball and his outstanding control piled up the outs. Ray Collins signed a professional baseball contract with the Boston Red Sox in 1909 at the age of 22 after graduating from the University of Vermont, and he went directly to the major leagues, joining Fred Lake's team on July 12, 1909. The six-foot, one-inch, 185-pound pitcher lost his debut to the Detroit Tigers on the 23rd by a 4–2 score but, in his next start, also against Detroit, he threw a shutout. Overall, Collins appeared in 12 games for the third-place Boston team during the season, with eight starts, compiling a respectable 4–3 record and a 2.81 earned run average. In 1910, under new manager Patsy Donovan, he pitched in 35 games, including 26 starts, for the fourth-place Red Sox. He tossed 18 complete games with four shutouts, won 13 games against 11 losses, and recorded a stellar 1.62 ERA, the sixth-lowest ERA in the American League. The next year, he went 11–12 for a fifth-place team that won just 78 games. He threw 14 complete games in 24 starts with a 2.40 ERA.

The 1912 Red Sox fielded one of their best teams ever. New manager Jake Stahl guided the Sox to their first pennant in eight years and Collins was a major contributor to their success. The big lefty missed the first two months of the season after suffering a spike wound during spring training, and he didn't record his first victory until June 22.[29] Over the final three months of the campaign, Collins contributed 13 victories (while dropping eight decisions) to the Red Sox cause, pitching in 27 games with a 2.53 ERA. Stahl's powerful contingent, with Harry Hooper, Tris Speaker, Larry Gardner, Smoky Joe Wood, and Collins, ran away with the American League pennant, winning 105 games against 47 losses, leaving the Washington Senators 14 games in arrears. In a hard-fought World Series confrontation against the New York Giants, the Red Sox eked out an eight-game-triumph. Ray Collins started the second game of the Series and pitched well, but two Boston errors in the eighth inning deprived him of a win, the game ending in a 6–6, 11-inning tie, called on account of darkness. He relieved Buck O'Brien in the second inning of Game 6 after O'Brien had been rocked for five runs in the opening stanza, and he threw seven scoreless innings in New York's 5–2 win. Overall, he pitched 14⅔ innings in two games in the Series with a 1.88 ERA but had nothing to show for it.

Ray Collins' career peaked in 1913 and 1914.

He went 19–8 in 1913, completing 19 of 30 starts with a 2.60 ERA, the fifth-best ERA in the league. He faced Walter Johnson four times during the season and came away with two victories. Three of the games ended in 1–0 decisions, and one of them, a 1–0 11-inning Collins victory, ended The Big Train's 14-game winning streak. He had other memorable games that year as well. On July 9, he blanked the St. Louis Browns, 9–0, with a four-hitter and hit a home run to help his own cause. Two weeks later, he tossed a five-hitter at the Chicago White Sox and slammed a bases-loaded triple to win the game, 4–1. The following year, the Vermont native held out for more money during spring training, threatening to jump to the newly formed outlaw Federal League if his demands were not met. After meeting with Red Sox owner Joseph Lannin and manager Bill Carrigan in Hot Springs, Arkansas, Boston's spring training camp, Collins signed a two-year contract for $5,400 a year, an increase of $1,800 over his 1913 salary. He rewarded his owner's faith in him with a 20-victory season, going 20–13 with 16 complete games in 30 starts, including six shutouts, with a 2.51 ERA. He won victories 18 and 19 on September 22 when he pitched and won both ends of a doubleheader in Navin Field, Detroit, by scores of 5–3 and 5–0, both complete game efforts.

Ray Collins' pitching skills mysteriously deserted him after his outstanding 1914 season and he was relegated to the bullpen for most of the 1915 season, pitching in just 25 games with nine starts and two complete games, and posting a record of 4–7 with a 4.30 earned run average. The 29-year-old southpaw retired at the end of the year saying he was "discouraged by his failure to show old-time form." His seven-year major league career, all with Boston, produced 84 victories against 62 losses, with a 2.51 ERA, number 30 all-time. As Tom Simon noted, "Collins returned to his native Colchester and struggled to eke out an existence as a dairy farmer for 42 years." The rustic lifestyle included no tractor, no automobile, and no indoor plumbing.[30]

Collins, Shano

Eight members of the Chicago White Sox baseball team were banned from organized baseball for life in 1920 for conspiring to throw the 1919 World Series, but Shano Collins was not one of them. He, along with the other honest players, struggled against overwhelming odds to win the Series, but it was all for naught. The Cincinnati Reds, thanks to the conspirators, won the World Championship five games to three.

John Francis "Shano" Collins was born in Charleston, Massachusetts, on December 4, 1885. His nickname was derived from his given name, John, which is Sean in Irish. Collins began his professional baseball career with Haverhill in the Class-B New England League in 1907, batting .208 in 15 games while holding down the shortstop position. The next year, he played second base for Springfield in the Connecticut League, batting .322 in 88 games. That performance brought him to the attention of Chicago White Sox owner Charles Comiskey, who purchased his contract from Springfield at the end of the season. The six-foot, 180-pound Collins began the 1910 season at first base for the White Sox, but after 28 games he was moved to right field where he developed into one of the game's best defensive outfielders. His batting, however, left something to be desired. He hit just .197 with 18 extra base hits and 24 RBI in 97 games in his rookie season.

His performance with the bat improved in his sophomore season, as he upped his average to .262, but it was never more than adequate, and it was erratic, year-to-year. He hit as high as .303 in 1920 and as low as .231 in 1923 and .234 in 1917. The right-handed-hitting Collins played in two World Series for the White Sox, batting .286 in 1917 when they defeated the New York Giants four games to two, and .250 in the infamous 1919 Fall Classic against Cincinnati. He was traded to the Boston Red Sox with Nemo Leibold for Harry Hooper in 1921, ending an 11-year career in Chicago.

Shano Collins played for his hometown Red Sox for four full years, but it was a difficult time in Boston during his tenure there. The team finished in the second division all four years, including two visits to the cellar. Still, Collins had some of his best years with the bat in Boston, hitting .286 in 1921, .271 the following year, and .292 in 1924.

Conigliaro, Tony

Tony Conigliaro is one of the most tragic figures in Boston Red Sox history. He was a tall, slim, powerfully built, right-handed slugger with unlimited potential who, like Pete Reiser, "flashed across the heavens like a blindingly beautiful meteor. For one brief moment, his dazzling brilliance illuminated the baseball world. Then he was gone, and only a memory remained."[31] Tony C. made his major league debut with Boston at the age of 19 at Yankee Stadium in New York on April 16, 1964. He played center field and batted in the seventh spot in the batting order, going 1 for 5 with a run scored in Boston's 4–3 victory. He played his last game on June 12, 1975. The years between 1964 and 1975 read like a Greek tragedy.

Anthony Richard Conigliaro signed a contract with the hometown Boston Red Sox following his graduation from high school in 1962. As David Nevard pointed out, Boston sent him to the instructional league in September and he "felt completely overmatched there, so he went home and lifted weights and swung a lead bat in the cellar all winter."[32] Tony C. joined his first professional baseball team in the spring of 1963, the Wellsville Red Sox in the Single-A New York–Pennsylvania League, and he literally destroyed New York–Penn pitching, smoking the ball to the tune of .363 with a league-leading 42 doubles, 24 home runs, and 74 runs batted in, in 333 at bats over 83 games.

That performance brought him a promotion to the parent club the next spring, thanks to the insistence of Red Sox manager Johnny Pesky. The local hero played his first major league game in Yankee Stadium, as noted above. The next night, at home, the Red Sox entertained the Chicago White Sox, and the youngster jumped on the first pitch from Joel Horlen in the fourth inning and sent it skyrocketing over the Green Monster in left field for his first major league home run. The six-foot, three-inch, 185-pound slugger "took a wide, flat-footed stance at the plate, with a slight crouch and the bat sticking straight up behind his head. He had what was known as quick wrists, and today would be called bat speed. He was a slashing, aggressive pull hitter, a .270 guy with power."[33] He challenged pitchers by crowding the plate when he batted, a practice that took its toll on him during his career. In his rookie season, he lost eight games after being hit by Moe Drabowsky of the Kansas City A's, and almost three months later, on July 26, "Pedro Ramos of the Indians hit Tony on the right arm with a pitch that fractured his ulna bone and sidelined him for six weeks."[34] He returned to action in early September, and he continued to torment opposing pitchers the rest of the season, stinging the ball to the tune of .329 with five doubles and four homers in 76 at-bats. His overall rookie season statistics included a .290 batting average with 21 doubles, 24 home runs, and 52 RBI.

The next year he established himself as a bona fide major league star. Now the regular right fielder for the Red Sox, he batted .269 with 82 RBI and he led the American League in home runs with 32, becoming, at 20 years old, the youngest player ever to lead a major league in home runs. Two years later, he became the youngest player ever to reach 100 career home runs. Jim Palmer said, "He might have been the guy to break Ruth's and Aaron's records. With his swing, in that ballpark, there's no telling how many he would have hit."[35] Tony Conigliaro was enjoying his baseball suc-

Tony Conigliaro

cess and he was also enjoying his celebrity. He made headlines wherever he went, some good and some bad. Ray Fitzgerald of the *Boston Globe* reported, "Tony Conigliaro, in the years I covered him, was often self-centered, ambitious, petty, crude, and impatient. But he was also gracious, charming, marvelous with kids (if the kids were polite), witty, and cooperative" (36).

Tony C. played 150 games with 558 at-bats in 1966, hitting .265 with 26 doubles, 28 home runs, and 93 runs batted in. The following year, on August 18, with Conigliaro batting .287 with 20 homers in 349 at-bats, the Red Sox hosted the California Angels, and a festive crowd of 31,027 was on hand to cheer for their surging heroes. As the evening got under way, Boston was in fourth place, but they only trailed the first place Minnesota Twins by three and a half games, and they had the momentum. Jack Hamilton, a noted spitball pitcher with control problems, was on the mound for Bill Rigney's team. As the fourth inning got under way, the game was still scoreless, and the Sox had George Scott and Reggie Smith coming up ahead of Conigliaro. Scott drilled a single to center field but was out trying to stretch it into a double. Smith flied out to right. Tony C. stepped in and disaster followed. Hamilton's first pitch hit him on the left cheekbone, dropping him to the dirt like he was shot. The sound was sickening, and players and fans alike knew Tony was badly hurt. He was carried off the field on a stretcher and taken to Sancta Maria Hospital in Cambridge, where he was diagnosed with a fractured cheekbone, a dislocated jaw, and damage to his left eye. He was released from the hospital eight days later, his left eye a swollen black mass and his vision badly impaired, but he worked hard all winter and by spring training he felt well enough to attempt a comeback.

Tony Conigliaro gave it his best shot during spring training but came up short. Before the regular season began, he returned home, his eyesight still not good enough to hit a baseball. He sat out the entire 1968 season, but returned to the game the next year, and this time he seemed well enough to play. And play he did. On opening day, in Baltimore, he launched a two-run homer into the Maryland sky, and he kept hitting all year. He played 141 games in right field for Boston in 1969, with a .255 batting average, 21 doubles, 20 home runs, and 82 RBI. He was rewarded with the American League's Comeback Player of the Year Award in recognition of his extraordinary performance. The next year was even better. He played 146 games with 560 at-bats, 89 runs scored, 20 doubles, and personal highs with 36 home runs and 116 runs batted in.

Red Sox Nation was shocked when their hero was traded to the California Angels during the off-season, but his sojourn on the west coast lasted only 74 games when deteriorating vision forced him to retire after hitting four homers with 15 RBI in 256 at-bats, for a .222 batting average. He was just 26 years old. Conigliaro made one last attempt at another comeback in 1975 with Boston, but finally had to call it a day after batting .123 with two home runs in 57 at-bats covering 21 games. Tony C.'s Boston career statistics consisted of a .267 batting average in 2,955 at-bats, with 790 base hits, including 162 home runs.

Conigliaro suffered a massive heart attack in 1982, leaving him bedridden. He died in Salem, Massachusetts, on February 24, 1990, at the age of 45. As Costello and Santa Maria noted, "Sometimes an accumulation of injuries and frustrations will wear a player out. So one day, the player quits. It was never that way with Tony C. Things just never got any better. No matter how often he came back — from broken bones, blindness, death — he would always get hit again, a little harder than before. He could always hit back better than most. He just couldn't escape the knockdowns."[37]

Cooke, Dusty

He was born in Swepsonville, North Carolina, on June 23, 1907. "Christened Allen Lindsay Cooke, he was a big guy, six-foot-two and 205 pounds. He was all bone and muscle, hard as a rock and strong as an ox."[38] He was signed by the New York Yankees in the late twenties, and worked his way through their minor league system, with stops in Asheville, NC and St. Paul, MN. With the Asheville Tourists in 1928, Cooke led the South Atlantic League in triples with 30, and the Tourists raced to the league title by 18 games over Macon. The next year, with St. Paul in the

American Association, the left-handed slugger won the league's Triple Crown, batting .358 with 148 RBI and 33 home runs. He was brought up to the big club in 1930, and was considered to be one of the team's top prospects. He gave manager Joe McCarthy a preview of things to come on June 25 in a 16–4 rout of the St. Louis Browns in Yankee Stadium. The big left fielder 3- for-5 in the massacre, with a double and a home run, driving in two runs and scoring three. His home run was one of the longest home runs ever hit in Yankee Stadium, the ball sailing over the running track in center field, a near-500-hundred foot blast. But after batting .255 with six home runs in 92 games in 1930 and .333 with a single home run in 27 games the following year, he suffered a separated shoulder while making one of his patented diving catches against the Washington Senators on April 26. He missed all but three games the following season and began the 1933 season with the Newark Bears of the International League, where he was hitting .203 in 19 games when he was rescued by the Boston Red Sox.

Boston acquired Cooke from the Yankees on May 15, 1933, beginning a four-year association with the North Carolina native. Dusty responded with a .293 batting average in his first year in Boston, slamming 35 doubles and ten triples. He followed that with averages of .244, .306, and .273, while giving Joe Cronin's team decent outfield defense, but he was injury-prone throughout his career, suffering from, among other things, a broken collarbone and a fractured leg that limited his playing time to a total of 404 games in four years. But when he was healthy, he was a tough out. On August 31, 1933, batting out of the third slot in the batting order, Cooke pummeled New York Yankees southpaw Herb Pennock and two relievers for four base hits in six at-bats, including a double and a triple, scoring three runs and driving in two as Boston romped over the proud Bronx Bombers by a 15–2 score. On August 29, 1935, Cooke homered off Johnny Marcum of the Philadelphia Athletics in Shibe Park to pace the Red Sox to a 6–2 victory as Wes Ferrell recorded his 20th victory of the season. He batted .273 in 111 games in 1936 and was optioned to Minneapolis for the 1937 season. He regained his health and found his batting stroke with the Millers, hitting .345 with 47 doubles and 18 home runs in 151 games, but with Vosmik, Chapman, and Cramer in the outfield, and Ted Williams on the way, there was no room for the 30-year-old Cooke on the Boston roster, and he was sold to the Cincinnati Reds at the end of the season. He batted .275 in 82 games for the Reds in 1938 and then went back to the minor leagues where he played another four years.

Cramer, Doc

The native of Beach Haven, New Jersey, starred for three American League teams — the Athletics, the Red Sox, and the Tigers — from 1929 to 1948, accumulating 2,705 base hits along the way, en route to a .296 career batting average. The left-handed hitter appeared in two World Series, going 1-for-2 for the A's in 1931 and pacing the Tigers to a World Championship in 1945 by hitting .379 in seven games with seven runs scored and four RBI.

Roger "Doc" Cramer was born on July 22, 1905, and began his career in organized baseball as a pitcher-outfielder for Martinsburg in the Class-D Blue Ridge League in 1929. After leading the league in batting with a .404 average, the 24-year-old Cramer was called up to Philadelphia at the end of the season, going hitless in six at-bats. He split the 1930 season between Philadelphia, where he batted .232 in 30 games, and Portland in the Pacific Coast League, where he pummeled PCL pitchers for a .347 batting average. He hit .260 for the A's in 65 games in 1931 and then broke out with a .336 average in 92 games the following season. Over the next 13 seasons, he never played fewer than 133 games a year.

Cramer developed into one of the American League's best leadoff hitters, slashing singles and doubles to all fields and hitting .300 or better eight times in 12 years. The six-foot, two-inch, 185-pound speedster was also considered to be one of the leagues best center fielders. Blessed with outstanding instincts, great speed, and a strong throwing arm, he roamed far and wide, turning would-be base hits into routine outs. In 1936 he was traded to the Boston Red Sox in a four-player deal, giving Boston a first-class center fielder for five years. He led the league in putouts and double plays in 1936 and in putouts in 1938. He also hit over .300 in four of those years with a high of .311 in 1939 and a low of .292 in 1936. He scored 116 runs for Boston in 1938 and 110 runs the following year. He led the league with 200 base hits in 1940, but was traded to Washington in December of that year for Gee Walker, who was then sent to Cleveland for pitcher Joe Dobson.

Criger, Lou

Lou Criger, like most of the early catchers, was a defensive specialist who was skilled in calling a game and keeping baserunners honest with a strong throwing arm. Over his career, he gunned down 48 percent of all base runners who challenged his arm, the highest caught-stealing percentage of any catcher in Red Sox history. When he joined the Cleveland Spiders in 1896, he struck up a relationship with pitcher Cy Young, and the two men established a rapport that kept Criger in the game for 16 years. Young liked the way Criger called a game, and he appreciated Criger's defensive skills, so every time Young changed teams, he took Criger with him. The two men were a battery for three years in Cleveland, two years in St. Louis, and eight years in Boston, before they parted company. Over the years Lou Criger was behind the plate in more than 200 of Cy Young's victories.

Louis "Lou" Criger was born in Elkhart, Indiana, on February 3, 1872, and began his major league career in 1896 as noted. When he first became a major leaguer, he handled the bat fairly well, hitting .279 for Cleveland in 1898, .256 for St. Louis the following year, and .271 for the Spiders in 1900. But the wear and tear of catching siphoned off his batting skills and, over the remaining 11 years of his major league career ending in 1912, he hit over .200 just three times with a high of .256 in 1902.

The five-foot, ten-inch, 165-pound right-handed hitter played for the Boston Pilgrims/Red Sox for eight years, from 1901 through 1908, and he caught every inning of the Pilgrims' first World Series in 1903, batting .231 with four RBI as Jimmy Collins' team defeated the Pittsburgh Pirates five games to three to claim the major league's first World Championship.

Crisp, Coco

The Boston Red Sox were suddenly without a center fielder after the 2005 season when Johnny Damon opted for free agency, subsequently signing with the New York Yankees. They solved that problem quickly, picking up Coco Crisp in a trade with the Cleveland Indians on January 27, 2006. Covelli Loyce "Coco" Crisp, a native of Los Angeles, California, began his major league career with Cleveland in 2002. He spent four years with the Indians with great success, batting .297 and .300 his last two years there, and hitting 42 doubles and 16 homers in 2005. The sleek, six-foot, 180-pound speedster became a member of the Boston Red Sox and their everyday center fielder in 2006, and he had a decent, but not outstanding season with Terry Francona's club, batting .264 with 22 stolen bases in 105 games, after missing seven weeks due to an injury.

The Red Sox were unhappy with their third-place finish in 2006 and after numerous roster changes during the off-season they flew high in 2007, but not so Coco Crisp. His season was a mixed bag. He played a sensational center field, roaming far and wide to take base hits away from opposing batsmen. But at the plate he looked lost. On April 29, as Boston raced to a four game lead with a 16–8 won-lost record, the California native was hitting a minuscule .235 with three stolen bases in 24 games. By the All-Star break, Terry Francona's cohorts had opened up a sizable ten-game bulge with a 53–34 record, but Crisp was still a marginal contributor with a .265 batting average and 16 stolen bases. Boston's big lead almost disappeared down the September stretch, but they hung on to beat the Yankees by two games, their 96–66 record giving them the home field advantage throughout the American League playoffs. Coco Crisp finished the season with a .265 batting average and 28 stolen bases.

The speedy center fielder started the first eight games of post-season play, three games in the American League Division Series and the first five games of the American League Championship Series. He hit .200 in the ALDS, and was bogged down at a barely visible .143 after five games of the ALCS when he was replaced by Jacoby Ellsbury for the last two games of that series and the four games of the World Series. Crisp's .182 batting average for the three post-season series necessitated battling Ellsbury for the center field job in 2008, with first one and then the other racing to the forefront. The Los Angeles native played in 118 games in 2008, batting .283 in 361 at-bats with 18 doubles, three triples, seven home runs, and 20 stolen bases. The post-season was just the opposite of the 2007 post-season as far as Ellsbury and Crisp were concerned. Crisp started only one game in the ALDS against the Los Angeles Angels, going 1-for-4, but in the ALCS, while Ellsbury went hitless in 14 at-bats over the first three games, Crisp started five games. He hit a lusty .450 overall, with nine base hits in 20 at-bats in six games, including two doubles and one RBI. But after the post-season ended, he was gone, traded to Kansas City on November 19.

Cronin, Joe

Joseph Edward Cronin, one of the great shortstops of the twentieth century, went on to become a manager, general manager and president of the American League before retiring at the age of 66. He was born in the Excelsior district of San Francisco on October 12, 1906, and was an outstanding high school athlete who won the city's junior tennis championship at the age of 14. After graduating from high school, Cronin took a job as a bank clerk and played semi-pro baseball until a scout for the Pittsburgh Pirates spotted him and signed him to a professional baseball contract in 1925.

The five-foot, eleven-and-a-half-inch, 180-pound right-handed hitter got off to a good start as a professional, batting .313 for Johnstown in the Middle Atlantic League. He hit .320 for New Haven in the Eastern League in 1926, spending parts of both seasons with the Pirates, but they were apparently unimpressed with his skills and his contract was sold to the Kansas City Blues of the American Association in 1928. He split the season between the Blues and the Washington Senators, who purchased his contract for $7,500 at the end of the season. The handsome Irishman spent the next seven seasons with Washington, developing into an all-star shortstop, both offensively and defensively, and eventually being promoted to player-manager in 1933. The fact that he was courting owner Clark Griffith's niece, Margaret, whom he married in 1934, probably didn't hurt his chances. In any case, the young manager led his team to the American League pennant in his first year at the helm, finishing seven games ahead of the New York Yankees. They lost the World Series to the New York Giants four games to one, although Cronin held up his end, batting a cool .318.

After one more season in Washington, where his team plummeted to seventh place, 34 games behind the pennant-winning Detroit Tigers, Joe Cronin was traded to the Boston Red Sox for Lyn Lary and $150,000. Boston's new player-manager took over a fourth-place club, but in spite of his offensive contributions he was unable to improve the team's fortunes, finishing fourth, sixth, and fifth his first three years at the helm. In 1938, Cronin batted .325 with a league-leading 51 doubles, 17 home runs, and 94 RBI, leading his team to a second-place finish. The Red Sox finished second three more times before finally grabbing the brass ring in 1946. Cronin retired as an active player in 1945, and he gave up the managerial reins two years later, becoming Boston's General Manager. In 1958, he left the GM post, and in January, 1959, he was elected President of the American League, a post he held until 1973.

Joe Cronin's playing career lasted 20 years, during which time he compiled a career batting average of .301 with a high of .346 in 1930. He was Boston's regular shortstop for seven years, and was an All-Star in five of those years. As a Red Sox player, he batted over .300 four times, hit 30 or more doubles six times, drove in over 100 runs three times, and scored over 100 runs twice. He was the first player to hit pinch-hit home runs in both ends of a doubleheader, a feat he accomplished on June 17, 1943, giving him three pinch-hit homers in four trips to the plate. His 15-year managerial record showed 1,236 victories against 1,055 losses. With Boston he won 1,071 games and lost 916, for a fine .539 winning percentage. Joe Cronin was elected to the National Baseball Hall of Fame in Cooperstown, New York, in 1956.

Culp, Ray

The journeyman right-handed pitcher, who spent five nondescript years with the Philadelphia Phillies and Chicago Cubs, suddenly became the ace of the Boston Red Sox staff when he was obtained in a trade with the Cubs for a minor league outfielder and cash. Ray Culp, a six-foot, 195-pound Texan, began his professional baseball career with Johnson City in the Appalachian League in 1959 at the age of 18, going 0–1 in four games. After three more years of seasoning, he was brought up to the big club in Philadelphia in 1963, and he responded with a fine 14–11 record for the fourth-place Phillies. He posted an excellent 2.97 earned run average for the year, but he led the league in bases on balls with 102 in 203 innings. After that season, his fortunes declined, as he won only 37 games over the next four seasons.

Ray Culp's first year in Boston in 1968 changed all that. With Boston's pitching staff in disarray after their pennant-winning season the previous year, the big right-hander suddenly found himself as the ace of the staff. Jim Lonborg, who had gone 22–9 in 1967, suffered through an injury-filled season in 1968, posting a 6–10 record in 23 games, and the rest of the staff was erratic. Culp gave manager Dick Williams a sterling effort, winning 16 games against six losses in 35 games with 30 starts, 11 complete games, six shutouts and a 2.91 ERA. The next year he posted a 17–8 record with nine complete games in 32 starts, and in 1970, he went 17–14 with 15 complete games in 33 starts with a 3.04 ERA.

The 30-year-old Texan reached the downside of his career in 1971 as he won just 14 games against 16 losses for Eddie Kasko's third-place outfit. He went 5–8 in 1972 and 2–6 the following year before hanging his glove up for good. During his six years in Boston, Ray Culp won 71 games and lost 58 for a .550 winning percentage.

Damon, Johnny

One of the leaders of the notorious "Bunch of Idiots" that roamed the Boston Red Sox dugout in 2004, Johnny Damon was a major contributor to the World Championship that put to rest the "Curse of the Bambino" forever. The Kansas speedster was born in Fort Riley on November 5, 1973, and was signed to a professional baseball contract by the Kansas City Royals 18 years later. He immediately impressed the KC brass with his bat-handling technique and his outstanding outfielding skills. He tattooed the ball at a .349 clip and stole 20 bases in 50 games in his professional debut with the Royals in the Gulf Coast League. He hit .290 for Rockford in 1993, .316 for Wilmington the following year, and a healthy .343 for the Wichita Wranglers in the Double-A Texas League in 1995. That performance brought about a quick promotion to the parent club midway through the season, and he responded as expected, batting .282 in 47 games for the Royals.

Johnny Damon was a main cog in the Kansas City machine for the next six years, covering center field like a blanket, batting around the .300 mark, scoring runs in bunches, and stealing anywhere from 16 to 46 bases a year. He hit .307 and .327 his last two years in Kansas City, scored over 100 runs in each of his last three years, and stole 26, 36, and 46 bases respectively. His 2000 season was a career year for Damon as he hit .327 with 42 doubles, 10 triples, 16 homers, and 88 runs batted in, while leading the league with 136 runs scored and 46 stolen bases. In 2001, the KC comet was traded to the

Johnny Damon

Oakland Athletics in a five-player deal. After one season in Oakland, he filed for free agency, eventually signing with the Boston Red Sox.

The six-foot, 205-pound left-handed hitting center fielder was a perfect fit in Boston as the team was being structured for a run at the pennant. Johnny Damon showed manager Grady Little his wares in 2002, batting .286 with 34 doubles, a league-leading 11 triples, 14 homers, 118 runs scored, and 31 stolen bases. With the addition of Bill Mueller, Kevin Millar, and David Ortiz in 2003, the Red Sox were poised to challenge the New York Yankees for the American League leadership. The final piece of the puzzle came in 2004 with the addition of closer Keith Foulke.

Without a bona fide closer, the Red Sox won 95 games against 67 losses in 2003, finishing six games behind the division champion New York Yankees. Damon had another good season, batting .273 with 103 runs scored. With the arrival of Foulke, Boston, under new manager Terry Francona, put more heat on Joe Torre's embattled athletes. Foulke appeared in 72 games with 32 saves during the run for the pennant. Other players who also played a big part in the Red Sox resurgence included Curt Schilling (21–6), Pedro Martinez (16–9), David Ortiz (41 homers and 139 RBI), and Manny Ramirez (43 homers and 130 RBI). Johnny Damon was the primary table-setter, batting .304 with 123 runs scored, 35 doubles, 19 stolen bases, and career highs to the point in both home runs (20) and runs batted in (94).

Although their 98 victories were three less than the New York Yankees, Boston entered the post-season playoffs as the American League wild-card entry. Matched against the Anaheim Angels in the ALDS, Francona's bombers swept the west coast contingent three straight with Damon pounding Angels pitching for a .467 batting average. The American League Championship Series pitted Boston against the hated Yankees, and it looked like it would be a short series as New York won the first three games, including a 19–8 thrashing in game three. They were up 4–3 in the ninth inning of Game 4 with all-world closer Mariano Rivera on the mound, when the miracle of Lansdowne Street rose up to bite the cocky Bronx Bombers, and Boston's determined warriors swept the final four games to capture the American League pennant. Damon hit a mediocre .171 in the series, but he drove in seven runs in seven games, four of them on a second-inning grand slam in Game 7 that put the last nail in the Yankees coffin. The Red Sox played host to the St. Louis Cardinals, the National League representative, in the first game of the 100th World Series, and they set the tone for the Series early, winning the opener, 11–9. Three more victories followed and Boston was crowned baseball's World Champions. Damon hit .286 in the Series with two doubles, a triple, a homer, and four runs scored. Damon played one more year in Boston, batting .316, and then filed for free agency at the end of the season, eventually signing with the hated Yankees on January 3, 2006. His reward for that move was a ringside seat for the 2007 World Series between Terry Francona's club and the Colorado Rockies.

Daubach, Brian

Brian Daubach was a six-foot, one-inch, 201-pound first baseman who had two tours of duty with the Red Sox, the first one from 1999 through 2002 and the second one in 2004. The Illinois native originally signed a professional baseball contract with the New York Mets in 1990, but after seven years of bouncing around the Mets farm system, he filed for free agency and signed with the Florida Marlins. Two more frustrating years followed, with just ten games of major league ball to show for his efforts. The Marlins released him in November, 1998, and he was signed to a Boston Red Sox contract one month later.

The 28-year-old first baseman played 110 games for Jimy Williams' team in 1999, batting a crisp .294 with 21 homers and 73 RBI in 381 at-bats. He made some significant contributions to Boston's wild card pursuit, including smashing two doubles and a homer and driving in five runs in an 11–6 Sox victory over the Seattle Mariners in Fenway Park on August 13, and going 5-for-5 with a homer and six RBI in a 13–2 rout of the Mariners. He batted .250 with a homer and three RBI in the Division Series win over the Cleveland Indians, and he had a homer and three RBI in the loss to the Yankees in the ALCS. The next year he suffered through the feared sophomore slump. His batting average fell off to .248, but he still hammered 21 home runs and drove in 76 runs in 495 at-bats. Daubach bounced back to hit 22 homers with 71 RBI in 2001, and 20 homers with 78 RBI the following year. The problem Williams had with Daubach was where to play him. He was known as a hard-nosed player who would eat dirt to get the ball, and he was also a player who produced big hits in the clutch. But he was slow afoot and his glove was a liability. He played first base, right field, and left field for Boston, and was the designated hitter in 112 games, but he became expendable when David Ortiz appeared on the scene. He spent the 2003 season with the Chicago White Sox before returning to Boston the following year as a member of the famous World Championship team, although he didn't play in the post-season. He finished his major league career with the New York Mets in 2005. Daubach's career may have suffered from the fact that he was one of the "scabs" that crossed the picket line in 1995 during the baseball players' strike. As a result, he was one of the few players who were not members of the Major League Baseball Players Association.

Delock, Ike

The five-foot, eleven-inch, 175-pound right-handed pitcher played his entire 11-year major league career with the Boston Red Sox except for seven games with the Baltimore Orioles at the end of his career in 1963. He won one game and lost three with the Orioles. Delock began his professional baseball career with Auburn in the Border League in 1948, splitting ten decisions with a 5.16 ERA in 24 games. He worked his way through the Boston Red Sox farm system over the next six years with two brief stops in Boston, where he pitched in 62 games with a 7–10 record. After putting together a brilliant 20–4 won-lost record with Scranton in the Eastern League in 1951, he was brought up to the parent club the following year but was found wanting, posting a 4–9 mark in 39 games. He split the 1953 season between Boston and Louisville of the Triple-A American Association, showing some improvement in Boston but not enough to stick. He finally put it all together in 1954, winning 17 games against 10 losses for Louisville, and he was rewarded with a one-way ticket to Boston. The 25-year-old curve ball artist from Highland, Michigan, became a permanent member of the Boston Red Sox in 1955.

Ike Delock pitched in 29 games in 1955, 18 of them as a starter, with a 9–7 won-lost record and three saves. He pitched out of the bullpen the next two years, pitching in 48 games in 1956 with 13 victories and seven losses, and pitching in 49 games with nine victories and eight losses the following year. Manager Pinky Higgins rescued Delock from the bullpen in 1958, adding him to the starting rotation along with Tom Brewer and Frank Sullivan. The right-hander responded with a fine 14–8 record and a 3.37 ERA. He won 11 and lost six in 1959 with a 2.95 ERA, but his career declined over the next three and a half years. His combined record from 1960 to 1963 was 20–26 in 75 games pitched. The 33-year-old pitcher was traded to Baltimore during the 1963 season and ended his career there.

DiMaggio, Dominic

Dominic DiMaggio may have been the second-greatest all-around center fielder in Boston Red Sox history, after Tris Speaker. As Mark Feeney reported, "Mr. DiMaggio, who stood 5-feet-9-inches tall and wore eyeglasses, was nicknamed 'The Little Professor,' a tribute to his intelligence on the field as well as his scholarly mien and small stature. Along with canniness, Mr. DiMaggio brought quickness and speed to the Red Sox lineup."[39] Boston's answer to Joe D. was a Red Sox mainstay for 11 years beginning in 1940, with three years out for military service from 1943 through 1945. He was a dangerous .300 hitter who specialized in sending line drives to the gaps or off the Green Monster for two bases. He was also a reliable contact hitter whose patience at the plate resulted in numerous bases on balls, a high on-base-percentage, and an average of 102 runs scored for every 550 at-bats. On defense, the Little Professor was a fleet-footed outfielder who covered acres of ground in the Fenway ballyard and who, according to some people, actually covered two positions, his own and Ted Williams.' It has been told that on many occasions when a ball was hit to left-center field, Ted would yell, "You take it, Dom!" DiMaggio thrilled Boston fans with his exciting catches

Dom DiMaggio

and his ability to scale the center field wall in Fenway Park to take base hits away from opposing batters. His speed, his dependable glove, and his strong throwing arm made him one of the best center fielders of his era, along with big brother Joe. He led the league in putouts and double plays twice, and assists three times during his career. He is still number four all-time in baseball history with 2.92 putouts per game as an outfielder.

The San Francisco native was the youngest of the three baseball-playing DiMaggio brothers, the other two being Joe and Vince. Young Dominic, like his brothers, began his professional baseball career with his hometown San Francisco Seals in the Triple-A Pacific Coast League. The 19-year-old outfielder batted an impressive .306 in his rookie season, with 33 doubles and 109 runs scored in 496 at-bats. He followed that with a .307 season in 1938, and then hit a sizzling .360 for the Seals in 1939, with 48 doubles, 18 triples, 14 home runs, and 165 runs scored, in the grueling 170-game PCL schedule.

That performance was enough for the Boston Red Sox, who had previously rescued Ted Williams and Bobby Doerr from their west coast hideaway. Dominic DiMaggio didn't miss a beat with the Red Sox in his rookie season, putting together an outstanding all-around game, playing center field with a graceful abandon and batting .301 with 32 doubles and 81 runs scored in 418 at-bats. He was a member of Boston's .300-hitting outfield that year, playing alongside Ted Williams and Doc Cramer. Dominic's batting average slipped slightly the next year to .283, but he increased his on-base percentage by 18 points by being more selective at the plate. He drew 90 bases on balls and hit 37 doubles while crossing the plate 117 times. It was the first of six years he would score 100 or more runs. His 1942 season was a mirror-image of the '41 season as he hit .286 with 110 runs scored and 36 doubles.

The call to military service in World War II took DiMaggio away from the playing field for three of his prime years, from ages 26 to 29, but when he finally returned in 1946, he picked right up where he left off, stinging the ball at a .316 clip with 85 runs scored in 142 games, and helping the Red Sox win 104 games to take the American League pennant by 12 games over the Detroit Tigers. He batted .259 with three doubles and three RBI in the World Series as Boston dropped a tough seven-game series to the St. Louis Cardinals. He scored the winning run in Boston's 6–3 victory in Game 5, but his injury in Game 7 may have cost Boston the title. In the top of the eighth inning DiMaggio doubled to drive in two runs to tie the game at three-all, but he pulled a hamstring going into second base and had to be replaced by Leon Culberson. In the bottom of the inning, with Enos Slaughter on first base, Harry Walker sent a drive to left-center field that DiMaggio might well have caught, but the slower Culberson was unable to reach the ball and then made a mediocre throw back to the infield while Slaughter raced around the bases all the way from first to score the eventual championship run. The Cardinals outfielder later confessed that "If they hadn't taken DiMaggio out of the game, I wouldn't have tried it."[40]

The Little Professor continued his outstanding all-around play for the Red Sox for another six years, batting over .300 twice with a high of .328 in 1950, when he led the league with

131 runs scored, 11 triples, and 15 stolen bases. He was also a member of another .300-hitting outfield, with Ted Williams and Al Zarilla. The previous year he had put together a 34-game hitting streak that was ended on August 9 on an outstanding catch by brother Joe. It was the 14th-longest hitting streak in major league history, and he followed that with a 27-game streak in 1951.

During his career, Dominic DiMaggio played in six All-Star games, batting .353. He played his entire career with the Boston Red Sox, accumulating 1,680 base hits in 5,640 at-bats over 1,399 games, good for a .298 batting average. His .383 on-base-percentage was 24 points higher than the league average. And his 2.92 range factor was a full 63 points higher than the league average.

Dinneen, Bill

A big, six-foot, one-inch, 190-pound fireballer from Syracuse, New York, "Big Bill" Dinneen began his baseball career as a semi-pro pitcher in his hometown, but he turned pro in 1895 with Toronto in the Eastern League, going 0–4 as a 19-year-old rookie. He improved his record to 11–12 the following year, and turned in an excellent 21–8 mark in 1897, drawing the attention of the Washington Nationals, who signed him to a major league contract for the 1898 season. He spent two years in D.C., compiling won-lost records of 9–16 and 14–20, and another two years with the Boston Beaneaters, where he put together won-loss records of 20–14 and 15–18 for a team that had a losing record both years.

In 1902, the big right-hander jumped to the Boston Somersets of the newly formed American League, where he spent the next six years. Dinneen went 21–21 for the third-place Somersets under manager Jimmy Collins in 1902, and then compiled a 21–13 log for Boston the following year as they raced to the American League pennant by 14_ games over Connie Mack's Philadelphia A's. Dinneen, who had a smooth, well-balanced delivery, was blessed with a sharp-breaking curveball to supplement his blazing fastball that was considered to be one of the fastest pitches in the American League. In the 1903 World Series, won by the newly-named Pilgrims over the National League representative, the Pittsburgh Pirates, five games to three, Big Bill won three games against a single loss, with two of his victories being 3–0 shutouts. He tossed a three-hitter at the Bucs in Game 2 and sent 11 of them back to bench dragging their bats behind them. In the Game 8 finale, he held the hard-hitting Pirates to four hits while fanning seven.

Dinneen won 23 games against 14 losses in 1904, with a 2.20 ERA, as Boston won the pennant again, but there was no World Series that year due to a disagreement between the leagues. On the last day of the season, Boston had a doubleheader against the New York Highlanders, who needed to win both games to slip past the Pilgrims for the title, but the Boston right-hander took care of that in short order. Matched against 41-game winner "Happy Jack" Chesbro in the opener of the twin-bill, he came away a winner by a 3–2 score when Chesbro uncorked a wild pitch with two men out and two strikes on the batter in the ninth inning, permitting the pennant-winning run to cross the plate. Dinneen set two American League records during the year: consecutive complete games

Bill Dinneen

(37) and the most consecutive innings pitched without relief (337⅔). But that year took its toll on Dinneen's 28-year-old arm. He was plagued by arm problems after the 1904 season, and his career began to slip into mediocrity. In 1905, Big Bill could do no better than a 12–14 record for a team that finished in fourth place, but he did have one day to smile about. On September 27, in the Huntington Avenue Baseball Grounds, the New York native tossed a no-hitter at the Chicago White Sox, winning 2–0.

After going 8–19 in 1906 and starting the following year at 0–4, Bill Dinneen was shuttled off to the St. Louis Browns, where he went 7–10. He compiled a record of 14–7 for St. Louis in 1908, and 6–7 in 1909 before hanging up his glove for good. During his Boston career he won 85 games against 85 losses, including three 20-win seasons. He was also a decent hitter with a .192 career batting average and 29 stolen bases to his credit. After his retirement from pitching, Dinneen became a major league umpire. He was the first person to both play in a World Series and umpire in one. He made the call in Yankee Stadium when Babe Ruth was thrown out trying to steal second base to end the 1926 World Series. He was also umpiring in Wrigley Field the day Babe Ruth called his shot in the 1932 World Series.

Dobson, Joe

Joseph Gordon Dobson was born in Durant, Oklahoma, on January 20, 1917. Known as "Burrhead" because of his wiry, curly hair, the youngster lost his thumb and left forefinger playing with a dynamite cap when he was nine years old, but that didn't stop him from playing baseball, and when he was 20 years old he began his professional baseball career with Troy in the Alabama-Florida League, going 19–12 with 200 strikeouts in 270 innings pitched and a 2.27 ERA. The next year he won 11 games and lost seven for New Orleans in the Southern League, bringing him an invitation to Cleveland to pitch for the Indians. He spent two years with the Indians, where he went a combined 5–10 in 75 games pitched, 65 of them out of the bullpen, and then was traded to the Boston Red Sox in a six-player deal that also brought the Red Sox catcher Frankie Pytlak.

Joe Dobson was one of Boston's big winners during the 1940s, winning 106 games against 72 losses with 17 shutouts in 257 games pitched, with 202 starts and 90 complete games. The six-foot, two-inch, 200-pound right-handed curveball specialist was treated roughly in his Red Sox debut on May 23, 1941, and found himself trailing 5–0 after three innings, but Boston rallied to tie the score at 9–9 in the late innings and the game was called on account of darkness at the end of the ninth inning. Dobson ran off eight consecutive victories at one point during the season and finished the year with 12 wins against five losses. He followed that with an 11–9 season in 1942 and a 7–11 season in 1943 that included a near no-hitter. On September 24, he had a no-hitter for six innings against the Cleveland Indians, but Lou Boudreau lashed a single to right field leading off the seventh inning, ending that scenario. Dobson finished with a two-hitter, winning 1–0 in ten innings. Then he was off to military service for the next two years in World War II. He was inducted into the U. S. Army on December 22, 1943, and spent most of the next two years at Camp Wheeler near Macon, Georgia. After his discharge from the Army on February 15, 1946, Burrhead returned to the playing field and gave manager Joe Cronin a sterling effort that season, going 13–7 in 24 starts with a 3.24 ERA as the Red Sox raced to the title by 12 games over Detroit. His most difficult game was played on June 8. He learned just before the game that his father had died in Arizona, but his brother told him that his father would want him to pitch, so he took the mound and coasted to a 15–4 win. His teammates exploded for 12 runs in the first three innings, permitting him to ease up the rest of the game. The 29-year-old veteran appeared in three games in the World Series against the St. Louis Cardinals. He pitched one inning in relief in Game 2, tossed a complete-game four-hitter in Game 5, winning 6–3 while yielding no earned runs, and pitched 2⅔ scoreless innings in Game 7. Overall, he held St. Louis to four base hits in 12⅔ innings while striking out ten batters and posting a perfect 0.00 ERA. According to Dobson, the key to his success was his "atom ball the pitch I used whenever I got into trouble. It was usually a down-breaking curve that exploded like 'Operation Crossroads.'"[41]

Burrhead had his best season for the Red Sox in 1947, winning 18 games against just eight losses, completing 15 of 31 starts, saving one game, and posting a 2.95 ERA in 228⅔ innings pitched, but Boston could do no better than third place, 14 games behind the New York Yankees. Dobson, however, had another close call with perfection on September 17 when he one-hit the St. Louis Browns in Fenway Park, winning 4–0. Walt Judnich's bloop single in the seventh inning was the only blot on his record. The Red Sox improved their position in 1948 but, in spite of Dobson's 16–10 record, they lost the American League pennant to the Cleveland Indians in a playoff. He won 14 games against 12 losses the following year, but the team once again came up short. They blew a one-game lead over the New York Yankees by dropping the last two games of the season to Casey Stengel's crew in Yankee Stadium. The big right-hander ended his first tenure in Boston in 1950, going 15–10 in 39 games with 27 starts and 12 complete games. He pitched three years for the Chicago White Sox with a combined record of 26–21 before returning to Boston to close out his major league career, pitching in two games with no record. Joe Dobson won 10 or more games for Boston seven times between 1941 and 1950, with a high of 18 games in 1947. His career ERA of 3.62 compared favorably with the league ERA of 4.05. In addition to his pitching prowess, he was also one of the better fielding pitchers in the American League, posting a .977 fielding average, 20 points higher than the league average.

Doerr, Bobby

In a recent study of baseball's greatest players reported in this author's *All-Stars for All-Time*, Bobby Doerr was rated the fourth-best all-around second baseman in baseball history. He was also named as the best second baseman ever to play for the Boston Red Sox. He was quiet, modest, and unassuming, a man Ted Williams once called "The Silent Captain of the Red Sox." The Los Angeles native was born on April 7, 1918, and began his professional baseball career 16 years later when he played second base for the Hollywood Stars of the Pacific Coast League while still in high school. He hit a decent .259 for the Stars in 201 at-bats as a rookie in

Bobby Doerr (courtesy Bob Doerr).

1934, and the following year, the skinny five-foot, eleven-inch, right-handed hitter upped his average to .317 over the full 172-game schedule, with 205 base hits in 647 at-bats. In 1936, still adding weight to his lanky frame, the 18-year-old phenom smoked the ball at a .342 clip with 37 doubles, 12 triples, two home runs, 100 runs scored, 77 runs batted in, and 30 stolen bases, in 175 games and 695 at-bats.

His athletic skills didn't go unnoticed in the Red Sox organization. General Manager Eddie Collins, who was on a mission to recruit slugger Ted Williams, made it a double-killing when he also signed the teenage second baseman. It was one of the best scouting trips in Boston Red Sox history. Doerr began his major league career the following year at the age of 19, and Williams followed two years later. The slick-fielding Californian played 55 games for Boston in his rookie season, backing up Eric McNair who was primarily an offensive second baseman. In 1938, Bobby Doerr settled in as the Red Sox regular second baseman, playing 145 games at the position, fielding brilliantly, leading the league with 118 double plays, and batting a solid .289. McNair was traded to the White Sox on December 21, 1938.

The 21-year-old infielder came of age in 1939. Now a solid 175 pounds, his power numbers began to surface, as he hit .318 with 28 doubles and 12 home runs in 525 at-bats. He also blossomed in the field as he fielded .976, eight points higher than the league average, and exhibited exceptional range, with an average of six chances per game, one more than the league average. The following year, he rattled the fences for a .291 average with 37 doubles, 10 triples, 22 home runs, and 105 RBIs. The Red Sox had an outstanding hitting club that year, posting a league-leading .286 batting average, but their poor 4.89 team ERA doomed the team to fourth place. The 1940 experience was a harbinger of things to come in Doerr's career. Most years the Red Sox had a powerful offensive team that lacked strong pitching, dooming them to playing the bridesmaid to the pitching-rich New York Yankees bride.

Boston finished second, second, seventh, and fourth over the next four years, usually showing the way in most offensive categories, but struggling to produce adequate pitching. In 1944, Bobby Doerr hit a career-high .325 with 30 doubles, 10 triples, 15 home runs, 95 runs scored, and 81 RBI, while leading the league with a .528 slugging average, earning him *The Sporting News* Player of the Year award. He hit for the cycle in a 12–8 loss to the St. Louis Browns on May 17 in the second game of a doubleheader, with Boston winning the opener 5–1 behind a Tex Hughson four-hitter. The following year, with most of the regulars, including Doerr, serving their country in World War II, the Red Sox limped home in seventh place with a 71–83 record, 17½ games behind the pennant-winning Detroit Tigers.

In 1946, the team returned to full strength, with Doerr, DiMaggio, Williams, and Pesky back from the war, and supported by a strong pitching staff that included Tex Hughson, Dave Ferriss, Mickey Harris, and Joe Dobson. The boys all responded with a dedication that brought Boston 104 victories and a 12-game bulge over second-place Detroit. Bobby Doerr was one of the big factors in the Red Sox surge, leading the league in putouts, assists, double plays, and fielding average, while stroking the ball at a .271 clip with 34 doubles, 18 homers, and 116 RBI. In the World Series against the St. Louis Cardinals, won by St. Louis in seven games, he led the Boston attack with a .409 batting average, one double, a home run, and three RBI. In Game 6, won by the Redbirds, Doerr drove in Boston's only run, and in the Game 7 finale, won by St. Louis, 4–3, he had two singles in four at-bats. He singled and went to third base with one out in the second inning, but died there as Wagner and Ferriss both flied out to left field. In the ninth, he followed York's single with one of his own but, after a force play sent pinch-runner Paul Campbell to third base, Ray Partee fouled out and Tom McBride hit into a force play to end the Series.

Bobby Doerr continued to play world-class baseball for Boston for another five years, leading the league in assists and double plays in 1947, and hitting for the cycle a second time, thus becoming the only Boston player ever to hit for the cycle twice. He reached that plateau in Fenway Park on May 13 by slamming a single and a double during a nine-run eighth inning, as the Red Sox thrilled their fans with a 19–6 rout of the Chicago White Sox. Boston starter Dave Ferriss fell behind 4–1 after four-and-a-half innings, but Joe Cronin's sluggers pushed over 18 runs in the next four innings to get him off the hook. The following year, the pride of L.A. batted .285 with 27 homers and 111 runs batted in, and he excelled in the field once again, handling 414 consecutive chances over 73 games without an error. He hit .309 in 1949 and .294 the following year with a league-leading 11 triples and 27 home runs, and career highs in runs scored (103) and runs batted in (120), while leading the league in putouts and fielding average. On June 8, 1950, he ripped three home runs as the Red Sox once again entertained the people of Boston with a hometown massacre, this time whipping the hapless St. Louis Browns to the tune of 29–4.

After the 1951 season in which he hit .289 with a .981 fielding average, the 33-year-old infielder, suffering from a bad back and unable to put forth an acceptable effort in the field, retired to his ranch in Oregon. During his career, Bobby Doerr led the league in double plays five times, fielding average and putouts four times each, and assists three times. He is number eight all-time in career putouts with 4,928, number 14 in career assists with 5,710, and number three in career double plays with 1,507. He was named to nine All-Star teams and played in eight All-Star games, and twice broke up no-hitters by Bob Feller. He did it the first time on a frigid Memorial Day in Fenway Park on May 25, 1939, by sending a soft single over the second baseman's head in the second inning, but confessed later that "I hit the ball off my ear and broke the bat." The second time was in League Park, Cleveland, on July 31, 1946, and this time it was a second-inning line drive over shortstop.

The admitted guess hitter spent his entire 14-year major league career in a Boston uniform, where his quick insight humbled opposing pitchers to the tune of a .288 average with 2,042 base hits in 7,093 at-bats over 1,865 games played. Robert Pershing Doerr was elected to the National Baseball Hall of Fame in 1986.

Dougherty, Patsy

Patsy Dougherty was a hot-headed Irishman who fought with his teammates, opposing players, umpires, and owners over a successful but tempestuous ten-year major league career. The future left fielder of the Boston Pilgrims was born in Andover, along Route 17 in southwest New York state, on October 27, 1876, and grew up in nearby Bolivar. He played for the Bridgeport Orators in the Connecticut State League in 1901, before joining Boston the following year. The six-foot, two-inch, 190-pound left-handed hitter started his major league career off with a bang, pounding the ball at a .342 clip and stealing 20 bases in 108 games for Jimmy Collins' crew, although his fielding left something to be desired as he could do no better than an .899 fielding percentage. In his sophomore season, the Pilgrims leadoff hitter was sensational, tattooing the ball to the tune of a .331 average with 35 stolen bases, while leading the league in base hits with 195 and in runs scored with 107 as Boston raced home in first place in the American League, 14½ games ahead of Philadelphia.

In the World Series against the Pittsburgh Pirates, Dougherty hit just .235 but he had a day to remember on October 2nd when he became the first player to hit two home runs in one World Series game. He hit an inside-the-park homer to right-center field leading off in the first inning, beating the throw from Claude Ritchey, to give the Pilgrims a quick 1–0 lead, and slammed another round-tripper in the sixth inning, this one over the left field fence, as Bill Dinneen blanked Fred Clarke's Buccaneers, 3–0. Boston, down three games to one in the Series, pounded Pittsburgh 11–2 in Game 5 with Dougherty contributing two triples and three RBI to the cause. The Pilgrims went on from there to sweep the final three games to claim the World Championship.

Boston won another American League pennant the following year, but no World Series was played because the two leagues were squabbling. Dougherty was traded to the New York Highlanders after playing 49 games for the Pilgrims that year, apparently because he was in club president John I. Taylor's doghouse. The pugnacious New Yorker batted .283 and .263 in his two years in New York, but was quickly shuttled off to the Chicago White Sox after engaging in a fistfight with Highlanders manager Clark Griffith.

Doyle, Denny

The 31-year-old second baseman was a valuable contributor to the Boston Red Sox pennant drive in 1975. Manager Darrell Johnson acquired Denny Doyle from the last-place California Angels on June 14 to replace the injury-prone Doug Griffin, and he notified his new infielder on arrival that he was there for his defense and any contributions he might make with his bat would be a bonus. Doyle went on to surprise everyone by contributing to the Red Sox pennant chase with both his glove and his bat. He made a game-saving defensive play in his first game with Boston, and hit a home run in his second game. He later contributed a 22-game hitting streak to the cause. For the season, he stung the ball at a .310 clip for the Red Sox, with 21 doubles and 51 runs scored in 310 at-bats over 89 games. Boston, with its new infielder in tow, went on to capture the Eastern Division title by four-and-a-half games over Baltimore. They took the Oakland Athletics to task in the American League Championship Series, winning the series three games to none. Denny Doyle batted .273 in the ALCS with three runs scored. In the World Series, a seven-game loss to the Cincinnati Reds, he hit .267 with a double, a triple, and three runs scored. He played two more years with the Red Sox, retiring in March, 1978, after Jerry Remy joined the team.

Drago, Dick

Dick Drago was a hard-throwing right-handed pitcher with a sinking fastball and a deadly slider, who enjoyed a 13-year major league career with Kansas City, Boston, California, Baltimore, and Seattle, from 1969 through 1981. His first step up the minor league ladder was at Daytona Beach in the Florida State League, where he went 4–7 as a 20-year-old in 1965. He won 15 games each for Rocky Mount, Montgomery, and Toledo, before finding a home with Kansas City. He played five years with the Royals, pitching over 200 innings each season and posting a 17–11 won-lost record with a 2.98 ERA in 1971. After going 12–14 in 1973, the Kentucky native was traded to the Boston Red Sox on October 24.

Drago pitched a total of five years in Boston, over two tours of duty, and was a big part of the 1975 pennant-winning season. In his first year in Boston in 1974, he split his time between starting and relieving, pitching in 33 games with 18 starts, eight complete games, three saves, and a 7–10 won-lost record. The next year, the six-foot, one-inch, 190-pound righty worked primarily out of the bullpen as the team's fireman, pitching in 40 games with 38 relief appearances, 15 saves, and a 2–2 record. In the ALCS, Drago pitched in two of the three games, with 4⅔ innings pitched and two saves. He pitched four innings in two games in the World Series, losing his only decision. He was traded to California for three players in March, 1976, returning to Boston in December, 1977, as a free agent. He went 4–4 in 1978, pitching in 37 games with one start and seven saves. The next year, he won ten games against six losses, pitching in 53 games with one start and 13 saves. And in 1980, he was 7–7 in 43 games pitched with seven starts and three saves. He was traded to Seattle on April 8, 1981, retiring after the season.

Drew, J.D.

David Jonathan Drew played baseball for Florida State University, where he set numerous NCAA records for batting and slugging. The six-foot, one-inch, 195-pound left-handed slugger was drafted by the Philadelphia Phillies in the 1987 amateur draft, but after bitter negotiations during which Drew refused to sign for less than $10 million, he opted to play in the independent Northern League, while becoming the poster-boy for greedy ballplayers. He re-entered the draft in 1998 and eventually signed a four-year, $8.5 million contract with the St. Louis Cardinals, who sent him to the Arkansas Travelers in the Double-A Texas League. Drew spent two months in the minor leagues, and was recalled to St. Louis on September 8. He batted a torrid .417 with the Cardinals, with five home runs in 36 at-bats down the stretch. Over the next five years, he proved to be a good ballplayer but not the superstar he was advertised to be. His batting average ranged from .242 to .323 from 1999 through 2003. He was also injury-prone, spending long periods of time on the disabled list, never playing more than 135 games in any one season, and three times playing between 100 and 109 games. Drew was traded to the Atlanta Braves in 2004, where he had a career year, batting .305 with 31 home runs and 93 RBI. He signed a free agent contract with the Los Angeles Dodgers the following year, but was a major disappointment on the west coast, playing in only 218 games in two years and batting .284 in 746 at-bats, with 35 home runs and 136 RBI.

He opted for free agency once again after the 2006 season and signed a long-term contract with the Boston Red Sox. During the exciting 2007 chase to the World Series title, Drew exasperated the Red Sox Nation faithful with his erratic play. He got off the mark quickly, ripping the ball at a .375 clip through most of April. Then suddenly his bat went cold, and hit just .189 from April 20 to June 1, dropping his season average to .222. He got hot again in June, hitting .345 in the 26 games prior to the All-Star Game, bringing his season average up to .258. He hit .231 from July 6 to September 6, but then reversed himself once again and scorched the ball at a .393 clip over the last 18 games of the season, to finish with an average of .270 with 30 doubles, four triples, 11 homers, and 64 RBI in 466 at-bats over 140 games.

In the post-season, Drew followed the same pattern. He was a non-factor in the American League Division Series, batting .182 as Boston took the measure of the Los Angeles Angels in three straight. In the American League Championship Series against the Cleveland Indians, he was more of a factor. He was 4-for-15 with no RBI in the first four games of the series as the Indians jumped out to a three-games-to-one lead, but in Game 5, with the Red Sox facing elimination, he went 1-for-1 with a double, a walk, and a run scored, as Boston won going away, 7–1. Back home in Fenway Park for Game 6, J.D. wore the hero's mantle. Coming to the plate in the first inning, with the bases loaded and two men out, as reported by Jeff Horrigan in the Boston Herald, "(Carmona) left a knee-high fastball over the plate to Drew, who crushed it with the speed, distance, and straightness of a well-struck 3-wood, sending it over the center field wall for the sixth grand slam in ALCS history."[42] Boston won the game, 12–2. Daisuke Matsuzaka took the ball for the Game 7 finale, and held Cleveland in check for five innings while his teammates pummeled Indians starter Jake Westbrook and two relievers, en route to a satisfying 11–2 victory. The World Series matched Terry Francona's charges against the National League champions, the Colorado Rockies. In this series, Boston took no prisoners, dispatching the western invaders in four games. In the opener, won by Boston by a 13–1 count, Drew doubled into the right field corner to drive in Boston's third run in the first inning and singled to drive in another run later in the game. Curt Schilling was the star of the next game, out-dueling Ubaldo Jimenez, 2–1. Drew was in the middle of the first rally, in the fourth inning, singling Mike Lowell to third base where he eventually scored on a sacrifice fly by Jason Varitek. For the game, Drew was 2-for-2 with a walk. Moving on to Colorado for Game 3, the Red Sox didn't miss a beat, pushing over six runs in the third inning en route to a 10–5 rout of the Rockies. Drew had a quiet 1-for-4 day. In the clincher the following day, he went 0-for-4 as Boston won by a 4–3 score on home runs by Mike Lowell and Bobby Kielty. Overall, Drew hit .333 for the World Series, with two doubles and two RBI. His total post-season numbers showed 16 base hits in 51 at-bats over 14 games, for a .314 average, with three doubles, one home run, and 11 RBI. Drew hit .280 with 19 homers and 64 RBI in 2008, .279 with 24 homers and 68 RBI in 2009, .255 with 22 homers and 68 RBI in 2010, and .222 with 4 homers and 22 RBI in 2011. His five year totals in Boston show a .268 batting average in 2,012 at-bats, with 532 base hits, including 80 home runs.

Dropo, Walt

Walter Dropo's nickname of Moose was derived from the name of his hometown of Moosup, Connecticut, where he was born on January 30, 1923. He signed his first baseball contract with the Boston Red Sox in 1947, and worked his way through their farm system over the next three years, finally joining the parent club in 1950 where he took over the first base job, sending Billy Goodman to the bench as a utility player. The six-foot, five-inch, 220-pound right-handed slugger had a career year in his rookie season, batting .322 with 28 doubles, 34 home runs, 101 runs scored, and a league-leading 144 runs batted in. He also led the league in total bases (326), and was second in home runs and slugging percentage (.583), earning him honors as the American League's Rookie of the Year. Dropo's explanation for his outstanding season was simple. "I was lucky. We had a strong lineup with Williams, Doerr, Stephens, Pesky, and DiMaggio, so the pitchers had to challenge the rookie and I got a lot of good pitches to hit."

That was the high-water mark of Dropo's 13-year major league career. He was struck down by the sophomore jinx in 1951, batting a lowly .239 with just 11 homers and 57 RBI in 99 games, eventually spending part of the season back in the minors, hitting .286 with five homers in 33 games with San Diego in the PCL. The next year, on June 3, the Red Sox traded him to Detroit in a nine-player deal and he responded with a .279 batting average, 32 homers, and 70 RBI for Fred Hutchinson's crew. On July 14 and 15 he tied the major league record of 12 consecutive base hits set by Pinky Higgins in 1938. He also tied the American

League record with 15 base hits in four consecutive games. Dropo played another ten years in the major leagues, with the Tigers, White Sox, Reds, and Orioles, retiring with a .270 career batting average and 152 home runs in 4,124 at-bats. Some years later he observed that "I was a .270 hitter with some power, and that .270 doesn't look so bad these days."

Easler, Mike

Mike Easler spent the first six years of his 14-year major league career bouncing back and forth between the major leagues and the minor leagues before gaining a permanent job with the Pittsburgh Pirates. He batted a crisp .307 for Pittsburgh in 1983 before being traded to the Boston Red Sox for John Tudor in December of that year.

The left-handed hitter, who had serious defensive deficiencies in the outfield with Pittsburgh, was converted to a first baseman in Boston, but that experiment was a failure also, and he spent his two-year tenure with the Red Sox primarily as a designated hitter. Easler himself thought that was a good move, noting, "The way I field, I was born to be a DH." There was never any doubt about Easler's hitting ability, however, and he gave the Red Sox a potent bat for two years, slugging .313 with 27 home runs and 91 RBI in 1984 and .262 with 16 homers and 74 RBI the following year. He was traded to the New York Yankees in 1986, retiring the following year.

Eckersley, Dennis

One of the most unique and versatile pitchers in baseball history, Dennis Eckersley was a starting pitcher for 12 of his 24 major league campaigns, and a world-class closer for the last 12 years.[43] The Eck was blessed with an explosive fastball early in his career but after he lost his velocity he relied on a devastating slider to record outs. The tall, lanky, six-foot, two-inch, 185-pound right-handed pitcher from Oakland, California, began his major league career with the Cleveland Indians in 1975, pitching in 34 games with 24 starts, and recording a 13–7 won-lost record with a 2.60 earned run average, and his efforts were rewarded when he was recognized by *The Sporting News* as the American League Rookie Pitcher of the Year.

Dennis Eckersley (George Brace photograph).

He fanned 200 batters in 1976 on his way to a 13–12 season, and on May 30, 1977, he realized a pitcher's dream by throwing a no-hitter at the California Angels, winning 1–0. He finished the year with 14 wins against 13 losses in 247⅓ innings pitched.

The following spring, Eckersley was traded to the Boston Red Sox, where he became the team's ace. He led all Boston pitchers in innings pitched and in victories his first year there, going 20–8 in 268⅓ innings pitched, and throwing 16 complete games in 35 starts, with a 2.99 ERA, as the Sox lost the American League East title to the New York Yankees by one game. The Eck won 17 games in 1979, but the following year he began to lose the zip on his fastball and he suffered through seven agonizing years on the mound, compiling a record of 74–78 between 1980 and 1986 as a starting pitcher for the Red Sox and the Chicago Cubs, who obtained him in a trade with Boston for Bill Buckner in 1984. Eckersley was subsequently traded by the Cubs to the Oakland Athletics in 1987, where he became an overnight legend. Tony LaRussa, the astute manager of the A's, immediately converted the tall right-hander with the buggy-whip delivery into the team's closer, a move that bordered on genius.

The new Oakland closer, with his new-found slider and pinpoint control, and throwing from a near-sidearm delivery, pitched in 54 games in 1987, compiling a 6–8 won-lost record with 16 saves and a 3.03 ERA. The next year he exploded on the major league scene as a closer par excellence, appearing in 60 games with a league-leading 45 saves and a minuscule 2.35 earned run average. From there it was onwards and upwards for the former fireballer. He was the American League's foremost closer from 1988 through 1995, appearing in 471 games with 35–23 won-loss record and 304 saves. He did have some ups and downs in post-season play, however. He was sensational in two Division Series, with three saves and a 1.93 ERA, and six Championship Series, with 11 saves, a 1–1 record, and a 2.70 ERA, but he endured some rough moments in the World Series. In 1988, against the Los Angeles Dodgers, he was the victim in one of the most dramatic blasts in World Series history. Coming into Game 1 in the bottom of the ninth inning to protect a 4–3 Oakland lead, he retired the first two Dodgers easily then, working carefully to Mike Davis, he walked him, bringing up a crippled Kirk Gibson, who had two bad legs that forced him to swing the bat with just his arms and wrists. It would be Gibson's only at-bat in the Series. As Gibson stepped into the batter's box he remembered the advice of the Dodgers' head scout, Mel Didier, who told him, "If the count goes to three and two, Eckersley will come in with a back-door slider, you can count on it." The Dodgers slugger fought off several pitches until he had worked a full count. Then, in a moment frozen in time, Eckersley tried to sneak a back-door slider past Gibson but the Dodgers slugger was ready for it and jerked it on a high arc to right field. A's right fielder Jose Canseco could only watch in stunned silence as the ball settled into the right field stands for a game-winning home run. That set the tone for the Series as the under-appreciated Dodgers took the powerful Oakland Athletics in five games. The Oakland closer saved one game in the 1989 World Series, a four-game sweep of the San Francisco Giants, but he was pummeled again the following year, absorbing one loss in two games pitched, with a 6.75 ERA as the Cincinnati Reds disposed of the A's in four games.

Dennis Eckersley returned to Boston to finish his career in 1998. His overall major league record consisted of 1,071 games pitched, number four all-time, 361 starts, 100 complete games, 197 victories against 171 losses, 20 shutouts, 710 relief appearances, 390 saves, a 3.50 earned run average — and one no-hitter. He also pitched in 28 post-season games, with one win, three losses, and 15 saves.[44] The well-deserving starter-closer was elected to the National Baseball Hall of Fame in 2004.

Ellsbury, Jacoby

Jacoby Ellsbury, who is of Navajo descent on his mother's side and of English and German descent on his father's side, grew up in Madras, Oregon, later moving to Arizona. As early as the second grade, Jacoby knew he wanted to be a major league baseball player and, when he was in Little League, his coach, Packy Sevada, noted, "He had the raw fundamentals to hit a baseball and run like no other in the 18 years I coached Little League. When I'd speak to the team or to Jacoby, he'd be the one to look you in the eye. He had the desire to learn and excel."[45] The Ellsburys returned to Madras in 1997 where the slim left-handed hitter attended high school, starring not only in baseball but also in track, football, and basketball. He attended Oregon State University, majoring in business and communications, and expanded his baseball skills. He batted .330, .352, and .406 during his three years at OSU, before signing a $1.4 million contract with the Boston Red Sox in 2005. One scouting report had called him "the best player in the NCAA in 2005. He has excellent instincts. His best tool is his speed and it's evident both on the bases and in center field where he catches everything hit his way."[46]

The 21-year-old outfielder began his professional baseball career that year with the Lowell Spinners in the Single-A New York–Pennsylvania League, and he responded with a .317 batting average and 23 stolen bases in 35 games. He split the 2006 season between Wilmington in the Carolina League and Portland in the Eastern League, batting .299 and .308 respectively, while stealing 41 bases in 111 games. His rapid rise through the Red Sox farm system continued through the 2007 season. He began the season with the Portland Sea Dogs, moved up to the Pawtucket Red Sox in mid-season, and up to the big club, where he electrified the Boston fans with his base hits and his flying feet, both on the bases and in the outfield. He played 33 games with Boston, 26 of them after September 1, smoking the ball at a .353 clip and stealing nine bases in nine attempts. His outstanding play was a major factor in Boston clinching the home field advantage throughout the playoffs.

Jacoby Ellsbury was the fourth outfielder in the Boston lineup, behind Drew, Crisp, and Ramirez, going into the post-season. He had just one at-bat in the three-game sweep of the Los Angeles Angels in the American League Division Series, but after Coco Crisp slumped to a .143 average in the first five games of the ALCS against the Cleveland Indians, the six-foot, one-inch, 185-pound speedster was inserted into the lineup to light a fire under the Boston offense, and he did his job well, particularly in the World Series. Boston finished off the Indians easily in the ALCS, winning the final two games by scores of 12–2 and 11–2.

Their opponent in the World Series was the upstart Colorado Rockies, the National League wild-card entry, and the winner of 21 of 22 games coming into the Series. Josh Beckett and the big Boston bats pounded the Rockies into submission in game one, winning 13–1. Curt Schilling won game two by a 2–1 score with Hideki Okajima and Jonathan Papelbon finishing up. Ellsbury, who took a collar in Game 1, went 1-for-3 with a walk in the Schilling victory. In Game 3, his bat came to life, and he combined with Dustin Pedroia for seven base hits in ten at-bats with four runs batted in, four doubles, and three runs scored, as the BoSox romped, 10–5. Ellsbury led off the third inning of a scoreless game with a double, moved to third on a bunt single by Pedroia and scored the game's first run on a double by David Ortiz. Later in the same inning, he rocketed another double to the left-center field gap, driving in the sixth run of the inning and becoming just the second player to hit two doubles in the same inning of a World Series game. Ellsbury finished the Game 4-for-5 with three doubles in the Boston massacre. Terry Francona's team completed the sweep of the Rockies the next day with Jon Lester chalking up the win. Jacoby Ellsbury led off the game with an opposite-field double down the left field line and carried the first run of the game across the plate on a double by Ortiz. The kid from Oregon added a single later in the game and Boston closed out Colorado 4–3. For the Series, Ellsbury batted .438 with seven hits in 16 at-bats, including four doubles.

The sophomore jinx nipped at his heels in 2008 but he finished the season strong, batting .280 with 98 runs scored and a league-leading 50 stolen bases. He hit .333 with six RBI in Boston's victory over the Los Angeles Angels in the ALDS, but he took the collar in the Championship Series, going 0-for-14 as the Red Sox bowed to the fired-up Tampa Bay Rays in seven games. The following year, the 25-year-old greyhound fought his way through good times and bad, beginning on April 12 when he broke Mike Greenwell's Boston record of 178 errorless games. Three days later he broke Coco Crisp's Sox record of 432 consecutive errorless chances

Jacoby Ellsbury

in Boston's 8–2 victory over Oakland. The New York Yankees were in town on the 26th with Andy Pettitte on the mound facing Justin Masterson, and Jacoby Ellsbury gave the hometown fans something to cheer about. In the Boston third, he reached on a fielder's choice, stole second base, and later scored the first run of the game. Two innings later, he drew a one-out walk, raced around to third base on David Ortiz's two-out double and, stayed there while Pettitte started to issue an intentional walk to Manny Ramirez. Ellsbury, one of the league's most dangerous baserunners, saw that Pettitte was ignoring him, and he made the Yankees southpaw pay for that mistake. He stretched his lead off third and then, as soon as Pettitte began his windup, he turned on the afterburners and headed home. When Pettitte realized what was happening, he rushed his windup and delivery, but the Boston speedster bounced across the plate on his stomach, easily beating Jorge Posada's tag as 38,154 Red Sox fans leaped to their feet screaming. They kept standing and screaming until Ellsbury came out of the dugout for a curtain call.

In May, he tied a major league record for outfielders with 12 putouts in a nine-inning game, but in June, after recording a mediocre .332 on-base-percentage with just ten bases on balls in 48 games, manager Terry Francona dropped the youngster from the leadoff spot to the seventh spot in the batting order, instructing him to take a more disciplined approach at the plate in order to add to his walk total and increase his OBP. Two weeks after his demotion, the Boston center fielder had his two Red Sox streaks broken. In a game against the Florida Marlins on June 17 he had a fly ball go off the tip of his glove in the first inning, ending his errorless streak at 222 games and 554 chances. The next night, his 22-game hitting streak came to an end as the Florida Marlins nipped Boston, 2–1, in a game called because of rain after five-and-a-half innings.

By July 20, Jacoby Ellsbury had improved his plate discipline to the point where he was returned to the leadoff spot in the batting order. His increased OBP and his flying feet stole the show as the season drew to a close. On August 21, he tied Tommy Harper's Boston stolen base record with his 54th in a game against the New York Yankees, and the victim, once again, was Yankees ace Andy Pettitte. Ellsbury walked and stole second base in the first inning but that was one of the few highlights for the Red Sox, who found themselves on the short end of a 20–11 score by the time the crowd filed out of Fenway Park. Four days later, he broke Harper's record in the first inning of a game against the Chicago White Sox. He led off the game with a double and promptly stole third base, eventually scoring the first run of the game. He finished with a 3-for-5 day as Boston came away a winner by a 6–3 score. For the season, Jacoby Ellsbury stung the ball at a .301 clip with 94 runs scored and a league-leading 70 stolen bases, finishing with a respectable .355 OBP.

The Boston speedster was sidelined most of the 2010 season after breaking six ribs in a collision with Adrian Beltre while chasing a fly ball down the left field line. He played just 18 games, but he returned to the baseball wars with a vengeance in 2011 and had a career-year. He recorded personal highs in batting average (.321), runs scored (119), doubles (46), home runs (32), and RBI (105), while stealing 39 bases. His home run output was 12 more than his four-year major league career total. Ellsbury's sensational effort was recognized by Major League Baseball and the beat writers who names him the American League Comeback Player of the Year.

Ellsbury keeps the fans on the edge of their seats day-in and day-out with his aggressive play and blinding speed. He makes impossible catches look routine, once pulling a Willie Mays highlight-reel catch with his back to the plate, taking the ball over his shoulder at the 420-foot mark. He has a reputation for being fearless, and that's reflected in his relentless pursuit of any ball hit into his territory. He dives onto the dirt warning track near the wall or scales the wall to make a catch if necessary. The excitement he brings to the game, and his sensational catches, will be retold in Back Bay and the Fens long after he has retired.

Engle, Clyde

Clyde Engle, the pride of Dayton, Ohio, had an eight-year major league career as a utility-man who played all infield and outfield positions. The five-foot, ten-inch, 190-pound right-handed hitter began his major league career with the New York Highlanders in 1909, playing left field and hitting .278 with 71 RBI in 492 at-bats. The following year, he was traded to the Boston Red Sox, beginning a four-and-a-half-year relationship with the Boston outfit. He became a jack-of-all-trades with Patsy Donovan's team, playing 106 games, 85 of them in the infield, and hitting .264. The next year was more of the same. He played in 146 games, mostly in the infield, and batted .270 with 24 stolen bases. In 1912, the Red Sox raced to the American League pennant by 14 games over the Washington Senators, but Engle saw action in only 58 games. He was limited to three pinch-hit appearances in the World Series, won by Boston over the New York Giants, four games to three, but in Game 8, "he was involved in one of the most celebrated plays in World Series history. With Boston trailing New York by a 2–1 score in the bottom of the tenth inning, Engle, pinch hitting for Smoky Joe Wood, hit an easy fly ball to right field that Giant outfielder Fred Snodgrass dropped, for what came to be known as the '$30,000 muff,' opening the floodgates for the Red Sox. Two walks, a single, and a sacrifice fly brought the World Championship home to Boston."[47] Clyde Engel played with Boston until midway through the 1914 season, when he jumped to the Buffalo Buffeds of the new Federal League. He returned to the American League to play for the Cleveland Indians in 1916, but retired after playing just 11 games.

Evans, Dwight

The Boston Red Sox have had several outstanding right fielders in their long history, including Harry Hooper and Jackie Jensen, but Dwight Evans may be the best of the lot. The eight-time Gold Glove winner was a master of Fenway Park's confusing right field foul area, and he had a cannon for a throwing arm that kept most runners glued to their bases.[48] Dwight Michael Evans was born in Santa Monica, California, on November 3, 1951. He was signed to a professional baseball contract by the Boston Red Sox in 1969 and began his professional career with the sixth-place Jamestown Falcons in the Single-A New York–Pennsylvania League,

Dwight Evans

where he batted .280 in 34 games. He made his way through the Boston farm system over the next three years, eventually completing his baseball internship with the Louisville Colonels, where he was named the International League's MVP in 1972, hitting an even .300 with 17 homers and 95 RBI in 144 games. He was called up to the big club on September 16, going 0-for-1 as a late-inning replacement in Luis Tiant's masterful three-hitter of the Cleveland Indians, Boston winning, 10–0. He played a total of 18 games at the end of the season with a .263 batting average and one home run. The next year, the man they called Dewey played in 119 games with 282 at-bats. He struggled at the plate, batting just .223, but he showed flashes of power with 13 doubles and 10 home runs. And he gained the immediate respect of opposing players and managers for his defensive skills that included above average speed and a cannon for a throwing arm.

In 1974, Evans brought his batting average up to a respectable .281 and drove in 70 runs in 463 at-bats, with 19 doubles and 10 home runs. He also led the league with a .990 fielding average. Over the next three years, the six-foot, three-inch, 204-pound right-handed hitter gradually increased his power numbers, but he also went through the most difficult period in his career. He battled a knee injury throughout the entire 1977 season, spending significant time on the disabled list that limited his playing time to 73 games. Still, he batted a respectable .287 with 14 homers and 36 RBI in 230 at-bats. The following season was almost as bad. On August 28, in a game against the Seattle Mariners, he was beaned by Mariners rookie Mike Parrott. He was rushed back into action after four games by manager Don Zimmer, who didn't understand Evans' problem. Zimmer, who had suffered a terrifying beaning himself that required having a metal plate inserted into his skull, railed at his right fielder for being plate-shy on his return to action, saying he had "the balls of a milk cow." In fact, Evans was suffering from vertigo, causing dizziness and double vision. Zimmer's action eventually cost Boston the pennant as they went 17–17 down the stretch, finishing one game behind the New York Yankees, and Evans struggled to hit a barely visible .161 with three extra-base hits and three RBI in 21 games, while striking out 19 times in 56 at-bats.

Once Dewey had fully recovered from his beaning and Ralph Houk had taken the helm in Boston, the right-handed slugger went on to have nine consecutive years of 20 or more home runs and four years of 100 or more RBI. During this period, Evans was a complete ballplayer, contributing to his team's success not only at the plate but in the field as well. He enjoyed a spectacular 1982 season, batting .292 with 32 homers, 122 runs scored, and 98 RBI, winning his fifth Gold Glove, being named to the American League All-Star team, and winning the T.A. Yawkey Award as the Red Sox MVP. His best year at the plate was 1987 when he hit a career-high .305 with 109 runs scored, 37 doubles, 34 home runs, and 123 RBI in 541 at-bats. He also had 32 homers, a league-leading 121 runs scored, and 104 RBI in 1984, and 29 homers with 110 runs scored and a league-leading 114 RBI the following year. During the strike-shortened 1981 season he led the American League with 22 home runs, 85 bases on balls, and 215 total bases. Over his career he averaged 30 doubles, 24 home runs, and 85 runs batted in for every 550 at-bats.

Dewey Evans' reputation in the field was beyond question. He was generally regarded as the best right fielder in the American League during the 1970s and 80s, winning eight Gold Gloves between 1976 and 1985. He led the league in fielding average twice, putouts four times, and assists and double plays three times each and, in addition, he helped his pitchers by keeping opposing base runners from taking extra bases on hits to right field. Dewey was particularly dangerous in the World Series, where he hit a combined .300 in two Series with three doubles, one triple, three home runs, and 14 RBI in 14 games. In Game 3 of the 1975 World Series against the Cincinnati Reds, he hit a two-run homer off Rawley Eastwick in the top of the ninth inning to tie the score at five-all, only to have the Reds push over the game winner in the tenth. The next day, in Game 4, he ripped a triple to the right field wall in the top of the fourth inning, driving in the first two runs of the game in an eventual 5–4 Red Sox victory. And in Game 6, the famous Carlton Fisk game, Evans gave Fisk a chance to bat with a sensational defensive play in the 11th inning. Cincinnati put a man on base with one out, and as Joe Morgan made his way to the plate, Evans stood in right field planning what he would do if a ball was hit his way. "When the ball was hit, I was ready for it," he said. "It wasn't the best catch I ever made, but it was the most important." Morgan, a left-handed hitter, drove the ball hard to right field and, Dewey had to reach back behind his head to make a spectacular leaping catch in front of the right field stands taking an extra-base hit away from "Little Joe." His quick throw to Yastrzemski and Carl's relay to Denny Doyle doubled off Ken Griffey, Jr., who was already standing on third base. Fisk ended the suspense one inning later on the second pitch thrown to him in the bottom of the 12th inning. In Game 2 of the 1986 Series, Evans paced the Sox to a 9–3 drubbing of the New York Mets with a single, a homer, and two RBI, and in the decisive seventh game, he gave John McNamara's team a 1–0 lead in the top of the second inning with a home run. His two-run double in the eighth inning trimmed New York's lead to 6–5, but Boston could get no closer, eventually falling, 8–5.

Ferrell, Rick

Richard Benjamin (Rick) Ferrell was one of the finest defensive catchers of his era, an excellent handler of pitchers, an artist at framing pitches and the possessor of a strong throwing arm who gunned down 41 percent of base runners attempting to steal. Unlike his hot-tempered brother, Wes, the slim, slightly balding receiver was a real gentleman, soft-spoken and considerate, and a leader by example. One of seven brothers including Wes, he was born on a farm in Durham, NC, on October 12, 1905. The Ferrell brothers all played sandlot baseball, and Rick won the catcher's job by default. No one else wanted to catch. In addition to Rick's 18-year major league career, Wes enjoyed a 15-year major league career and George played minor league ball for 20 years.

Nineteen-year-old Rick Ferrell was signed to a professional baseball contract by the St. Louis Cardinals in 1925 and spent several weeks riding the bench in St. Louis without getting into a game. The next year, with Kinston in the Class-B Virginia League, the five-foot, 11-inch, 170-pound backstop batted .265 and was a standout on defense. He hit .249 and .333 during two years with Columbus in the American Association, the Cardinals' top farm club, and when Commissioner Kenesaw Mountain Landis declared him a free agent after the 1928 season, he signed with the St. Louis Browns, where he spent four years, refining his craft and establishing a reputation as a fine defensive catcher with a dangerous bat. On April 29, 1931, he was on the field when his brother Wes tossed a 9–0 no-hitter at the Browns in League Park, Cleveland. But he almost ended Wes' bid for immortality. He smashed a ball back through the middle that looked like a sure base hit, but Cleveland shortstop Bill Hunnefield made a spectacular stop, then threw the ball wide to first base, allowing Rick to reach. Rick went on to bat .306 that year and .315 the following year, before being traded to the Boston Red Sox on May 11, 1933.

Ferrell, who would be joined on the Red Sox by his brother in 1934, continued his strong hitting with Boston from 1933 to 1937, posting a combined batting average of .302. The right-handed hitter had little power, but he had an outstanding .393 on-base percentage during his Red Sox stay thanks to an exceptional batting eye that drew an average of 83 walks, with just 23 strikeouts, for every 550 at-bats. He stroked the ball at a .301 clip with 34 doubles and 65 bases on balls in 458 at-bats in 1935, and .312 with 27 doubles and 65 walks in 410 at-bats the following year. More important than his offense, however, was his defense. When his brother Wes joined him in Boston, he told Wes, whom he had caught since before they were teenagers, "Throw me anything you please. You can't fool me." Wes agreed, noting, "He was a real classy receiver. You never saw him lunge for a ball. He'd get more strikes for a pitcher than anybody I ever saw because he made catching look easy." Rick was unexpectedly traded to Washington on June 10, 1937, after hitting .308 in 18 games.

Ferrell, Wes

Wes Ferrell was a big, strong, handsome, hot-tempered, right-handed pitcher who stood six-foot, two-inches tall and weighed a muscular 195 pounds. He was born in Greensboro, NC on February 2, 1908, and grew up playing baseball with his six brothers. He graduated from Guilford College in 1927 and joined the Cleveland Indians that summer, appearing in one game with no record. The 19-year-old pitcher was blessed with a blazing fastball that had batters diving into the dirt. After one year in the minors, where he went 20–8 with Terre Haute in the Class-B Three-I League, he joined the big club in 1929 and promptly ran off four 20-plus-victory seasons under manager Roger Peckinpaugh. His four-year totals in Cleveland were 21–10, 25–13, 22–12, and 23–13, setting a major league record in the modern era for winning 20 or more games his first four years in the majors. During an era when men were men and pitchers finished what they started, he completed 96 of 129 starts for a sensational 74 percent completion rate.

Wes reached the pinnacle of pitching supremacy on April 29, 1931, when he threw a no-hitter against the St. Louis Browns with brother Rick in the St. Louis lineup. Rick almost ruined his Wes' gem. He lined a ball back through the middle that looked like a sure base hit, but shortstop Bill Hunnefield ran the ball down and made an off-balance throw to first base that was wide of the mark, permitting Rick to reach base. The friendly home-town score gave Hunnefield an error on the play, one of three errors he was charged with on the day. Wes struck out eight batters and walked three in his classic. He also paced the offense, smashing a double and a home run, and driving in four runs.

Ferrell injured his arm in 1933 and his record fell to 11–12 that year. But the big, rawboned right-hander didn't let that curtail his career. He changed from a hard-throwing flamethrower to a curveball pitcher, giving himself five more years of pitching excellence. In 1934, at the suggestion of his brother Rick, the Boston Red Sox obtained Wes in a trade and were rewarded with three years of outstanding pitching. Throwing to his brother, he went 14–5 his first year in Boston, with 17 complete games in 23 starts. The next year he had a career year, leading the American League with 25 victories, 38 games started, 31 complete games, and 322⅓ innings pitched. But his temper was as noteworthy as his pitching. Teammate Billy Werber remembered one game when Ferrell had been knocked out of the box by the Philadelphia A's. He went to the dugout and "struck himself in the jaw with his fist and slammed his head into the concrete wall. Bucky (manager Bucky Harris) had to pin his arms to his sides to keep him from doing further damage. Another time I saw him get so mad after being taken out of a game that he jumped up and down on an expensive watch he owned, crunching it beyond repair."[49] Ferrell won 20 games again the following year, going 20–15, again leading the league in games started (38), complete games (28), and innings pitched (301).

Wes Ferrell's teammate in Boston from 1934 to 1937 was Lefty Grove, giving Boston two of the most tempestuous players ever to step on a baseball diamond. The two pitchers combined for 45 victories in 1935 and 37 victories the following year, but Ferrell, who was hit hard early in 1937, going 3–6 with a 7.61 ERA, was shipped off to Washington where he finished the year with a record of 14–19. He went 15–10 the next year, essentially ending his career. With Boston, he won 62 games against 40 losses for a fine .608 winning percentage, while completing 81 of 110 starts, a 74 percent completion rate.

Wes Ferrell was also one of the best-hitting pitchers ever to play major league baseball. His career batting average was .280, based on 329 base hits in 1,176 at-bats. His 38 career home runs are a record for major league pitchers, and were ten more than brother Rick hit in 6,028 at-bats. Wes slammed nine home runs and batted .319 in 116 at-bats in 1931, hit seven home runs in 140 at-bats two years later, and hit another seven home runs with 32 RBI and a .347 batting average, in 150 at-bats in 1935. As Werber noted, "Ferrell wanted the ball, and if he was not pitching, he wanted to pinch hit. In the late innings of a close ball game, Wesley could sense when a pinch hitter might be needed almost before the manager. He would go to the bat rack, select his bat, and walk to and fro in front of manager Bucky Harris, waving that bat. He wanted to be at the plate no matter who was pitching and he could be counted on to get the bat on the ball. He even played 13 games in the outfield in 1933 and hit .271 for the year."[50] After he left the major leagues in 1941, Wes Ferrell played in the minor leagues for another eight years, off and on, and in 1942 played second base and outfield for Lynchburg in the Class-C Virginia League and led the league in batting average (.361) and home runs (31) in 410 at-bats.

Ferris, Hobe

Albert Samuel "Hobe" Ferris, a native of Trowbridge, England, had a well-earned reputation as a hard-nosed baseball player who played the game all-out all the time. The pugnacious infielder, who stood only five-foot, eight-inches tall and who weighed a feathery 162 pounds, was a famous umpire baiter who suffered several suspensions during his career. He was also quick with his fists, engaging in numerous fights with opposing players and teammates, much to the dismay of his managers and owners.

Ferris began his baseball career with North Attleboro, Massachusetts, in 1898, moving up to Pawtucket in the New England League the following year, where he stung the ball at a .295 clip. In 1900, he hit .292 for Norwich in the Connecticut League, with 31 of his hits going for extra bases. Throughout his major league career, the slender infielder earned a reputation as a slugger, with 28 percent of his hits going for extra bases, a figure exceeded by only ten other American League players during the Deadball era, according to Dennis H. Auger in *Deadball Stars of the American League*. In 1901, Ferris was drafted by the Cincinnati Reds, but chose to join the Boston entry in the newly formed American League instead. He was an immediate standout with the bat in Boston, rapping 16 doubles and 15 triples in 523 at-bats, and driving in 63 runs, but his defense was atrocious, primarily because he was learning a new position at second base after playing shortstop previously. He was charged with 61 errors in his rookie season, the second-highest total for a second baseman in American League history, but he quickly refined his defense, and, over the next six years, he was considered to be the premier defensive second baseman in the league, dazzling the fans with spectacular plays that short-circuited many an enemy rally. One writer said his defense made Nap Lajoie "look like a second-rater."[51]

During the Pilgrims' World Championship season in 1903, Hobe Ferris batted a respectable .251 and played a sensational second base despite leading the league in errors. On June 5, at the Huntington Avenue Baseball Grounds, he slammed an inside-the-park home run to pace the Pilgrims to a 10–8 victory over the Chicago White Sox. On August 23, in a doubleheader against the Browns in St. Louis, he displayed his sensational glove work in Boston's 5–3 and 4–2 sweep. In game one he short-circuited a Brownie rally by starting a triple play, saving the game for Long Tom Hughes. In the nightcap, he came to Cy Young's rescue by starting a double play to kill another rally and quieting 19,000 St. Louis fans.[52] In the World Series against the Pittsburgh Pirates, won by Boston five games to three, he committed the first error in World Series history when he bobbled a grounder off the bat of Kitty Bransfield in the top of the first inning, leading to three unearned runs in a 7–3 Pittsburgh victory. But he more than made up for that miscue as the Series progressed. In the fourth inning of Game 2, with Boston on top by a 2–0 score, and Pirate runners on second and third, Honus Wagner hit a line drive that he corralled and turned into an inning-ending unassisted double play. In the game eight finale, the little right-handed hitter drove in all the runs in a 3–0 victory. In the fourth inning, he hit a one-out dying quail to center field to plate Freeman and Parent with the first two runs of the game, and in the sixth inning, he lined a two-out single to center field to send Candy LaChance across the plate with the final run. Overall, Hobe Ferris hit .290 in the Series with a triple and five RBI.

The following year, when the team visited Cleveland, a fire broke out in the hotel, and Ferris, Bill Dinneen, Freddy Parent, and Norwood Gibson risked their lives fighting the fire and were afterward hailed as heroes. The little Englishman could be a hero if the opportunity presented itself, but he could also bring the wrath of the establishment down on his shoulders when his fiery temper exploded. In 1902 he was suspended for an altercation with umpire Jack Sheriden. And four years later, he self destructed. "His nasty temper flared up during a September 6, 1906 game against the New York Highlanders in Hilltop Park (when) Boston outfielder Jack Hayden took a leisurely route on a fly ball hit to short right field, which Ferris himself failed to go after, resulting in an inside-the-park home run. Returning to the bench at the end of the inning, Ferris initiated a vile verbal attack on Hayden for what he perceived to be a lackadaisical play. Hayden, in turn, landed three stingers to Hobe's jaw. After their teammates separated them, Ferris braced himself on a rail and thrust his foot into Hayden's face, knocking out several teeth."[53] When the smoke cleared, both players were ejected from the game, and Ferris was arrested on assault charges and suspended for the rest of the season. He later tried to justify his actions by saying, "I suppose I'm a fool for being in earnest and trying to win, but that is my way."[54]

Hobe Ferris was traded to the St. Louis Browns in 1908, where he played out the final two years of his major league career. He drifted back to the minors in 1910, eventually retiring in 1914. During his seven years in Boston, Ferris stroked the ball at a deceptively low .237 clip with 876 base hits in 3,689 at-bats. In the field he was brilliant, posting a .954 fielding average that was five points higher than the league average, and displaying outstanding range. He led the league in fielding average once, putouts twice, assists twice, and double plays twice.

Ferriss, Dave

David Meadow "Boo" Ferriss, born on December 5, 1921, was a true country gentleman out of Shaw, Mississippi. He acquired his nickname as a toddler when his attempt to say "brother" kept coming out "Boo." Ferriss received an early baseball education from his father, who played, coached, and umpired baseball around Shaw, and he grew into an outstanding athlete at Shaw High School, not only in baseball where he compiled a 19–2 record, but in football, basketball, and tennis as well. He was already being scouted by major league scouts, but his father told him he needed to get a college education before he pursued his baseball dream, so the lanky right-hander, who grew to six-foot, two-inches tall and topped the scales at a husky 208 pounds, entered Mississippi State University on a full baseball scholarship in 1939. He excelled at Mississippi State both in the classroom and on the diamond for three years. In the spring of 1942 the 20-year-old right-hander was drafted by the Boston Red Sox and left college to try his hand with Boston's Greensboro farm team in the Class-B Piedmont League. He went 7–7 with a 2.22 ERA for the pennant-winning Red Sox and, as he told me, he was called "the hero of the league playoffs and league championship series" by his manager, former major league player and Future Hall Of Famer Heinie Manush. In the semi-finals against the Charlotte Hornets, he won one game and saved two, all in relief, as Greensboro won four straight. Then, in the finals against Portsmouth, he saved one game and threw a four-hitter to win the fifth game, as Greensboro prevailed in six.

As he was about to make his mark on the game, Ferriss, like many other young men in that era, was sidetracked by World War II. He received his draft notice after the 1942 Piedmont League season ended, and he was soon on his way to Randolph Field in Texas, as a member of the U.S. Army Air Corps, his home for the next 26 months. He was a physical training instructor on the base, and a pitcher on the baseball team under manager Bibb Falk, a 12-year major league outfielder who compiled a .314 career batting average. In 1944, Boo Ferriss went 20–8 on the mound for Randolph Field, and walked off with the batting championship as well, posting a .417 average to nose out Enos "Country" Slaughter by three points. Ferriss was hospitalized with asthma during the winter, and subsequently received a medical discharge in February, 1945. He reported to the Boston Red Sox's Louisville farm team in the International League in the spring, but was called up to the parent club before he ever appeared in a game for the Colonels.

He joined the Boston Red Sox in April and set the American League on its heels, pitching a two-hitter against the Philadelphia Athletics in Shibe Park in his major league debut on the

Dave "Boo" Ferriss

29th, winning 2–0, and going three for three at the plate against Bobo Newsome. One week later he blanked the New York Yankees in Fenway Park by a 5–0 count, and contributed a single and a double to the Boston offense. He went on to set two American League records along the way, 22⅓ consecutive scoreless innings at the start of his career and winning his first eight games, four by shutout. Armed with a devastating sinker and slider, plus a deceptive windup, he took the league by storm. As one American League hitter said, "I know why I can't hit Ferriss. He hides that ball behind his back and he uses his glove to shield the ball from the hitter. The glove screens the ball, and the hitter doesn't get a look at the ball at all until it is almost on top of him."[55] Boo Ferriss won 21 games against just 10 losses for a seventh-place team in 1945, completing 26 of 31 games started with five shutouts, and throwing 264⅔ innings with a 2.96 earned run average, 40 points lower than the league average. The next year, joined by Mickey Harris (17–9) and Tex Hughson (20–11), Ferriss won 25 games against six losses, for a league-leading .806 winning percentage, and the Red Sox made a historic journey from seventh place to the American League pennant. The big right-hander continued his dominating ways that year, completing 26 games in 35 starts with six shutouts, and pitching 274 innings with a 3.25 ERA. In the World Series, a seven-game loss to the St. Louis Cardinals, Ferriss threw a six-hit shutout at the Redbirds in Game 3, winning 4–0, and he had a no-decision in Game 7, won by St. Louis on Slaughter's daring baserunning maneuver.

Sadly for Boo Ferriss, his career began a downward spiral in 1947, due to a painful injury suffered on July 14. As he reported it to me, "I tore something in my shoulder in a night game in Cleveland in 1947. I tried to snap a 3–2 curveball and I heard something pop. I finished the game and Bobby Doerr hit a home run in the ninth and we won, 1–0. The next day I couldn't get my arm up to my three-quarter delivery. I could only pitch sidearm. Next start against Chicago, I lost the zip on my fastball. I never had the power again."[56] He struggled through the remainder of the year, pitching in pain most of the time, while throwing 218⅓ innings and compiling a 12–11 won-loss record. The next year, in what turned out to be his swan song, he pitched 115⅓ innings in 31 games with nine starts, posting a 7–3 record. He pitched just 7⅔ innings in five games with the Red Sox over the next two years, and spent three years in the minor leagues attempting a comeback before calling it a day. He was the pitching coach for the Red Sox from 1955 to 1959, and then left organized baseball to assume the duties of baseball coach and athletic director at Delta State University in Cleveland, Mississippi, a position he held for 26 years before retiring in 1988.

Over his abbreviated six-year major league career, all with Boston, Ferriss won 65 games against 30 losses for a superb .684 winning percentage. He completed 67 of his 103 starts for a 65 percent completion rate, a feat that is unheard-of today. In addition to his pitching credentials, he also helped himself at the plate with a .250 career batting average that produced 19 RBI in both 1945 and 1947. According to *The Ballplayers*, he was used as a left-handed pinch-hitter 41 times. He was also an exceptional defensive player, with quick reflexes and a reliable glove.

Finney, Lou

SABR historian Doug Skipper wrote in, "Lou Finney," "Lou Finney was a tough man to strike out, a fast, feisty left-handed hitter with line-drive power. A scrappy curly-haired Alabaman who spoke with a Southern drawl, fanned only once for every 24.9 official turns, one of the 50 best ratios in major league history." Jimmie Foxx added, "He's a guy that'll cut your heart out to win a game." An outfielder-first baseman, Lou Finney enjoyed a 12-year major league career without ever finding a permanent position. He played 688 games in the outfield, playing all three positions at one time or another, and 415 games at first base. His defense was just average or slightly below average in all positions, but wherever he played, he could always hit. He produced a .287 career batting average, mostly with the Philadelphia Athletics and the Boston Red Sox, including three years over .300.

Finney joined the Red Sox in May, 1939, and played with them into the 1945 season, when he was sent to the St. Louis Browns. Boston finished in second place three times during Finney's stay there, but they could never grab the brass ring. The six-foot, 175-pound left-handed hitter served as a valuable utility man or as a fill-in for Jimmie Foxx at first base, but his lack of power prevented him from nailing down a permanent job. He contributed more than his share to Boston's season in 1939, batting .325 while playing 32 games at first base and 24 games in the outfield. He led the American League with 13 pinch hits. In 1940 he put together his best season, slugging the ball at a .320 clip with 31 doubles, 15 triples, and 73 RBI in 130 games. His effort was rewarded when he was selected for the American League All-Star team that year. Finney's statistics began to decline gradually after 1940 when he passed his 30th birthday, and he finally left the major leagues in 1947.

Fisk, Carlton "Pudge"

Backstop, a book that compared the 50 greatest catchers in the history of major league baseball, rated Carlton Fisk the 14th-greatest all-round catcher of all time. He was number 15 on offense and number 30 on defense. He was considered to be one of the foremost sluggers ever to don the tools of ignorance, and his above-average speed was reflected in his 128 career stolen bases as well as in his low grounded-into-double play totals. He was also an outstanding defensive catcher, adept at calling a game, blocking pitches in the dirt to prevent passed balls and wild pitches, and at blocking the plate. He was an expert at framing pitches to give his pitchers more than their fair share of strike calls. His fielding average was superior to his contemporaries, and his above-average quickness and foot speed gave him a decided advantage in running down pop-ups or pouncing on bunts. His only weakness behind the plate, and the primary reason for his low defensive rating, was his caught-stealing record. He threw out just 33 percent of runners attempting to steal compared to a league average of 36 percent.

The future Hall Of Fame catcher was born in Bellows Falls, Vermont, on December 26, 1947. "As a catcher on a kid's baseball team, the chubby youngster was called 'Pudgy,' later reduced to just Pudge. The nickname stuck. Carlton 'Pudge' Fisk attended the University of New Hampshire where he dreamed about being a power forward for the Boston Celtics, but he was sidetracked when the Boston Red Sox drafted him in the first round of the 1967 baseball draft."[57] After serving a year in the army, Fisk joined the Waterloo Hawks in the Single-A Midwest League, and he immediately made his mark on the game, hitting a crisp .338 with 12 homers in 62 games. He played for the Pittsfield Red Sox in the Double-A Eastern League the following year, but his average fell to a disappointing .243. After a .229 season with the Pawtucket Red Sox in the same league in 1970, he found his stroke with the Louisville Colonels of the International League, batting .263 with 10 home runs in 94 games, not a sensational record, but something to build on.

Manager Eddie Kasko called Pudge Fisk up to Boston in September, and he responded with a healthy .313 batting average in 48 at-bats. The big backstop, who had melted away the blubber of his younger days, was now a muscular 220 pounds, well distributed over his six-foot, three-inch frame.[58] Beginning in 1972, Fisk was the first-string catcher for the Red Sox, a position he filled for the next nine years, although the journey was never smooth. The right-handed-hitting slugger had a stellar season in 1972, rapping the ball at a .293 clip with 28 doubles, a league-leading nine triples, 22 home runs, and 61 RBI in 457 at-bats. He, like the rest of the Red Sox, was disappointed when the team lost the American League pennant to the Detroit Tigers by a scant one-half game, but his pain was alleviated somewhat by his unanimous selection as the American League's Rookie of the Year. He also won his only Gold Glove that year. Fisk caught 135 games in 1973, hitting a so-so .246 but hammering 26 home runs and driving in 71 runs.

The next two years were difficult ones for Pudge as he was hampered by injuries to his collarbone, knee, arm, and groin, limiting his playing time to 52 games in 1974 and 79 games the following year. When he was healthy, however, he wielded a dangerous bat, slugging the ball at a combined .318 average in 450 at-bats, with 26 doubles, 21 homers, and 78 RBI. He hit the ball hard in the 1975 ALCS, batting .417 in the three-game sweep of the Oakland Athletics. His World Series average was a lukewarm .240, but he provided one of the enduring memories of World Series play when he smashed

Carlton Fisk

had hit more home runs (351) and caught more games (2,226) than any catcher in major league history. His home run record was subsequently eclipsed by Mike Piazza, and the games-caught record by Ivan Rodriguez. He was a 2000 inductee into the National Baseball Hall of Fame in Cooperstown, New York. He is also the catcher on the Boston Red Sox all-time, all-star team.

Flagstead, Ira "Pete"

Pete Flagstead was an outstanding, all-around major league center fielder for 13 years, including seven years with the Boston Red Sox. The Montague, Michigan, native stood just five-foot, nine-inches tall and weighed 165 pounds soaking wet, but he was a talented contact hitter who rarely struck out and who had an excellent on-base percentage. In the field, he was a fleet-footed center fielder with a strong throwing arm and a reliable glove. Flagstead began his baseball odyssey in 1917 as a 23-year-old right-handed-hitting third baseman with Tacoma in the Class-B Northwestern League, where he pummeled opposing pitchers to the tune of a .376 average, losing the batting title by a single point. The following season, now settled in center field, he tattooed the ball at a .381 clip for Chattanooga in the Southern Association, resulting in his recall by the Detroit Tigers. His rookie season in the major leagues was a memorable one as he hit American League pitchers for a .331 average in 287 at-bats with 22 doubles and a .416 OBP. Flagstead played in Detroit for three more years, but he couldn't break into the starting all-world outfield of Bobby Veach, Ty Cobb, and Harry Heilmann, so he was sold to Boston at the beginning of the 1923 season.

Detroit's loss was Boston's gain as Pete Flagstead put together two consecutive .300 seasons, batting .312 for the Red Sox in 1923 and .307 in 1924. He didn't have much power but he was able to hit the alleys frequently enough to produce as many as 41 doubles in a season and, as one source noted, his bat and his hustle delighted Boston fans. In 1925, he hit a strong .280 for the Red Sox, leading the team with 38 doubles, 160 base hits, 63 bases on balls, and 84 runs scored. He also sparkled in the outfield, running down fly balls with mo-

a historic 12-inning, game-winning home run off the left field foul pole in Game 6, hopping down the first base line and waving his arms frantically, trying to will the ball into fair territory.

Pudge Fisk returned to action full-time in 1976 and gave the Boston faithful five more years of sensational backstopping, although he was limited to 91 games in 1979 after spending 38 days on the disabled list. Overall he played in Boston for 11 years, playing in 1,078 games, with 1,097 base hits in 3,860 at-bats, for a .284 batting average. Much to the chagrin of Boston fans, their favorite receiver opted for free agency at the end of the 1980 season, eventually signing a long-term contract with the Chicago White Sox, where he played for the next 13 seasons, retiring from the wars in 1993.

Pudge Fisk set a major league record with just four passed balls in 151 games in 1977.

In the same year, he became the fifth catcher in major league history to score and drive in 100 or more runs, when he scored 106 runs, drove in 102 runs, and batted a solid .315 with 26 doubles and 26 home runs. During his career, he was an 11-time all-star, and appeared in seven All-Star Games. When he retired, he notorious regularity, and keeping baserunners honest with his accurate throws. His hustle was rewarded when he was voted Boston's Most Valuable Player at the end of the season. On April 19, 1926, the little center fielder tied the major league record for the most double plays started by an outfielder in a game, with three. Unfortunately for Flagstead, he played with the Red Sox at a time when they fielded cellar-dwelling teams year after year. During his six years in Boston, the team finished last five times and seventh once. In 1928, Flagstead's last full year in a Boston uniform, he played in 140 games, batting .290 with 41 doubles and 84 runs scored. Late in the season he was honored by the team and the fans with "Flagstead Day," and he was showered with numerous gifts including $1,000 in gold and a new car. Pete Flagstead was claimed on waivers by Washington 14 games into the 1929 season and was sold to Pittsburgh the same year. The 36-year-old outfielder returned to the minor leagues after hitting .250 in 1930. He played one year in the Pacific Coast League, batting .231, and then retired to his home in Olympia, Washington, where he coached the local baseball team, leading them to the Timber League playoffs three consecutive years. He also enjoyed fishing with his wife Reita and raising game roosters and call ducks. He died on March 13, 1940, at the age of 46.

Fornieles, Mike

Jose Miguel "Mike" Fornieles was born in Havana, Cuba, on January 18, 1932. His first year of minor league baseball was 1951, when he went 17-6 with a league-leading 2.86 ERA with Big Spring in the Class-C Longhorn League. He pitched for his hometown Havana club in the Florida International League the following year, winning 14 games against 12 losses, before being brought up to Washington late in the season, where he had a memorable debut on September 2 facing the Philadelphia Athletics in a night game in Griffith Stadium before a sparse weeknight crowd of 6,413. The Senators presented the handsome right-hander with four runs in the opening stanza on two base hits, two walks, and two errors. In the top of the second inning catcher Joe Astroth of the A's lined a one-out single to center field, putting runners on first and third, but Fornieles struck out the next batter and escaped the inning unscathed. That was the last serious threat Philadelphia posed as Fornieles went on to pitch a one-hitter, striking out four and walking six in a 5-0 shutout. He finished the season with a 2-2 record in four games. He was sold to the Chicago White Sox over the winter, went 8-7 in 1953, and split the 1954 season between Chicago, where he went 1-2, and their Charleston farm club in the American Association where he recorded a mark of 7-7. Over the next three years, Fornieles pitched for the White Sox, Toronto of the International League, and Baltimore. He was traded from Baltimore to the Boston Red Sox on June 14, 1957, in exchange for Billy Goodman.

Mike Fornieles pitched for the Red Sox until June 14, 1963, when he was sold to Minnesota. The five-foot, eleven-inch, 170-pound right-handed pitcher was an important cog in the Boston machine for seven years, during which time he pitched in 286 games, including 28 starts, while compiling a record of 39-35. Fornieles reportedly had a complete repertoire of pitches including a fastball, a curve, and a knuckler, with an occasional screwball and slider thrown in. He was a starting pitcher his first year in Boston in 1957, going 8-7 in 25 games, with 18 starts, seven complete games, one shutout, and a 3.52 ERA. Manager Pinky Higgins sent Fornieles to the bullpen the next year where he evolved into the team's fireman. His best year with Boston was 1960 when he appeared in a league-leading 70 games, posting a 10-5 won-loss record, and earning what would be 11 saves under today's rules with a 2.64 ERA. His outstanding performance was rewarded when he was selected as the American League's Fireman of the Year by *The Sporting News*. He was 9-8 in 1961, appearing in 57 games with what would be 12 saves today, and 3-6 in 42 games the following year, his last year in the Hub. He was sold to Minnesota in mid-June, 1963, where he finished the season and then retired.

Foster, Eddie "Kid"

Edward Cunningham Foster, a native of Chicago, Illinois, played major league baseball from 1910 to 1923. His 18 year professional adventure got underway with Coffeyville in the Class-D Kansas State League in 1906, where the 19-year-old shortstop hit .275 in 62 games and led the league in runs scored with 44. He bounced around the minor leagues for the next three years before he was rescued by the New York Highlanders. After one season in the Bronx where he saw action in only 30 games, batting a near-invisible .133 and committing 10 errors in 22 games, he found himself back in the minors in 1911. The itinerant infielder resurfaced the next year with the Washington Senators, beginning an eight-year hiatus in the nation's capital where he was converted to a third baseman, and did a workmanlike job both offensively and defensively for Clark Griffith's team. The Boston Red Sox obtained his services on January 20, 1920, and he played with the Sox for two-and-a-half years. His first season in the Hub, he hit .259, and he followed that up with a fine .284 season, but in 1922, bogged down with a .211 average after 48 games, he was claimed by the St. Louis Browns off waivers. His Boston career ended after 285 games in which he produced 240 base hits in 907 at-bats for a .265 average. Kid Foster was an average hitter, but he had a reputation as a clutch hitter who, in 1917, spoiled Eddie Plank's bid for a no-hitter with a two-out double in the ninth inning. He led the league in assists and double plays once each, but overall was considered to be a below-average defensive player.

Foster, George "Rube"

The Golden Era of Boston Red Sox baseball ran from 1912 through 1918. They won four World Championships in seven years, and for two of those World Championships they had the services of a tough, little right-handed pitcher named George "Rube" Foster. Foster was born in Lehigh, Oklahoma, on January 5, 1888, and he entered professional baseball with Tulsa in the Western Association 20 years later. He was an outfielder early in his career, but soon switched to the pitcher's mound where he flourished. After bouncing around the bushes for three years, he was signed by Houston of the Texas League in 1911 where he went 7–13 and 24–7 over the next two years. He was drafted by the Boston Red Sox in 1913, and he compiled a record of 3–3 with them in 19 games. After Smoky Joe Wood showed him how to control his fastball during spring training in 1914, the five-foot, seven-and-a-half-inch, 170-pounder went into the season armed and confident. He ran up a string of 42 consecutive scoreless innings that was finally ended in Cleveland on May 26 when the Naps pushed over a run in the fifth inning en route to a 3–2 victory. When the season ended Rube had compiled a fine 14–8 record in 32 games with a minuscule 1.70 ERA, second-best in the American League. That set the stage for his career season.

Foster evolved into the ace of the Boston Red Sox staff as the 1915 season progressed, posting a 19–8 record with 21 complete games in 33 starts, five shutouts, 255⅓ innings pitched, and a 2.11 ERA. He also wielded a potent bat, batting .277, with seven doubles, a home run, and nine RBI in 83 at-bats. Thanks in large part to Foster's performance, Bill Carrigan's team won the American League pennant by two-and-a-half games over the Detroit Tigers and faced the National League champion Philadelphia Phillies in the World Series. Rube Foster pitched Game 2 of the Series after the Phillies had defeated Ernie Shore, 3–1, in the opener. The stocky Oklahoman responded with a wonderfully crafted three-hitter, winning his own game, 2–1, by ripping a two-out single to center field in the ninth inning, driving in Larry Gardner from second base with the winning run. He was on the mound again four days later in Game 5, and closed out Pat Moran's stubborn crew by a 5–4 count. He scattered nine base hits, fanned five and walked two, finishing the Series with a 2–0 record, two games pitched, two complete games and a 2.00 ERA. He also went 4-for-8 at the plate with a double and an RBI. Over the winter, Foster's salary was increased to $2,700 in appreciation of his outstanding season.

The 1916 season was a mixed bag for the 28-year-old Foster. According to Leigh Grossman, the little right-hander suffered from arm problems that prevented him from pitching on a regular basis. The highlight of his season occurred in Fenway Park on June 21, when he set down the New York Highlanders without a hit, winning 2–0. He retired the first 16 men in order before issuing a base on balls to Leslie Nunamaker with one out in the sixth inning, but Nunamaker died on second. The Boston hurler walked Hugh High leading off the seventh, but Carrigan quickly ended that threat by cutting the Highlanders' fleet-footed left fielder down trying to steal second base. In the eighth inning, Lee Magee drew a one-out walk but was left stranded as Foster retired Joe Gedeon and Nunamaker on fly balls. In the ninth, he set the Highlanders down in order to preserve his masterpiece, afterwards receiving a $100 bonus from owner Joe Lannin. Overall, the regular season was less than satisfying for Rube. Even though he put together a fine 14–7 record, manager Carrigan, trying to protect his pitcher's arm, started him in only 19 games, while using him out of the bullpen 14 times. Foster threw nine complete games with three shutouts, and posted four wins in relief. He was now the number five man in the starting rotation as Babe Ruth, Dutch Leonard, Carl Mays, and Ernie Shore all won 15 or more games. In the World Series against the Brooklyn Robins, he pitched in just one game, throwing three scoreless innings of relief in a losing cause. The following year was even more disappointing as the top four threw 1,136⅓ of the team's 1,421⅓ innings (80 percent), limiting Foster to an 8–7 record in 124⅔ innings pitched in 17 games, with 16 starts and nine complete games.

Foster refused to report to spring training in 1918 because Red Sox management wanted him to take a salary cut. He was traded to the Cincinnati Reds before the season started but, hampered by his still-aching arm and unhappy with his salary offer, he refused to report there either, choosing instead to go home to his ranch in Oklahoma, ending his major league career. Rube Foster's career was brief, just five years, all with the Boston Red Sox, but it was noteworthy. He compiled a 58–33 won-lost record, an outstanding .637 winning percentage, and a 2.36 career ERA. His World Series record was 2–0 with a 1.71 ERA. Foster also contributed to his team's success with both his hitting and his defense. He was a career .215 hitter who hit .268 in 1917 and .277 in 1915.

Foulke, Keith

The year 2004 could be considered Keith Foulke's best season. It was a year in which he became a legend in Boston and in the entire New England region, a year in which he was a major contributor to the Red Sox World Championship, and a participant in that historic event that destroyed forever the mythical "Curse of the Bambino." The famous Boston closer was born in Ellsworth Air Force Base in Rapid City, South Dakota, on October 19, 1972. He attended Galveston Community College in Texas and Lewis-Clark State College in Lewiston, Idaho, before signing a baseball contract with the San Francisco Giants in 1994. His baptism of fire came with the Everett Giants in the Northwest League that year, and he posted a 2–0 record with a 0.93 ERA. He was 13–6 with San Jose in the California League the following year, 12–7 with Shreveport in the Texas League in 1996, and 5–4 with Phoenix in the Pacific Coast League in 1997 before he was recalled to San Francisco, where he lost five of six decisions. On July 31, he was traded to the Chicago White Sox where he ran up a 3–0 record with Terry Bevington's team. He spent five more years in the Windy City, where he worked his way from middle relief to the team's closer by 2000.

According to NationMaster.com, "He has an effective 90 MPH fastball and what many people consider to be one of the best circle change-ups in the game. While he is solid against right-handed hitters, he is particularly lethal against lefties. His strikeout pitch is usually an inside

Red Sox General Manager Theo Epstein (left), with Keith Foulke as Foulke is introduced to the Boston media (courtesy Julie Cordeiro and Boston Red Sox).

circle changeup."⁵⁹ Foulke used his changeup to perfection with the White Sox, pitching in 72 games in 2000, with 34 saves, a 2.97 ERA, and 91 strikeouts in 88 innings. The next year he appeared in 72 games with 42 saves and a 2.33 ERA. His save percentage over the two-year period was a world-class 90 percent. The six-foot, 195-pound right-hander suffered from a "dead arm" in 2002 and lost his closer's job, but he still pitched in 65 games with 11 saves, before being traded to Oakland in the off-season. With the A's, he led the league with 43 saves in 48 save opportunities, was selected for the American League All-Star team, and won the Rolaids Relief Award as the league's best closer, but he lost his only decision in the American League Division Series as the A's were bested by the Red Sox three games to two. He filed for free agency at the end of the season and joined the Red Sox, who were attempting to build a World Championship team. In addition to Foulke, the Red Sox also added Curt Schilling to the staff.

Many players contributed to Boston's success in 2004, but no one contributed more than Keith Foulke. He pitched in 72 games with a 5–3 won-loss record, and he saved 32 games with a 2.17 earned run average. In the post-season, he was virtually untouchable. He had one save as the Red Sox swept the Anaheim Angels three straight in the ALDS, another save as Terry Francona's boys disposed of the New York Yankees in seven hard-fought games in the ALCS, and picked up a win and a save in Boston's World Series victory over the St. Louis Cardinals. And he got his wish to be on the mound when the last out of the Series was recorded.

Injuries hampered Foulke's last two years in Boston. He pitched in pain for three months in 2005 before going on the shelf with an injury to his left knee. The fickleness of baseball fans was never more evident than when Foulke, one of the heroes of the 2004 miracle, struggling with injuries and with a 6.03 ERA in June, was booed lustily by the Fenway Park faithful. He just shrugged off the boos. "They don't bother me as much as it bothers me to get up every morning and have to look in the mirror." His injuries limited his season to 43 games with 15 saves and a 5.91 ERA. He had two knee surgeries during the off-season, but he was inconsistent in the spring and in the early-season games, forcing Francona to use him in middle relief and move Jonathan Papelbon to the closer's role. Elbow tendonitis sent him to the DL for another two months beginning on June 12, ending any hopes he might have had of returning to the closer's role. He finished the season with a 4.35 ERA in 44 games, with no saves. Foulke filed for free agency in the fall, signing with the Cleveland Indians, but he sat out the 2007 season with an elbow problem, and pitched one year with Oakland before retiring. Keith Foulke's three years in Boston produced 13 wins, nine losses, and 47 saves in 159 games pitched.

Fox, Pete

Ervin "Pete" Fox was born in Evansville, Indiana, on March 8, 1909. He was a semi-pro pitcher in his youth, but was converted to an outfielder after he was signed by the Detroit Tigers in 1930. He spent three years in the Tigers farm system, hitting over .300 every year with a high of .357, and winning the batting title for the pennant-winning Beaumont Exporters in the Class-A Texas League in 1932. Fox joined the Detroit Tigers in 1933 and was a fixture on the team for eight years. He was one of the top all-around outfielders in the American League during that time, with a reputation as a reliable .300 hitter, a daring baserunner, and an aggressive outfielder. He was a major factor in the success of the great Tigers teams of the 1930s, helping them capture two American League pennants and one World Championship. He hit over .300 for three consecutive seasons, from 1935 through 1937. He had a career year in 1937 with personal highs in batting average (.331), base hits (208), runs scored (116), and doubles (39). The five-foot, eleven-inch, 165-pound, right-handed hitter also hit 12 home runs and drove in 82 runs. Pete Fox was not a power hitter, but he was an expert at finding the gaps in the outfield and piling up the two-base hits. He also legged out 13 triples in 1933, and launched 15 home runs in 1935. He was formidable on defense with a strong arm and a dependable glove. His .977 career fielding average was six points higher than the league average.

The Detroit Tigers captured the American League pennant in both 1934 and 1935. They lost a hard-fought seven-game World Series to the legendary St. Louis "Gashouse Gang" led by Pepper Martin and Joe Medwick in 1934, but Fox held his own, batting .286 in the Series and leading both teams with six doubles in 28 at-bats. In Game 2, a hard-fought 3–2 ten inning victory for the Tigers, Fox kept them in the game during regulation by driving in their first run with a double down the left field line in the fourth inning, and then carrying home the tying run in the bottom of the ninth after leading off the inning with a single to right field. In Game 5, a 3–1 Detroit victory, he drove in the first run of the game with a two-out double to center field. In Game 7, an 11–0 Cardinal win, he had two of the Tigers' six hits, both doubles. The next year, Mickey Cochrane's charges took the measure of the Chicago Cubs in six games, and Pete Fox led both teams in batting average (.385), at-bats (26), base hits (10), doubles (three), and triples (one). In Game 3, a 6–5, 11-inning Detroit triumph, Fox tripled in their first run in the sixth inning and then singled during a four-run rally in the eighth. He drove in their only run in a 3–1 loss in game five, and he had a double and a single with an RBI in the Game 6 finale, won by the Tigers, 4–3.

Pete Fox was sold to Boston on December 12, 1940, where he ended his career. He played with the Red Sox for five years, often as the fourth outfielder. When he took a regular turn in the outfield, in 1943 and 1944, he responded as of old. He batted .288 in 1943 with 24 doubles and 22 stolen bases. The next year, he stroked the ball at a .315 clip with 37 doubles, 70 runs scored and 64 RBI in 496 at-bats.

Foxx, Jimmie

The man known as "The Beast" and "Double X" was one of the most prodigious sluggers in the history of the game. When he retired from baseball in 1945 he was the only player other than Babe Ruth and Mel Ott to have more than 500 career home runs to his credit. This gentle giant was born on a farm in Sudlersville, Maryland, on October 22, 1907. He grew into a powerful physical specimen after years of chopping wood, plowing fields, "and often loading and unloading supplies such as sacks of fertilizer, grain, and other items. Farm work, Jimmie would later claim, helped him to develop strong wrists, arm, leg, and back muscles."[60]

Foxx developed into a superb athlete by the time he was 13, particularly on the track. In 1923, sportswriters covering the state Olympiad in Baltimore voted "fifteen-year-old Jimmie Foxx, the muscular 165-pound youngster from Sudlersville High School the star athlete of the year."[61] He was also a high school standout in weightlifting, basketball, and soccer. But his favorite sport was baseball, a game taught to him by his father when he was just old enough to walk. Del Foxx was an outstanding baseball player in his own right but gave up an opportunity to play professionally to stay at home, run the farm, and raise a family. Instead, he concentrated on teaching his son how to catch, hit, and throw.

Jimmie's training must have been exceptional because he was signed to a professional baseball contract in 1924 when he was just 16 years old. In his first minor league season, he caught 76 games for Easton in the Class-D Eastern Shore League, where he hit a respectable .296, slammed ten home runs in 260 at-bats, and led the league's catchers in assists. After being sold to the Philadelphia Athletics for $2,500, he spent

Jimmie Foxx

the last month of the season with the A's, mostly sitting on the bench next to Connie Mack, absorbing the manager's words of wisdom about all aspects of the game. Young Foxx returned to Sudlersville in September to begin his senior year in high school, and the following summer, after graduation, he joined Providence in the International League, where he stroked the ball at a crisp .327 pace in 41 games. He arrived in Philadelphia in the spring of 1926 to find another catcher already there, a fellow named Mickey Cochrane. Foxx may well have been a better defensive catcher than Cochrane, but Cochrane could not play any other position, while the versatile Foxx could play just about anywhere, catcher, first base, third base, or the outfield. He even pitched ten games during his major league career, posting a 1–0 record and a 1.52 ERA. By 1929, the pride of the Eastern Shore was Philadelphia's full-time first baseman. And what a first baseman he turned out to be. He and Lou Gehrig are generally rated as the two greatest first basemen in the history of the game, and it was a tossup as to who was the greater.

Jimmie Foxx was the heart and soul of the great Philadelphia Athletics teams of the late 1920s and early 30s, leading them to three consecutive American League pennants and two World Championships from 1929 to 1931. He batted a combined .344 in the three World Series, with four home runs and 11 RBI in 18 games. He also fielded .994. Foxx played with the A's for 11 years with spectacular results. He hit .364 while leading the league with 58 home runs and 169 RBI in 1932, and won the Triple Crown with a .356 batting average, 48 home runs and 163 RBI the following year. Connie Mack had a habit of selling off his high-priced players at regular intervals to maintain financial stability in the organization. As a result, Lefty Grove was traded to the Boston Red Sox after the 1933 season and Jimmie Foxx followed him two years later.

The Red Sox were not able to win an American League pennant during Foxx's stay there, but it wasn't his fault. He just missed a second Triple Crown in 1938, when he led the league in batting (.349), RBI (175), on-base percentage (.462), slugging average (.704), total bases (398), and bases on balls (119), but lost the home run crown when his 50 home runs finished second to Hank Greenberg's 58. The following year, he slugged the ball at a .360 clip with a league-leading 35 homers and 105 RBI. Double X hit more than 30 home runs and drove in more than 100 runs his first five years in Boston. He spent a total of seven years with Joe Cronin's club before being released on waivers to the Chicago Cubs on June 1, 1942.

Jimmie Foxx led the league in home runs four times, runs scored once, RBI three times, bases on balls twice, on-base percentage three times, slugging average five times, and batting average twice, during his 20-year major league career. As Bill Werber noted, "No one hit the ball as far as Jimmie Foxx. He hit them over the roof in left field in Shibe Park, over the roof in Detroit's Navin Field, and out of sight everywhere else. He was a beautiful physical specimen, with muscular forearms, thick wrists, big thighs and calves, a flat belly, and muscles bulging from his chest. He cut his shirtsleeves high, not out of showmanship, but to give his big arms enough room, but the sight had a powerful effect on opposing pitchers."[62] Another teammate claimed that Foxx wasn't born. He was trapped. The Philadelphia strongman holds the major league record for most consecutive years with 30 or more home runs with 12, and he shares the major league record for most consecutive years with 100 or more RBI with 13. He is current number eight in career RBI with 1922, number ten in career on-base percentage with .428, and number five in career slugging average with .609. He twice hit 50 or more home runs in a season, hitting 58 homers in 1932 and 50 in 1938. In the field, he led all American League first basemen in putouts once, assists three times, and fielding average three times. He was voted the American League's Most Valuable Player three times and was selected for the American League All-Star team nine times. Jimmie Foxx was elected to the National Baseball Hall of Fame in 1951. He is quite obviously the first baseman on the all-time Boston Red Sox team.

Foy, Joe

Joseph Anthony Foy, a six-foot tall, 210-pound infielder out of the Bronx, New York, was ignored by most major league scouts because he was too roly-poly. He eventually signed a baseball contract with the Minnesota

Twins in 1962 and spent his first year of professional baseball with the Erie Sailors in the Class-D New York–Pennsylvania League, where he caught and played first base, batting .285 in 113 games. At the end of the season, he was drafted by the Boston Red Sox, who thought he had unlimited potential, and he was groomed to be the team's third baseman of the future during his minor league apprenticeship. In 1965, with the Toronto Maple Leafs in the Triple-A International League, Joe Foy led the league in batting with a .304 average, while banging out 21 doubles and 14 home runs in 500 at-bats. His all-around play resulted in his selection as the International League's MVP and *The Sporting News* Minor League Player of the Year, and brought about his promotion to the Boston Red Sox.

The right-handed-hitting third baseman spent the next three years in Boston, giving the Red Sox adequate if not sensational third base play. His rookie season was one of his best seasons as he batted .262 with 23 doubles, 15 homers, 97 runs scored, and 63 runs batted in. During the famous 1967 "Impossible Dream" season, Joe Foy batted .251 with 22 doubles and 16 homers, and he made several highlight reels along the way. On Friday afternoon, April 14, he was a major factor in pitcher Billy Rohr's memorable major league debut in Yankee Stadium. The six-foot, three-inch, 170-pound southpaw tossed a one-hitter at Ralph Houk's crew, winning by a 3–0 count, and Foy made a dazzling defensive play in the sixth inning to protect his pitcher's bid for a no-hitter. Bill Robinson, a .196 hitter, lined a ball back through the box that deflected off Rohr's glove and bounced toward the third base foul line for what looked like a sure base hit, but Foy raced in, barehanded the ball, and fired it to first in time to nip the batter and keep 14,375 cocky New York fans under control. Two innings later, he sent a two-run homer into the New York sky to give his pitcher some breathing room, but in the bottom of the ninth inning, with two men out and the bases empty, Elston Howard stepped to the plate and dropped a single into right field for the only Yankee's hit of the day.

Two months later, Joe Foy was a central figure in a wild, bench-clearing brawl in the Bronx. On June 20, he hit a fifth-inning grand-slam home run off Mel Stottlemyre, pacing Boston to 7–1 triumph. Foy was brushed back in a later at-bat and when he was hit in the helmet by Thad Tillotson in the second inning the next night, Boston pitcher Jim Lonborg wasted no time getting even. He plunked Tillotson in the ribs, igniting a dugout–emptying free-for-all. Foy was nowhere to be seen during the melee but Boston strongman Rico Petrocelli picked Tillotson up over his head and slammed him to the ground before order could be restored.

Joe Foy's batting average declined to .225 in 1968 and, when he was left unprotected in the expansion draft at the end of the season, Kansas City selected him. He spent the last three years of his major league career with the Royals, New York Mets, and Washington Senators. The Bronx native was hampered by a weight problem during his career, and also by reported alcohol and drug problems. When he was with the Mets in 1970, as reported in Wikipedia, he showed up at Shea Stadium for a doubleheader one day looking like he was high on some kind of drug after a night on the town with some of his old friends. In spite of his unsteady demeanor, Gil Hodges started him at third base in the second game. The first batter hit a hard shot past third that Foy never even saw and, as one player noted, he was still standing in his crouched position punching his glove and yelling, "Hit it to me. Hit it to me."

Freeman, Buck

He was the first great slugger of the twentieth century. The secret of his success, according to some of his peers, was that, unlike most batters of his time, who were contact hitters, he swung from the heels on every pitch, fully intending to drive the ball out of the park.[63] Also, unlike most other players, in the off-season, Buck Freeman "kept himself in shape by walking 12 miles a day in addition to weightlifting, parallel bars, boxing, and other activities. 'What work I have done as a batsman I owe in large measure to my exercise in the gymnasium,' Freeman said, 'which ... developed the muscles that come into play when I hit the ball.'"[64]

John Frank "Buck" Freeman was born in Catasauqua, Pennsylvania, on October 30, 1871. Born into a poor Irish family in the coal-mining region of Pennsylvania, he began work in the coal mines at the age of 12, but he spent most of his free time playing baseball. He pitched for the Washington Nationals of the American Association in 1891, but lasted only five games. He was released with a 3–2 record after walking 33 batters in 44 innings. Back in the minors, the five-foot, nine-inch, 165-pound southpaw pitched for Troy in the Eastern League in 1892, but was gradually converted to an outfielder, much like Babe Ruth, to take advantage of his powerful bat. He terrorized pitchers wherever he played during the 1890's, smashing 34 home runs for Haverhill in the New England League in 1894, hitting 20 and 23 homers for the Toronto Canucks in the Eastern League in 1897 and 1898 respectively, and putting 25 balls into orbit for Washington in the National League in 1899.

Freeman joined the Boston Beaneaters in 1900, but jumped to the Boston Somersets in the new American League the following year. He was an immediate hit with the Boston fans, leading his team at bat with a .339 average while slugging 23 doubles, 15 triples, and 12 home runs, and driving in 114 runs. The next year he hit .309 and led the league with 121 RBI, while sending an assortment of extra-base hits to all parts of the Huntington Avenue Baseball Grounds. After finishing second and third their first two years in the American League, the team, now known as the Pilgrims, won the pennant in 1903, and Freeman once again paced the Boston attack, batting just .287 but hammering 39 doubles and 20 triples in 567 at-bats, and leading the league with 13 home runs, 104 RBI, 72 extra-base hits, and 281 total bases. He was the first player to lead both the National and American Leagues in home runs.

The first World Series was played that year and matched the Pilgrims against the National League champion Pittsburgh Pirates. Fred Clarke's warriors jumped out to a three-game-to-one lead behind the pitching of Deacon Phillippe, who won all three games, but the Pilgrims bounced back to sweep the final four games and claim the World Championship. Buck Freeman batted .281 in the Series with three triples, six runs scored, and four RBI. In the Series finale, the left-handed-hitting slugger walloped a triple to deep center field off Pirates ace Deacon Phillippe leading off the bottom of the fourth inning of a scoreless game and carried the Championship run across the plate on a single by Hobe Ferris.

The sweet-swinging outfielder played in Boston for three more years, but after 1904 his batting average slipped to .240 and then .250 and his power mysteriously disappeared, with just four round-trippers in 847 at-bats. After playing only four games for Boston in 1907, Freeman was waived to Washington who released him before he ever played a game for them. He bounced around the minor leagues for another six years before retiring to his home in Wilkes-Barre.

Frye, Jeff

Jeffrey Dustin Frye, a native of Oakland, California, was drafted out of Southeastern Oklahoma College by the Texas Rangers in the 1988 amateur draft, and was sent to the Butte Copper Kings of the Rookie Pioneer League to begin his climb to the top of the professional baseball hierarchy. The 21-year-old infielder hit a steady .286 for the Copper Kings in 55 games while alternating between shortstop and second base. From Butte, he made his way through Gastonia, Charlotte, Tulsa, and Oklahoma City between 1989 and 1992, batting an even .300 with the pennant-winning Oklahoma City 89ers in the Triple-A American Association, before his call-up to the parent Texas Rangers midway through the season. He hit a respectable .256 with Texas while doing a decent job defensively at second base, but his career got sidetracked the next spring when he was placed on the disabled list and lost the entire 1993 season to a knee injury. It was a demon that would plague Frye throughout his career. He also lost the entire 1998 season when he injured his knee in spring training, and he was on the disabled list at least six other times in eight years.

Jeff Frye spent four seasons with Texas, but his injuries prevented him from enjoying a rewarding major league career, and he was released by the team in December 1995 after playing in just 214 games from 1992 to 1995. Boston took a chance on the five-foot, nine-inch, 165-pound infielder, signing him to a contract on the recommendation of manager

Kevin Kennedy, and he spent four seasons with the Red Sox, where he had moderate success. In 1996, his first year in Boston, he batted .286 in 105 games, had an excellent .372 on-base percentage, and did a commendable job at second base. The following year, Frye played a career-high 127 games, stung the ball at a .312 clip with 36 doubles and 19 stolen bases, and posted a sensational .991 fielding average. Then disaster struck. He missed the entire 1998 season as noted above, and he played just 41 games for Boston in 1999 and 69 games the following year before he was traded to the Colorado Rockies. He retired after the 2001 season.

Garciaparra, Nomar

The major leagues were blessed with no less than five world-class shortstops as the twenty-first century got under way, and Anthony Nomar Garciaparra was one of the best, a five-tool point player who hit for average, hit with power, and had exceptional speed, a reliable glove, and a strong throwing arm. As noted in *The Red Sox Fan Handbook*, "Although he was a free swinger — like Mike Greenwell before him, Garciaparra frequently swung at the first pitch he saw — Garciaparra hit for high averages with good power and seldom struck out. In the field his great range and strong throwing arm led to both spectacular plays and occasional wild throwing errors (particularly since he threw to poor defensive first basemen for much of his career)."[64]

Boston's all-time greatest shortstop was born in Whittier, California, on July 23, 1973, and he grew up playing and starring in soccer. But by the time the lanky youngster had showcased his baseball skills at Georgia Tech while majoring in business, his name was well-known to baseball scouts across the country. After his junior year of college, he was drafted by the Boston Red Sox and sent to their Sarasota farm team to refine his skills.

The 21-year-old right-handed hitter posted a .295 average with 10 extra-base hits in 28 games with Sarasota, and was promoted to Trenton, Boston's Double-A Eastern League affiliate, for the 1995 season. Garciaparra hit a respectable .267 for the Thunder, with 36 extra-base hits and 35 stolen bases in 125 games. The following year he spanked the ball at a .343 clip in 43 games with the Pawtucket Red Sox in the Triple-A International League, bringing about his promotion to the parent club, where he made his major league debut on August 31, going 0-for-1 as a late game replacement for Jeff Frye at second base in an 8–0 loss to the Oakland Athletics in the Oakland-Alameda County Coliseum. The next day, he started at shortstop for Kevin Kennedy's team and pounded out three base hits, including his first major league home run, in five at-bats in an 8–3 Red Sox victory. In the fourth inning, with Boston up 1–0, Garciaparra leaned into one of John Wasdin's heaters and drove it out of the park. He singled and scored in the sixth, and hit an RBI single in the ninth. Overall, Nomar hit .241 in 24 games with Boston over the last month of the season with four home runs and 16 RBI in 87 at-bats, and he handled the defensive responsibilities with the finesse of

Nomar Garciaparra

a veteran. His rapid rise through the Red Sox farm system forced John Valentin, Boston's incumbent at shortstop, to become a third baseman.

Nomar Garciaparra, at the age of 24, had filled out to a muscular 190 pounds by 1997 and, with his tight, quick swing and his exceptional batting eye, he was ready to fulfill his potential. His rookie year was, to put it mildly, sensational. He played 153 games at shortstop, batted .306, scored 122 runs, launched 44 doubles and 30 home runs, drove in 98 runs, stole 22 bases, and led the American League with 684 at-bats, 209 base hits, and 11 triples. In the field, he led American League shortstops with 249 putouts and 113 double plays. Needless to say, he was selected as the American League's Rookie of the Year in a runaway. The sophomore jinx did not find a home in Nomar's head. In fact, he upped his average to .323, hit 35 home runs, and drove in 122 runs.

Two magnificent years followed for the Boston shortstop. He led the American League in batting in 1999 with a .357 average, while vslugging 42 doubles and 27 home runs, with 104 RBI. The following year he led the league with a stratospheric .372 batting average, with 51 doubles, 21 homers, and 96 RBI. Then, just when Garciaparra was at the peak of his career, fate intervened. He aggravated an old wrist injury during spring training that, in spite of having it surgically repaired, continued to hamper him throughout the 2001 season, eventually limiting his appearances to just 21 games. He bounced back the following year to hit a resounding .310 in 156 games, with 24 homers, 101 runs scored, 120 RBI, and a league-leading 56 doubles. In 2003 he had another banner season, stroking the ball at a .301 clip with 37 doubles, 13 triples, 28 home runs, 120 runs scored, 105 RBI, and 19 stolen bases.

The 2004 season promised to be a year to remember in Boston after they had gone to the free agent market and acquired a proven ace in Curt Schilling and a solid closer in Keith Foulke. The team's goal was nothing short of a World Championship. Unfortunately, Nomar Garciaparra was not able to accompany them to the Promised Land. He suffered an Achilles tendon injury in spring training and, along with injuries to his wrist and his groin, he was sidelined from March 26 to June 9. At the end of July, he was traded for shortstop Orlando Cabrera and Doug Mientkiewicz. Nomar spent two injury-filled years with the Chicago Cubs followed by three injury-filled years with the Los Angeles Dodgers. He spent the 2009 season with the Oakland Athletics, batting .281 in 65 games, but after battling injuries all season, he called it a day after the season ended.

Garciaparra played for the Boston Red Sox for six full seasons and parts of three others. He stung the ball at a .323 clip for the BoSox, with 1,281 base hits in 3,968 at-bats, and he was just as reliable in post-season play. He played in four Division Series batting .321 in 16 games with five doubles, five homers, and 17 runs batted in. In three Championship Series, the handsome Californian batted .321 with two doubles, a triple, two home runs, and seven RBI. He was a shoo-in for the position of shortstop on the all-time Red Sox team.

Gardner, Larry

William Lawrence "Larry" Gardner was a simple country boy from the tiny hamlet of Enosburg Falls, Vermont, just ten miles south of the Canadian border. He was born on May 13, 1886, and attended the University of Vermont, where he majored in chemistry, hoping to take his profession west after graduation to be an assayer in the gold mine region. He was a friendly student with a keen sense of humor, who reportedly caused his chemistry professor to change his seat several times during the year to keep him from socializing during class. Outside class he thrilled the students and local fans with his baseball skills that eventually brought him to the attention of the Boston Red Sox. He signed a baseball contract with the Sox during his junior year, and spent the summer traveling with the team. The Enosburg Falls native made his major league debut in the Huntington Avenue Baseball Grounds on June 25, 1908, going into the game in the late innings and becoming an instant hero by slamming a game-winning double to beat Washington, 2–1. He played in ten games in September, batting .300 with three hits in ten at-bats, then returned to UVM for his senior year. After graduation, he was loaned to Lynn in the Class-B New England League, where he received his baptism of fire in organized baseball. He played shortstop for the Shoemakers because when he played third base in Boston, opposing batters bunted him off the field. He hit a respectable .305 in 61 games for Lynn and the next year he was back in Boston, but saw limited action in 19 games, batting .297 in 37 at-bats with a double and two triples. He played 113 games at second base for the Red Sox in 1910, batting .283 with 10 triples in 413 at-bats, but his range in the field was considered to be too limited for a second baseman, so the following year he moved to the third base position where he would spend the next seven years.

Larry Gardner earned a reputation as a good hitter and a dependable fielder during the dead ball days after he learned how to defend against bunts. He was also a popular presence in the clubhouse where his light-hearted banter and mischievous ways kept the players on their toes and their morale high. He often entertained his teammates with his skills as a ventriloquist and as a member of Boston's barbershop quartet. On the field, he hit a Boston career high of .315 in 1912, with 24 doubles, 18 triples, 88 runs scored, and 86 runs batted in, as the Boston Red Sox juggernaut raced to the American League pennant, winning 105 games against 47 losses. At one point it was feared that Gardner would be lost for the World Series because of an injury. On September 21, during an 11–4 Boston victory in Detroit, he dove for a ground ball and broke the little finger of his bare hand at the first joint, with the bone protruding, but the gutty New Englander was back in the lineup on October 6 and played all eight games of the World Series with his fingers taped together. Boston outlasted John McGraw's New York Giants in the hard-fought Fall Classic, thanks to one of the most famous miscues in baseball history. In Game 4 in the Polo Grounds, Gardner paced the Sox and Smoky Joe Wood to a 3–1 triumph with a single, a triple, and two runs scored. He carried home the first run of the game after leading off the second inning with a mighty triple high over Red Murray's head in right field, and then scoring on a wild pitch. He walked leading off the fourth, but was forced at second by Jake Stahl, who eventually scored Boston's second run. Finally, in the ninth with the Sox protecting a slim 2–1 lead, Gardner led off with a single and raced home on a one-base knock by Wood. In game seven, won by New York 11–4, the pride of Enosburg Falls hit the only Boston home run of the Series. The next day, in the deciding game eight, played in newly-built Fenway Park, game two having ended in a tie, Christy Mathewson and Hugh Bedient crossed swords with neither hurler giving an inch. New York scored one run in the third and Boston tied it in the bottom of the seventh on Olaf Henriksen's double to left field, scoring Jake Stahl. The Giants scored off Bedient in the tenth inning and, with Mathewson on the mound, hopes of Red Sox fans were at low ebb. But suddenly Boston got a life when a fly ball by Clyde Engel, batting for Wood, was dropped by Fred Snodgrass in center field in what has become known as "The $30,000 Muff." Snodgrass recovered to rob the next batter, Harry Hooper, of a base hit with a sensational catch, with Engle tagging up and moving over to third base. After Steve Yerkes walked, Tris Speaker singled sharply to right field, scoring Engle with the tying run, and both runners moved up a base on the throw-in. Duffy Lewis was walked intentionally to load the bases, and Larry Gardner became an instant Red Sox legend by sending a long sacrifice fly to Snodgrass in center field, sending the Championship run across the plate.

The village of Enosburg Falls, Vermont, went crazy over their new hero, and they readied a huge celebration for his return home. When the train carrying Larry Gardner pulled into the station, fireworks lit up the Vermont sky, a band played, and 500 people who had descended on the tiny village from all over Franklin County cheered wildly as the 26-year-old third baseman alighted from the coach. He was welcomed home by friends and relatives, and by the usual politicians who never missed a photo op. Larry and his father sat in the back seat of the first car, leading a 16-car parade down Main Street to the Town Hall, where speeches were made and gifts were presented. It was a hectic off-season for the unassuming hero, who was in demand for numerous speaking engagements all over Vermont including one at the Hotel Vermont in Burlington where he was presented with a silver loving cup.

Larry Gardner was relieved when it was time for him to depart for Hot Springs, Arkansas, for spring training. The solitude, the joy of playing baseball again and socializing with his teammates, were welcomed by him. The Red Sox followed their World Series triumph with two disappointing seasons, limping home in fourth place in 1913 and second place the following year. In 1915, Bill Carrigan's charges were loaded to the hilt, both on the mound and in the field. Led by Tris Speaker and a powerful pitching staff, they edged the Detroit Tigers by two-and-a-half games to capture the American League pennant. Gardner played a minor role in the victory as he battled injuries most of the season and hit a respectable .258 in 127 games. Boston's opponents in the World Series were the Philadelphia Phillies, who had outlasted Brooklyn in the National League, and Boston disposed of them rather easily in five games. Larry Gardner was fairly quiet at the plate, batting just .235 with a triple, but he was flawless in the field, leading all fielders with 13 assists and playing errorless ball.

The 1916 Boston Red Sox team was almost as good as the 1915 contingent. Gardner was one of their top offensive weapons as he hit .308 with an excellent .372 on-base percentage. Their opponents in the World Series were the Brooklyn Robins and, as in 1915, they disposed of the Senior Circuit representatives in five games. Gardner batted just .176 for the Series, but he contributed two home runs and a Series-high six RBI. His second homer of the Series was an inside-the-park job in the second inning of game four. It was a three-run shot to deep left-center field that wiped out a 2–0 Brooklyn lead and provided the winning runs in a 6–2 Boston victory. They closed out the Series the next day in Fenway Park, winning 4–1 behind Ernie Shore. Gardner was 0-for-2 but he drove in Boston's first run with a sacrifice fly in the second inning. Boston's star third baseman batted .265 in 1917 and then was traded to the Philadelphia Athletics in the off-season, ending his Boston tenure.

Gaston, Milt

Nathaniel Milton Gaston joined the New York Yankees in 1924 at the age of 28, moving to the Boston Red Sox five years later. Most baseball experts consider Gaston to have been a decent pitcher who, playing with good teams, might have compiled a winning record instead of his actual record 97–164. Gaston had the misfortune of playing with one of Boston's worst ball clubs. They finished in last place in both 1929 and 1930 and sixth place in 1931. The six-foot, one-inch, 185-pound right-hander was blessed with a good fastball and a deceptive forkball, but he had difficulty controlling the forkball and it often eluded his catcher with disastrous results. On July 10, 1928, he blanked the Washington Senators, 9–0, yielding 14 base hits, still the major league record for the most hits allowed in a shutout. He also tied another major league record for pitchers by participating in four double plays in one game. Gaston won 12 games and lost 19 with the cellar-dwelling BoSox in 1929 even though his ERA was 51 points better than the league average. The next year, he was 13–20 for a team that won only 52 games, and his 3.92 ERA was 73 points better than the league average. In his last year in Boston, he went 2–13 and was traded to the Chicago White Sox in December. Milt Gaston's Boston career produced 27 victories against 52 losses in three years.

Gedman, Rich

Richard Leo Gedman was another Massachusetts native who gravitated to the hometown Boston Red Sox when he decided to play professional baseball. Gedman was a pitcher and a first baseman at St. Peters High School in Worcester, Massachusetts, graduating in 1977. He went unclaimed in the June draft, but was subsequently signed as a free agent by the Boston Red Sox, who sent him to the Instructional League to learn to be a catcher. He was assigned to Boston's farm club in Winter Haven in the Single-A Florida State League in 1978, where he hit an even .300 in 98 games. His advance through the Boston farm system was rapid and he made his major league debut on September 7, 1980, punching out two base hits in his first game.

Rich Gedman spent most of the 1981 season with the Boston Red Sox after playing 25 games in Pawtucket. He split catching time with Gary Allenson his first three years with the Red Sox, refining his game at the major league level. The six-foot-tall, 210-pound left-handed hitter played in 62 games with Boston in 1981, with

205 at-bats, and he hit a hard .288 with 15 doubles and five homers. As a result of his fine season *The Sporting News* selected him as the American League Rookie of the Year. His 1982 season ended prematurely when he broke his right clavicle in Detroit on September 17. By 1984, Gedman was ready to assume full responsibility for the catching duties in Boston, and Allenson was on the way out. He played 133 games in 1984, slamming 26 doubles and 24 home runs, driving in 72 runs, and batting .269. The next year, he hit a career-high .295 with 30 doubles, 18 homers and 80 RBI, and on September 18, he hit for the cycle and drove in seven runs as the fifth-place Red Sox embarrassed the division leading Blue Jays by a 13–1 score. He launched a one-out home run in the third inning, came back with a bases-loaded triple in the fourth, had an RBI single in the fifth, and closed out his big day with a two-run double in the seventh as John McNamara's team entertained a festive Fenway Park gathering of 17,598.

He played 135 games in 1986 and hit .258 with 29 doubles 16 homers, and 65 RBI. Gedman's defensive skills kept pace with his offensive contributions during these three years, his peak years as a major league catcher. He was particularly adept at handling the pitching staff, and his strong throwing arm kept runners anchored to their bases. He cut down 44 percent of all base runners who attempted to steal against him from 1984 to 1986, including a phenomenal 49.5 percent caught-stealing percentage in 1986. He went 2-for-4 with a double and had the game-winning RBI against Toronto on September 28 as the Red Sox clinched the American League Eastern Division title by nine games over the Blue Jays. And he was one of the heroes of the American League Championship Series, going 10 for 28, a .357 batting average, with a double, a homer, and six RBI, and played errorless ball as Boston rallied to defeat the California Angels in seven games. In Game 5, with Boston down three games to one, he went 4-for-4 with a second inning home run that gave the Sox a 2–0 lead in Anaheim Stadium. After the Angels came back to open up a healthy 5–2 lead after eight innings, Boston rallied for four runs in the ninth. Gedman took one in the ribs to keep the rally going, and carried the third run of the inning across the plate. He also contributed a bunt single in the 11th inning that led to the game-winner. He went 2-for-4 in Boston's 10–4 rout of California in Game 6 and, although he drew the collar in four at-bats in the finale, his second-inning ground ball drove in the first run of the game in an 8–1 Red Sox triumph. Roger Clemens went seven innings for the win.

The World Series against the New York Mets was something he would rather forget. He hit just .200 in the Series with one home run and one RBI, but it was Game 6 that stuck in his craw. With Bob Stanley on the mound, two men out, two Mets on base, and Boston one out away from winning the World Championship, Stanley uncorked a wild pitch that many people thought Gedman should have blocked, but he missed it and the tying run crossed the plate, with the winning run moving into scoring position at second base. Moments later, Mookie Wilson's ground ball brought in the game-winner, and the rest is history.

Boston's top catcher missed the first month of the 1987 season as he negotiated a free-agent contract, eventually re-signing with Boston on May 1, but things went downhill from that point on. He was on the disabled list from July 7 to July 22 with a groin injury, and then was knocked out for the rest of the season on July 30 when he suffered torn ligaments in his thumb after a home plate collision. His season amounted to just 52 games, 151 at-bats, and a disappointing .205 batting average. He came back to play 95 games the following year, but missed six weeks of play from April 11 to May 30. In the ALCS, a four-game loss to the Oakland A's, he batted .357 with a homer and an RBI and fielded flawlessly. After the season ended, he filed for free agency, eventually re-signing with the Red Sox. He played 93 games for Boston in 1989, splitting time with Rick Cerone, and after the Red Sox signed defensive specialist Tony Pena to backstop for them, on November 27, Gedman became expendable. Boston cut him loose on June 7, 1990, sending him to the Houston Astros.

Geiger, Gary

Gary Geiger patrolled the outer garden in Boston for seven years, from 1959 through 1965, but injuries and illnesses prevented him from reaching his potential.⁶⁵ The slender six-foot-tall, 165-pound outfielder from Sand Ridge, Illinois, joined the Red Sox after spending the 1958 season with the Cleveland Indians. Manager Pinky Higgins made Geiger a full-time outfielder in 1959 and he eventually became an outstanding center fielder. He had good range, a dependable glove, and a strong throwing arm, but his first season with the Red Sox gave an omen of things to come. During a spring training exhibition game in Scottsdale, Arizona, he collided with shortstop Don Buddin chasing a foul ball down the left field line and was knocked unconscious. It was the first of many health issues that prevented the likeable outfielder from realizing his potential. It also kept him on the bench for almost half of Boston's 1,118 scheduled games during his seven-year hiatus in the Hub. He said he liked to play at 171–175 pounds, but he had difficulty maintaining that weight. He had a decent, although not spectacular, introduction to the fanatical Fenway fans in 1959, showing his defensive skills, both in left field and center field, and hitting 11 homers with 48 RBI in 335 at-bats despite a mediocre .245 batting average. In 1960, he held down the right field post for the Red Sox, hitting a brisk .302, but his season was cut short on July 29 when he was operated on for a collapsed lung that kept him out of the lineup the rest of the season.

He had his two best seasons with the Red Sox in 1961 and 1962, leading the league in outfield assists both years and giving his team some pop with the bat even though his batting averages were still below the .250 level. On April 17, 1961, before a small Monday afternoon gathering of 5,289 in the friendly Fens, the left-handed batter deposited a ball into the bullpen in right field to give the home team a 5–4 victory over the Los Angeles Angels. One month later, the Sand Ridge native wore the goat's horns as Baltimore defeated Boston's best, 5–4, before 6,777 fans in Memorial Stadium. The first two Baltimore batters were retired in the bottom of the ninth inning of a 4–4 game before pitcher Dick Hyde touched Bill Monbouquette for a single and then surprised the Boston ace by stealing second. The next batter, Brooks Robinson, hit a soft fly ball into center field for what should have been the final out of the inning, but when three Boston fielders converged on the ball, disaster struck. Gary Geiger took his eye off the ball and dropped it as the winning run crossed the plate. On August 23, against Washington, he hit a two-run homer to break a tie and propel his team to a 9–4 victory, sending the 5,316 Fenway Park faithful home happy. Geiger only hit .232 for the year but he connected for 21 doubles and 18 home runs, driving in 64 runs in a career-high 140 games. He also posted a .988 fielding average and led the league with 12 assists.

The injury bug struck Geiger again on June 10, 1962. In a game against the Cleveland Indians at home, as reported in Wikipedia, Tito Francona, leading off the game for Cleveland, hit a long drive to left-center field, with Gary Geiger in hot pursuit. Geiger looked like he had the ball in his sights as he hit the warning track, but he suddenly made a last-second leap and hit the wall head-first as the ball caromed back toward the infield. He grabbed his head and sank slowly to his knees before collapsing on the Fenway turf. He was eventually carried off the field on a stretcher and taken to the hospital.⁶⁶ Francona ended up at third base with a triple and later scored. It was the first run in a slugfest that saw Cleveland outlast Boston, 14–10, in 13 innings. Gary Geiger was back in the lineup the next day, and he was one of the few bright spots in the Red Sox lineup for the season as the team limped home in eighth place in a ten-team league. The slender outfielder batted .249 with 16 homers and 54 RBI in 131 games. He also played a sensational center field, posting a .987 fielding average and leading the league with eight assists.

Gary Geiger played 121 games in 1963, stroking the ball at a respectable .263 pace and once again gave Boston outstanding defense, roaming far and wide to pull down potential base hits from opposing batters. One of his most satisfying days that summer occurred on May 26 when his two-run homer in the eighth inning at Tiger Stadium gave Johnny Pesky's team the eventual winning runs in a 6–5 Boston triumph, as the Sunday afternoon crowd of 21,149 Detroit fans sat in stunned silence. The following season was disappointing for the 27-year-old outfielder. On February 24, as he was on his way to Arizona for spring training, he was stricken with stomach pains and hospitalized at St. Luke's Hospital in St. Louis, where he was operated on for a bleeding ulcer. He made one attempt at a comeback, playing five games, but with his weight down to 135 pounds, and in a weakened condition, he finally went on the voluntary retired list and sat out the rest of the season. He was still in a weakened condition as 1965 got under way and on June 7, his comeback came to an abrupt halt. The Red Sox paired off against the Chicago White Sox at home and, with Chicago up by a 7–3 count in the eighth inning, White Sox first baseman Tom McGraw hit a shallow fly ball to center field. Geiger, racing in from his position in deep center field, made a desperate dive for the ball, landing on his glove hand and fracturing his hand in three places. He went on the DL a few days later, missing the rest of the season, and was released outright to Toronto that fall.

Gernert, Dick

Richard Edward Gernert was a big, rawboned right-handed slugger who spent eight years with the Boston Red Sox as a first baseman-left fielder. He was born in Reading, Pennsylvania, on September 28, 1928, and grew into an outstanding baseball player in his hometown, playing high school ball and American Legion ball. The six-foot, three-inch, 210-pound athlete attended Temple University, where he played both baseball and basketball. Gernert went unclaimed in the 1949 amateur baseball draft, but he was later signed by the Boston Red Sox, who sent him to San Jose in the Class-C California League. He moved up the Red Sox's minor league ladder quickly, ripping the ball at a .383 clip for San Jose, earning a promotion to Scranton in the Single-A Eastern League, where he hit .265 with six homers and 40 RBI in 60 games. He finished the season with Louisville in the Triple-A American Association, batting .219 in 26 games. The following year, he hit .306 for Scranton in 124 games, and .315 with Louisville in 19 games.

Dick Gernert was with the Boston Red Sox in 1952, where he began the season sharing the first base duties with Walt Dropo. After Dropo was traded to the Detroit Tigers on June 3, Gernert became Boston's regular first baseman, and he took advantage of his opportunity by slamming 20 doubles and 19 home runs and driving in 67 runs, leading the Red Sox in both categories even though he had just 367 at-bats. In 1953, the Red Sox first baseman played a major part in two of Boston's most historic games. On June 17, he carried the big bat as the Red Sox demolished Detroit, 17–1, at home, launching two home runs into the upper atmosphere. He slugged a two-run homer over the Green Monster in left field in the bottom of the first to give his team a quick 2–0 lead and open the flood gates. A seven-run fourth stretched Boston's advantage to 11 runs, ending any suspense about the outcome. Gernert put another ball into orbit leading off the fifth, and the Sox added a five-spot in the eighth for good measure. In all, the big first baseman enjoyed a 3-for-4 day with two homers, four RBI, and four runs scored. The next day, with Lou Boudreau's team leading the Tigers by a 5–3 score after six-and-a-half innings, they went on a rampage in the bottom of the seventh, sending 17 runners across the plate before a meager weekday crowd of 3,626 in the Fenway ballyard. Gene Stephens set a major league record with three base hits in the same inning. Dick Gernert whacked a one-out, three-run home run during the uprising and later drew a bases-loaded walk, giving him four RBI in the inning. He went 2-for-5 on the day, and the Red Sox won by a final score of 23–3. Their 40 runs scored in two consecutive games is still a modern major league record. The Reading, Pennsylvania, native hit 21 homers during the year, the seventh-highest total in the American League, drove in 71 runs, and batted .253.

Unfortunately, he missed most of the next two seasons because of illness, playing in just 21 games with 43 at-bats over the two-year period. He returned to the Red Sox lineup in 1956, but found himself without a regular position. He spent the next four years as a platoon player, alternating between first base and left field, where he spelled the aging Ted Williams from time to time. He was considered to be the regular first baseman although he played in more than 100 games at the position only one year. In 1958, he had one of his best years with Boston, both offensively and defensively. He hit 20 homers and drove in 69 runs in 431 at-bats, and in the field, he led all American League first basemen in putouts (1.101), assists (93), and double plays (118). The following year he shared the first base duties with Vic Wertz, hitting .262 with 11 homers in 298 at-bats. He was traded to the Chicago Cubs on November 21, 1959, ending his Boston Red Sox career after eight years.

Goodman, Billy

He was, quite literally, the man without a country, or at least without a position. He was a .300 hitter whose specialty was placing singles beyond the reach of outfielders during a time when the leagues were looking for long-ball hitters. William Dale Goodman was born on a dairy farm in Concord, NC, on March 22, 1926. He spent his youth working on the farm, milking cows, chopping wood, plowing cotton and, when time permitted, playing pickup baseball games in a cow pasture. He began his professional baseball career as a skinny 18-year-old outfielder with the Atlanta Crackers in the Class-A1 Southern Association in 1944. The five-foot, eleven-inch, 160-pound left-handed hitter batted a cool .330 for the Crackers and led the league with 122 runs scored and 13 triples. Goodman missed the 1945 season while serving in the United States Navy in the South Pacific during the last days of World War II, but after the war, he returned to Atlanta and stroked the ball at a stratospheric .389 clip for the Crackers in 1946. He was sold to the Boston Red Sox after the season ended, and started the 1947 season with Boston, but after going 2-for-11 in 12 games, he was farmed out to the Louisville Colonels of the American Association, where he hit a resounding .340.

The next spring, manager Joe McCarthy made Goodman his first baseman, and he held that position for two years, during which time he demonstrated his skills both offensively and defensively. He batted .310 in 1948 and led all American League first basemen in total chances per game. The next year, he hit .298 and led the league with a .992 fielding average. However, as 1950 got under way, his days as a regular were numbered. Walt Dropo, a six-foot, five-inch, 220-pound behemoth from Moosup, Connecticut, arrived on the scene after slugging 19 homers for Louisville and Sacramento, and assumed the first base duties, sending Goodman to the dugout. The tall, skinny, frail-looking six-footer was at a disadvantage when competing for a position on a major league baseball team. He had no power and, in spite of being one of the most versatile players ever to play the game, he was forever being bumped by a player with more muscle. "Joe Cronin, the General Manager of the Red Sox called Goodman 'a ragbag player' which is as good a description as any for a guy who looks as though he is a refugee from an oxygen tent when he is enjoying the best of health." "It's a lucky accident whenever I hit one over the fence," Goodman admits. "I've given up trying to hit 'em far because the harder I try the worse the results I get." He said when he gets a home run "it's usually the case of trying to bring in a runner from third base with an outfield fly and a sudden gale, or something, giving the ball a ride."[67]

Although he was always at a disadvantage, Goodman would not be denied. He was a line drive hitter with good bat control who struck out only half as often as he walked, giving him an excellent on-base percentage, and his ability to play any outfield or infield position kept him in the lineup throughout the season. In 1950, he led the American League in batting with an average of .354, becoming the first player to win the title without having a permanent position. He played 45 games in the outfield, 27 games at third base, 21 games at first base, five games at second base, and one game at shortstop, becoming the team's regular left fielder after Ted Williams fractured his elbow in the All-Star Game. Overall, he played in 110 games with 424 at-bats, and Johnny Pesky deserved an assist on Goodman's batting title because he took himself out of the lineup over the final weeks of the season so Goodman could reach the minimum number of at-bats to qualify for the title. When Bobby Doerr retired after the 1951 season, Goodman became the regular second baseman, a position he held for four years, before being traded to Baltimore on June 14, 1957. Goodman retired in 1962 after 16 years of Big League service during which he batten an even .300, with 1,691 base hits in 5,644 at-bats.

Gordon, Tom "Flash"

Tom "Flash" Gordon, a five-foot, nine-inch, 160-pound flamethrowing right-hander, was taught to throw the curveball by his father in Sebring, Florida, and, in conjunction with his fastball, he brought major league scouts to Sebring in droves. The Kansas City Royals drafted the slender pitcher in the sixth round of the 1986 amateur draft and sent him to their Sarasota farm club in the Gulf Coast League, where he went 3–1 in nine games with a minuscule 1.01 ERA. He made his way through the Royals' farm system over the next two years, with stops in Omaha, Eugene, Fort Myers, Appleton, and Memphis, finally arriving in Kansas City on September 8, 1988.

He pitched two innings of scoreless relief in his major league debut, striking out two, in Oakland's 5–1 win over the Kansas City Royals in Royals Stadium.

The following year, his rookie season, the 21-year-old fireballer racked up a 17–9 record in 49 games, including 16 starts. He fanned 153 men in 163 innings, and posted a 3.64 earned run average. The 17 wins were a high-water mark for Flash Gordon during his seven years in Kansas City. Three times he won 12 games and once he won 11, as he struggled with his control and consistency. He filed for free agency after a 1995 season that saw him go 12–12 in 31 starts with a 4.43 ERA. The Boston Red Sox eventually signed him to a contract on December 21, 1995, and made him part of their starting rotation with Roger Clemens, Aaron Sele, and Tim Wakefield. Gordon posted a 12–9 mark in 1996, starting 34 games with a 5.59 ERA. The following spring, Red Sox pitching coach Joe Kerrigan converted him from a starting pitcher to a relief pitcher, and eventually a closer. In 1997, the Florida native won six games against ten losses, but posted 11 saves with just two blown saves. Flash Gordon had finally found his niche. After the 1997 season, he never started another game, appearing in a total of 540 games through 2009, all of them out of the bullpen. The little right-hander pitched in 73 games for the Red Sox in 1998, going 7–4 and saving a league-high 46 games. He set a major league record with 56 consecutive saves for Jimy Williams' team between 1998 and 1999, but lost most of the 1999 season because of Tommy John surgery to repair a torn ligament in his elbow. He pitched in just 21 games that year with 11 saves. After the surgery that he fought against for almost a year, he sat out the entire 2000 season. He was not offered a contract by Boston for 2001, and signed with the Chicago Cubs. He went on to pitch for six different teams between 2001 and 2009, going 35–33 with 87 saves in 446 games pitched. He was primarily a setup man after 2001, and the 41-year-old bullpen specialist was still active in 2009, although he was on the disabled list most of the season, appearing in just three games. He was released by the Arizona Diamondbacks on August 11.

Flash Gordon was a three-time All-Star and appeared in seven post-season games, going 0–1 with no saves. He took the loss in the 1998 Division Series finale against the Cleveland Indians in Fenway Park on October 3, blowing a 1–0 lead in the eighth inning as 33,537 rabid Red Sox fans sat in disbelief. He replaced Derek Lowe to start the inning and was touched up for a one-out single by Kenny Lofton, who moved to second base on a hit to center field by Omar Vizquel. After Lofton stole third on the 30-year-old right-hander, David Justice ripped a double to center field to plate the two winning runs. Tom Gordon's 21-year major league record included 890 games pitched with a 138–126 won-lost record, and 158 saves. He is the only pitcher in major league history with more than 100 victories, 100 saves, and 100 holds.

Greenwell, Mike

Mike Greenwell, a native of Louisville, Kentucky, began his professional baseball career in the Boston Red Sox organization in 1982 at the age of 19, batting .269 in 268 at-bats with the Elmira Pioneers in the Single-A New York-Pennsylvania League. Three years later, after hitting .256 with 13 homers for Pawtucket in the tough Triple-A International League, he went up to Boston for a cup of coffee at the end of the season. His first major league hit was a game-winning two-run homer in the 13th inning against the Blue Jays in Toronto on September 25, and he finished the season batting .323 in the Big Show with 10 base hits in 31 at-bats. The next year, he put it all together, batting .300 with Pawtucket, with 18 homers in 320 at-bats. Recalled by Boston on July 24, he banged out 11 base hits in 35 at-bats for a .314 average for John McNamara's club. He also made five post-season appearances with Boston that season, going 1-for-2 as a pinch-hitter against the California Angels in the ALCS and 0-for-3 as a pinch-hitter against the New York Mets in the World Series.

In 1987, the 23-year-old outfielder, the heir apparent to Williams, Yastrzemski, and Rice, "rapidly established himself as one of baseball's best hitters. With a smooth left-handed batting stroke modeled after George Brett's,"[68] he put together a sensational rookie season, batting .328 with 31 doubles, 19 home runs, and 89 RBI in 412 at-bats. His fine effort was rewarded when he was named to the Topps and Baseball Digest All-Rookie Teams. Somewhere along the line, he acquired the nickname "Gator" for entertaining guests at his family fun park in Cape Coral, Florida, in the offseason by wrestling alligators.

The following spring, he beat out Jim Rice for the left field job, and he defied the sophomore jinx, crafting a career season with a .325 batting average, 39 doubles, 22 home runs, 119 RBI, and 16 stolen bases in 590 at-bats. Mike Greenwell played for the Red Sox for eight more years, batting over .300 three times, but his numerous injuries curtailed what might have been a Hall of Fame career. He made seven trips to the disabled list for periods up to three-and-a-half months between 1989 and 1996. In 1992, he played in just 49 games, and in 1994, he was limited to 95 games. In all, he appeared in over 147 games only twice. When he was healthy, he was one of the top outfielders in the American League, being named to the 1988 and 1989 All-Star teams. His biggest day in a Red Sox uniform came on September 2, 1996 at the Kingdome in Seattle, Washington. The two teams engaged in a slugfest that saw Boston starter Roger Clemens gone after five innings as the Mariners jumped out to a 5–0 lead before the Sox got their bats unlimbered, particularly the heavy lumber of Mike Greenwell who accounted for all nine RBI in a 9–8 ten-inning victory. Gator got his team on the board with a two-out, two-run homer into the right field seats in the top of the fifth inning, cutting the Seattle lead to 5–2. Two innings later, he put

Mike Greenwell

the BoSox on top with a grand-slam homer following a Reggie Jefferson double and walks to Troy O'Leary and Tim Naehring. After the Mariners took out their frustration on the Boston bullpen for a three-spot in the bottom of the inning, Boston erupted again in the eighth. With Seattle closer Norm Charlton, on the mound, Greenwell sliced a two-out double to left field, plating the tying runs. The game remained tied into the tenth when Gator came through yet again. Rafael Carmona, another southpaw, walked two men with two out, bringing Mr. Greenwell to the plate, and the Boston terminator quieted the crowd of 24,470 by poking a base hit to left field, sending Wil Cordero scampering home with the winning run. Greenwell went 4-for-5 in the game with a single, a double, two home runs, two runs scored and nine RBI.

The big Kentuckian appeared in five post-season series with the Red Sox, going a combined 7-for-48 for a barely visible .145 batting average. The lone bright spot in his post-season career was in game three of the 1988 ALCS when he slammed a double and a home run with three RBI in a 10–6 loss to the Oakland Athletics. Mike Greenwell's 12-year career statistics with Boston included 4,623 at-bats in 1,269 games played with 1,400 base hits for a .303 batting average. In the field he had a dependable glove and a strong, accurate throwing arm. His .981 fielding average was three points better the league average.

Griffin, Doug

Red Sox fans will remember Doug Griffin — "Dude" to his friends — as a sure-handed second baseman and a tough clutch hitter, but also an injury-plagued player.[69] The six-foot-tall, 160-pound infielder from South Gate, California, began his professional baseball career with Idaho Falls in the Pioneer League in 1965 after being drafted by the California Angels in the June amateur draft. After hitting .200 in 31 games with Idaho Falls, he was promoted to the Quad Cities Angels in the Class-A Midwest League, and he responded with a respectable .276 batting average in 98 games. He spent the next two years in the submarine service at the U.S. Naval Base in Hawaii, playing baseball on military teams. Returning to the organized baseball scene in 1969, he split the season between Quad Cities and the El Paso Sun Kings in the Double-A Texas League, hitting .308 in 50 games with El Paso. In 1970, the 25-year-old Californian spent a comfortable summer with the league-leading Hawaii Islanders in the Pacific Coast League, where he stung the ball at a .326 clip, scored 119 runs, led the league with 35 stolen bases, and was voted to the league's All-Star team. The flashy fielder, who was known for his glove and his great speed, finished the season with the California Angels, but was traded to the Red Sox in the off-season.

Doug Griffin was Boston's regular second baseman his first three years in the American League, displaying exceptional defensive skills, while hitting in the .250 range. Pitcher Ken Tatum appreciated having the human vacuum cleaner behind him. "He's not big, but he's a great competitor. He dives for balls. He can hit and run, and he will sacrifice himself to move along a base runner. He has very quick hands and he can make the double play."[70] Unfortunately the slender infielder was injury-prone, spending too much time on the disabled list. He dazzled fans with his spirited play during the first half of 1971, producing three three-hit games and fielding flawlessly with just two errors in his first 200 chances. Then, on June 28, going back for a pop fly during a Monday night game in Fenway Park, he suffered back spasms and had to be helped off the field, spending the next 28 days on the DL. The following year, he suffered a broken hand when hit by a Gaylord Perry fastball on August 9, limiting his season to 129 games. But he still impressed the voters enough to award him a Gold Glove. He impressed manager Eddie Kasko as well. "I have ceased to be amazed at the plays he makes. He did something spectacular every day. He gets to balls I cannot believe he can reach."[71] In 1973, an errant pitch by Billy Champion fractured his hand again and put him on the shelf from May 25 to July 13, but he still put together his best season defensively, fielding .990 with just six errors in 584 chances. His good luck didn't last long, however. On April 30, 1974, he was knocked unconscious by a Nolan Ryan heater, causing a concussion and a temporary hearing loss, and sending him to the DL from April 30 until July 1. And last but not least, he was put out of action again by Oakland's Dick Bosman on August 30, 1975. He shared second base duties with Denny Doyle that year as the Red Sox captured the Eastern Division title, defeated the Oakland A's in the American League Championship Series, but were beaten by the Cincinnati Reds in a seven-game World Series. Doyle held down the second base duties in the post-season, limiting Griffin to one at-bat in the World Series.

Doug Griffin played in 49 games in 1976 and five games the following season before being released on June 21. He subsequently retired. During his stay in Boston, from 1971 to 1977, the refugee from a hospital bed played in 614 games, or just 63 percent of the scheduled games. Leo Durocher once said, referring to Brooklyn Dodgers outfielder Pete Reiser, "He had everything but luck." The same thing could be said of Griffin.

Grove, Lefty

As noted in *The Ballplayers*, he "had a blazing fastball and a temper to match," reportedly tearing a clubhouse to shreds after a losing effort. Yet he was one of the greatest pitchers in baseball history and, arguably, the greatest southpaw pitcher ever to unleash a heater.[72]

Lefty Grove

Robert Moses Grove was born in Lonaconing, MD on March 6, 1900. He made his professional baseball debut at the age of 20 with Martinsburg in the Class-D Blue Ridge League where he went 3-and-3 in six games, and was then sold to the Baltimore Orioles of the International League. The tall, slender fireballer threw nothing but smoke in his early years, but he didn't always know where the ball was going. He led the International League in bases on balls three straight years and in strikeouts four straight years, averaging a strikeout an inning. He fanned 330 batters in 303 innings in 1923, an IL record that still stands. Grove's records for Baltimore were 12–2, 25–10, 18–8, 27–10, and 27–6. That was all Connie Mack needed to see, and the owner of the Philadelphia Athletics immediately made Baltimore owner Jack Dunn, an offer he couldn't refuse, $105,000 in cash, to obtain the rights to the future Hall Of Famer.

The six-foot, three-inch, 190-pound hurler suffered through a losing season with the A's in 1925, winning 10 games and losing 12 for a second-place team. The chink in Grove's armor was his bases on balls total of 131 in 197 innings. He reduced his walks to just 79 walks in 262⅓ innings by 1927, and the improvement showed in his won-lost record that brought him his first 20-victory season at 20–13. The talented southpaw went on to enjoy seven consecutive seasons of 20 or more victories, including four years where he led the league in victories. He also led the American League in strikeouts his first seven years in the league, and showed the way in ERA five times. Lefty Grove's best year was 1931 when he pitched the A's to a 13½-game margin over the New York Yankees in the American League pennant race. He won 31 games against four losses that year for an .886 winning percentage, while pitching in 41 games, 30 of them starts, with 27 complete games and four shutouts. He led the league in victories, winning percentage, complete games, shutouts, strikeouts, and earned run average, his 2.06 ERA being a fantastic 2.32 runs below the league average. During the Philadelphia Athletics' three-year run of American League pennants and two World Championships from 1929–1931, Grove went 20–6, 28–5, and 31–4 as noted previously. He pitched in eight World Series games, winning four and losing two in five starts with four complete games, and a 1.75 earned run average.

In addition to his pitching skills, Grove's temper was legendary. "On the day he was pitching," wrote biographer Jim Kaplan, "It was suicide for a photographer to take his picture. He'd throw the ball right through the lens." If he lost a game, according to one of his teammates, it was best to stay clear of the clubhouse. As noted in Shatzkin's *Ballplayers*, he "shredded uniforms, kicked buckets, ripped-apart lockers, and alienated teammates."[73] Doc Cramer added, "Lose a one-to-nothing game and you'd be ducking stools and gloves and bats and whatever else would fly."[74]

The 34-year-old hurler, having lost the zip on his fastball, was traded to the Boston Red Sox on December 12, 1933, in one of Connie Mack's periodic house-cleaning maneuvers. He spent his first year in Boston re-inventing himself, changing from a fastball pitcher to a finesse pitcher, but the first year was a difficult one as he nursed a sore arm in addition to working to offset the loss of his fastball. He won just eight games that year against eight losses, but by the next spring, he was ready to crank it up. He went on to give Joe Cronin's cohorts some outstanding pitching over the next seven years, beginning with 1935 when he went 20–12 for a fourth-place team, while leading the league with a 2.70 ERA. He compiled a 17–12 record the following year and once again led the league in ERA with a 2.81 mark. The 37-year-old southpaw won another 17 games in 1937, losing just nine times, went 14–4 with a league-leading 3.07 ERA the following year, and 15–4 in 1939, leading the league in winning percentage (.789) and ERA (2.54). With his career winding down, and his heater a distant memory, he struggled through two more seasons, going 7–6 and 7–7 in 1940 and 1941 respectively, before hanging up his glove for good. He won his 300th and final major league victory on July 25, 1941, when he defeated the Cleveland Indians, 10–6, in Fenway Park. During his memorable 17-year major league career, the temperamental southpaw won 300 games and lost 141. He led the American League in victories four times, winning percentage five times, strikeouts seven times, and earned run average a major league-record nine times. He was inducted into the National Baseball Hall of Fame in 1947.

Harper, Tommy

Tommy Harper was born in Oak Grove, Louisiana, on October 14, 1940. He played the outfield for San Francisco State University until 1960, when he was signed as an amateur free agent by the Cincinnati Reds, who sent him to their farm team in the Class-B Three-I League, where he batted .254 and stole 26 bases in 79 games. The following year, the five-foot, ten-inch, 168-pound speedster, still with Topeka in the Three-I League, led the league with 131 runs scored, 11 triples, and 31 stolen bases, while pounding out 27 doubles, 15 home runs, and batting .324 in 124 games. After one more year of seasoning with San Diego in the Pacific Coast League, where he hit .333 with 26 homers and 84 RBI, Harper was called up to the big club to begin his major league career in 1963.

The 22-year-old outfielder never lived up to management's expectations in Cincinnati, with his batting average fluctuating between .225 and .278. His one standout year was 1965, when he hit .257 with 28 doubles, 18 homers, 35 stolen bases, and a league-leading 126 runs scored. He was traded to Cleveland in 1968, and the Cubs' Ferguson Jenkins was one man who was happy to see him leave the National League. "I'm glad he's out of my hair. He's a 100 percent type. First time I ever faced him, he hit one in the upper deck. He's got great speed and he's smart on the bases, the type to distract an infield and upset a pitcher."[75] Harper moved to Seattle a year later, where he led the American League with 73 stolen bases, and after the franchise moved to Milwaukee he spent two years there. In 1970, he became the sixth 30–30 player in major league history with 31 home runs and 38 stolen bases. His averages plummeted in 1971 and he was traded to the Boston Red Sox in the off-season.

Tommy Harper's tenure in Boston lasted three years where he displayed his blinding speed, scoring 92 runs, hitting 14 homers, and stealing 25 bases in 1972, and being selected as the team's MVP the following year after stroking the ball at a .281 clip with 23 doubles, 17 home runs, 92 runs scored, 71 RBI, and a league-leading 54 stolen bases. He played one more year in Boston, batting .237, before being traded to the California Angels. He retired after the 1986 season, but remained active in baseball. He was a coach for the Boston Red Sox from 1980 through 1984 and from 2000 to 2002. Nick Cafardo of the Boston Globe said one time that Tommy Harper was his favorite coach. He said Harper had an "off the chart incredible baseball mind."

Hatteberg, Scott

Scott Allen Hatteberg, a native of Salem, Oregon, signed a contract with the Boston Red Sox after graduating from Washington State College in 1991. The six-foot, one-inch, 195-pound receiver began his professional baseball career with Winter Haven in the Single-A Florida State League, and made two short visits to Fenway Park in 1995 and 1996, before becoming a full-time member of Jimy Williams' squad in 1997. He replaced Mike Stanley as the regular catcher and surprised everyone with his timely hitting. He batted a brisk .277 in his rookie season, with 23 doubles and 10 home runs in 350 at-bats, and followed that with almost identical stats the following year, batting .276 with 23 doubles and 12 home runs in 359 at-bats. Unfortunately, his defense didn't measure up to his offense. He had come to the Red Sox with a reputation as a strong defensive catcher, but his glove seemed to be overrated. He had difficulty throwing out baserunners attempting to steal and was plagued by passed balls. In May 1999, he injured his elbow and was out of the lineup for four months recovering from surgery. When he returned, he discovered that his arm, which was not one of his strong points prior to the injury, was even worse after surgery. His caught-stealing percentage, 28 percent in 1997 and 1998, dropped to 21 percent in 1999, then to 19 percent and 9 percent, the next two years. He lost his regular job to Jason Varitek when he hurt his elbow but the situation was reversed in 2001 when Varitek broke his elbow, midway through the season and Hatteburg stepped in to fill the breach.

One of his fondest memories in a Boston uniform was August 6, 2001, during a Monday night game in Fenway Park. A noisy crowd of 33,977 jammed the little park along Yawkey Way to cheer for their favorites against the last-place Texas Rangers. In the bottom of the fourth, with Boston on top by a 4–2 score, they threatened to add to their total when Brian Daubach drew a base on balls and Chris Stynes followed with a single, sending Daubach to second base, but the rally died there when Hatteburg hit a line drive right at shortstop Alex Rodriguez, who tossed the ball to Randy Velarde at second base to double-up Daubach, and Velarde tagged Stynes coming down from first base to complete a triple play. Two innings later, Hatteburg had a chance to redeem himself when he came to the plate with the bases loaded and Texas protecting a 7–6 lead. The big receiver promptly unloaded, sending a screamer into the right field bleachers for a grand-slam home run, giving the Back Bay Bombers their winning runs in a 10–7 triumph. Scott Hatteburg's dramatics gave him the honor of being the only player in major league history to hit into a triple play in one at-bat and hit a grand-slam homer in his next at-bat.

Hatteburg's joy was short-lived, however. His inability to throw a baseball essentially ended his career as a catcher and the Red Sox did not renew his contract for 2002. The big left-handed hitter filed for free agency at the end of the season and played first base for Oakland for four years before retiring. Scott Hatteberg's seven-year statistics with the Red Sox included a decent .267 batting average, but his defense was suspect. He was charged with an average of 25 passed balls for every 154 games played, about double the league average, and his caught-stealing percentage of 21 percent was at least ten percent below the league average.

Higgins, Pinky

Michael Frank "Pinky" Higgins made his major league debut with the Philadelphia Athletics on June 25, 1930. He appeared in 14 games for the A's that year, hitting .250, and was farmed out to Dallas and San Antonio in the Texas League for seasoning in 1931, where he hit a combined .284 in 131 games. The following year, the six-foot, 180-pound third baseman played for the league-champion Portland Beavers in the Pacific Coast League, where he had a career season, stroking the ball at a .326 clip with 51 doubles, 33 home runs, 145 runs scored, and 132 RBI in 189 games played.

Connie Mack quickly recalled him to Philadelphia for 1933, and he responded with an excellent .314 batting average, including 34 doubles, 11 triples, 14 homers, and 99 runs batted in, in 567 at-bats. On August 6, as the A's were outhitting the Washington Senators 12–8 in Griffith Stadium, Pinky Higgins hit for the cycle, going 4-for-5 with five RBI and four runs scored. Disdaining the sophomore jinx, Higgins tortured opposing pitchers to the tune of a .330 average in 1934 with 37 doubles, 16 homers, and 90 RBI in 543 at-bats. His batting average dropped to .296 and .289 the next two years, and combined with his erratic defense, encouraged Mack to trade him to the Boston Red Sox on December 9, 1936.

The 28-year-old Texan enjoyed two good seasons in Boston, batting .302 with 106 RBI in 570 at-bats in 1937 and .303 with 106 RBI the following year. Higgins began one of baseball's historic streaks in the first game of a doubleheader against the Chicago White Sox in Comiskey Park on June 19, 1938, when he stroked a single in his last at-bat. He went 3-for-3 in the nightcap with a walk, a double, and an RBI as Boston defeated the White Sox, 6–1, completing a sweep of the doubleheader. Two days later, in Briggs Stadium, Detroit, in the first game of a Tuesday twin bill, he paced the Red Sox to an 8–3 triumph over the Tigers by hammering four straight hits including a double, and drawing a walk in his fifth at-bat.

He kept up his abuse of Tigers pitching in game two, raking the hometown hurlers for four more hits in four at-bats, while driving in one run in a 5–4 Boston victory. The next day his streak came to an end when he struck out in his first trip to the plate against Chicago southpaw Vern Kennedy, but when the smoke had cleared, he had set a major league record with 12 consecutive base hits in 14 plate appearances, with two bases on balls. On August 23, in the first game of a Tuesday doubleheader at the Fens, Boston's slugging third baseman unleashed his offensive pyrotechnics once again when he ripped five base hits in five at-bats, with two doubles and five RBI as the Sox crushed the Cleveland Indians, 13–3. He went two-for-five in the nightcap as Boston won again, by a 14–12 score. Jimmie Foxx, who had six RBI in the game, hit a ninth-inning grand slam to win it.

The right-handed-hitting Higgins was fortunate to have played baseball during the 1930s when the American League intentionally used a much livelier ball than the National League. The ball, known as the number 3 ball, was in play through the 1938 season, after which both leagues agreed to use a slower ball in 1939. He departed Boston in December, 1938, taking his offensive skills to Detroit where he stayed for more than six years. He continued to hit although with more modest averages that ranged from .267 to .298. He starred for Detroit in a losing effort in the 1940 World Series, batting .333 with five extra base hits and six RBI in seven games. Higgins returned to Boston midway through the 1946 season, batting .275 in 64 games and then retiring from active duty. He managed the Red Sox from 1955 through 1962, winning 560 games and losing 566 for a .502 winning percentage.

Hillenbrand, Shea

Thirty-seven years after the original Dr. Strangeglove, aka Dick Stuart, showcased his defensive magic around the Fens, another good hit-no field infielder sent chills up the spines of the Boston faithful whenever a ball was hit in his direction. Shea Matthew Hillenbrand, who was born in Mesa, Arizona, on July 27, 1975, spent two years as the shortstop for the Mesa Community College baseball team, after which he was drafted by the Boston Red Sox, who assigned him to their Lowell farm team in the Single-A New York-Pennsylvania League. The six-foot, one-inch, 210-pound, right-handed free-swinger hit a brisk .315 for Lowell, but was found wanting defensively as a shortstop, making 14 errors in 10 games. He was subsequently tried at third base and first base without success. Still, his hitting was so impressive that he was moved through Boston's minor league system, spending three years in Single-A ball while the team searched for a position he could handle. They even tried him at catcher, but a knee injury ended that experiment. His best year in A-ball was 1998, when he scorched the ball at a .349 clip for Michigan in the Midwest League, with 33 doubles, 19 home runs, and 93 runs batted in, splitting his time between catcher, first base, and third base. He played first base and third base for Trenton in the Double-A Eastern League in 2000, batting .323 with 35 doubles, 11 homers, and 79 RBI in 135 games, and giving him a spot on the Red Sox 2001 spring training roster.

Shea Hillenbrand impressed manager Jimy Williams in Florida, posting a healthy .423 batting average, and he was subsequently handed the starting third base job in Boston. He had a decent, but not outstanding, rookie season, batting .263 with 12 homers, but he drove in only 49 runs in 139 games, drew only 13 bases on balls, and had an embarrassing .291 on-base-percentage. On defense, playing almost exclusively at third base, he committed 18 errors, for a .941 fielding average, six points below the league average. "Hillenbrand got off to another fantastic start in 2002, highlighted by a game-winning homer off Yankee closer Mariano Rivera on April 13, and a game-winning pinch-hit grand slam off the catwalk in Tampa Bay's Tropicana Field on May 4."[76] Boston's handsome third baseman started the All-Star Game for the American League in Milwaukee's Miller Park on July 9, going 0-for-2 with a strikeout. The game was the first All-Star Game to end in a tie when the pitching staffs were depleted after 11 innings with the game deadlocked at 7–7. As in his rookie year, the Mesa native tailed off after a fast start, finishing the year with a .293 average, 43 doubles, 18 homers, 25 bases on balls, 83 RBI, and a .330 OBP, in 634 at-bats. Once again he was found wanting on defense, committing a major-league high 23 errors in

156 games for a .943 fielding average. In January, 2003, general manager Theo Epstein signed both third baseman Bill Mueller and first baseman David Ortiz, making Hillenbrand expendable, and he was subsequently traded to the Arizona Diamondbacks on May 29.

Hoblitzell, Dick

Richard Carleton "Doc" Hoblitzell, a native of Waverly, West Virginia, was an intelligent player who was well liked and respected by his teammates as well as by opposing players. He attended Marietta College in 1905 and 1906, where he was a star halfback on the football team, later transferring to Western University of Pennsylvania, where he played end. He began playing professional baseball with Clarksburg in the Class-D Western Pennsylvania League in 1907, playing under an assumed name in order to protect his amateur status while in college. The next year Clarksburg sold him to the Cincinnati Reds of the National League on August 13 for $2,750. The 19-year-old Hoblitzell hit .254 in 32 games for the Reds in 1908, and upped his average to .308 in 142 games the following year. He also returned to school during the off-season, studying dentistry at Ohio College of Dental Surgery. Doc, as he was now called, stayed in Cincinnati for another four years, averaging between .278 and .294, and leaving his mark on opposing teams. "He stands well up at the plate, takes a healthy swing at the ball, and is a long driver at opportune times," wrote one reporter. "In fact, he is looked upon by opposing pitchers as one of the most dangerous men at the bat they are called upon to face."[77] He also contributed to the team's success on the bases, stealing from 17 to 32 bases a year in Cincinnati. In addition to his offensive output, he contributed on defense with his quickness, his exceptional range, and his dependable glove-work.

The Boston Red Sox purchased the contract of the six-foot-tall, 172-pound left-handed hitter from the cellar-dwelling Cincinnati Reds in July, 1914, for $1,500, and he was stationed at first base, replacing journeyman Clyde Engel, who had held the position since Jake Stahl retired the previous year. Hoblitzell was assigned to room with rookie pitcher Babe Ruth, but that association apparently didn't affect his batting eye as he hit a solid .319 in 69 games for Bill Carrigan's team that year, usually hitting from the third or fourth spot in the batting order. He hit .283 in 1915 for the American League champions, and .313 in the World Series, won by Boston in five games over the Philadelphia Phillies. The following year he batted .259 during the season and .235 in the World Series, a five-game victory over the Brooklyn Robins. Two years later he was hitting .159 after 25 games when he injured a finger in a May 6 exhibition game in Clifton, New Jersey, and was replaced at first base by Babe Ruth. One month later, on June 6, with World War I in full bloom, he was commissioned a First Lieutenant in the U.S. Army Dental Corps, ending his major league career.

Hobson, Butch

"Before Curt Schilling and the bloody sock in 2004, one player who personified toughness in a Boston Red Sox uniform was Butch Hobson. Hobson's legacy is that of a power hitting third baseman who brought a football mentality to the diamond in the way he played through pain and gave every ounce of effort on the field that his body could muster."[78] Clell Laverne "Butch" Hobson was born in Tuscaloosa, Alabama, on August 17, 1951, and matriculated at his hometown college, the University of Alabama, where he played football under the legendary Paul "Bear" Bryant, and also lettered in baseball, leading the team in hits (38), home runs (13), and RBI (37) in his senior year. The rugged six-foot, one-inch, 190-pound right-handed slugger was drafted by the Boston Red Sox in 1973 and spent the last month of the season with the Winston-Salem Red Sox in the Single-A Carolina League, where he hit .179 in 17 games. The former football player spent his first full season in organized baseball shuffling between the outfield, third base, and first base, playing in 119 games and striking the ball at a crisp .284 pace with 14 homers and 74 RBI in 119 games. By 1975, he had found a home at third base and played 138 games there for Bristol in the Double-A Eastern League, hitting .265 with 15 homers and 73 RBI for Bill Slack's second-place Red Sox. He was recalled to Boston late in the season and made his major league debut on September 7 as a pinch runner.

He started at third base for the American League Champions in Fenway Park on the 28th, going 1-for-4 during an 11–4 drubbing by the Cleveland Indians.

Butch Hobson split the next year between Rhode Island in the International League and the parent Boston Red Sox. He hit .286 with Rhode Island in 90 games with 25 home runs and 72 runs batted in. Recalled to Boston, he made his 1976 Fenway Park debut on June 28, playing third base in a 12–8 win over the Baltimore Orioles, and cracking two base hits in five trips to the plate with a double off Jim Palmer and an inside-the-park homer off Rudy May. The sixth-inning home run was a line drive to center field that got past Paul Blair when he tried to make a shoestring catch and rolled to the wall, scoring Cecil Cooper ahead of Hobson. In general, however, he was outmatched at the plate during his rookie season, batting .234 with eight homers and 34 RBI in 269 at-bats. In 1977, the 26-year-old infielder had a career season, batting .286 with 33 doubles, 30 home runs, nine behind Jim Rice's league-leading total, and 112 RBI, two behind Rice. In the field, he had a .946 fielding average and a league-leading 57 double plays, for the third place Red Sox. The gritty third baseman was hampered by a variety of injuries in 1978, including bone chips in his right elbow, cartilage damage in both knees, and a torn hamstring muscle, that Andrew Blume noted "contributed to a nightmarish season defensively and made every throw from third base an adventure."[79] Reportedly, Hobson adjusted his bone chips after every throw. He played through the pain, seeing action in 147 games and slugging 18 homers. He drove in 21 runs in ten games in April but his game suffered as the year wore on, and he ended the season with just 80 RBI, and an .899 fielding average, the lowest fielding average for any third baseman since 1907. After off-season elbow surgery Hobson came back to hit 28 homers with 93 RBI and a .935 fielding average the following year, but in 1980, after spending a month on the disabled list with a shoulder injury, he was limited to playing in just 93 games, hitting .228 with 11 homers and 39 RBI in 324 at-bats. He was traded to the California Angels on December 10, retiring from the game one year later.

The hustling, hard-nosed third baseman was loved and appreciated in Boston for his all-out aggressiveness and for his willingness to destroy his body for the good of the team. He himself noted, "Boston Red Sox fans are supportive ... whether a guy goes 0-for-20, as long as you are out there and giving 110 percent every day. That's all they care about. They're rooting for that blue collar guy that runs through walls. They want the guy who will dive into the stands for the ball." Butch Hobson was that guy.

Hoffman, Glenn

Glenn Edward Hoffman was drafted by the Boston Red Sox in 1976 and sent to the Single-A New York–Pennsylvania League, where he batted .272 in 60 games and handled the shortstop position with flair. Over the next three years, the strong-armed infielder moved through the Red Sox farm system, playing all the infield positions, and even pitching an inning. In 1978 and 1979, playing with Boston's top farm club in Pawtucket, he batted .282 and .285 respectively, and showed exceptional defensive skills at both third base and shortstop.

The six-foot, one-inch, 175-pound, right-handed hitter, who joined the parent club as a utility infielder in 1980, played 110 games at third base while Butch Hobson was nursing an injured shoulder, and he stung the ball at a .285 clip but, as it turned out, that would be his career high-water mark with the bat. The following year, with all-star third baseman Carney Lansford on board, Hoffman's playing time decreased to 78 games, most of them at shortstop, where he moved after Gold-Glover Rick Burleson was traded to California. He took over the position on a full-time basis in 1982 and 1983, fielding well and displaying a strong, accurate throwing arm and exceptional range. Unfortunately, while his glove was earning its keep, his bat did not keep pace. He hit a lowly .209 in 1982 and .260 the following year. He lost his shortstop job to Jackie Gutierrez in 1984, spent the year primarily as a defensive replacement, and had just 74 at-bats with a .189 average. He split the 1985 season with Gutierrez, out-fielding him by a wide margin and out-hitting him by 58 points, with his .276 batting average in 279 at-bats the second-highest average of his career. But just when it looked like Hoffman's career was stabilized, he was struck down with a sprained ankle and an irregular heartbeat that sidelined him for most of the 1986 season. He made an unsuccessful comeback with Boston in 1987, and was finally traded to the Los Angeles Dodgers on August 21.

Hooper, Harry

Harry Bartholomew Hooper, from Bell Station, California, attended St. Mary's College, earning a degree in Civil Engineering in 1907. After graduation, he joined the Sacramento club in the California State League because he was promised a surveying job when not playing ball. As he said, "I never had any intention of taking up baseball as a career. I expected to be an engineer."[80] Hooper never became an engineer. After two years in Sacramento, where he hit .301 and .344 respectively and fielded brilliantly, he was enticed to go to Boston, where he could play baseball for the Red Sox and, later, work as an engineer on the construction of a new ballpark. Hooper took the bait, relocated to Boston and developed into one of the greatest right fielders in Red Sox history.

In 1909, the 21-year-old outfielder patrolled left field at the Huntington Avenue Baseball Grounds for Fred Lake's third-place Red Sox. He hit a respectable .282 in 81 games in his rookie season, with 15 stolen bases. The next year he moved to right field, where he stayed for ten years. From 1910 to 1915, he teamed up with Tris Speaker and Duffy Lewis in what was called "The Million Dollar Outfield." Harry Hooper never developed into a slugger or even into a consistent .300 hitter, but he had an excellent .368 on-base-percentage, and he scored an average of 89 runs a year, thanks to his sharp batting eye that rewarded him with 71 bases on balls a year against just 33 strikeouts. He was considered the best leadoff man of his era, and was generally regarded as the best defensive right fielder in the major leagues. He had good speed, a dependable glove, and a strong, accurate throwing arm. His .966 career fielding percentage was seven points higher than the league average and his 81 career double plays is number five all-time.

Harry Hooper stroked the ball for a cool .311 average for Boston in 1911, but slumped to .242

Harry Hooper

in their World Championship year of 1912. He did rebound in the Series, however, batting .290 with two doubles and one triple in eight games, as Boston took the measure of the New York Giants, four games to three. He had another off-year in 1915, batting a mediocre .235 as the Red Sox raced to another American League pennant. But once again, he came through in the World Series, this time against the Philadelphia Phillies. The five-foot, ten-inch, 165-pound, left-handed hitter tortured Philly pitching for a .350 batting average and, in the Game 5 clincher, he powered the Sox to the World Championship by becoming the second player in World Series history to hit two home runs in a single game. He sent a screamer over the 408-foot mark in center field at Baker Bowl in the third inning, and he put the finishing touches on another Boston World Championship by hitting the game-winning home run into the center field bleachers in the ninth inning. The following year, he hit a crisp .271 with 20 doubles and 11 triples as Boston edged the Chicago White Sox by two games for the American League pennant. This time the Sox met the Brooklyn Robins in the World Series and once again they emerged victorious, four games to one. Hooper was at the top of his game in the Series, batting .333 with a double, a triple, and a Series-high six runs scored. Boston's right fielder had a big year in 1918, batting .289 with 26 doubles and 13 triples, but he suffered through his worst World Series, batting a lowly .200. Still, the Red Sox captured their fourth World Championship in seven years, defeating the Chicago Cubs four games to two. Even when Harry Hooper's bat was silent, his pitchers appreciated his outstanding outfield play. According to Babe Ruth, "Hooper's instinct for knowing where the ball was going to be was uncanny. I'm sure too that he made more diving catches than any other outfielder in history. With most outfielders, the diving catch is half luck; with Hooper it was a masterpiece of business."[81]

Boston owner Harry Frazee, as part of his fire-sale campaign that decimated the Red Sox between 1919 and 1921, dealt Hooper to the Chicago White Sox after the right fielder hit a career-high .312 in 1920, the first year of the lively ball era. Hooper hit even better in the Windy City, tattooing the ball at a .327 clip in 1921, .304 the following year, and .328 in 1924. He retired to enter the real estate business after hitting .265 in 1925, and 46 years later he was elected to the National Baseball Hall of Fame in Cooperstown, New York.

Hughson, Tex

Cecil Carlton "Tex" Hughson came out of the University of Texas in 1937 at the age of 21, and received his baptism of fire in professional baseball with Moultrie in the Class-D Georgia-Florida League, winning eight games against six losses with a 2.38 earned run average. The six-foot, three-inch, 180-pound right-hander, who had a full repertoire of pitches including a sinking fastball, a hard overhand curve ball, a slider, a screwball, a change of pace, and an occasional knuckleball, pitched for Canton in the Class-C Middle Atlantic League the following year, leading the league with 22 victories against seven losses.

After three more years of seasoning in the Boston Red Sox farm system, with Scranton and Louisville, the native of Kyle, Texas, was called up to Boston at the end of the 1941 season and responded with a 5–3 record in 12 games, with four complete games. In his first major league start against the Washington Senators in Fenway Park on July 6, he was hammered for two doubles and a single straight out of the gate but, after a conference on the mound, he settled down and threw a complete-game, 4–3 victory. Over his career he developed a reputation for being "a fearless competitor on the mound who was not averse to throwing inside on hitters, mixing in a hard fastball with an overhand curveball."[82] Unfortunately his body did not always respond as it was told, as in 1941 when he pulled a deltoid muscle in his pitching arm in August and missed the rest of the season. The following season, with Lefty Grove retired and Mickey Harris in military service, Tex Hughson suddenly became the team's ace, a responsibility that may have, in the long run, damaged his career. He came down with a sore arm in spring

Tex Hughson

training, but forced himself to pitch through the pain, appearing in 38 games with 30 starts, and leading the league in victories (22) against just six losses, complete games (22), innings pitched (281), and strikeouts (113). He loved pitching against the New York Yankees and compiled a 5–1 mark against them for the season. In reflecting on his success against the Bronx Bombers, he admitted, "I would rather beat the Yankees once than any other team twice."

The big Texan, like most of the Red Sox, suffered through a disappointing 1943 season that saw Boston plummet from second place to seventh place after the loss of key players like Ted Williams, Johnny Pesky, and Dom DiMaggio to military service. Hughson's sub-par season could be traced back to a mid-season game against the Detroit Tigers when Jimmy Bloodworth hit a line drive back through the box that broke his thumb. He had difficulty gripping the ball the rest of the season, and he suffered through two painful months, winning just one game against nine losses. He finished the year with an excellent 2.64 ERA but a mediocre 12–15 won-loss record, with a team that finished next to last in both batting average and runs scored. Boston rebounded the following year, thanks in part to the addition of "Indian Bob" Johnson, and they led the league in batting and runs scored. With that kind of support, Tex Hughson won 18 games against five losses, leading the league with a .782 won-loss percentage and posting a barely visible 2.26 ERA. Tigers General Manager Jack Zeller, one of his admirers, said, "Compared with Hughson, the others are only throwers. He has an arm too, but he puts more headwork into his pitching. He's one of the most cunning pitchers in years."[83]

Hughson spent the 1945 season in the U. S. Army, serving in the Pacific Theatre, but he came back to the baseball wars as strong as ever in 1946. He pitched the opening game in Washington on April 16, winning 6–3, and from there he went on to record a 20–11 mark with 21 complete games in 35 starts, as Joe Cronin's Back Bay Bombers won 104 games, leaving their closest challengers, the Detroit Tigers, a whopping 12 games in arrears. Hughson won four 1–0 games during the season, including the pennant-clinching victory over the Cleveland Indians in Municipal Stadium on September 13 that broke a six-game Boston losing streak. Ted Williams hit the only inside-the-park home run of his career to provide The Red Sox with the winning margin. Boston met the National League Champion St. Louis Cardinals in a thrilling seven-game World Series battle, won on Enos "Country" Slaughter's mad dash around the bases in Game 7. Hughson pitched in three games in the Series, including two starts, and posted a fine 3.14 ERA in spite of losing his only decision. The lanky right-hander took the mound in Game 1 in Sportsman's Park and held the Redbirds in check for eight innings, holding them to two runs on seven base hits, striking out seven, walking two, and leaving for a pinch-hitter on the short end of a 2–1 score. Boston tied the game in the ninth inning and won it in the tenth on a Rudy York home run. Hughson returned to action four days later in Game 4, but was driven from the mound in the third inning after being raked for six runs, in a game won by Eddie Dyer's team, 12–3. He came out of the bullpen in the third inning of Game 6 after St. Louis had scored three runs off Boston starter, Mickey Harris, and he blanked the Cardinals over 4 1/3 innings, but it was too little, too late, as St. Louis prevailed by a 4–1 score.

In a strange quirk of fate, both Dave Ferriss, who went 25–6 in 1946, and Tex Hughson had career-ending arm miseries during 1947. Ferriss hurt his arm in an early-season game in Cleveland and won only 19 more games over four years before retiring. Hughson's problem was different. He had suffered with arm and shoulder problems for much of his major league career, but it finally reached the point of no return in 1947. He had another sore arm in the spring and, in typical Hughson fashion, threw a two-hit, 1–0 shutout over New York on April 24, but in May he experienced bone chips in his elbow and numbness in the middle finger of his pitching hand. He continued to pitch in pain for another four months, but on September 3, in the first game of a doubleheader against the New York Yankees in the friendly confines of Fenway Park, he reached the end of the line, being forced to leave the game in the fifth inning, trailing 4–1 in a game the Yankees eventually won, 11–2. He pitched 189 innings in 29 games that year with 26 starts and 13 complete games, but his earned run average ballooned to 3.33. He had surgery on his arm and his shoulder in the off-season, and he pitched out of the bullpen the next two years trying to rehabilitate his arm but to no avail. He pitched 19 innings in 15 games in 1948, with no starts, finishing with a 3–1 record, and the following year he appeared in 29 games with two starts, pitching 78 innings and compiling a 4–2 won-loss record with a 5.33 ERA. He retired at the end of the season, at the age of 33.

One American League umpire paid him the highest compliment when he said, "Tex was the best. With his stuff, he should have won every game he pitched. He got licked usually when he got mad. It upset him when a .220 hitter hit one of his good pitches. If he had kept his temper, they never would have beaten him."[84] When he was healthy, Tex Hughson was one of the best starting pitchers of his time, and the pitcher his teammates wanted on the mound in a crucial game. During his eight-year Boston career, he won 96 games against 54 losses for an outstanding .640 winning percentage.

Hurst, Bruce

Bruce Vee Hurst was born in St. George, Utah, on March 24, 1958. After graduating from Dixie High School, where he pitched and played first base, the 1976 All-State selection was drafted by the Boston Red Sox in the June draft. The 18-year-old southpaw spent the summer with Elmira in the New York-Pennsylvania League, pitching in nine games and recording a 3–2 won-lost record with a 3.00 ERA in 42 innings. Hurst moved up the organizational ladder over the next three years, making stops in Winter Haven in the Florida State League and Bristol in the Eastern League before jumping from Double-A ball to the major leagues in 1980, debuting on April 12. The husky 22-year-old pitcher, who had blossomed into a six-foot, three-inch, 219-pound power pitcher, was eventually farmed out to Pawtucket for further seasoning. He went 2–2 in 12 games for Boston and 8–6 in 17 games with Pawtucket. He spent most of the 1981 season with Pawtucket, going 12–7 in 32 games covering 157 innings, before moving up to Boston, where he finished the season with a 2–0 mark in five games.

The Utah native became a major leaguer to stay in 1982. He pitched in 28 games with the Red Sox in his rookie season, with 19 starts, but suffered growing pains as attested to by his 3–7 record and 5.77 ERA. Following a November operation for the removal of bone chips from his elbow, he went 12–12, 12–12, and 11–13 over the next three seasons, before teaming with Roger Clemens and "Oil Can" Boyd to bring Boston its first American League pennant in nineteen years in 1986, compiling a record of 13–8 with an excellent 2.99 earned run average. He spent six weeks on the disabled list but still pitched in 25 games, all starts, with 11 complete games and four shutouts. He fanned 167 men in 174 innings while issuing just 50 bases on balls. In the ALCS, a seven-game victory over the California Angels, Hurst went 1–0, winning Game 2 by the count of 9–2 in a route-going effort. In the World Series, a disappointing seven-game loss to the New York Mets, the big lefty pitched in three games, with a 2–0 record and a 1.96 ERA in 23 innings pitched. He was on the mound in the World Series opener in Shea Stadium and blanked Davey Johnson's sluggers, 1–0. He came back in Game 5, posting a 4–2 victory and giving Boston a three-games-to-two lead in the Series, but Clemens and the Boston bullpen were unable to take advantage

Bruce Hurst

of the situation, dropping Game 6 by a 6–5 count after holding two leads in the late innings. Hurst started Game 7, but left after six innings with the score deadlocked at three-all.

He pitched well for Boston over the next two years, winning 15 games against 13 losses in 1987 and going a career-best 18–6 the following year, but as noted in the *Red Sox Fan Handbook*, "Hurst, a deeply religious man, was deeply offended by a number of sordid scandals involving Red Sox players,"[85] and he left the team as a free agent after the 1988 season, signing with the San Diego Padres. He pitched six more years in the major leagues before retiring at the age of 36, leaving an excellent career won-lost record of 145–113. During his nine-year Boston sojourn, the crafty southpaw "kept right-handed

sluggers at bay with a mix of slow breaking pitches and a sneaky fastball," as reported in *The Ballplayers*. He won 88 games for the Red Sox against 73 losses, and his 56 victories in Fenway Park are second only to Mel Parnell for southpaws.

Janvrin, Hal

He was just a .232 career batter with no power and a mediocre fielder with a leaky glove who was tried at all the infield positions with little success, yet he managed to carve out a ten-year major league career for himself. Harold Chandler Janvrin was nicknamed "Childe Harold" as a youth after the hero of Lord Byron's epic poem, but he was known as Hal as he grew older. He was born in Haverhill, Massachusetts, on August 27, 1892, and was a four-sport athlete at English High School in hockey, baseball, football, and track. Following graduation, he played semi-pro baseball around the Boston area, eventually signing a professional baseball contract with the hometown Boston Red Sox.

Janvrin made his major league debut with Boston on July 9, 1911, at the age of 18. He played nine games for Patsy Donovan's club that year, five games at third base where he fielded a ragged .733, and four games at first base, batting .148 in 27 at-bats. The next year he was sent to the Jersey City Skeeters in the International League for more seasoning, but was reclaimed by Boston after the season ended. He spent the next ten years in the major leagues, with the exception of 1918 when he served in the U.S. Army during World War I.

The five-foot, eleven-and-a-half inch, 168-pound, right-handed hitter played for the Boston Red Sox from 1913 to 1917, playing 201 games at shortstop, 152 games at second base, 67 games at first base, and 49 games at third base. He was found lacking defensively at all positions, posting a career fielding average of .907 at shortstop, 31 points below the league average, .933 at second base, 26 points below the league average, and .891 at third base, 41 points below the league average. He was just as futile with a bat in his hands, with batting averages that ranged from .207 to .269, and his baserunning skills left much to be desired, with a 52 percent stolen base percentage in 1914 and 1915. His one fleeting moment of glory occurred in the final game of the 1913 season against the Washington Senators in Griffith Stadium. Washington owner Clark Griffith made a farce of the game, using eight pitchers including five in the ninth inning, and he even pitched one inning himself. Janvrin was Boston's offensive hero with two inside-the-park home runs. His second homer, in the ninth inning, was a line drive to right field that 43-year-old Clark Griffith misplayed, the ball rolling past him to the wall while Janvrin scooted around the bases for Boston's ninth run, but the Senators won the game, 10–9.

In the 1916 World Series, won by the Red Sox over the Brooklyn Robins in five games, he wore one set of goat's horns in the classic duel between Sherry Smith and Babe Ruth, won by Boston 2–1 in 14 innings. Boston had a chance to win the game in the ninth inning when Janvrin hit a long drive to left field that Zack Wheat just missed catching after a long run. Janvrin coasted into second base with a double and advanced to third on a Mike Mowrey error. The next batter, Dick Hoblitzell, hit a line drive to center field that was caught by Hy Myers coming in, and Myers fired a quick strike to Otto Miller, who put the tag on the sliding Janvrin trying to score, putting a damper on the Sox rally that was ended when Larry Gardner fouled out to Miller.

Somehow, Hal Janvrin survived. After hitting .197 in 1917, he went off to serve his country in the armed forces during World War I, returning to the majors with Washington in 1919. He also played with St. Louis and Brooklyn before returning to the minor leagues after 1922.

Jefferson, Reggie

Reginald Jirod Jefferson was drafted by the Cincinnati Reds after graduating from high school in 1986, and spent the next five years navigating through Cincinnati's minor league maze before being brought up to the big club, making his major league debut on May 18, 1991. The six-foot, four-inch, 215-pound left-handed slugger, who was noted for his power but was only fair to middling on defense, played just five games for the Reds before he was traded to Cleveland on June 14. The Indians sent him to their Triple-A farm club in Colorado Springs in the Pacific Coast League, where he stung the ball at a .309 clip in 39 games. Cleveland recalled him midway through the season, but he struggled with a .198 batting average for the Indians in 26 games. Three years later, following a fine .327 season with the Seattle Mariners, he was declared a free agent and signed with the Boston Red Sox.

Manager Kevin Kennedy utilized Jefferson primarily as a designated hitter against right-handed pitchers, and the Florida native responded to the call with a .289 average in 46 games. Over the next five years, Reggie Jefferson proved to be an outstanding run-producer for the Boston crew, averaging 39 doubles, 20 home runs, and 85 RBI per season. The year 1996 was his best year with the Red Sox. Alternating between designated hitter and left field, he played in 122 games with 386 at-bats, scorching the ball at a .347 clip with 30 doubles, 19 home runs, and 74 RBI. He continued his cannonading in 1997, batting .319 in 136 games with 33 doubles and 13 home runs in 489 at-bats. His last two years in a Boston uniform were difficult years for Jefferson. He missed the last half of the 1998 season with a stress fracture in his lower back, limiting him to just 62 games and 192 at-bats, and when spring training rolled around, he had a new assignment, as he recalled. "I know basically what my situation is. I'm a backup now. That's been made clear to me and it's a role I accept." He played in 83 games during the season, batting .277 in 206 at-bats, but when he was left off the post-season roster, he went home and never returned. The Red Sox released him at the end of the season, ending his major league career. The free swinger, whose 300 strikeouts and 96 bases on balls produced a modest .349 on-base-percentage during his Boston tenure in spite of a .316 batting average, posted a healthy .474 slugging average, 45 points higher than the league average.

Jensen, Jackie

Jack Eugene Jensen, better known as "The Golden Boy," was an all-around athlete at Oakland High School and, after a short stint in the U.S. Navy, he went on to carve out a legendary career for himself at the University of California. He was All-American in both baseball and football, and is the only player to play in both the Rose Bowl and the NCAA College World Series. He averaged six yards per carry on the gridiron, and pitched his team to the 1947 NCAA College Baseball World Series title

Jackie Jensen

against future president George Bush's Yale Bulldogs. He signed a professional baseball contract with the Oakland Oaks of the Pacific Coast League in 1949 and the following year was traded to the New York Yankees.

Jensen spent the next four years, bouncing around between the minor leagues, the New York Yankees, and the Washington Senators, never becoming a star. The Senators traded him to the Boston Red Sox for Mickey McDermott and Tom Umphlett on December 8, 1953, and his career suddenly exploded. He quickly became one of the best right fielders in Boston Red Sox history. He was an excellent defensive player with exceptional speed, as well as a solid contact hitter with long-ball power to all fields, and a fleet-footed baserunner with good instincts. In his first year in Boston, the five-foot, eleven-inch, 190-pound right-handed hitter batted .276 with 25 homers, 117 runs batted in, and a league-leading 22 stolen bases. The following year, he put together a .275 season with a league-leading 116 RBI, and in 1956 he scorched the ball at a .315 clip while leading the league with 11 triples.

Jackie Jensen enjoyed his greatest season as a major leaguer in 1958 when he rattled the fences to the tune of a .286 average with 31 doubles, 35 home runs, and a league-leading 122 RBI. His efforts were rewarded when he was voted the American League's Most Valuable Player, in spite of the fact that Pinky Higgins' club could do no better than a third-place finish. "The Golden Boy" played two more years with the Red Sox, leading the league in RBI once again in 1959 with 112, and capturing a Gold Glove along the way, but when the major leagues expanded to the west coast in 1958, with the Dodgers and Giants leaving Brooklyn and New York for greener pastures, making air travel a necessity, Jensen, who was deathly afraid of flying, retired at the age of 32. He attempted a comeback in 1961, but hung up his glove for good after a nerve-wracking season of air travel and frequent panic attacks in airports. He also missed his family. "I have only one life to live and I'll be happier when I can spend it with my family. Being away from home with a baseball team seven months a year doesn't represent the kind of life I want or the kind of life my wife and children want."[86]

The durable outfielder played seven seasons with the Red Sox, posting a .282 batting average while missing just 22 games between 1954 and 1959. He exhibited outstanding range in the field and possessed a strong throwing arm. He led the American League in triples and stolen bases once each, RBI and sacrifice flies three times each, assists four times, double plays twice, and fielding average once. Ted Williams paid him the ultimate compliment when he said, "Right field in Boston is a bitch, the sun field and few play it well. Jackie Jensen was the best I saw at it."[87]

Johnson, Bob

Although he was less than one-half Cherokee, Robert Lee Johnson was called "Indian Bob" throughout his major league career. Born in Pryor, Oklahoma, on November 26, 1905, he was the younger brother of Roy Johnson, who enjoyed a ten-year major league career of his own. Bob Johnson began his long climb up the minor league ladder as a 23-year-old outfielder with Wichita-Pueblo in the Single-A Western League in 1929, batting .273 with 16 home runs in 66 games. After two lackluster years with the Portland Beavers of the Pacific Coast League, the right-handed slugger who stood five-foot, eleven-inches tall and topped the scales at a muscular 175 pounds, matured as a consistent hitter on the west coast. He posted averages of .337 and .330 with the Beavers in 1931 and 1932, and was quickly purchased by the Philadelphia Athletics' Connie Mack to replace the recently traded Al Simmons.

Indian Bob responded like a true professional, stinging the ball at a .290 clip with 44 doubles, 21 homers, and 93 runs batted in, in 142 games in his rookie season of 1933. The husky slugger played with the A's for ten years and was a model of consistency year after year. He hit over .289 eight times, slugged over 20 homers nine times, and drove in over 100 runs in seven consecutive seasons. And he had several memorable games along the way. On June 16, 1934, Johnson went 6-for-6 with a double and two home runs, both off Whitlow Wyatt, as the A's edged the White Sox, 7–6, in 11 innings. He also put together a 26-game hitting streak that year. Three years later, on August 29, 1937, Philadelphia's cleanup hitter set a major league record broken with six runs batted in one inning, slamming a grand-slam home run and a double off Chicago White Sox ace Monty Stratton, who gave up six of the A's 12 first-inning runs in one-third of an inning in a 16–0 blowout. The next year, on June 12, the Oklahoma native drove in all his team's runs with three home runs, one a grand slam in the first game of a doubleheader in Shibe Park, as the A's downed the St. Louis Browns, 8–3, behind right-hander Buck Ross.

Johnson played for the Washington Senators in 1943, but exhibited little power. That brought about a December 4 trade to the Boston Red Sox, and the 38-year-old outfielder gave Joe Cronin's team two solid years as a left fielder. He ripped the ball at a .324 clip in 1944, slammed 40 doubles, 17 home runs, drove in 106 teammates, and led the league with a .431 on-base-percentage. He also hit for the cycle on July 6. The following year, after batting .280 with 12 homers and 74 RBI in 143 games, he was released by the Red Sox on December 27.

Bob Johnson, a seven-time All-Star, was one of the most consistent players of his era. He hit over .300 five times and over .289 four other times, scored over 100 runs ten times, hit over 20 home runs nine times, and drove in more than 100 runs eight times. He also had an excellent batting eye, drawing 85 bases-on-balls for every 550 at-bats against 68 strikeouts, giving him a career .393 on-base-percentage. And his .506 slugging average was 105 points higher than the league average. The 175-pound slugger, who was also a fine defensive outfielder with a strong, accurate throwing arm, has been called by many baseball experts the most underrated player in baseball history, a player who deserves his own niche in the Baseball Hall of Fame, but is still on the outside looking in.

Johnson, Roy

Roy Cleveland Johnson, the older brother of Bob Johnson, was born in Pryor, Oklahoma, on February 23, 1904, and entered organized baseball with the San Francisco Seals of the Pacific Coast League in 1926, where he batted .260 in 25 games before being optioned to Idaho Falls in the Utah-Idaho League. He powdered the ball at a .369 clip for Idaho Falls while playing 112 games in the outfield. The five-foot, nine-inch, 175-pound left-handed hitter patrolled the outfield for the Seals for two more years, batting .306 and .360, bringing about his sale to the Detroit Tigers.

The 25-year-old Johnson tortured American League pitchers to the tune of .314 in his rookie season with the Tigers in 1929, cracking 201 base hits including a league-leading 45 doubles, 14 triples, and ten home runs, scoring 128 runs, driving in 69, and stealing 20 bases. He was the first rookie in major league history to accumulate 200 base hits. He also set an American League record for errors by an outfielder with 31. He hit .275 the following year and .279 with 37 doubles, a league-leading 19 triples, and 107 runs scored in 1931. After falling to .251 in 49 games in 1932, he was traded to the Boston Red Sox for Earl Webb on June 12, and his bat suddenly came alive. He batted a crisp .298 for Shano Collins' cellar-dwellers in 94 games, with 24 doubles and 11 home runs. The next season, holding down the right field spot in the Boston lineup, Roy Johnson hit .313 with 95 RBI in 133 games, and in 1934 he had a career year as he sparked the Red Sox to a fourth-place finish, their highest finish in 16 years and the first time they had a winning percentage during that period. He hit .320 in 143 games with 43 doubles, 10 triples, seven home runs, and 119 RBI. The next year he batted .315 and led the league with 21 assists. But Red Sox management was unhappy with his power numbers and his RBI totals, and he was dealt to the New York Yankees in the off-season.

Roy Johnson was a contact hitter who specialized in hitting line drives into the outfield gaps. He had a career batting average of .296 with an on-base percentage of .369 and a slugging average of .437, both well over the league average. On the other hand, he was just a fair defensive outfielder with average range though he had a strong throwing arm that produced 128 assists in 1,066 games, well above average, and he led the league in assists twice and in double plays once.

Jones, Dalton

James Dalton Jones was signed by the Boston Red Sox out of high school on June 4, 1961, and was assigned to their Alpine farm team in the Sophomore League where he posted a fine .322 average in 77 games. Three years later, the six-foot, one-inch, 180-pound left-handed swinger made the big jump to Boston, beginning a nine-year major league career. He made his major league debut on April 17, 1964, playing second base and batting leadoff as the Red Sox defeated the Chicago White Sox, 4–1, and he was a major factor in the victory, slashing a triple in four at-bats and scoring one run while driving in another. Unfortunately, he was a handicap at the plate most of the season, hitting a mediocre .230 for Johnny Pesky's club. He showed occasional flashes of offensive fireworks during his career, batting .270 in 1965 and .289 in 1967, but was bogged down between .220 and .234 the other three years he played in Boston. He did produce some big hits during his career, probably the biggest coming in Fenway Park on May 19, 1964, before a small crowd of dedicated Red Sox fans. Southpaw Bo Belinsky of the Los Angeles Angels, who enjoyed the L.A. night life more than he did pitching, took a 3–0 three-hitter into the ninth inning, retired the first two Red Sox, but was gone from the scene after just two more batters. A walk to Dick Stuart and a double by Tony Conigliaro sent Bo to the showers. Two batters later big Don Lee arrived on the scene to face pinch-hitter Dalton Jones with the bases loaded and a 3–1 lead. Jones worked the count to 3–2 and then jumped on a Lee fastball and sent it on a line over Dick Simpson's head in center field, clearing the bases with a walk-off double as the 7,027 fans erupted, sending tremors down the east coast. Jones later told the *Boston Globe's* Ray Fitzgerald that he was scared out of his mind when Pesky sent him up to pinch-hit.[88] On July 9, 1965, he had a five-hit game against the Washington Senators, and on September 10, he supported Dave Morehead's brilliant no-hitter with a run-scoring triple off Luis Tiant in the sixth inning for the first run of the game. The ninth-place Red Sox added another run in the seventh to complete the 2–0 masterpiece before a near-empty Fenway gathering of 1,247. The next year, on July 6, 1966, in the first game of a doubleheader in Yankee Stadium, he hit a one-out, two-run homer in the ninth inning to knock off the Bronx Bombers by a 5–3 score.

The Mississippi native played a big part in Boston's "Impossible Dream" run for the pennant in 1967. On May 24 he sent one of Denny McLain's fastballs into the upper atmosphere in Tiger Stadium to give Jim Lonborg a 1–0 win. On August 20, he had two key hits as the Red Sox came back from an 8–0 deficit to beat the California Angels, 9–8. Two days later, Boston's pinch-hitter extraordinaire broke a scoreless tie with a two-run triple in the seventh inning against Phil Ortega of the Washington Senators to propel the Red Sox to a 2–1 win that left Boston in a virtual tie with the Chicago White Sox in the race for the brass ring. Dick Williams' Back Bay Bombers visited Tiger Stadium to take on the Tigers in the heat of the pennant race on September 18, and they came away with a hard-fought, 6–5, ten-inning victory, thanks in large part to the efforts of Dalton Jones who went 4-for-5 with two RBI. His single in the first inning gave Boston its first run and his home run off Tigers reliever Mike Marshall in the top of the tenth brought Boston's last run home. To finish off his remarkable day, he speared a line drive off the bat of Bill Freehan in the bottom of the inning to end the game. After the game, he told the *Globe*'s Cliff Keane, "This has to be the best game of baseball I've ever played."[89] The tension grew as the last week of the season played out, leading to a fateful two-game series between the two leaders in Boston on the final weekend. Boston went to Baltimore mid-week and on the 24th all the gears seemed to be meshing as the Sox jumped out to a 7–0 lead behind Jim Lonborg. Dalton Jones' two-run triple in the first inning set the tone in the early going. At the end of six innings, with Boston up, 7–0, Dick Williams took Lonborg out of the game to rest him for the Minnesota series, but that move came close to being the blunder of the century as the Sox bullpen almost blew the game. Fortunately the offense added four more runs in the ninth and Boston withstood a four-run Baltimore ninth to win 11–7. Jones once again starred, ripping four base hits in six at-bats, with a double, a triple, and five RBI.

Boston hosted Minnesota for the final weekend, trailing the Twins by one-and-a-half games and needing a two-game sweep to claim the crown. On the final Saturday of the season, right-hander Jose Santiago, with a record of 11–4, faced off against Minnesota's 16-game winner, Jim Kaat, in the Fenway ballyard with 32,909 wild Red Sox fans hanging on every pitch. With the Twins on top 1–0 after four-and-a-half innings, Jones pinch-hit a single and scored the go-ahead run in a two-run Sox fifth. Both teams added a run in the sixth, and Boston pushed over three runs in the seventh to win 6–4. As Sunday dawned, 35,770 pennant-starved Red Sox fans pushed their way through the turnstiles at the Fens, grabbed a beer, and waited for the first pitch. With Boston's 21-game winner, Jim Lonborg, matching pitches with Minnesota's 20-game winner, Dean Chance, the Twins broke out on top, scoring unearned runs in the first and third innings to open up a 2–0 lead. But Dick Williams' charges came to life in the bottom of the sixth, scoring five runs on four hits, a walk, an error, and a fielder's choice, and Lonborg made it stand up for a 5–3 victory—and the pennant. Dalton Jones started at third base, batted second, and went 2-for-4, including a key single in the big sixth that loaded the bases. He eventually scored Boston's game-winning run. In the World Series, a losing effort against the St. Louis Cardinals, the Mississippi native played in six games as a third baseman and a pinch-hitter, and he rapped seven base hits in 18 at-bats for a .389 batting average.

Two years later, after struggling through another unproductive season with the bat that saw him hit just .220 with 33 RBI in 111 games, he was traded to the Detroit Tigers on December 13. His Boston career covered six years from 1964 through 1969, during which time he played all infield positions, with 137 games at first base, 208 games at second bases, three games at shortstop, and 131 games at third base. His defense was marginal at best and his .243 batting average was unacceptable, but he had some big hits in clutch situations and he is still Boston's all-time pinch-hit leader with 55.

Jones, Sam

Samuel Pond Jones was born in the tiny village of Woodsfield, Ohio, on July 26, 1892, and supposedly developed his strong pitching arm by throwing potatoes with his brother Robert on his grandfather's farm. He became a professional baseball player in 1913, pitching for last-place Zanesville in the Interstate League, winning two games and losing seven. He joined the Cleveland Indians in 1914 for one game, compiled a 4–9 record in 1915, and then was shuttled off to the Boston Red Sox in a trade that brought Tris Speaker to Cleveland.

The 22-year-old pitcher spent most of the next two seasons on the bench, appearing in just 21 games over that period, watching and waiting. In 1918, the six-foot tall, 175-pound, right-handed pitcher was added to the Red Sox starting rotation by manager Ed Barrow and began to earn his keep. He fit in well with the other pitchers on the Red Sox staff, who were primarily fastball pitchers. Jones was a finesse pitcher whose sidearm delivery, a la Don Drysdale, earned him the moniker "Horsewhip Sam." His repertoire consisted of a sharp-breaking curveball, a devastating change of pace, and a sneaky fastball. In his first start, on May 23, he lost a tough 1–0 decision to Guy Morton in Cleveland's Dunn Field, but in his second start, in the second game of a doubleheader in Fenway Park on May 29, he out-pitched Walter Johnson, winning 3–0 with a five-hitter. Eight days later, he blanked the Indians in Cleveland, 1–0, in ten innings, yielding just five base hits. Over the course of the season, he pitched in 24 games, with 21 starts, 16 complete games, and five shutouts. His 16–5 won-lost record, second on the Red Sox staff to Carl Mays' 21–13, gave him a league-leading .762 winning percentage, causing Tris Speaker to remark, "Sam Jones is the best pitcher Boston has. Those two years Sam sat on the bench made him. He simply absorbed everything that went on in the games. He's smart and learns rapidly. That slow ball of his simply floats up there and you swing your head off, and then he has a fast one that is on top of you before you realize it. In addition, he has as good a curve ball as anyone in the league."[90] Jones appeared in one game in the 1918 World Series, losing a 3–0 decision to Hippo Vaughn of the Chicago Cubs.

The lanky right-hander, who was given the moniker "Sad Sam" because of his sorrowful countenance on the mound, explained it this way. "Actually what it was, I would always wear my cap down real low over my eyes. And the sportswriters were more used to the fellows like Waite Hoyt, who'd always wear their caps way up so they wouldn't miss seeing any pretty girls."[91] An Associated Press obituary called him a "whimsical and quietly humorous man, brimful of quips and backwoods humor." Jones pitched inconsistently over the next two seasons as owner Harry Frazee began to dismantle his powerhouse club to get money to support his Broadway ventures. Sad Sam posted a record of 12–20 in 1919 and in 1920 he went 13–16 although he did contribute to the downfall of the defending American League champion Chicago White Sox by defeating them six times. He bounced back in 1921 to go 23–16 with a league-leading five shutouts for the fifth-place Red Sox, and was then traded to the New York Yankees who were on their way to establishing a dynasty. Sad Sam Jones spent six years with the Boston Red Sox, winning 64 games against 59 losses. He was one of the few pitchers who had more walks than strikeouts to his credit. With Boston, he walked an average of 2.9 men per nine innings while striking out 2.6.

Kinder, Ellis

Ellis Raymond Kinder, from Atkins, Arkansas, was picking cotton in the fields by the time he was ten. He worked five-and-a-half days a week, then went fishing with his mother on Sunday. He worked in construction after leaving school in the eighth grade, got married, and pitched amateur ball around Atkins until he was finally "discovered" by baseball scouts at the age of 24. He kicked around the minor leagues for seven years before reaching the Big Show. The St. Louis Browns purchased Kinder from Memphis at the end of the 1944 season, but they had to wait a year to begin collecting a dividend because he was called to military service with the U.S. Navy in 1945. He was a 31-year-old rookie with St. Louis when he made his major league debut on April 30, 1946. He went on to pitch in 33 games that year with seven starts and one complete game, winning three games, losing three, and posting a fine 3.32 ERA. Kinder was soon tabbed with the moniker "Old Folks" by his teammates because of his advanced baseball age, and he wore the nickname proudly the rest of his major league career. After going 8–15 in 1947 he was traded to the Boston Red Sox on November 18, one of the best deals Boston ever made.

Kinder arrived in Boston with a reputation as a party player who liked to have a drink or

Ellis Kinder

two, chase women, and stay out late at night. His manager, Joe McCarthy, spent many sleepless nights worrying about what effect Kinder's nighttime excursions would have on his pitching, but his fears quickly faded after watching Old Folks dispense of batter after batter, day after day. One evening, years after Kinder had retired, Birdie Tebbetts spoke at a Providence College dinner and, during a question and answer session, he was asked about the current whereabouts of Kinder. "Without missing a beat, Tebbetts looked at his watch and cracked, 'Right now I'd say he's at Jimmie O'Keefe's (Boston watering hole).'"[92]

The curve ball artist was a starting pitcher in Boston from 1948 through 1950, with 75 starts in 119 games pitched, including 40 complete games and eight shutouts. His best year was 1949, when he went 23–6 while leading the league in both winning percentage with .793 and shutouts with six. He pitched 252 innings in 43 games that year with 30 starts, 19 complete games and a 3.36 ERA, and was named the

American League Pitcher of the Year by *The Sporting News*. He got off to a slow start and was just 4–4 after being manhandled by the St. Louis Browns, 11–0, on June 9. He lost in relief to the Browns on July 24, and that was his last loss until the final day of the season. Along the way, he won 12 consecutive games as a starter, his last victory being a 3–0 whitewashing of the Yankees in Fenway Park on September 24. On the final Sunday of the season, in Yankee Stadium with the American League pennant on the line, Kinder took the mound against Vic Raschi, and promised his team a victory if they could get him three runs. Unfortunately, the Sox bats went dry when they needed them the most, and Kinder left the game after seven brilliant innings, trailing 1–0. The Yankees jumped on the Red Sox bullpen for four big runs in the bottom of the eighth, making Boston's three-run ninth too little, too late.[93]

Manager Steve O'Neil converted the rubber-armed right-hander to Boston's fireman two years later and Kinder responded with an 11–2 won-loss record while leading the league with 63 appearances, 14 saves, and 10 relief wins. On July 12, he entered a game against the White Sox in the eighth inning of a tie game and threw ten scoreless innings before Boston could push across the game-winner in the 17th. Pitching coach Bill McKechnie was duly impressed with his new fireman. "He's got a heart, a head, and a low sharp-breaking slider that's as tough a pitch to hit as anybody throws."[94] Bobby Doerr was just as impressed. "In all the years that I have been with this team, we have never had a relief pitcher like Ellis. The way he can come in and stop a rally or hold a lead is something at which I marvel."[95] In 1953 Old Folks once again led the league with 69 appearances, 27 saves, and 10 relief wins, while losing six times. He had 15 saves in 48 appearances in 1954 and 18 saves in 43 appearances the following year. He was selected off waivers by the St. Louis Cardinals on December 4, 1955, ending his Boston sojourn. He played two more years before retiring at the age of 43.

Kinder was not a noted batsman, but he had a few memorable days at the plate during his career. On August 6, 1950, he blasted a grand slam off Chicago White Sox ace Billy Pierce in the fifth inning, and set an American League record for pitchers with six RBI for the game. In 1953, the career .142 hitter tortured opposing pitchers to the tune of .379. On September 3, 1955, he came into a game against the Orioles in Memorial Stadium with the bases loaded and one out in the eighth inning, fanned Dave Philley, then retired Bob Hale on a soft fly ball to left field. He blanked the O's for four more innings before singling in the winning run himself in the top of the 12th.

Ellis Kinder's Boston tenure lasted eight years, from 1948 through 1955. He pitched in 365 games for the Red Sox, winning 86 and losing 52. He had 89 starts, 276 relief appearances, 55 complete games, 10 shutouts, and 91 saves. He was one of the greatest pitchers in Boston Red Sox history, both starting and relieving.

Klaus, Billy

William Joseph Klaus was an outstanding defensive player with good range, a strong, accurate throwing arm, and the ability to throw across his body quickly, according to one of his teammates. The five-foot, ten-inch, 165-pound native of Spring Grove, Illinois, was not a strong hitter average-wise, but he was a contact hitter who could bunt or hit-and-run with the best of them. He embarked on a professional baseball career as an infielder-outfielder for Appleton in the Wisconsin State League in 1946, where he batted .297 in 175 at-bats over 46 games. He continued to hit opposing pitchers at a better-than-.300 clip in the lower minors, but when he reached Triple-A ball, his batting average dipped to the .275 to .296 range. In 1954, he hit a steady .280 for Minneapolis in the American Association, and showed surprising power with 33 doubles and 21 home runs in 150 games, something he would not be able to duplicate in the Big Show. The New York Giants, who owned the rights to Klaus, traded him to the Boston Red Sox on December 14, 1954, beginning an 11-year major league career.

Billy Klaus went to spring training with Boston in 1955 and won the shortstop job from Milt Bolling. The 26-year-old left-handed hitter rapped the ball to the tune of .283 in his first full year with the Red Sox, with 83 runs scored and 60 RBI in 541 at-bats, finishing second in the Rookie of the Year voting. On June 17, he enjoyed one of his finest days as a major leaguer. In the first game of a doubleheader, Klaus, batting second, thrilled the Fenway faithful by hammering out four base hits in five at-bats with five RBI. His two-out, three-run homer in the fourth inning gave Boston a 5–0 lead, and they went on to defeat Cleveland by a 6–1 score. The following year, now playing third base in place of Grady Hatton, he batted .271 with 90 bases on balls, 91 runs scored, and a career-high .378 on-base percentage. On July 14, 1956, Mel Parnell threw a no-hitter at the Chicago White Sox, winning 4–0, and Billy Klaus was a major factor in the masterpiece with two putouts and four assists in the field, and two base hits in four at-bats at the plate. He doubled and scored the first run of the game in the fourth inning and singled to drive in the third run of the game in the sixth inning. He was bumped back to shortstop in 1957 with the arrival of Frank Malzone, and his batting average continued to slide, settling out at .252 in 127 games. But he had another day to remember on June 28 when he once again brought the Fenway fans to their feet as he stroked four base hits in five at-bats with two home runs, three runs scored, and five RBI in Boston's 9–2 thumping of the Detroit Tigers. The next year, with Don Buddin taking over the shortstop job, Klaus became a man without a home. He played in just 61 games with 88 at-bats, hit a barely visible .159, and was traded to the Baltimore Orioles in the off-season.

Billy Klaus was a popular teammate during his time in Boston. He had a happy-go-lucky personality, and he never took himself too seriously. In 1960 John F. Steadman reported, "Few things ever happen to Billy Klaus that he can't smile or joke about. He's an immensely likeable individual, completely honest with himself and self-effacing in 0-for-4 and 4-for-4 situations. Baseball exists, not for the superstars but because there are a lot of others like Billy Klaus around willing to work at the trade for a journeyman's wage and give the game all that's in him."[96]

Lee, Bill

William Francis Lee III was a six-foot, three-inch, 205-pound southpaw, called "Spaceman" because of his colorful personality. He attended the University of Southern California before joining the Boston Red Sox organization in 1968 with

Bill Lee

Waterloo in the Midwest League and with Winston-Salem in the Carolina League, both Single-A leagues. He started the 1969 season with Pittsfield in the Double-A Eastern League, going 6–2 before being called up to Boston in June.

Lee went 1–3, 2–2, 9–2, and 7–4, pitching out of the bullpen during his first four years in the Hub, when converted to a starting pitcher in 1973 his career blossomed. Using a sinker and an overhand curve, he recorded a 17–11 record in 1973 with 18 complete games in 33 starts, and a 2.75 ERA. He followed that performance with a 17–15 mark the next year and a 17–9 mark in 1975 as the Red Sox raced to the Eastern Division title. He didn't pitch in the three-game ALCS, but started two games in the World Series. He pitched eight-plus innings against the Cincinnati Reds in Game 2, leaving with a 2–1 lead, but reliever Dick Drago gave up two runs in the ninth to take the loss. Lee also started the fateful Game 7, pitching 6⅓ innings and leaving with a 3–2 lead, but once again the Sox bullpen blew it, Cincinnati winning the World Championship by a 4–3 score.

The Spaceman was an outstanding pitcher

during his ten years in Boston but his off-field antics disturbed some people, friend and foe alike, and he was finally traded to Montreal in 1979. Some of his statements were innocent enough. On his first view of Fenway's left field wall, he asked, "Do they leave it there during games?"[97] But other statements, including outbursts against manager Don Zimmer who he referred to as "The Gerbil," and a number of fights he was involved in, as well as his reported use of marijuana (he said he only sprinkled it on his cereal or buckwheat cakes), led to his downfall. One day during a game in Puerto Rico, he KO'd a batter who charged the mound. Later, several of the batter's relatives jumped him and did significant damage to his countenance. Lee shrugged off the incident, saying, "The set of teeth I got was better looking than my old ones anyway."[98]

Leonard, Dutch

Hubert Benjamin Leonard, a native of Birmingham, Ohio, was signed and released by the Philadelphia Athletics in 1911, then signed by the Boston Red Sox, who sent him to Worcester in the New England League. When he refused to report to Worcester, he was transferred to Denver in the Western League, where he came of age. He went 22–9 for Denver in 1912, and the Red Sox quickly recalled him at the end of the season.

The stocky five-foot, eleven-inch, 180-pound left-handed pitcher, called Dutch because he looked like a Dutchman, possessed an overpowering fastball, a sharp-breaking curveball, and good control. He started throwing a spitball late in his career and was one of the pitchers who were grandfathered when the pitch was banned in 1920. Leonard immediately became one of the aces of the Boston rotation in 1913, along with Smoky Joe Wood, Hugh Bedient, and Ray Collins. In his rookie season, the lanky Californian appeared in 42 games for Jake Stahl's fourth-place team with 14 victories and 17 losses. He started 28 games, threw 14 complete games, and posted an excellent 2.39 earned run average. The next year, he was almost unhittable, setting a major league record with a 0.96 ERA that still stands. He won 19 games against five losses, with 17 complete games in 25 starts, pitching 225 innings in 36 games. His victory total, along with Collins' 20 wins, Rube Foster's 14 wins, and the arrival of southpaw Babe Ruth, helped the Red Sox to a second-place finish, eight-and-a-half games behind Philadelphia, and had them poised to make a run for the pennant.

Boston edged Detroit by two-and-a-half games to capture the 1915 American League pennant, and Dutch Leonard played a key role in the result, going 15–7 in 32 games with 21 starts and 10 complete games. In the World Series, a five-game victory over the Philadelphia Phillies, he started Game 3 against Phillies ace Grover Cleveland Alexander, with the Series tied at one game apiece. Boston's home games were played in the new Braves Field instead of Fenway Park to take advantage of the larger seating capacity. Leonard was touched up for a run in the top of the third inning, but that was all the offense Pat Moran's crew would muster as Boston's crafty southpaw retired the last 20 batters in succession. The Red Sox tied the game in the fourth inning on a triple by Tris Speaker and a sacrifice fly by Dick Hoblitzell, as the 43,200 Bostonians who helped set a new World Series attendance record roared their approval. The game continued tied until the bottom of the ninth when lightning struck. Harry Hooper opened the inning with a sharp single to right field against the Philadelphia ace, moved around to third on two infield outs, and carried home the winning run on a single over second base by Duffy Lewis. Leonard was touched up for three base hits, struck out six men and didn't issue a single base on balls in his victory.

The Boston fireballer achieved baseball immortality in Fenway Park on August 30, 1916, when he stopped the St. Louis Browns, 4–0, with a no-hitter, keeping Bill Carrigan's cohorts atop the American League in a tight pennant race. It was a wild game witnessed by 8,500 fans who saw several brilliant plays by the Boston defense. Harry Hooper made a sensational running catch in deep left-center field in the first inning, crashing into the fence but holding onto the ball. Shortstop Everett Scott took a base hit away from Hank Severeid in the fifth inning. Leonard finished the 1916 season with an excellent 18–12 record with 17 complete games in 34 starts, six shutouts and a 2.36 ERA, as the Red Sox swept to another

American League pennant, this time defeating the Chicago White Sox by two games. They met the Brooklyn Robins in the World Series and the result was another five-game triumph, with Leonard contributing another complete game victory, with three strikeouts and four bases on balls. He took the mound in Game 4 facing Rube Marquard, with Boston leading in the Series, two games to one. It took him awhile to get his bearings in this game as he was touched up for two runs in the bottom of the first inning on a triple, a single, a walk, and an error, but like the previous year, he settled down and blanked the Robins over the last eight innings. Boston meanwhile jumped on Marquard to take the lead in the top of the second. After Hoblitzell walked and Duffy Lewis sent him scampering around to third base with a ringing double off the right field wall, Larry Gardner sent a rocket into the left-center field gap and raced around the bases for a three-run homer before Hy Myers could retrieve the ball. Bill Carrigan's opportunistic crew added single runs in the fourth, fifth, and seventh innings, en route to a 6–2 triumph.

After going 16–17 the next season, the hard-throwing southpaw reached the pinnacle of his profession one more time, on June 3, 1918, tossing a 5–0 no-hitter at the Detroit Tigers in Navin Field before a stunned home crowd of 3,500. Bobby Veach, who drew a two-out base on balls in the first inning, was the Tigers lone base runner, as Leonard exhibited pinpoint control, hitting the corners routinely while retiring the last 25 Detroit batters in succession, including Ty Cobb, who fouled out to third base as a pinch-hitter in the ninth inning. Babe Ruth's long home run into the center field bleachers in the first inning was all the help Leonard needed. Three weeks after his masterpiece, Dutch Leonard enlisted in the U.S. Navy, missing the last half of the season as well as the World Series. He was traded to the New York Yankees after the 1918 season, and they sold him to the Detroit Tigers, where he pitched for five years before retiring.

Dutch Leonard's six-year Red Sox career consisted of 90 victories against 64 losses with a microscopic 2.13 ERA. According to David Jones in *Deadball Stars of the American League*, the Ohio native was "one of the era's most controversial figures. Regarded as a selfish, cowardly player by many of his contemporaries, Leonard frittered away much of his major league career, alternating periods of brilliance with long bouts of inertia."[99]

Lepcio, Ted

Thaddeus Stanley Lepcio was born in Utica, New York, on July 28, 1930. After graduating from Seton Hall University in 1951, he became one of the era's "bonus babies," signing a $60,000 contract with the Boston Red Sox and being sent to their Roanoke farm club in the Piedmont League for seasoning. The five-foot, ten-inch, 176-pound, right-handed hitter played 54 games at third base for Roanoke, hitting a respectable .268 with seven homers in 190 at-bats. He was promoted to Louisville late in the season, splitting his time between third base and second base, and striking the ball at a .263 clip with 13 extra-base hits in 137 at-bats.

The 21-year-old infielder was added to the Boston roster as a utility man in 1952 and performed satisfactorily, playing 57 games at second base and 25 games at third base. He batted .263 in 84 games with 17 doubles and five homers in 274 at-bats. Lepcio held down the utility spot for Boston for seven years, but he never demonstrated enough skills, either offensively or defensively, to win a permanent job at any one position. He split the second base duties with Billy Goodman in 1954, but was displaced by Goodman in 1955. He played 57 games at second base in 1956 and 68 games at that position the following year, but gave way to Pete Runnels in 1958. During his seven-year Red Sox tenure he batted .247 with 53 home runs in 1,622 at-bats. Defensively, his fielding average was five to 12 points below the league average at both second base and third base, and his range was about average.

Lester, Jon

Jonathan Tyler Lester was born in Tacoma, Washington, on January 7, 1984, and entered professional baseball 18 years later. He signed with the Boston Red Sox in 2002 and was sent to their farm team in the Florida Rookie League for one game. Over the next four-and-a-half years he moved up Boston's minor league ladder, generating rave reviews every step of the way. He started the 2006 season with Pawtucket but was promoted to the big club in mid-season after going 3–4 with a 2.70 ERA at the Triple-A level. He pitched well for Boston over a two-month period, showing a 7–2 record with a 4.76 ERA, when his world came crashing down. The six-foot, two-inch, 190-pound southpaw was diagnosed with a rare form of non–Hodgkin's lymphoma, a blood cancer, on September 2, but after a four-course regimen of chemotherapy, he was declared to be free of the disease on December 5.

Jon Lester arrived at the Red Sox spring training camp in Fort Myers, Florida, on February 12, 2007, just three pounds under his playing weight. One month later, he pitched in his first game, throwing one perfect inning in a "B" game and hitting 89–90 mph on the radar gun. His comeback continued into the season, beginning with Greenville in the South Atlantic League where he pitched in three games with no record. With Portland in the Eastern League, he posted a 1–0 mark in one game, before moving up to Pawtucket where he went 4–5, pitching 71⅔ innings in 14 games with a 3.89 ERA. The Boston Red Sox recalled him after the All-Star game and, on July 23, the sneaky-fast lefty was touched up for just two runs in six innings in a win over the Cleveland Indians. In all, he pitched in 12 games for Boston, posting a perfect 4–0 mark as Terry Francona's charges headed into the post-season after winning the American League East Division. Lester did not see any action in the ALDS, but pitched 3⅔ innings in two games in relief in the ALCS with no record. His big chance finally came on October 28 when he was selected to pitch in the fourth game of the World Series against the Colorado Rockies with the Sox up three games to none. He was up to the challenge, blanking the Rockies on three base hits over 5⅔ innings with three strikeouts and three walks, and leaving with a 2–0 lead. He was the winning pitcher as Boston held on to win the game, 4–3, and the World Championship along with it.

Jon Lester came of age in 2008, relying heavily on his full repertoire of pitches that includes a 92–94-mph four-seam fastball, a cut fastball, a slider, and a changeup, all thrown from a low three-quarters arm angle. After going 2–2 in his first two starts, he scaled the heights on May 19, shackling the Kansas City Royals without a hit, striking out two and walking two in a 7–0 masterpiece. The no-hitter, the 18th no-hitter in Red Sox history, was a complete surprise to Lester because his bullpen session prior to the game was terrible and left the 24-year-old southpaw worrying if he could survive the first inning. But his command improved with each pitch, and on his 130th pitch of the game, a 94-mph heater, Alberto Callaspo went down on strikes to end the drama. From there, Lester went on to dominate American League opponents, posting a 16–6 record with an outstanding 3.21 ERA. He threw two complete-game shutouts during the season and participated in three other shutouts, pitching an average of 6⅓ innings per start. His post-season performance, however, ended on a disappointing note. He was dominant in the ALDS, pitching 14 innings in two starts against the Los Angeles Angels

Jon Lester

with a 1–0 won-lost record and a perfect 0.00 ERA. He threw seven innings in the opener, yielding one unearned run, and came away a 4–1 winner. In Game 4, he was on his game again, leaving after seven innings with a 2–0 lead, but the bullpen blew it. In the ALCS, he lost game 3 to the Tampa Bay Rays by a 9–1 score, leaving with two men out in the sixth inning after being raked for five runs. He came back in the Game 7 finale, in a rematch with his Game 3 opponent, Matt Garza, and although he pitched better this time, the result was the same. He yielded single runs in the fourth, fifth, and seventh innings, dropping a tough 3–1 decision. He was touched up for six base hits but he struck out eight men and didn't walk a batter.

He had another outstanding season in 2009, winning 15 games against eight losses, pitching 203⅓ innings with a 3.41 ERA. After dropping his first two starts, he defeated Baltimore by a 2–1 count before 37,869 noisy fans in the Fens, holding the O's scoreless while fanning nine men and walking two during his seven-inning outing. Mike Lowell singled in a run in the fifth inning and Dustin Pedroia knocked in the second run with a two-out single. Baltimore pushed over a run in the ninth to close out the scoring. On July 10, the lanky southpaw pitched eight innings in a 1–0 victory over the Kansas City Royals, holding KC to four base hits while striking out eight and walking two. Boston finally dented the plate in the bottom of the eighth on a single by Mark Kotsay and a double down the left field line by Dustin Pedroia. Boston's closer, Jonathan Papelbon, set the Royals down in order in the ninth for save number 23. Lester entered the All-Star break with an 8–6 record, but stepped it up a bit over the last half of the season, going 7–2 down the stretch. He participated in two more shutouts along the way, pitching eight innings in a 4–0 victory over Tampa Bay, and pitching 6⅓ innings in a 3–0 victory over Cleveland, both at home.

Jonathan Lester, Boston's classiest lefty since Mel Parnell, turned in his best season in 2010, winning 19 games against just nine losses, with 225 strikeouts in 208 innings and a 3.25 ERA. He went 5–0 in May with a 1.84 ERA and was named the American League Pitcher of the Month. He upped his record to an enviable 11–3 by the All-Star break, but suffered through four consecutive losses coming out of the break before turning things around. From August 27 to September 25 he ran off a six-game winning streak beginning with a 3–1 win over the Tampa Bay Rays on the strength of two home runs by Victor Martinez, who lit up the Florida sky in the first and seventh innings. The game also marked the first of four consecutive games in which the talented southpaw struck out at least ten batters. He began the last week of the season by hurling his team to a convincing 7–3 victory over the New York Yankees in Yankee Stadium, bringing his record to 19–8. Lester had another fine season in 2011, pitching 192 innings in 31 starts while compiling a 15–9 won-loss mark. He was at his best during the first half of the season when he went 10–4, but after being forced out of a game against Toronto with a back strain on July 5 while pitching a no-hitter through four innings, he went a month without a decision before defeating the Chicago White Sox by a 10–2 margin. The talented southpaw battled command problems over the last half of the season and, after running off a four-game winning streak in late August, his high pitch counts caught up with him and he dropped his last three decisions.

Lewis, Darren

Darren Joel Lewis was a very good defensive center fielder with good instincts and blazing speed but a weak throwing arm, and played four years with the Boston Red Sox near the end of his career. The six-foot tall, 175-pound, right-handed hitter was drafted by the Oakland Athletics on June 1, 1988, and spent most of the summer with Madison in the Midwest League, batting a mediocre .246 in 199 at-bats with just six extra base hits and 20 stolen bases. He worked his way through the minor league maze between 1989 and 1991, spending time with Modesto in the California League, Huntsville in the Southern League, Tacoma in the Pacific Coast League, and finally with Oakland in the American League.

He made his major league debut with the A's on August 21, 1990, batting .229 in 35 at-bats. The following year he was traded to the San Francisco Giants, where he spent the next five years. He was the Giants' regular center fielder in 1993 and 1994, batting .253 and .257 respectively, earning his keep with his speed and his defense. He led the National League with a perfect 1.000 fielding average in 1993 and with nine triples in 1994. He was traded to the Cincinnati Reds in 1995 in a multi-player deal, and two years and two teams later, the California speedster was signed as a free agent by the Boston Red Sox.

He quickly became a favorite of manager Jimy Williams in 1998 with his excellent outfield coverage, and by getting the most mileage out of his .268 batting average with 70 bases on balls, 29 stolen bases, and 95 runs scored. In the American League Division Series that year he tattooed Cleveland pitching to the tune of .357 in a four-game Boston loss. The following year, he slumped to .240 with 16 stolen bases and 63 runs scored, but his defense was solid and Boston once again qualified as the wild card entry in the post-season. Jimy Williams' sluggers defeated the Cleveland Indians in five games, sweeping the last three games by scores of 9–3, 23–7, and 12–8 after Cleveland had taken a two-games-to-none lead in the series, and Lewis chipped in with a hefty .375 batting average with five runs scored. Unfortunately, the Sox made a quick exit from the Championship Series, falling to the New York Yankees in five games. That was the end of Darren Lewis' career as a starting outfielder with Boston. He was relegated to being the fourth outfielder on the team with the arrival of Carl Everett in 2000, and he played just 97 games for the Red Sox that year and 82 games in 2001 before he was released. After playing one year with the Chicago Cubs, where he batted .241, he retired.

Lewis, Duffy

George Edward "Duffy" Lewis, one of the members of Boston's famous "Million Dollar Outfield," that included Tris Speaker and Harry Hooper, was born in San Francisco, California, on April 18, 1888. He attended St. Mary's College of California from 1907 to 1909 and played baseball up and down the west coast during the summer, first with Alameda in the outlaw California State League and then with Oakland in the Pacific Coast League. After hitting a crisp .279 in 200 games with the Oaks in 1909, the five foot, seven-inch, 160-pound outfielder, who acquired his nickname from his mother's maiden name, was drafted by the Boston Red Sox.

Duffy Lewis had an outstanding rookie season in Boston, hitting .283 with 44 extra-base hits, but he had a few run-ins with his teammates. He "did not take too kindly to the treatment accorded to rookies, refusing, for example, to limit his time in the batting cage or to back down from confrontations with his fellow players.[100] His relationship with Tris Speaker got off to a rough start and remained rocky throughout his career. But none of that interfered with his play on the field. He was an excellent defensive player who covered acres of ground with short, quick strides. He didn't have much power at the plate but he was a reliable contact hitter whose line drives produced a .284 career batting average with 26 doubles and six triples a year. The little left-handed hitter was considered to be a clutch hitter and a good RBI man, accounting for 79 runs batted in for every 550 at-bats. On June 6, the rookie's single deprived Chicago White Sox ace Ed Walsh of a no-hitter. Lewis continued to stroke the ball with authority in 1911, batting .307, one of only two times in his career he would go over the .300 mark. His 86 RBI was tops on the team, and his batting average trailed only Hooper and Speaker. One of his more timely clutch hits of the year came on May 13 when his ninth inning grand-slam home run brought Boston back from a 10–1 fifth-inning deficit to a tie, and the Red Sox went on to win by a 13–11 score in ten innings.

The following year was a momentous year in Boston Red Sox baseball. They moved into a new ballpark, Fenway Park, at its time one of the most beautiful stadiums in the country. It only had one slight problem. There was a ten-foot-high incline in front of the left field wall, requiring fielders to climb the hill for fly balls. It was cause for concern for all left fielders, many of who came tumbling down the hill after losing their balance, much to the enjoyment of the fans. Duffy Lewis was one of the few outfielders who mastered the ill-advised construction, but it took him countless hours of practice to do it. "I'd go out to the ballpark mornings," he later told a sportswriter, "and have somebody hit the ball again and again out to the wall. I experimented with every angle of approach up the cliff until I learned to play the slope correctly. Sometimes it would be tougher coming back down the slope than going up. With runners on base, you had to come off the cliff throwing."[101] Over the years, the incline became known fondly in Boston as "Duffy's Cliff."

Boston romped to the 1912 American League pennant by 14 games over the Washington Senators, and Lewis contributed a tough .284 batting average and a team-leading 109 runs batted in. On September 6, his single drove in the only run of the game as Smoky Joe Wood outpitched the great Walter Johnson. Jake Stahl's boys dispatched the New York Giants in eight games in the World Series, though Lewis who suffered through a .188 Series. Boston slipped to fourth place in 1913, moved back up to second place the following year, and grabbed another brass ring in 1915, edging the Detroit Tigers by two-and-a-half games. Their opponents in the World Series were the Philadelphia Phillies, and Carrigan's cohorts took care of the National League upstarts in five games, with Duffy Lewis tattooing the ball at a torrid .444 clip with a double, a home run, and five RBI. In Game 3, with the Series tied at one game apiece, he singled home Harry Hooper in the ninth inning to give Boston a hard-fought 2–1 win. The next day he doubled home the eventual game-winning run in the sixth inning. In the Game 5 finale, he hit a game-tying two-run homer into the center field bleachers in the eighth inning, in a game won by Boston, 5–4.

The following year, the Red Sox repeated as the American League champion and took the measure of the National League representative, this time the Brooklyn Robins, in five games. Once again Lewis was one of his opponent's main tormentors, batting .353 and slugging two doubles and a triple with three runs scored. The Sox finished second in 1917 with Lewis batting .302 with 65 RBI, but by 1918, when Boston won their fourth World Championship in seven years, their left fielder was among the missing. He spent the year in the U.S. Navy, stationed at Mare Island, California, and serving as player-manager on their baseball team. After his discharge late in the year, he was traded to the New York Yankees as part of Harry Frazee's infamous fire sale. He played in the major leagues three more years before retiring at the age of 33.

Lonborg, Jim

James Reynold Lonborg joined the Boston Red Sox as an amateur free agent on August 14, 1963, after graduating from Stanford University, and two years later he was added to a Boston starting rotation that included Earl Wilson and Bill Monbouquette. The six-foot, five-inch, 210-pound, right-handed power pitcher made his major league debut in Baltimore on April 23, pitching six innings and being touched up for three runs in a 4–2 loss. He had good stuff in his first start but he was wild, walking the bases full in the second inning and then laying the ball down the middle to pitcher Robin Roberts, who promptly hammered it down the left field line for a bases-clearing double, one of only two hits Lonborg yielded in the game. Gentleman Jim, as he was called, received a rude welcome to the major leagues overall, winning just nine games against 17 losses with a 4.48 ERA. The next year, he lowered his ERA to 3.86, pitching 181⅔ innings in 45 games, and

Jim Lonborg

posting a 10–10 won-loss record for a team that finished ninth in a ten-team league.

Not much was expected of Boston in 1967, but, as all Red Sox fans know, it was the year the "Impossible Dream" came true, when manager Dick Williams guided his charges to a most unlikely American League pennant. Big Jim Lonborg was the drum major leading the parade. The 25-year-old flamethrower had a full repertoire of pitches that included a live fastball, a sinker, a slider, and a curve, and he was at the top of his game all year long. His fastball was humming on Friday evening, April 28, when the Red Sox welcomed the Kansas City Royals to the friendly confines of Fenway Park, before a sparse crowd of 9,026. The big right-hander disposed of 13 of the enemy batters via the strikeout route, ten of them going down between the third and sixth innings, on his way to a six-hit, 3–0 shutout. Mike Andrews and Reggie Smith had run-scoring singles in the fifth inning and the Sox added a run in the seventh on two walks and two errors. One month later, Lonborg blanked the Detroit Tigers, 1–0, with an 11-strikeout performance in Tiger Stadium, and Dalton Jones provided the Sox ace with all the offense he needed by slamming a leadoff home run in the top of the second inning. The Tigers mounted two threats along the way but couldn't capitalize on either one. In the second inning, the first two batters singled, but Dalton Jones started a quick double play to nip that rally in the bud, and in the eighth inning, after Al Kaline had opened the inning with a line drive double to left field, Lonborg retired the next three men in order, two of them via the strikeout route. Dick Williams brought his cohorts back to Tiger Stadium again on July 9, a sweltering Sunday afternoon with the temperature hovering in the nineties. Boston's flamethrower turned finesse pitcher on this day to conserve his energy, but he was still forced to leave the game after seven innings, suffering from heat exhaustion, turning the reins over to his closer, John Wyatt. Between the two of them, they held Detroit to just four base hits in a 3–0 Red Sox victory. Boston scored two runs in the second inning on a triple by Jerry Adair and a home run by Reggie Smith, and they added a run in the eighth on a Carl Yastrzemski round-tripper.

Boston visited Minneapolis on August 6 to do battle with the Twins in the red-hot American League pennant race. There were still five teams jockeying for position, with just five games separating number one from number five. Boston led Minnesota by one game at the start of the day, but they were in a virtual deadlock for second place by the time the sun went down. Dean Chance, the Twins ace, faced off against Jim Lonborg, with Chance winning a rain-shortened, five-inning encounter by the score of 2–0, but the Minnesota ace had mixed feelings about the victory because he was flirting with a perfect game, having retired all 15 Boston batters he had faced. Gentleman Jim faced the New York Yankees twice in a period of nine days late in the season and held them in check in both games. On August 29, in The House That Ruth Built, he outpitched Mel Stottlemyre 2–1, sending 11 Yankees back to the dugout dragging their bats behind them. He also drove in what proved to be the winning run with a single to left field in the seventh inning. Then, on September 7, Ralph Houk brought his ninth-place rag-tag outfit into the Fens to have another go at Big Jim. But the second time was no blessing. Lonborg was in command throughout and the New Yorkers succumbed to his fastball again, this time by a 3–1 score that saw ten of them go down on strikes. Rico Petrocelli got Boston off on the right foot by launching a home run into the left field screen in the second inning. They added another run in the sixth inning and, after New York had dented the plate in the seventh, they pushed over run number three in the bottom of the eighth.

The 1967 pennant race went down to the wire, with four teams still in the running. The Red Sox entered the final day of the season tied with the Minnesota Twins with 92 wins each, and the Detroit Tigers were only one-half game behind the league leaders. When Detroit was eliminated from the race after dropping the second game of a doubleheader to the California Angels, it left the Boston-Minnesota game to determine the American League pennant winner. The game matched two 20-game winners, Jim Lonborg and Dean Chance, with Lonborg coming away the winner. The game was played in Fenway Park with a full house of 35,770 wild

Red Sox fans cheering their team on. The fans grew strangely quiet early in the game as Minnesota scored an unearned run in the first inning on an error by George Scott and added another unearned run in the third inning on a misplay by Carl Yastrzemski, but the Boston bats finally came to life in the bottom of the fifth inning, and it was Jim Lonborg who started the rally. He led off the inning with a bunt single, bringing the Fenway faithful to their feet, and filling the little park with loud screams and whistles. Jerry Adair followed with single to center field and Dalton Jones singled to left to load the bases. Yaz then came through big-time, lining a base hit to center field to send the two tying runs scampering across the plate. Ken Harrelson reached base on a fielder's choice ground ball that plated the third run of the inning, bringing the Twins closer, Al Worthington, into the game. Worthington immediately uncorked two wild pitches that scored Yaz, and a fifth run came across on an error. That was all the help Lonborg needed, but he did get another boost in the eighth inning, when the Twins mounted their last attack. Rich Reese opened the inning with a single, but Cesar Tovar squelched that bid at a rally by hitting the ball to Jerry Adair, who started a fast second-to-first double play with George Scott on the receiving end. Tony Oliva, Harmon Killebrew, and Bob Allison then followed with singles, with Oliva scoring on Allison's hit, but the big, slow-moving left fielder was gunned down by Yaz at second, trying to take an extra base. A short time later, the Boston Red Sox were crowned American League Champions.

Boston met the St. Louis Cardinals in the World Series, losing a tough seven-game confrontation. The *Boston Globe* reported, "No player in the history of the World Series, before or since, did what Jim Lonborg did in 1967. Lonborg still holds the record for the fewest hits given up in back-to-back starts, when he was simply brilliant in games two and five of the great Series with the St. Louis Cardinals."[102] The 24-year-old right-hander tossed a one-hitter at Red Schoendienst's mighty Cardinals in Game 2, winning 5–0. The only hit off the Red Sox ace was a two-out double by Julian Javier in the eighth inning. He handcuffed the Redbirds again in Game 5, winning 3–1 on a three-hitter, with the Cardinals' only run coming on a ninth-inning home run by Roger Maris. Boston's gutty ace tried to come back on two days' rest in Game 7, but his tank was empty, and he dropped a 7–2 decision to Bob Gibson, who won his third complete-game victory of the Series.

Gentleman Jim won the 1967 American League Cy Young Award after leading the American League with 39 starts, 22 victories (against nine losses), and 246 strikeouts in 273⅓ innings, with a 3.16 earned run average. The California native, who also was named the American League Pitcher of the Year by *The Sporting News*, should have been at the peak of a distinguished pitching career in 1967, with many successful seasons ahead of him, but fate determined otherwise. Lonborg broke his leg in a skiing accident on December 24, 1967, and was never the same. He pitched for the Red Sox for four more years, with a combined record of 27–29, spending several months on the disabled list, as well as a short rehabilitation stint in Louisville. Boston's World Series hero was subsequently traded to the Milwaukee Brewers on October 10, 1971, joining the Philadelphia Phillies one year later, where he had a minor rejuvenation, going 17–13 in 1974 and 18–10 two years later. He retired from baseball after the 1979 season, attended Tufts University Dental School, and became a practicing dentist.

Lord, Harry

Harry Donald Lord was born in Porter, Maine, on March 8, 1882. He began playing professional baseball in Kesar Falls, Maine while he was still in college, eventually breaking "into organized baseball at age 24 in 1906 with Worcester in the New England League, and the next year moving up the Providence in the Eastern League. His performance there caught the attention of the Boston Pilgrims and, at 26 years of age, he broke into the big leagues on September 25, 1907," in a losing effort as Boston dropped a 4–3 decision to the Detroit Tigers.[103] He was installed as Boston's starting third baseman in 1908, and he played 144 games at that position in his rookie season, batting a respectable .259 with 23 extra-base hits and 23 stolen bases. The five-foot, ten-inch, 165 pound, left-handed hitter dismissed the sophomore jinx the following year by smoking the ball at a .315 clip with 19 extra-base hits, as the team, now known as the Red Sox, moved into third place in the American League with 88 victories against 63 losses. His 89 runs scored and his 36 stolen bases were fourth-best in the American League and his 168 base hits were fifth-best. Harry Lord was known as a hustling player who was once timed in 3.4 seconds going from home to first base. He showed good speed on the bases and was always ready to take an extra base on an unsuspecting outfielder.

The 1910 edition of the Boston franchise, under the direction of Patsy Donovan, was battling for a spot in the first division when, on July 10, a Walter Johnson fastball broke Lord's finger, sending him to the sidelines. By the time he recovered, Clyde Engle was holding down third base, making Lord expendable, and he was traded to the Chicago White Sox on August 9. He played 368 games for the Red Sox between 1907 and 1910, and he was "selected as third baseman on Baseball Magazine's American League All-Star team in 1908, 1909, and 1910."[104] He was a decent hitter but he lacked power and, in the field, he was below average in both fielding average and range. According to one historian, he was virtually immobile in the field.

Lowe, Derek

He forever endeared himself to the fans of the Boston Red Sox by his remarkable performances in Boston's historic 2004 post-season run that led to their first World Championship in 86 years. He pitched in four games in three post-season series and was the winning pitcher in the final game of each series. Derek Christopher Lowe was born in Dearborn, Michigan, on June 1, 1973. At Edison Ford High School, he lettered in four sports — golf, baseball, basketball, and soccer — achieving all-league honors in all sports and All-State honors in basketball. After graduating from high school in 1991, he passed up a basketball scholarship offer from the University of Michigan to sign a baseball contract with the Seattle Mariners. The six-foot, six-inch, 230-pound, right-handed power pitcher spent a total of seven years in the Mariners' minor league system with moderate success, making his major league debut on April 26, 1997. He pitched 3⅓ innings of relief against the Toronto Blue Jays in the SkyDome, yielding the winning run in the bottom of the ninth inning to take the loss. He won his first major league game six weeks later, pitching 5⅓ innings on June 6, yielding three runs in a 6–3 win over the Detroit Tigers. Lowe pitched in 12 games for Seattle, winning two games and losing four, before being traded to the Boston Red Sox on July 31.

The big right-hander was sent to the bullpen by manager Jimy Williams, going 0–2 in eight games at the end of the season. In 1998, the hard-working Lowe pitched in 63 games with ten starts, posting a 3–9 record with four saves. He began the following year as the setup man for closer Tom Gordon, who had led the American League with 46 saves in 1998, and then for Tim Wakefield who assumed the closer role when Gordon went down with an elbow injury, but he moved into the closer role himself late in the season and recorded 15 saves with a 6–3 won-loss record. He became the team's official closer in 2000, relying on his hard slider to induce ground ball outs as opposed to the strikeout route followed by Gordon and most major league closers. Lowe's repertoire also included a curve, a change of pace, and a cut fastball, but it was his slider that was his out pitch. He

Derek Lowe

responded magnificently, leading the American League with 42 saves in 47 save opportunities for an excellent 89 percent success rate.

The year 2001 was a mixed bag for Derek Lowe as he struggled with his pitches and with his confidence in mid-season, and eventually lost his closer's job to Ugueth Urbina, who was obtained in a trade with Montreal at the trading deadline. Boston's new manager, Grady Little, inserted Lowe into his starting rotation in 2002, and the change proved to be a brilliant move on the part of Little. Lowe proceeded to have a career season. As reported in *The Red Sox Fan Handbook*, "In his first game of the season, Lowe retired the first 12 hitters he faced, and took a no-hitter into the eighth inning. On April 27, Lowe pitched the first no-hitter at Fenway in 38 years. Amazingly, this was also Lowe's first career complete game."[105] A Saturday afternoon crowd of 32,837 chilled fans roared their approval as Rickey Henderson, leading off the bottom of the first inning, sent a fly ball over the Green Monster to give the Sox a 1–0 lead over the Tampa Bay Devil Rays. They put the game on ice two innings later when they unleashed a six-run barrage against Delvin James, who was touched up for four singles plus a double by Jason Varitek. Lowe had the Tampa Bay batters pounding his sinker into the ground all day, with 13 of them being retired on ground balls, and six more striking out. Brent Abernathy, who led off the third inning with a base on balls, was the only Devil Ray baserunner of the game, a 10–0 Boston victory. The big right-hander was selected to start the All-Star Game after compiling a dominating 12–4 record with a 2.36 ERA through early July, and he threw two innings in the midsummer classic's first tie game, an 11 inning 7–7 disappointment. He finished the season with a sensational 21–8 record and a 2.58 ERA as Boston came home in second place in the Eastern Division, trailing the perennial Division Champion New York Yankees by ten-and-a-half games. He had another fine year in 2003, going 17–7, but his ERA ballooned to 4.47 and he seemed to lose his confidence in critical situations.

The 2004 season would be one that Derek Lowe, his Boston teammates, and Red Sox fans nationwide will remember and relive forever. The Michigan native compiled a 14-12 won-lost record for the year, but he pitched poorly, with a 5.42 ERA, and was rescued only by Boston's potent offense. In the post-season, he was banished to the bullpen, serving in middle relief. In game three of the ALDS against the Anaheim Angels, with Boston on top two games to none in the best-of-five series and their pitching staff depleted with thirteen pitchers having been used in the first two-plus games, manager Terry Francona was down to the bottom of the barrel in the 6–6 game as the tenth inning arrived. He nervously waved Derek Lowe in from the bullpen and Lowe, like the mythical phoenix, rose from the ashes to live again and shut down the Angels, leaving two men on base. He became the winning pitcher when, with two men out and Johnny Damon on base, David Ortiz put a charge into an outside curve ball and lofted a two-run homer into the Monster Seats, another magical walk-off moment for Big Papi. Lowe was rewarded for his effort when manager Terry Francona handed him the ball to start Game 4 of the ALCS against the New York Yankees, with Boston down three games to none, imploring his pitcher to fend off the inevitable for one more day. As a full Fenway Park crowd watched the proceedings, Lowe responded with a strong effort in a game that went into extra innings thanks to the flying feet of Dave Roberts. In the bottom of the 12, Manny Ramirez led off the inning with a single to left field and Big Papi drove one into the right field seats for another walk-off celebration. After the Red Sox had captured the next two games, Lowe was back on the mound for Game 7 in "The House That Ruth Built," and he silenced the Yankees bats for a 10–3 series-clinching victory, yielding one run on a single base hit in six innings, leaving with an 8–1 lead. In the World Series against Tony LaRussa's St. Louis Cardinals, he pitched Game 4 in Busch Stadium with 52,037 rabid Cardinal fans trying to rally their team from a three-games-to-none deficit. But it was too late for the Redbirds. Johnny Damon hit a leadoff homer in the top of the first inning, the Sox added another brace of runs in the third and Lowe tossed seven brilliant shutout innings, holding Pujols and company to three hits and a single walk while striking out four men to secure Boston's historic World Championship. With that victory, he became the first pitcher in baseball history to be the winning pitcher in all three post-season series. Derek Lowe filed for free agency in the off-season and eventually signed with the Los Angeles Dodgers, leaving the Red Sox as a bona fide Boston legend. He pitched for the Atlanta Braves in 2011.

Lowell, Mike

Michael Averett Lowell, "the son of Carlos Lowell, a Cuban exile of Irish and German descent who established residency in Puerto Rico from 1962 to 1974 while pitching for the Puerto Rico National Team," was born in San Juan on February 24, 1974.[106] He was raised in Miami, Florida, and graduated from Coral Gables High School in 1992, where he starred on the baseball team. He went on to star for the Florida International University baseball team, three times being selected to the All-Conference team. He was drafted by the New York Yankees in 1995, forcing him to juggle his college career and his baseball career for two years before he received his Bachelor's degree in Finance.

The six-foot, three-inch, 210-pound, right-handed slugger began his organized baseball career in 1995 with Oneonta in the New York-Pennsylvania League, playing 72 games and hitting .260. Two years later, on September 13, 1998, after working his way through the New York minor league network, he made his debut with Joe Torre's team, and played eight games at the end of the season, going 4-for-15 for a .267 average. He was traded to the Florida Marlins on February 1, 1999, and by June became the team's regular third baseman. In 2000, his power numbers began to evolve as he slugged 22 homers in 508 at-bats with 91 RBI and a .270 batting average. He continued to hit for average and power over the next three years and helped the underdog Florida team capture the 2003 World Championship, batting .276 with 32 home runs and 105 runs batted in during the season, but missing 32 games late in the season with a broken hand. The Marlins, under the deft handling of replacement manager Jack McKeon, jumped up from fourth place to a second-place finish and a wild-card berth in the post-season. The young Marlins defeated San Francisco in the NLDS, Chicago in the NLCS, and finally the New York Yankees in the World Series. Mike Lowell, who was still recovering from his injury, was of little help in the NLDS but crushed tow home runs in the NLCS including a game-winning homer in Game 2 and another two-run homer in Game 5. He batted only .217 in the World Series but contributed a two-run single in the fifth inning of the Game 5 finale.

The financially strapped Marlins began to sell off their star players after 2003, including Brad Penny, Josh Beckett, Ivan Rodriguez, and Derek Lee. Lowell's number came up two years later and, on November 24, 2005, after a tough season in which he hit a mediocre .236, he was traded to the Boston Red Sox. The Sox, who had won the World Championship in 2004, were reloading for another shot at the championship. The hard-hitting, slick-fielding third baseman fit right in with the Red Sox cast of characters, and he stung the ball at a hard .284 in 2006 with 20 homers and 80 RBI. The following year he was Boston's MVP as he had one

Mike Lowell

day in Chicago, Illinois, on February 3, 1952. After graduating in 1974, from USC where he lettered in both baseball and football, Fred Lynn was signed by the Boston Red Sox and sent to their Bristol farm team in the Double-A Eastern League, where he hit .259 in 53 games. The next year, he hit .282 with the Triple-A Pawtucket Red Sox, and was brought up to the parent club after the International League season ended. He saw action in 15 games with Boston and smoked the ball at a .419 clip with six extra-base hits in 43 at-bats.

He joined Jim Rice, who was also in his rookie season, and Dewey Evans, who was entering his third full season, in the Red Sox outfield in 1975, and the trio excited Boston fans with their exploits on the field, particularly Fred Lynn, whose acrobatic catches turned enemy hits into outs. As Maury Allen noted, "(Lynn) is a young player who plays defense as hard as he hits the ball, thinks nothing of making an impossible catch, and can run and throw with the game's finest defensive outfielders. 'I was a flanker back in college at USC,' says Lynn. 'It was routine catching passes diving through the air. I am not concerned when I catch fly balls diving through the air.'" All three outfielders had outstanding seasons in 1975. Rice hit .309 with 22 homers and 102 RBI, Evans batted .274 with 13 homers, and Lynn tormented opposing pitchers to the tune of .331 with 21 homers and 105 runs batted in. Lynn also led the league with 103 runs scored, 47 doubles, and a .566 slugging average. His greatest day in baseball occurred on the evening of June 17, 1975, when he pummeled Detroit Tigers pitching for three homers, a triple, a single, and ten runs batted in. The 23-year-old Chicagoan's spectacular rookie season was amply rewarded, as he became the first player to win both the Rookie of the Year Award and the Most Valuable Player Award in the same year. He also won the first of his four Gold Gloves for fielding excellence. The Red Sox, who were the Eastern Division Champions that year, swept the Oakland A's three straight in the ALCS, but came up short in the World Series, losing to the Cincinnati Reds in seven hard-fought games. Fred Lynn did everything he could to help his team in the post-season, hitting .364 in the ALCS and .280 with a double, a homer, and five RBI in the World Series.

The smooth-swinging lefty, who stood six-foot, one-inch tall and tipped the scales at 185 pounds, played in Boston for five more years, winning three more Gold Gloves and hitting the ball hard and often. His best year was 1979, when he slugged 39 home runs, scored 116 runs, and drove in 122 runs, while leading the league in batting average (.333), on-base percentage (.423), and slugging average (.637). Toronto manager Roy Hartsfield noted at the time, "Lynn is the most complete player in our league." The Chicago native batted .301 in 110 games in 1980 and was then traded to the California Angels. In the 1983 All-Star Game, he hit a grand-slam home run, and was voted the game's MVP, as the American League defeated the National League, 13–3. He also hit home runs in the 1976, 1979 and 1980 games.

Fred Lynn's talent was virtually limitless, but his fragile body prevented him from realizing his full potential. He was able to play in 150 games only once in 17 years and, after batting over .300 in four of his six full seasons in Boston, he never again reached that magic number, often sidelined with nagging injuries such as pulled muscles and strains, as well as more serious injuries like broken ribs and torn knee ligaments that put him on the disabled list five times during his career.

Malzone, Frank

Frank Malzone was one of the greatest third basemen in Boston Red Sox history. He was a dangerous hitter with above-average power at the plate, and in the field the six-time All-Star and three-time Gold Glove winner led the league in fielding average and putouts once each, in assists three times, and in double plays five times. He was selected as a member of the all-time Boston Red Sox team in 1995. Frank James Malzone was born in Bronx, New York, on February 28, 1930. Baseball was the major activity in his neighborhood so he and his siblings played a lot of ball on a field near their home. He attended Samuel Gompers High School and played baseball there as well as playing semi-pro baseball. He played in a high school all-star game in the Polo Grounds in 1947 and smashed two triples, after which he was offered a contract by the New York Giants, but he turned it down because he was planning to be an electrician. Later he was offered a contract by the Boston Red Sox and this time he accepted the offer, $150 a month and no bonus. He was assigned to Milford in the Eastern Shore League, where he stung the ball at a crisp .304 pace with 32 doubles, 10 homers and 77 RBI in 424 at-bats. He batted .329 with a league-record 26 triples for Oneonta in the Canadian-American League the following year, missed most of 1950 with injuries, and hit .283 with Scranton in the Eastern League in 1951.

His baseball career was interrupted after the 1951 season when he was drafted into military service during the Korean War, spending the next two years with the United States Army in Hawaii and playing shortstop on the Army baseball team. After his discharge, he got back in shape by playing winter baseball in San Juan, Puerto Rico, before joining Louisville in the top-rated American Association. Frank Malzone played for the Colonels for two years, hitting .270 in 1954 and .310 with 88 RBI the following year. He even had a cup of coffee with the Red Sox at the end of the 1955 season, stroking seven hits in 20 at-bats for a .350 average. In his second major league game, on September 20, he went 6-for-10 in a doubleheader with Baltimore. Over the winter, he suffered a tragedy that seriously affected him for many months. He lost his first child, Suzanne, to illness and, as he noted, "When I went to spring training, I was out of it. I did make the ballclub, but by the trading deadline they sent me to the Triple-A San Francisco club of the Pacific Coast League."[107] Malzone hit a barely visible .165 with Boston in 1956 but recovered to post a .296 average in 324 at-bats with the Seals.

Frank Malzone's major league career began in earnest in 1957, and it was one of the best seasons he had during his career. The five-foot, ten-inch, 180-pound, right-handed hitter ripped the ball at a .292 clip with 31 doubles, 15 home runs, and 103 runs batted in, in 634 at-bats. "His defense won raves, and he set a record for third baseman, since broken, with ten assists in a game against Washington. Malzone also became the first player to lead his position in games played, putouts, assists, errors, fielding percentage, and double plays in the same season."[108] He also won the first of his three Gold Gloves and was selected to the first of his six All-Star teams, from 1957 to 1960, 1963 and '64. In 1958 he hit a career-high .295 with 30 doubles, 15 homers, and 87 RBI, and he carried home his second Gold Glove. The following year was more of the same, a .280 batting average, 34 doubles, 19 homers, 92 RBI, and another Gold Glove. Leo Durocher, a former player and major league manager, who was doing color commentary for the NBC "Game of the Week," said, "The guy's got a weakness? Dandruff maybe."

Malzone continued his superb play for another five years, batting between .264 and .291 and playing outstanding defense. He led the American League in double plays a record five straight years, from 1957 to 1961. In 1962 he had another fine offensive season, hitting .283 with a career-high 21 home runs and 95 runs batted in. His career began to wind down in 1964 when he hit .264 with 13 homers and 56 RBI, and he was released on November 24, 1965, after struggling through a .239 season where he hit just three home runs and drove in 34 runs in 364 at-bats. Over the years he had

Frank Malzone

been one of Boston's most popular players, and it was painful for Red Sox fans to see someone else stationed at third base when the 1966 season opened. Frank Malzone played all but 82 of his 1,441 games with Boston, batting .276 in 5,273 at-bats with 131 home runs. His dependable glove and outstanding range supplemented his offensive contributions.

Mantilla, Felix

Felix Lamela Mantilla signed a professional baseball contract with the Milwaukee Braves in 1952, joining the parent club four years later as a defensive replacement at shortstop and third base and hitting a respectable .283 in 53 at-bats over 35 games. The six-foot, 160-pound, right-handed hitter played with the Braves, as a utility infielder, through 1961, giving Fred Haney, and later Charlie Dressen, adequate defensive play at all infield positions, primarily second base, but somewhere along the line, his bat went dead, with averages ranging from .215 to .257. He was drafted by the New York Mets in the expansion draft on October 10, 1961, and played one year in New York, batting .275 in 141 games.

The Mets traded him to the Boston Red Sox on December 11, 1962, beginning a three-year sojourn in the Hub. Felix Mantilla played in just 66 games in 1963, 27 of them at shortstop, but his leaky glove and limited range ended that experiment almost before it began. He played only six games at shortstop during his last two years in Boston. He did exhibit a strong bat in 1963, however, batting .315 with eight doubles and six homers in 178 at-bats, so manager Johnny Pesky tried to find a position he could play to get his bat in the lineup. The next year, he played in 133 games, including 47 games in the outfield and 46 games at second base, with just one error at each position. He hammered a stunning 30 home runs along with 20 doubles while batting .289 with a .553 slugging average in 425 at-bats. Mantilla was Boston's regular second baseman in 1965 and put 18 balls into orbit with 92 RBI in 534 at-bats, earning a spot on the American League All-Star team, but that wasn't enough to satisfy new manager Billy Herman, and he dealt Mantilla to Houston on April 3, 1966. He played just 77 games with the Astros before retiring.

Martinez, Pedro

Pedro Martinez has been called the most intimidating pitcher of his era. All the evidence seems to substantiate that claim. He could, in fact, challenge Walter Johnson as the greatest pitcher of all time, but that depends on the magnitude of his downside as his career draws to a close. Through the 2009 season, Pedro's adjusted earned run average (AERA) is 154, six points higher than the number two man, Lefty Grove, and his .687 winning percentage is number two all-time behind Whitey Ford's .690. He is number six in fewest hits allowed per game (7.1), and number two in strikeouts per game (10.0), trailing only Randy Johnson (10.7).

Pedro Jaime Martinez was born in Manoguayabo, Dominican Republic, on October 25, 1971, the fifth of six children born to Paolino and Leopoldina Martinez. Pedro's father, who was called freakishly strong, was a talented pitcher in his own right during the 1950's, the possessor of what was described in Jockbio as a murderous sinker that batters beat into the ground, and he instructed his children in the fine points of pitching. Pedro's older brother,

Pedro Martinez

Ramon, signed a contract with the Los Angeles Dodgers in 1985 when Pedro was only 13 years old, but Dodgers scout Ralph Avila clocked young Pedro's fastball at 80 mph on the radar gun, with good movement, and made a mental note to revisit the boy at a later date. When he turned 16, three years later, Pedro signed with the Dodgers and embarked on a magical journey from the dirt streets of the Manoguayabo barrio to big-city stardom in the United States.

The Dominican teenager spent two years playing in the Dominican Summer League, posting a combined record of 12–3, following which the 135-pound, right-handed power pitcher, using his newly-found 90 mph fastball to perfection and demonstrating excellent command of his pitches, was sent to the Dodgers farm club in Great Falls in 1990 for further seasoning. He worked his way through the Dodgers farm system, finally reaching L.A. in 1992, where he went 0–1 in two games at the end of the season. The following year, Pedro appeared in 65 games for the Dodgers, posting a 10–5 record and a fine 2.61 ERA. But manager Tommy Lasorda didn't think the tall, skinny kid could stand the wear and tear of a full major league season, and he traded the 22-year-old flamethrower to the Montreal Expos. Pedro pitched for the Expos for four years, blossoming into a world-class starting pitcher. His last year in Canada, the five-foot, 11-inch, 170-pounder posted a record of 17–8 with a league-leading 1.90 ERA, and walked off with the National League Cy Young Award. For some strange reason, the Expos traded their All-World pitcher to the Boston Red Sox on November 18, 1997, for Carl Pavano and Tony Armas.

Pedro came to the Red Sox well-armed, according to the experts. He "has a pair of fastballs and curves, plus a wicked change, soft scroogie, cutter, and slider. He can alter his arm angle and release point, and he can make seasoned hitters look like rookies even without his best stuff."[109] Manager Jimy Williams welcomed the young pitching phenom with open arms, and Pedro paid immediate dividends. He tossed a 2–0 shutout, sprinkled with 11 strikeouts, in the Oakland Coliseum in the A's 1998 home opener, and ten days later, in Boston, he blanked the Seattle Mariners, 5–0, with 12 strikeouts. In September, in Yankee Stadium, Pedro held the powerful Bronx Bombers to one hit, fanning 17 of them along the way. For the season, he posted a 19–7 record that helped the Red Sox make a quantum leap from fourth place in the American League Eastern Division to second place, a position they would hold for the next seven years. The following year, Pedro Martinez had a career season. He breezed through the best of the American League, winning 23 games against just four losses. He led the American League in victories, winning percentage (.852), strikeouts (313), and earned run average (2.07). The ERA was particularly impressive when it was compared to the league ERA of 4.86. The 2.79 ERA differential was the largest differential in major league history. Naturally, the Boston ace won his second Cy Young Award in a runaway. He was also named the American League Pitcher of the Year by *The Sporting News*, and was selected as the right-handed pitcher on the American League All-Star Team. This after being named the Most Valuable Player in the 1999 All-Star Game after fanning five of the first six batters he faced in a two-inning stint that brought him the victory. In post-season play he was sensational, pitching 17 innings overall, with two victories, no losses, 23 strikeouts, and a perfect 0.00 ERA. He was forced out of Game 1 in the ALDS after four innings with a strained back, leading 2–0, but the bullpen couldn't hold the lead and Cleveland won the game, 3–2. He volunteered for relief duty in the Game 5 finale, and even though he was unable to control his fast ball or his changeup, he stymied the Cleveland batters with curveballs, tossing six no-hit innings and striking out eight batters as the Red Sox roared back from an 8–7 deficit to win the division series by a 12–8 count. He pitched Game 3 in the Championship Series against the New York Yankees, winning 13–1, but Boston went down to defeat in five games.

In 2000, Boston finished in second place, two-and-a-half games behind the Yankees, and they failed to qualify for post-season play. But Pedro held up his end, going 18–6 and leading the league in both strikeouts (284) and ERA (1.74). His 3.17 ERA differential broke his own record set the previous year. He almost added a no-hitter to his resume. In an August 29 game against the Tampa Bay Devil Rays, the Boston ace, on his way to an 8–0 win, carried a no-no into the ninth inning before John Flaherty broke it up. The flamboyant Dominican missed three months of the 2001 season with a sore shoulder, finishing with a 7–3 record in 18 games pitched. He came back strong the following season, winning 20 games against four losses, pitching 199⅓ innings in 30 games and leading the league with 239 strikeouts and a 2.26 ERA. Pedro went 14–4 in 2003, but missed a month of the season with a recurrence of his shoulder problem. In post-season play, he went 1–0 against Oakland in the ALDS as Boston won the series in five games, but he was not as fortunate in the ALCS against the Yankees. He pitched Game 3 against Roger Clemens, and got a no-decision in New York's 4–3 win. But he did get a decision in the fight that accompanied the beanball war between himself and Clemens. Both benches emptied after Clemens had brushed Manny Ramirez back with a heater, and during the melee Don Zimmer lunged at Pedro, but the younger man deftly sidestepped the 72-year-old Yankees coach and threw him to the ground. There were no injuries as a result of the brawl and no one was ejected, but Pedro received reams of bad press from the New York media. Coming back in game seven, Boston's ace held a commanding 5–2 lead after seven innings, but when he ran into trouble in the bottom of the eighth, manager Grady Little held a conference at the mound and decided to leave Pedro in the game after Pedro assured him he still had gas in his tank. But Pedro was wrong. New York rallied for three runs to tie the game, and went on to win it in 12 innings. The decision cost Little his job, but Pedro was back at the same old stand under new manager Terry Francona.

The 2004 season turned out to be a magical season for the Red Sox and their tortured fans. Boston broke out to a big lead early and held off a late Yankees charge to win their first American League Eastern Division title in ten years by three games. They raced through the Division Series, sending the Anaheim Angels home in three straight. Pedro won his start, 8–3, pitching seven innings. The ALCS was more challenging. Manager Joe Torre's cohorts opened a quick three-games-to-none lead, beating Boston's aces, Curt Schilling and Pedro Martinez, in the process. Pedro lost Game 2 by a 3–1 score. Francona's charges, on the brink of a humiliating sweep at the hands of their hated rivals, rallied from a 4–3 deficit in the bottom of the ninth inning against Yankees closer Mariano Rivera, thanks to Dave Roberts, whose baserunning skills tied the game, and the clutch hitting of David Ortiz, whose home run in the 12th inning won it. Pedro pitched six innings in Game 5, but got a no-decision in a game that Big Papi won with a walk-off single in the 14th. Boston went on to sweep the last two games of the series to advance to the World Series, where they met the St. Louis Cardinals. The Red Sox were in high gear now, and blew the Redbirds away in four straight. Pedro did his bit, pitching seven shutout innings in Game 3, fanning six and retiring the last 14 batters in a row, in a 4–1 Boston victory. Derek Lowe completed the sweep in Game 4, winning 3–0.

That was Pedro's swan song with the Red Sox. He filed for free agency at the end of the season and signed with the New York Mets. He pitched for the Philadelphia Phillies in 2009 but injuries slowed him down over the last four years. His career through 2009 produced a 219–100 won-loss record with a 2.93 ERA. He was an eight-time All-Star, a three-time Cy Young Award winner, and led the league in ERA five times, strikeouts three times, won-loss percentage twice, and victories, complete games, and shutouts once each. He won 117 games against 37 losses for a magnificent .760 winning percentage with a glittering 2.52 ERA during his seven-year stay in Boston. Pedro Martinez was always a fiery competitor who took no prisoners. He was a pitcher for the ages.

Matsuzaka, Daisuke

Daisuke Matsuzaka was a high school baseball star and a national hero at Yokohama High School after unleashing his 90 mph fastball at overmatched opponents. In the now-famous 1998 National High School Baseball Tournament called Summer Koshien, in which 4,102 high schools competed for the national championship, with 55 schools advancing to the finals in Koshien Stadium, "The Monster," as he was called, rose to the challenge. He pitched 36 innings in four games over a period of four days, winning four games without a defeat, with three complete games and two shutouts, one of which was a no-hitter. On August 19, Yokohama's ace pitcher and cleanup hitter tossed a 148-pitch shutout, and the next day, in the quarterfinals, "he pitched a 250-pitch, 17-inning game at age 17 for the victory. In the semi-finals he pitched one inning in relief and won again as his team rallied from a six-run deficit for a comeback victory. He then cemented his legend with a 3–0 no-hitter against Kyoto Seisho High School in the finale. He became the only high-schooler to go undefeated all year long, and he set a record for strikeouts with 208. He set a Koshien record with 14 K's in a game. He also led Japan to the world amateur championship title, getting the MVP award for the tournament."[110] The Seibu Lions drafted the precocious right-hander in 1999 for a 50-million yen signing bonus and a 13-million yen salary.

The husky, six-foot, 185-pound fireballer cruised through his rookie season in the Japan Pacific League, winning 16 games against five losses, with 151 strikeouts in 180 innings and a 2.60 earned run average. His performance was rewarded when he won the Rookie of the Year award and was voted to the Best Nine team as the best pitcher in the league. As noted on baseball-reference.com, "In his first match-up with Ichiro Suzuki, he struck out Ichiro in three consecutive at-bats."[111] Overall, in the two years Ichiro played against Matsuzaka in Japan before departing for America, Daisuke held Japan's greatest hitter to a .235 batting average with one home run and four RBI in 10 games. The Monster enjoyed a highly successful eight-year career in Japan, winning 108 games against 60 losses, with 60 complete games and 16 shutouts. He led the league in strikeouts four times, victories three times, ERA twice, and earned the coveted Sawamura Award as the league's best pitcher once. He also won seven Gold Gloves for his fielding ability. He left the Japan Pacific League in 2006 in a blaze of glory, posting a 17–5 record with a 2.13 ERA. That same year, he was named MVP of the first World Baseball Classic, running up a 3–0 record with a 1.30 ERA. He defeated Cuba in the finals, tossing four innings of one-run ball, and leaving with a 6–1 lead in a game eventually won by Japan, 10–6. The handsome right-hander became the property of the Boston Red Sox in 2007 after spirited bidding against the New York Yankees and Seattle Mariners. Boston paid the Lions $51.1 million for the rights to negotiate with Matsuzaka, eventually signing Japan's top pitcher to a six-year, $52 million contract on December 14.

Within days, or perhaps weeks of the signing, the new Boston ace was dubbed Dice-K by the Boston media and, armed with a 91–96 mph fastball, a slider, a changeup, a cutter, and a forkball, he made his major league debut with the Red Sox on April 5, 2007, facing the hapless Kansas City Royals in Kauffman Stadium, and whipping them 4–1 with a strong, seven-inning, ten-strikeout performance. Dice-K reportedly also had a mysterious pitch known as a "gyroball," but no such pitch has ever been identified. Like many rookies, the Japanese flamethrower had some growing pains during the season, but he recorded a fine 15–12 won-

Daisuke Matsuzaka

lost mark, pitching 204⅔ innings in 32 games and sending 201 batters back to the bench shaking their heads as the Red Sox raced to the American League East Division title. He pitched the pennant-clincher for Boston against the Minnesota Twins on September 28, yielding two runs over eight innings. He pitched one game in the ALDS with no record and finished the ALCS with a 1–1 mark. He started Game 3 of the ALCS against the Cleveland Indians in Jacobs Field and was touched up for four runs in 4⅔ innings, striking out six batters in a 4–2 defeat. He came back in Game 7 and was the winning pitcher in an 11–2 Boston victory. He pitched five innings with three strikeouts and no walks, leaving with a 3–2 lead, and Hideki Okajima and Jonathan Papelbon each tossed two innings of relief to wrap up the championship. When Boston met the Colorado Rockies in the World Series, Daisuke Matsuzaka had the honor of pitching Game 3 in Coors Field, and he was the winning pitcher in a 10–5 Red Sox rout, hurling 5⅓ innings and fanning five batters. He was replaced by Javier Lopez with two runners on base and one out in the sixth inning with the Red Sox holding a comfortable 6–0 lead, and Lopez allowed both runners to score. Boston had broken the game open with a six-run uprising in the top of the third inning while 49,983 dedicated Rockies fans could only suffer through the debacle. Jacoby Ellsbury ripped two doubles in the inning, one leading off the inning and the other to drive in the sixth run. Mike Lowell had a bases-loaded single and Dice-K knocked in two runs with a single of his own.

In 2008, the talented 28-year-old hurler had a career season, posting an outstanding 18–3 record with 154 strikeouts in 167⅔ innings and a 2.90 earned run average. Boston qualified for the playoffs as a wild-card entry, and had to face the powerful Los Angeles Angels in the ALDS. Dice-K started in Game 2, but had a no-decision in Boston's 7–5 victory. After disposing of the Angels in four games, Terry Francona's team met the East Division champions, the Tampa Bay Rays, in the ALCS, and Matsuzaka was picked to pitch the opener at Tropicana Field in St. Petersburg, Florida, on October 10. The hard-throwing right-hander responded to the challenge brilliantly, retiring 16 of 17 batters between the first and sixth innings, and shackling the Rays on four hits with nine strikeouts in his seven-inning effort, en route to a 2–0 Boston victory. Dice-K was handed the ball again in Game 5 with his team down three games to one, but he didn't have his "A" game with him on this day, and the Rays pounded him for five runs in four innings. The Red Sox, however, were not done. In the biggest comeback in post-season play in 79 years, Terry Francona's troops fought back from a 7–0 deficit to score eight runs over the last three innings, winning 8–7. Tampa Bay won the series in seven games.

Daisuke Matsuzaka missed most of the next three seasons with various arm and back miseries before resorting to Tommy John surgery in June 2011 to repair his ailing elbow. His combined record for 2009–2011 showed a 16–15 won-loss mark with 207 innings pitched in 45 games. The 31-year-old right-hander is hoping for a return to form in the 2013 season.

Mays, Carl

He is unfortunately best known as the man who killed Ray Chapman and not as a pitcher who won 208 games during a notable 15-year major league career. Mays, who threw underhand, pitched inside and Chapman, the Cleveland shortstop, always crowded the plate, a recipe for disaster. The disaster came on August 16, 1920, when a Mays delivery struck Chapman, who was leaning over the plate, in the head, dropping him like a load of bricks. He died 12 hours later without ever regaining consciousness. Mays, the ace of the New York Yankees staff, went on to finish the season with a 26–11 won-loss record.

Carl William Mays, a native of Liberty, Kentucky, began his professional baseball career with Boise in the Western Tri-State League, winning 22 games against nine losses with a 2.08 ERA. He was paid $90 a month for his efforts. He went 10–15 with Portland in the Northwest League the following year, and 24–8 with Providence in the International League in 1914. The Boston Red Sox, who had a working agreement with Providence, brought Mays up to the big club for the 1915 season. According to Rob Neyer and Bill James, "Carl slings the ball from his toes, has a weird looking windup, and in action looks like a cross between an octopus and a bowler. He shoots the ball in at the batter at such unexpected angles that his delivery is hard to find, until along about five o'clock, when the hitters get accustomed to it — and the game is about over."[112] Another baseball writer noted that Mays threw "with a submarine motion so pronounced that he sometimes scraped his knuckles on the ground while delivering the ball."[113]

Carl Mays pitched in 38 games for Bill Carrigan's crew in 1915, most of them out of the bullpen, winning six and losing five. Boston won the pennant by two-and-a-half games over the Detroit Tigers, but Mays didn't see any action in the World Series, won by Boston in five games. The next year, the five-foot, eleven-inch 195-pound right-hander won his stripes, appearing in 44 games with 24 starts and 14 complete games, while compiling a record of 18–13 with a 2.39 ERA. In the Fall Classic against the Brooklyn Robins, Mays lost Game 3, 4–3, but the Red Sox won in five. In 1917, Mays went 22–9 with a sparkling 1.74 ERA in 35 games covering 289 innings. Boston made it back to the winner's circle in 1918, edging Cleveland by two-and-a-half games in a season cut short by World War I. In the World Series against the Chicago Cubs, won by the Red Sox in six games, Carl Mays pitched two complete-game victories. He won Game 3 and the Game 6 clincher, both by 2–1 scores as he had the Cubs batters pounding the ball into the dirt inning after inning. In Game 6, he carried Boston's first run across the plate after walking to lead off the third inning.

The 27-year-old pitcher got off to a slow start in 1919, going 5–11 through July, when he was unceremoniously traded to the New York Yankees. According to *Deadball Stars of the American League*, Mays was "perhaps the most disliked player of his era. A noted head hunter even before the Chapman beaning, Mays refused to apologize for how he pitched. 'Any pitcher who permits a batter to dig in, is asking for trouble,' he once said. 'I never deliberately tried to hit anyone in my life. I throw close just to keep the hitters loose in there.'"[114] Carl Mays pitched for Boston from 1915 into 1919, winning 72 games against 51 losses with a brilliant 2.16 ERA. He was also a dangerous .268 career hitter and a solid defensive player with a dependable glove and quick reflexes.

McInnis, Stuffy

John Phalen "Stuffy" McInnis was one of the best-fielding first basemen of all time, in addition to being a career .300 batter. He was a contact hitter who rarely struck out while sending line drives to all sections of the ballpark, but he was also adept at executing a hit-and-run play or sacrificing a runner along. His 384 sacrifice hits are still number three all-time. McInnis grew up playing baseball in and around Boston and by the time he was a teenager in the Boston suburban leagues, his defensive prowess was already evident to the fans, and whose shouts of "that's the stuff, kid" whenever he made a sensational defensive play led to his nickname. The handsome, five-foot, nine-inch, 170-pound infielder joined the professional baseball ranks in 1908 with New Bedford in the Class-B New England League for $100 a month. Playing shortstop with New Bedford and Haverhill, he batted a cool .301 in 51 games, and his contract was immediately sold to Connie Mack of the Philadelphia Athletics, where he would spend the next nine years. His time with the A's was an exciting time for the New Englander as Mack's teams were the class of the league. The infield, consisting of McInnis, Eddie Collins, Jack Barry, and Frank "Home Run" Baker, all defensive specialists and all except Barry .300 hitters, soon became known as "The $100,000 Infield."

Stuffy McInnis made his major league debut in 1909 as a backup for the shortstop, Jack Barry, but by 1911, Connie Mack, realizing McInnis was not going to displace Barry anytime in the near future and noting McInnis' skill with the bat, converted him to a first baseman. The 20-year-old infielder set out to hone his skills. "During infield practice, he urged his teammates to throw the ball high, low, and wide to make him reach for them."[115] The result was the best-fielding first baseman in the major leagues. The right-handed hitter did not have outstanding power but his line drives to the alleys produced some key doubles and triples, and his excellent bat control made him an excellent hit-and-run man. McInnis stroked the ball at a better-than-.300 clip six times in the next seven years, with a high of .327 in 1912, but on January 10, 1918, Connie Mack traded his first baseman to the Boston Red Sox after a salary dispute. Unfortunately for McInnis, he joined Boston as the team was beginning its descent into mediocrity. But during his first year in a Red Sox uniform, they were still the cream of the crop. They won the American League pennant in a war-shortened season, and carried off the World Championship trophy as well. They disposed of their World Series opponent, the Chicago Cubs, in six games, although McInnis, who had hit .272 during the regular season and led the league in fielding with an average of .992, hit just .250 in the Series with two runs scored.

During McInnis' last three years in the Hub, the Red Sox finished sixth once and fifth twice. In 1919, as Boston slipped into the second division, Stuffy batted .305 and fielded .995. The following year, he hit .297 and once again led the league's first basemen with a fielding average of .996. He batted .307 in 1921 and struck out just nine times, the fewest strikeouts ever for any Red Sox player with more than 500 at-bats. The slick-fielding first baseman also set an American League record with a .999 fielding average, making only one error in 152 games. He set another record, handling 1625 chances without an error, from May 31, 1921, to June 2, 1922. But that was Stuffy McInnis' farewell to Boston fans. He was traded to the Cleveland Indians in December and played five more years in the major leagues, retiring after playing one game in 1927.

When Stuffy McInnis finally called it a day after 19 seasons, he left with a career .307 batting average and a reputation as one of the American League's finest defensive first basemen. His fielding average of .993 was five points above the league average and his range factor put him in the upper echelon of wide-ranging first basemen. "Wearing the small, rounded mitt of his day, Stuffy McInnis set still-standing fielding records for first baseman."[116] He led the American League in fielding average six times, double plays four times, putouts three times, and assists twice.

McNair, Eric

Donald Eric McNair was born in Meridian, Mississippi, on April 12, 1909, and began his professional baseball career with Meridian in the Class-D Cotton States League in 1928. The 19-year-old shortstop found Cotton States pitching to his liking, rattling the fences to the tune of a .317 average with 89 runs scored and 23 stolen bases in 123 games. He started the following year with Knoxville in the Class-B South Atlantic League, but after hammering opposing pitchers at a .391 clip in 91 games, he was moved up to Memphis in the Class-A Southern Association, where he continued his offensive pyrotechnics, batting .310 in 24 games. That was all Connie Mack needed to see, and the venerable owner of the Philadelphia Athletics purchased his contract and brought him to the City of Brotherly Love that September. The five-foot, eight-and-a-half-inch, 160-pound, right handed hitter made his major league debut on September 20 and punched out four base hits in eight at-bats over four games at the end of the season.

McNair, nicknamed Boob after a Rube Goldberg cartoon character named Boob McNutt, split the 1930 season between shortstop and third base, hitting .266 in 78 games. The following year, in 79 games, mostly at third base, the Mississippi native upped his average to .271, and in 1932 he had a career season. He compiled a solid .285 batting average with 18 homers, 95 runs batted in, and a league-leading 47 doubles, while holding down the shortstop job full-time. One spring day, when the A's were visiting Chicago, McNair, "Sugar" Cain, and several other players went out to view the choppy water on Lake Michigan. Cain said he would give $100 to anyone who would jump off the jetty into the lake. McNair, who didn't like Cain, jumped into the lake, quickly scrambled back to land, and ran to the hotel before he froze to death. He said he "paid the bellboy $2 to get my suit pressed and $1 to dry out and shine my shoes. Made $97 off old Sugar."[117] He played another three years for Connie Mack, batting between .261 and .280, and then fell victim to Mack's periodic housecleaning, being traded to the Boston Red Sox during the 1935 off-season.

The speedy little infielder played under Joe Cronin from 1936 through 1938, giving Red Sox fans tight infield defense and a timely bat. According to teammate Bill Werber, McNair was "good-natured, pleasant, and well liked, in addition to being a fine shortstop."[118] He batted

.285 for Boston in 1936, and followed that up with a .292 season where he hit 29 doubles and 12 home runs, driving in 76 runs in 126 games. After a torn ligament in his left knee sidelined him for all but 46 games in 1938, he was traded to the Chicago White Sox, where he hit a career-high .324, in what turned out to be his last full season in the major leagues. He retired in 1942 and died tragically in 1949 at the age of 35. Baseball historian Bill Nowlin called him the "little chap with dynamite in his powerful wrists."

Menosky, Mike

Michael William Menosky began his professional baseball career in the Federal League before catching on with the Washington Senators in 1916. Menosky spent most of the year with Minneapolis in the Double-A American Association, where he stroked the ball at a .267 clip, but he did manage to get into 11 games with Washington, batting .162 with six hits in 37 at-bats. The five-foot, ten-inch, 160-pound, left-handed hitter played left field for the fifth-place Senators in 1917, batting .258 in 322 at-bats. He quickly gained the reputation for being an all-out player who was known as "Leaping Mike" for his daring, fence-crashing catches. After spending the 1918 season in the U.S. Army in World War I, he hit .287 in 1919 and was then traded to the Boston Red Sox on January 20, 1920, joining a Boston team that had been decimated by owner Harry Frazee to satisfy his Broadway theatrical productions.

Mike Menosky was a good hitter on a bad team with good speed and power to the alleys, and he played left field with abandon over the next four years, producing some timely hits along the way. He played under three managers during his tenure in Boston, but nothing helped as the club finished fifth twice and eighth twice. He batted .297 in 1920, followed by a career-season in 1921, where he scorched the ball at a .300 clip with 60 bases on balls and a .388 on-base-percentage, while giving manager Hugh Duffy strong outfield defense. Menosky enjoyed some of his greatest days in a Red Sox uniform that year, including a Friday afternoon doubleheader on June 17 when he ripped five base hits in six at-bats, four for extra bases. In the opener, batting out of the second spot in the batting order against Pol Perritt of the Detroit Tigers, he thrilled the Fenway Park crowd by banging out three base hits in four at-bats, a single, double, and triple, with three runs scored, as Boston defeated Howard Ehmke in relief, 5–4, in ten innings. In the nightcap, he went two-for-two, with a triple, a home run, and two bases on balls, scoring four runs and driving in one in a 6–5 Boston triumph, also against Ehmke. In all, Menosky scored seven of Boston's 11 runs on the day. Two months later, on August 18, he went four-for-five with a double and two runs scored as Hugh Duffy's warriors took a 6–5, ten-inning decision from the Tigers in Briggs Stadium. On the 24th, the Red Sox dropped a hard-fought 12–11 decision to the St. Louis Browns in Sportsman's Park, but Menosky held up his end by pounding out four base hits in six at-bats, with a double, three runs scored, and two RBI.

After another solid season in 1922 where he batted .283, he slipped to .229 the following year and, at the age of 28, he hung up his glove for good. But before he retired, he participated in two historic games. On September 7, 1923, in Shibe Park, playing left field behind his new teammate Howard Ehmke, he had three putouts and one assist as Ehmke threw a 4–0 no-hitter at the A's, assisted by Lady Luck. "In the bottom of the sixth inning, Ehmke's masterpiece seemingly came to an abrupt end when (A's pitcher Slim) Harriss slammed a clean double to left-center. Slim, who stood 6–6 and weighed 180 pounds ran like a scared rabbit. But he neglected to touch first base when he darted straight as a whippet to second. Perched on that base, he surveyed the scene with all the might and ease of a conqueror until — much to Slim's embarrassment, umpire Red Ormsby ruled Harriss out," negating his base hit.[119] In the eighth inning, Frank Welch sent a line drive to left field that Menosky ran down but couldn't hold. It was originally called a hit but was later changed to an error, once again saving Ehmke's no-no. Four days later, Ehmke was on the mound again, this time in Yankee Stadium before a small gathering of 18,000 New Yorkers. There was another controversial call in this game, and this time Lady Luck deserted the Red Sox pitcher. "The first batter for the Yankees was Whitey Witt.... He hit a chopper down the third base line to Howard Shanks, a former outfielder who was playing third. The ball took an odd hop and Shanks muffled it against his chest. By the time he was ready to throw, he saw there was no chance to get Witt, so he didn't throw.[120] Official scorer Fred Lieb ruled the play a hit. The game was still scoreless for six innings but in the seventh Boston pushed across three runs, the first run scoring on a single by Ehmke, who went 3-for-4 in the game, and the last two runs coming across on a home run by Val Picinich. Ehmke lost his no-hitter but he still holds the American League record for the fewest hits allowed by a starting pitcher in two consecutive games — one.

Metkovich, George

He was a wartime replacement for Dominic DiMaggio, and he went on to enjoy a ten-year major league career before calling it a day. George Michael Metkovich, from Angel's Camp, California, signed a professional baseball contract with the Detroit Tigers as an amateur free agent after graduating from high school in 1939. He spent his first year in organized baseball with the Fulton Tigers in the Kitty League and had a rousing rookie season, stinging the ball at a .313 clip with 40 doubles, 10 triples, and 12 home runs, in 530 at-bats. Unfortunately his career cooled off after that debut. After being granted free agency in January, 1940, and subsequently signing with the Boston Bees, he played two years with Evansville in the Triple-I League and one year with Hartford in the Eastern League, with mixed results. It was about this time that he received the nickname Catfish from Bees manager Casey Stengel during spring training in 1943. Metkovich stepped on a catfish while trying to dislodge a hook from its mouth and a barbed fin cut into his foot, putting him out of action most of the spring, and causing the Bees to sell his contract to the San Francisco Seals of the Pacific Coast League for $5,000. He batted .325 in 71 games with the Seals, bringing about a trade to the Boston Red Sox, who had a void in their outfield after the recent losses of Dom DiMaggio and Ted Williams to military service in World War II.

Metkovich gave Boston some decent, though not exceptional, outfield play from 1943 through 1946. He played his first game for Joe Cronin's team on July 16, 1943, and went on to hit .246 in 78 games. The next year, the six-foot, one-and-a-half-inch, 180-pound, left-handed hitter upped his average to .277 with 45 extra base hits in 134 games for the fourth-place Red Sox and, at one point, he enjoyed a 25-game hitting streak. He tailed off to .260 in 1945 and on August 4 he struck out against Bert Shepard, a veteran of World War II and the only man ever to play in the major leagues with an artificial leg. His batting average further declined to .246 in 1946, but he did manage to pound out a double in two at-bats as a pinch hitter in the World Series before being sold to the Cleveland Indians on April 2, 1947.

Miller, Rick

Richard Alan "Rick" Miller was a valuable member of the Boston Red Sox team from 1971 through 1977 and again from 1981 through 1985. He was a sensational acrobatic defensive outfielder with a strong, accurate throwing arm who dazzled Fenway Park fans with his sliding catches. He was Boston's fourth outfielder from 1971 through 1977, filling in for such stalwart gardeners as Yastrzemski, Lynn, Rice, Evans, and Reggie Smith.

Miller, an All-American baseball player at Michigan State University, was drafted by the Boston Red Sox in 1969 and sent to their Double-A farm team in Pittsfield, Massachusetts, where he gave the Pittsfield team outstanding defensive play and hit a respectable .262 in 77 games. He rose rapidly through the Boston farm system on the strength of his strong defensive play, and made his major league debut as a pinch-runner on September 4, 1971, at the age of 23. In his first at-bat tow innings later, he faced Phil Hennigan of the Cleveland Indians. Miller admitted later, "I came in late in the game as a pinch hitter and I was really nervous." Hennigan's first pitch was a high fastball and Miller chased it, lining it to the opposite field off the Green Monster for a double. He went on to hit a cool .333 in 15 games at the end of the season. The Michigan native joined a team that already had an outfield of Carl Yastrzemski, Tony Conigliaro, and Reggie Smith, so he became the number one bench player, who was used primarily for late inning defensive purposes or to spell a player who needed a rest or who was injured. "I got great jumps, I knew how to play players, I would cheat, I knew the counts, I always moved on each pitch according to the count," he said, describing his forte as a defensive specialist in Fenway's tough center field. "Thurman Munson just hated me, because I would play him perfect. I took more hits away from him. He'd be all over me from the catcher's position when I came up to bat. I'd just step out and say, 'Are you done yet?'"[121]

During his 12-year, two-stint tour of duty with the Red Sox, Miller went to bat more than 400 times just twice. Still, he was a key member of the team. He was selected as the team's "Unsung Hero" twice, once in 1972 and again in 1981, the BoSox Club Man of the Year in 1974, and the Comeback Player of the Year in 1976. The lanky, six-foot, 180-pound, left-handed hitter was mainly a singles hitter, but he had a decent .346 on-base-percentage. During his first tour of duty in Boston, his batting average ranged from .194 to .283. After spending three years with the California Angels, during which time he won a Gold Glove, he returned to the Red Sox in 1981 and posted a solid .278 batting average in 1,155 at-bats, until his retirement in 1985. He said he was glad to return to Boston because it was an exciting place to play baseball. He also noted, "I'd like to be known as someone who gave everything all the time, and was a complete player who did every phase of the game well. I came in as a defensive specialist and left as an offensive specialist."[122]

He enjoyed two big offensive outbursts during his career that should be noted. On Sunday, July 7, 1974, in the first game of a doubleheader in Fenway Park against the Kansas City Royals, he went 5-for-5 with a double, a home run, three runs scored, and five RBI in an 11–9 defeat. His sixth-inning grand-slam homer had given Darrell Johnson's team a brief 8–5 lead, but the bullpen gave the lead away two innings later. He had an equally impressive game on May 11, 1981, pounding out five base hits in five at-bats against the Toronto Blue Jays in Exhibition Stadium. His hits included four doubles, tying a major league record, and after his last double in the ninth inning he came around to score the winning run in a 7–6 Red Sox victory.

Mirabelli, Doug

Doug Mirabelli, a light-hitting catcher with a knack for catching the elusive butterfly pitches of Tim Wakefield, carved out a seven-year career for himself in Boston as Wakefield's personal catcher, first from 2002 through 2005 and then, after a 14-game hiatus in San Diego in 2006, the rest of that year and all of 2007. He also caught Wakefield in the 2007 ALCS, going 0-for-2 at the plate.

Douglas Anthony Mirabelli was born in Kingman, Arizona, on October 18, 1970, and attended Wichita State University, where he starred in baseball. The three-time All-American scorched the ball at a .341 clip over the three-year period with 30 home runs and 190 runs batted in, in 198 games. He was also a member of the Shockers' 1990 National Championship team. He was signed by the San Francisco Giants after graduation from Wichita State in 1992 and was sent to their farm club at San Jose in the California League for seasoning, where he hit a lowly .232 in 53 games. He played for six teams over the next three years, working his way through the Giants' farm system and trying to get his bat untracked. The six-foot, one-inch, 220-pound backstop made his major league debut with San Francisco on August 27, 1996, going 0-for-1 in a 3–2 loss to the Philadelphia Phillies. He finished the year batting .222 in nine games. From 1996 through 1999, Mirabelli was on a merry-go-round between San Francisco and both Phoenix and Fresno in the Pacific Coast League, fine-tuning his defensive skills and trying unsuccessfully to master major league pitching. The lumbering right-handed hitter was a solid Triple-A hitter with good power, but he was overmatched at the major league level. After hitting just .230 with the Giants in 2000, he was sold to the Texas Rangers in 2001 and eventually found his way to the Hub, being traded to the Red Sox on June 12, 2001.

Doug Mirabelli batted .270 for Boston after the trade, with nine homers in 141 at-bats, and earned his stripes by demonstrating his ability to catch the dancing pitches of Tim Wakefield. He caught 201 games for Boston between 2002 and 2005, giving the team outstanding defense while slamming 28 home runs and driving in 93 runs in 610 at-bats, although his batting averages fluctuated widely between .225 and .281. He was traded to the San Diego Padres on December 7, 2005, but, when his replacement in Boston had serious problems handling Wakefield's deliveries, Boston was able to reacquire the big catcher on May 1, 2006, giving Wakefield his first relaxing night's sleep in months. Mirabelli's second tour of duty with Boston lasted less than two years. He was released prior to the 2008 season, ending his major league career.

Monbouquette, Bill

"Monbo," as he was called, was a durable pitcher who had a good fastball and a devastating slider that enabled him to start 30 or more games, and pitch more than 200 innings, for six straight years."[123] The husky five-foot, eleven-inch, 195-pound, right-handed pitcher was signed to a professional baseball contract with his hometown team, the Boston Red Sox, for a $4,000 bonus after his graduation from high school in 1954.

Monbo was a finesse pitcher who relied on changing speeds and pitching to spots to keep enemy batters off-balance, but it took him a couple of years in the minor leagues to get untracked. After three more years in the bushes, he was called up to the Red Sox in July, 1958, and made his major league debut in a night game against the Detroit Tigers in the friendly confines of Fenway Park on July 18. But Fenway Park was anything but friendly to Monbo as he was raked for five runs, three of them earned, in five innings in a game eventually won by Boston, 11–9. Detroit scored two runs out of the gate on a walk, an error, and a single, and to add insult to injury, Billy Martin stole home against him. In the third, Bill Norman's team pushed across three more runs on two singles, two doubles, and a wild pitch. Two-and-a-half weeks later, Monbo recorded his first major league victory, a complete-game, seven-hit effort before a Tuesday night gathering of 23,030 screaming Fenway fans. Pinky Higgins' Back Bay Bombers scored four runs in the third inning to make Monbo's job easier, with three of them scoring on a Jimmy Piersall fly ball into the left field screen. They added single runs in the sixth, seventh, and eighth innings, for a final score of 7–1. The 21-year-old kid from Medford

Bill Monbouquette

finished his rookie season with a 3–4 won-lost mark and a decent 3.31 ERA in 54⅓ innings pitched over ten games. The following year, he appeared in 32 games, with 13 starts and two complete games, going 7–7 with a 4.15 ERA.

By 1960, Monbouquette had become the ace of Pinky Higgins' staff, and he was more than up to the task, posting a 14–11 record with a 3.64 ERA in 36 games pitched with 30 starts, for a seventh-place team that won only 65 games and lost 89 during the season. He also started the first All-Star Game that year, but was roughed up by the National League sluggers who took him downtown twice and sent four runners across the plate in his two innings on the mound, pinning him with the 5–3 loss. His best day on the mound was May 7, when he stopped the Detroit Tigers on one hit in Fenway Park, winning his third game against two losses, by a 5–0 count. There was no suspense in the game regarding a possible no-hitter since the only hit was a one-out double to left field by Neil Chrisley in the first inning. Monbo walked two men in the game and retired the last 11 men he faced. Boston gave its pitcher a three-run cushion in the second inning, two of them coming on a single by Frank Malzone. Vic Wertz homered for the BoSox in the seventh inning, and Malzone drove in another run with a double in the eighth.

Bill Monbouquette went 14–14 for a sixth-place team in 1961, starting 32 games with 12 complete games and a 3.39 ERA. The cagey right-hander fanned 161 men but had some trouble with his control, walking 100 batters in 236⅓ innings. He didn't have any trouble with his control on May 12, however, when he beat the Washington Senators in Griffith Stadium, 2–1 with a five-hitter. He sent 17 Washington batters back to the bench on strikes while issuing four walks. The Red Sox scored what proved to be the winning run in the top of the seventh inning on a bases-loaded walk to Monbouquette himself. The next year, with his pinpoint control operating on all cylinders once again, he walked only 65 men in 235⅓ innings, while recording a fine 15–13 won-lost mark for a team that won 76 games while losing 84. The Red Sox ace struggled early in the season, compiling an 8–10 record through July, but he was still in the starting rotation as the team moved into Chicago for a short two-game series against Al Lopez's tough Go-Go White Sox. As manager Pinky Higgins explained, "Monbo had been a disaster in his last four starts, no wins, 19 hits and 17 runs in 11 innings. But when your team is in eighth place with a record of 46–56, you don't have too many options. Besides, somebody has to start the game."[124] Monbo not only started the August 1 game, he finished it and tossed a masterpiece, a 1–0 no-hitter against Chicago's cagey veteran, 42-year-old Early Wynn, as 17,185 White Sox rooters sat glued to their seats, quietly hoping for a miracle. Monbouquette fanned seven men and walked only one, retiring the last 22 batters in succession. The Red Sox scored the only run of the game with two men out in the eighth inning on consecutive singles by Jim Pagliaroni, Pete Runnels, and Lou Clinton. The only close play of the game for Monbo occurred in the second inning when, with one out, Charlie Maxwell sent a screamer into the right field corner, ticketed for four bases, but Lou Clinton raced back to the 360-foot mark and made a sensational leaping catch against the fence to take a home run away from the Tigers left fielder.

The 1963 season was Monbo's best. He went 20–10 in 36 starts with 13 complete games, and a 3.81 ERA in 266⅔ innings pitched. The next year, pitching for another poor Red Sox representative that finished eighth in a ten-team league, he was 13–14 with a 4.04 ERA, but he did have another gem to put in his scrapbook. On September 6, he threw his second one-hitter, this time against the Minnesota Twins in Metropolitan Stadium but, to no one's surprise, he lost the game, 2–1 on a sixth inning error followed by a two-run homer by Zorro Versalles. In 1965, he won 10 games and lost 18 with a 3.70 ERA for Billy Herman's pitiful ninth-place club that finished the season with a mark of 62–100. Bill Monboquette's Boston career ended that year as he was traded to the Detroit Tigers in the off-season. The four-time all-star pitched three more years in the major leagues before retiring in 1968 at the age of 31. His Boston statistics from 1958 through 1965 included 254 games pitched with 228 starts, 72 complete games, and a 96–91 won-lost record.

Montgomery, Bob

Robert Edward Montgomery was born in Nashville, Tennessee, on April 16, 1944. He signed with the Boston Red Sox out of high school in 1962 and was assigned to their Olean farm club in the New York-Pennsylvania League, where he played outfield and third base and batted .273 in 46 games. Over the next eight years, Monty made the rounds of the Boston farm system, playing in no fewer than five leagues, including five years in Triple-A ball where settled in as catcher for Toronto and Louisville in the International League.

After ripping the ball at a .324 clip for the Louisville Colonels in 1970, with 30 doubles, 14 home runs, and 89 runs batted in, in 131 games, the 26-year-old receiver was finally recalled to Boston to back up the incumbent, who was, from 1972 to 1978, Carlton Fisk. He never escaped the backup role due to his weak bat, but he spent his entire ten-year major league career with the Red Sox, giving them reliable backstopping and occasional power. As he said, "When I catch a game, I don't worry about hitting too much. I'm like a blind hog in a cornfield up at the plate; I just swing and that's it. If I get a hit and drive in a run, fine. But my main job is helping the pitcher."[125] The six-foot, one-inch, 203-pound, right-handed batter usually hit in the low .200's, but three times he put it all together and batted over .300. In 1973, he stroked the ball at a .320 clip in 128 at-bats, with seven home runs and 25 RBI. Four years later, he hit an even .300 in 40 at-bats, and in 1979 he hit .349 in 86 at-bats covering 32 games. He played his last game in the major leagues on September 5, before 34,419 of the Fenway Faithful, going 1-for-2 with a run scored as the Baltimore Orioles were in the process of demolishing the pride of Boston by a 16–4 count. Montgomery also had the distinction of being the last major league player to bat without a batting helmet.

Mueller, Bill

William Richard Mueller was drafted by the San Francisco Giants in 1993 and made his professional debut with the Everett Giants in the Class-A Northwest League that summer, playing second base and shortstop and stroking the ball at a .300 clip with 11 extra-base hits in 200 at-bats. The five-foot, eleven-inch, 175-pound switch-hitter was primarily a singles hitter, but he showed some power on occasion, and he was a contact hitter who sprayed the ball to all fields from either side of the plate. He worked his way through the Giants' minor league system over the next three years, with way stops in San Jose, Shreveport, and Phoenix, hitting at a .300-plus pace in each location.

He spent part of the 1996 season with San Francisco, making his debut with the team as a pinch-hitter on April 18. The next day, also as a substitute, he got his first major league base hit against the Chicago Cubs. Mueller played 106 games with Phoenix that year, batting .302, and 55 games with San Francisco, where he showed a .330 batting average in 200 at-bats. That performance made Bill Mueller a major leaguer for good. He spent four more years with the Giants, holding down third base and hitting between .268 and .294. Jackie Krentzman, in the "Giants Magazine," paid Mueller the ultimate compliment in 1998 when he wrote, "this small, nondescript 26-year-old has earned one label, and it's quite an exclusive one, Ballplayer."

Bill Mueller was traded to the Chicago Cubs after the 2000 season, was traded back to San Francisco late in 2002, and filed for free agency on October 28 of that year. He was signed by the Boston Red Sox as a free agent to a two-year $4.5 million contract on January 14, 2003, and he helped them into the post-season playoffs for the first time in four years. The smooth-swinging switch-hitter was a major contributor to Boston's offensive pyrotechnics that produced a league-leading 961 runs scored, and he even walked off with the American League batting championship, caressing the ball to the tune of a .326 average. Mueller also showed surprising power in 2003 with 45 doubles, 19 home runs, 85 runs scored, and 85 RBI in 146 games. During the season, he had several game highlights, in particular the games of July 4 and July 29. On the Fourth of July against the New York Yankees in Yankee Stadium, all the fireworks belonged to Terry Francona's Back Bay Bombers. They blasted the New Yorkers by a 10–3 count with Bill Mueller chipping in with two home runs, three bases on balls, three runs scored, and two RBI. On the 29th, the Red Sox took the Texas Rangers to task at the Ballpark in Arlington, 14–7. Mueller became the first player in major league history to hit two grand-slam homers from opposite sides of the plate in the same game. He hit three round-trippers in all, and drove in nine runs to pace the Boston attack. He homered into the upper atmosphere leading off the third inning for Boston's first run of the game, launched a grand slam to left field off southpaw Aaron Fultz during a seven-run Red Sox uprising in the seventh that wiped out a 4–2 Rangers lead, and followed that with another grand slam, this one from the left side of the plate, in the eighth inning off hard-throwing Jay Powell. The Boston hitting machine also had 13 three-hit games during the season. The Red Sox finished the season in second place in the American League Eastern Division, six games behind the Yankees, but they qualified as the wild-card entry in the post-season playoffs. They won the Division Series against the Oakland Athletics in five games, but dropped a painful Championship Series to New York when Aaron Boone sent a Tim Wakefield pitch into the left field stands in the 11th inning, sending the Francona boys into a fit of depression. Mueller's bat was quiet throughout the playoffs as he hit just .174.

The year 2004 was a different story. The team was dedicated to seeking revenge from day one, and they got it, but it wasn't easy. In an early-season preview of what was to come, they took three out of four games from the mighty Yankees in the friendly confines of Fenway Park by scores of 6–2, 5–2, 3–7, and 5–4. They got excellent pitching from Wakefield and Schilling and timely hitting from Bill Mueller, who went 8-for-15 for a .533 average with a homer, three RBI, and four runs scored. The man who was considered to be the consummate professional by his teammates came to their rescue on July 8 at home against the Oakland Athletics. Francona's cohorts had opened up a 7–1 lead after five innings but the bullpen couldn't hold it and the game was deadlocked at seven-all after nine-and-a-half innings. In the bottom of the tenth with two men out, Johnny Damon lashed a single to left field and Mueller sliced a two-base hit down the line, scoring the fleet-footed Damon all the way from first. But by July 23, the Red Sox locomotive had run out of steam and was languishing in second place, nine-and-a-half games behind the high-flying Yankees. They had lost the first game of a three-game series in Fenway Park to New York by an 8–7 score and were trailing 3–0 in the third inning of the second game when the famous Varitek-A Rod confrontation seemed to light a fire under the lethargic Bostonians. The Red Sox fought back in what was considered to be the turning point of their season, and won the game in the bottom of the ninth inning when Bill Mueller, known alternately as "The Pro" and "Billy Ballgame," lifted a 3–1 pitch from All-World closer Mariano Rivera high into the Boston evening sky for a game-winning two-run home run. From there, it was onwards and upwards for Terry Francona's troops. They made a valiant run at the Yankees down the stretch, but came up three games short. Still, they qualified once again for the post-season, and this time they went all the way. First, they swept the Anaheim Angels three straight in the ALDS, earning the right to meet the Yankees again in the American League Championship Series. New York jumped out to a quick three games to none lead in the series before the Red Sox woke up. But when they did wake up, it was all over. They swept the final four games against Joe Torre's team and then swept the St. Louis Cardinals four straight in the World Series to claim their first World Championship in 86 years. Bill Mueller played a big part in the triumph, batting .333 in the ALDS, .267 in the ALCS, and a hefty .429 in the World Series, and he had perhaps the key hit of the entire post-season when, in the ALCS, he took a Mariano Rivera pitch back up the middle in the ninth inning of Game 4 to drive in the tying run, setting the tone for Boston's ultimate triumph.

The hard-working third baseman played one more year with the Red Sox, batting .295 in 150 games, leaving for free agency at the end of the 2005 season. He played just 32 games with the Los Angeles Dodgers before a knee injury ended his career. When all was said and done, Bill Mueller "was a ballplayer who never brought attention to himself. He was a classy player who played the game the right way. He was quiet in the clubhouse, and a very religious family man from Missouri."[126]

Myer, Buddy

Buddy Myer was, according to teammate Bill Werber, "one of the finest bunters ever to play, and as a left-handed hitter, he was particularly adept at dragging the ball for a base hit. He is said to have beaten out 60 bunts one season."[127] He was also an intense and combative competitor who was involved in a number of fights during his career, including one with his good friend Werber. That happened when Myer spiked Werber sliding into third base. Werber took offense at Myer's slide, a bench-clearing brawl ensued, and Werber had to have six stitches to close the wound in his arm. The 163-pound infielder was also involved in another fight that has been called the most violent on-field brawl of the twentieth century. The defending World Champion New York Yankees invaded Griffith Stadium on April 25, 1933 to do battle with the upstart Washington Senators. After starting the season 7–0, the Bronx Bombers were humbled in the first two games of the series by scores of 5–4 and 11–10 and came into game three with fire in their eyes. In the fourth inning of an eventual 16–0 New York blowout, Ben Chapman, a 190-pound outfielder and a notorious racist, slid hard into Washington's Jewish second baseman and slit his leg open. Myer got to his feet, kicked Chapman in the back, Chapman threw a couple of anti-semitic comments Myer's way, fists flew, and the brawl was on. The two combatants were eventually separated and were ejected from the game. But as noted in *The Baseball Page*, "Chapman, who had to walk through the Senators bench, suddenly pounced on Washington pitcher Earl Whitehill — knocking him out with his fists. Senators climbed onto the Yankee outfielder as teammates fought to Chapman's rescue. While the brawl continued in the dugout, Yankee Dixie Walker became embroiled in a dispute with Senator fans who had scaled the low barriers next to the dugout, grabbed bats, and joined the fray. Bill Dickey, Tony Lazzeri, and Lefty Gomez came to Walker's rescue, battling their way through the spectators."[128] After 20 bloody minutes order was restored and the field was cleared. Three players were injured in the fracas, five fans were arrested, and Myer, Chapman, and Walker were suspended for five games and fined $100 each.

Charles Solomon Myer was born in Ellisville, Mississippi, on March 16, 1904, and joined New Orleans in the Class-A Southern Association in 1925. Owner Clark Griffith of the Washington Senators was so impressed with the youngster, who was hitting .336 for New Orleans, that he brought him up to the big show at the end of the season. The next year he was Washington's first-string shortstop and he rewarded the Senators for their faith in him by hitting .304 with ten stolen bases and 62 runs batted in, in 132 games. Griffith, in what he later called the dumbest deal he ever made, traded Myer to the Boston Red Sox on May 2, 1927, with Myer battling through a 15-game, .216 slump.

The 23-year-old infielder played for the Red Sox for two years, showcasing his skills, both with his bat and his glove. He held down the shortstop job for Bill Carrigan's team in 1927, then moved to third base in 1928 where he outfielded his peers by 16 points. The left-handed hitter batted .288 after the trade, with 22 doubles and 11 triples in 469 at-bats. The following year, he stroked the ball at a .313 clip while leading the league with 30 stolen bases. Surprisingly, Boston traded Myer back to Washington for five players on December 15, 1928. He went on to have an outstanding career at second base with the Senators over the ensuing 13 years. The career .303 hitter won the batting title in 1935, going 4-for-5 in the last game of the season to finish at .349, edging Cleveland's Joe Vosmik, who sat out the game thinking he had the championship won.

Naehring, Tim

Timothy James Naehring, out of Cincinnati, Ohio, was a star-crossed third baseman for the Boston Red Sox from 1990 through 1997. After signing a free-agent contract with the organization in 1988 and making his way through Boston's farm system over the next three years, the six-foot, two-inch, 205-pound, right-handed hitter flexed his muscles in Pawtucket in the Triple-A International League in 1990, slugging 15 homers in 82 games and playing solid defense, bringing about his recall to Boston to fill a hole at shortstop.

Naehring made his major league debut as a defensive replacement on July 15. The following night he started at shortstop against Minnesota but went hitless in four at-bats with three strikeouts, and he also committed an error. But he more than made up for it on the 17th when his first major league base hit, a sharp single to center field, drove in the only run of the game in the fifth inning. Later in the game he doubled to left field but was erased when Jody Reed grounded into a fast triple play, third to second the first. In 1991, Naehring played just 24 games before he was shut down after hitting a barely visible .109 that included an 0-for-39 run. Leg and back problems slowed his progress and held him to a .231 average in 72 games in 1992 before the root cause of his problem was discovered — one of his legs was shorter than the other leg. After he was fitted with a platform to adjust for the imbalance, he went on to have the best season of his career in 1993, hitting .331 in 39 games for Butch Hobson's team. Having been displaced by John Valentin at shortstop, Naehring served in a utility role for two years before moving to third base to replace Scott Cooper, who had been traded to St. Louis. He and Mo Vaughn teamed up to have a day to remember against the Oakland Athletics in a Fenway Park afternoon game on April 19, 1994, before 21,745 loyal Sox rooters. The two men hit back-to-back home runs off A's starter Bob Welch in the second inning and repeated the feat off Carlos Reyes in the sixth inning. In all, Naehring enjoyed a 4-for-4 day with three RBI and three runs scored. His two best years in a Red Sox uniform were 1995 and 1996, the only two years where he was able to play in more than 100 games in a season. He played a solid third base for Kevin Kennedy in 1995, displaying a good glove with excellent range and batting .307 with 27 doubles and ten home runs in 126 games. In the ALDS, won by Cleveland over the Red Sox in three games, Naehring batted .308 with four hits in 13 at-bats and fielded flawlessly. His home run in the 11th inning of Game 1 gave his team a 4–3 lead, but the bullpen couldn't hold it and the Indians won the game 5–4 in 13 innings. Naehring played 116 games in 1996, batting .288 with 17 home runs and once again providing strong defense at the hot corner. But that was the end of the road for the 30-year-old infielder. He hit .286, hit nine home runs, and was a sensation in the field in 70 games in 1997, before elbow problems sent him to the sidelines. But he went out in a blaze of glory. On May 22 in Yankee Stadium, before a modest weekday crowd of 28,255, he went 4-for-6 with a double as Boston embarrassed Joe Torre's proud Bombers by an 8–2 count. A month later, on June 23, playing against the Toronto Blue Jays in the Sky Dome, he ripped three base hits in five at-bats, including a seventh-inning home run that proved to be the difference in a 7–6 Red Sox victory. He never played another major league game.

Tim Naehring played his entire major league career with the Boston Red Sox, but injuries that put him on the disabled list six times in eight years prevented him from realizing a long, memorable career. Naehring left a career batting average of .282 in 1,872 at-bats. He also gave Boston outstanding defense at third base with exceptional range and a .962 fielding average, nine points higher than the league average.

Newsome, Skeeter

"Skeeter" Newsome, so nicknamed because he was small, fast, and an irritant to opposing players, fashioned a 12-year major league career for himself with a modicum of talent and an excess of desire and effort. The five-foot, nine-inch, 170-pound infielder from Phenix City, Alabama, began his professional baseball career with Talladega in the Class-D Georgia-Florida League as a shortstop in 1930 and batted a respectable .284 in 83 games. He roamed minor league clubhouses for another three years, working his way through the Class-B leagues to A-ball, the highest rated league at the time, and up to the majors. His batting averages ranged from a low of .250 with Decatur in the Class-B Three-I League to a high of .286 with Tulsa in the Single-A Texas League.

The Philadelphia Athletics rescued him from the bushes in 1935, giving him a considerable amount of playing time at shortstop as well as at second base and third base. He hit a mediocre .207 in his rookie season, playing in 59 games, but the following year, playing 127 games at shortstop, the Alabama native, in addition to giving Connie Mack's club sensational defense at shortstop, increased his average to .225 while striking out only 27 times in 471 at-bats. Newsome upped his average to .253 in 122 games in 1937 but just when it looked like he had found a regular position he was hit in the head with a pitched ball in a spring training exhibition game against Portsmouth of the Piedmont League and played in just 17 games during the season. He played 99 games for Philadelphia in 1939 but was farmed out to the Baltimore Orioles of the International League the next year.

The 28-year-old infielder was traded to the Boston Red Sox after the season ended, and he spent the next five years in the Hub, playing shortstop or second base, as needed. He spelled the 35-year-old Joe Cronin at shortstop in 1941, was relegated to a utility role in 1942 with the arrival of Johnny Pesky, replaced Pesky, who was drafted into military service in World War II, in 1943 and 1944, and filled in for the departed Bobby Doerr at second base in 1945, handling both positions with equal skill and dexterity. Johnny Pesky once called him "a veteran player and a wonderful little guy." He was a wonderful little guy except when it came to striking out. Skeeter took pride in making contact with the ball and he was embarrassed when he struck out. One day, after he was called out on strikes by umpire Bill McGowan, he let the umpire know what he thought of the call. "I'll bet you wouldn't have called Joe D. out on that pitch," he said to which McGowan replied, "You're right, I wouldn't have called Joe out on that pitch because he would have hit it up next to the 457 foot sign in left-center field." The scrappy little infielder subsequently became part of Red Sox lore in 1945 when he slapped a base hit down the right field line in Fenway Park and tried to stretch it into a double. Philadelphia right fielder Hal Peck ran the ball down and uncorked a throw in the direction of second base. As fate would have it, the ball struck a low-flying pigeon and deflected right to second baseman Irv Hall, who laid the tag on a sliding Newsome. The pigeon flew away unharmed, but reportedly demanded an assist on the play. With both Pesky and Doerr returning from the war, Newsome was sold to the Philadelphia Phillies on December 12, 1945. He played two years with the Phillies before retiring in 1947 at the age of 37. Skeeter Newsome's Boston sojourn included terrific defense with a fielding average that was 16 points better than the league average. He batted .260 in 497 games with the Red Sox, and he also moved countless base runners along with deftly placed sacrifice hits, finishing in the top five in sacrifices in three of his five years in Boston.

Nixon, Russ

Russell Eugene Nixon was born in Cleves, Ohio, on February 19, 1935. The husky backstop was signed to a free agent baseball contract by the Cleveland Indians in 1953 and was assigned to their farm team in Green Bay in the Class-D Wisconsin State League, where he received his baptism of fire in professional baseball, and came away unscathed with a batting average of .336. The following year, with Jacksonville Beach in the Class-D Florida State League, he slammed 11 triples in 465 at-bats, led the league with 36 doubles, and captured the batting championship with an average of .387. He won another batting title in 1955, ripping Class-B Triple-I League pitching for a .385 average while playing with Keokuk. That performance brought him a promotion to the Indians' top minor league team, the Indianapolis Indians of the American Association. The six-foot, one-inch, 195-pound, left-handed hitter stroked the ball at a solid .319 clip for Indianapolis, ending his minor league seasoning.

Russ Nixon joined the Cleveland Indians in 1957, backing up the veteran Jim Hegan, and when Hegan was traded to the Detroit Tigers the following year, the 23-year-old Nixon became the Indians' first-string catcher. After batting .281 in 62 games in his rookie season in the big leagues, Nixon stung the ball at a robust .301 pace in 113 games in 1958, but that would be his high-water mark for batting average and games played in a season, as well as for runs scored, base hits, home runs, and RBI. Injuries reduced his playing time to 82 games in 1959 and he was traded to the Boston Red Sox to replace the veteran Sammy White on June 13, 1960, after playing in just 25 games for Cleveland.

The big catcher shared catching responsibilities with Jim Pagliaroni in Boston from 1960 to 1962, hitting .298 in 80 games in 1960, .289 in 87 games in 1961, and .278 in 65 games the following year. He was behind the plate on October 1, 1961, when Roger Maris, batting in the fourth inning with one out, deposited a Tracy Stallard pitch ten rows deep in the right field stands at Yankee Stadium for his 61st home run of the season, breaking Babe Ruth's long-held record of 60 home runs. Nixon was 2-for-3 with a triple in the game, but the Sox were blanked by Bill Stafford, losing 1–0. From 1963 through 1965, he served as backup catcher to Bob Tillman, appearing in 238 games over that period with batting averages between .233 and .270. He was traded to the Minnesota Twins on April 6, 1966, and spent two years in the Twin Cities before returning to Boston in 1968. He hit just .153 in 29 games for Dick Williams' team before retiring.

Russ Nixon played in 524 games for Boston in two tours of duty, batting .268 in 1,337 at-bats. He holds one ignominious record. He failed to steal a base during his major league career, in seven attempts, establishing a record for the most games played (906) without a stolen base.

Nixon, Trot

Trot Nixon coined the phrase "Dirt Dog" in 2001 and epitomized that description during his stay in Beantown. On the field, he often resembled a grubby street person with stubble on his face, wearing a dirty uniform and a filthy hat. One source noted, "The combination of perspiration, rotted tobacco, bacteria, and some other toxins from playing a series in Yankee Stadium has brought Trot's hat to a dangerously high level of filth." Manager Terry Francona just smiled when he heard the comments about Trot's appearance, saying, "He might look like Pigpen from the Charlie Brown cartoons, but I love Trot. Man, that's some beautiful filth there."[129] In addition to his appearance, Nixon also had a reputation for being a hard-nosed, fiery player who hustled from the first pitch to the last, and was a vocal leader in the dugout.

Christopher Trotman Nixon was drafted by the Boston Red Sox in the first round of the 1993 amateur draft and made his major league debut three years later when the Sox brought him up for a cup of coffee. He was used as a pinch runner on September 21, 1996, and started the last game of the season, a 6–5 win over the New York Yankees. He went 2-for-4 with a double and scored two runs, including the tying run in the sixth inning. The six-foot, two-inch, 195-pound, left-handed hitter spent the next two years with Pawtucket in the International League refining his talents, returning to Boston to stay at the end of the 1998 season.

Trot Nixon settled in as Boston's full-time right fielder in 1999, replacing Darren Bragg, who was released during the off-season, and he quickly established himself as one of the best right fielders in the American League. He became an expert at tracking down balls in Fenway Park's quaint right field corner, and his rifle-like throwing arm, typical of a former quarterback, kept baserunners glued to their bases. Nixon's rookie season at the plate was an adventure as he got off to a slow start, hitting a weak .105 in April, but manager Jimy Williams stuck with him and he came on strong down the stretch, finishing the year with a respectable .270 batting average with 15 home runs and 52 runs batted in, in 381 at-bats. His most satisfying day of the year was July 24, when he smashed three home runs with five RBI against the Detroit Tigers in Tiger Stadium, as the Red Sox routed the Bengals by an 11–4 count. His first home run was a three-run shot into the friendly right field stands off right-hander Jeff Weaver in the second inning that gave Boston a 4–1 lead. He homered again off Weaver in the fourth inning, and put number three into orbit in the eighth inning with Willie Blair on the hill.

Nixon spent a month on the disabled list in 2000 but still played in 123 games, batting .276 in 427 at-bats. The following year, he celebrated his good health with a .280 batting average in 535 at-bats, with 100 runs scored, 31 doubles, 27 home runs, 88 runs batted in, and a .505 slugging average. Trot Nixon had his best year in the majors in 2003 when he stroked the ball at a crisp .306 pace with 24 doubles, 28 home runs, 87 RBI, and a .578 slugging average in 134 games. In Game 3 of the ALDS against the Oakland Athletics, he thrilled the 35,460 Fenway fanatics who crammed the little park along Yawkey Way to cheer for their heroes, by slamming a pinch-hit, two-run, walk-off homer in the bottom of the eleventh inning to give Boston a hard-fought 3–1 victory.

Boston's original Dirt Dog suffered from a herniated disc during much of the team's march to the American League pennant in 2004, appearing in only 48 games with 149 at-bats and a .315 batting average, but he was healthy in time to play in all three of the post-season series and he punished the ball to the tune of a .357 average with three doubles and three RBI in Boston's four-game sweep of the St. Louis Cardinals in the World Series. His two-run double in the third inning of Game 4, one of his three doubles in the game, paced the Sox to a 3–0 World Championship victory. The game, played in Busch Stadium before 52,037 strangely silent Cardinal fans, was played under a full lunar eclipse, but that didn't deter Derek Lowe, who blanked the Redbirds on three hits for seven innings, becoming the first pitcher to be the winning pitcher in all three post-season series.

The husky right fielder played two more injury-filled years with Boston, batting .275 and .268 in 124 and 114 games respectively. He filed for free agency after the 2006 season and signed with the Cleveland Indians on January 19,

2007. During his time in Boston Trot Nixon was known as a guy who hustled on every play. As noted in the "Red Sox Fan Handbook," he was popular with fans, both because he was a gutty player who helped give birth to the "dirt-dog" notion and because he developed something of a "Yankee-killer" reputation. He was also seen as a stabilizing influence in the clubhouse.[130] Nixon played with the Red Sox from 1996 through 2006, appearing in 982 games with 912 base hits in 3,285 at-bats for a .278 batting average with a .366 on-base percentage, and a .478 slugging average.

Offerman, Jose

He was another of the outstanding shortstops to emerge from San Pedro de Macoris, a city of 20,000 people in the Dominican Republic. At one point during the 1980's, six of the 26 major league shortstops were born there, prompting the city to post a sign advertising itself as "the birthplace of shortstops." Jose Antonio Offerman was plucked from the dusty streets of his hometown by the Los Angeles Dodgers in 1988 at the age of 19 and was sent to their farm team in Great Falls, Montana, in the Pioneer League, where he hit a resounding .331 with a league-leading 57 stolen bases in 60 games. He made his way through the Dodgers farm system over the next three years, eventually finding a home in Los Angeles. He gave the Dodgers mediocre defense at shortstop over the next six years, with good range but a leaky glove that produced a .943 fielding average, 24 points below his peers. His bat was erratic as well, fluctuating between .210 and .287.

After a three-year stint in Kansas City, where he did a decent job defensively at both first base and second base and stung the ball at a .300 plus clip, the switch-hitter was signed by the Boston Red Sox as a free agent. He spent three and a half years in Boston before being sold to the Seattle Mariners on August 8, 2002. During his Boston tenure, the lanky six-footer played primarily second base and first base for Jimy Williams' team. He was Boston's regular second baseman for three years before splitting his final season between first base and designated hitter.

Jose Offerman provided Boston with adequate defense at second base in 1999, and he hit a crisp .294, with 107 runs scored, 37 doubles, a league-leading 11 triples, eight homers, 69 RBI, 18 stolen bases, and an excellent .391 on-base percentage. A knee injury hampered his play in 2000, limiting his range at second base, cutting his batting average by 39 points, and eliminating his stolen bases completely. He rebounded somewhat the following year, but not enough to justify keeping him in the lineup on a regular basis. His batting average was still a respectable .267 in 128 games, but his on-base percentage slipped to .342 and his defense was shaky. His Boston career ended on August 8, 2002, when he was sold to the Seattle Mariners after hitting just .232 in 72 games.

Okajima, Hideki

Hideki Okajima was another of the exceptional Japanese baseball players who joined the major leagues in recent years, and he was a major factor in the Boston Red Sox successful World Championship quest in 2007. Okajima was born in Kyoto, Japan, on December 25, 1975. After graduating from Higashiyama High School in 1994, he was drafted by the Yomiuri Giants of the Japan Central League, but didn't begin pitching for them until 1995. Pitching mostly out of the bullpen as a setup man, the sneaky-fast southpaw often pitched multiple innings and, on August 31, 1999, he threw nine shutout innings in relief. He became the Giants closer in 2000, but after saving 25 games in 2001, he was returned to his role of setup man the following season. Over the next four years, Okajima appeared in from 41 to 53 games a season for Yomiuri, but was then traded to the Nippon Ham Fighters in 2006. He pitched in 55 games for the Ham Fighters, going 2–2 with a 2.14 ERA and helping his team win the league championship.

Okajima became a free agent in 2006 after completing ten years of service in the Japan League and signed a two-year $2,500,000 contract with the Boston Red Sox. According to Wikipedia, "Okajima has a distinctive pitching form in which he turns his head downwards just before he releases the ball, and after release jerks it hard towards third base.... (His) fastball is usually in the 85–89 mph range, rarely ever reaching 90 mph. His out pitch in Japan was his sharp rainbow curveball in the 70–75 mph range, which left-handed hitters find hard to hit. He also occasionally throws a circle changeup, a slider in the 80–84 mph range and a changeup usually 82–84 mph." During an early-season rainout, "Red Sox pitching coach John Farrell tweaked Okajima's changeup delivery. The result was a devastating changeup with screwball motion dubbed the 'Okie-Dokie' by bullpen coach Gary Tuck. Detroit Tigers slugger Gary Sheffield declared Okajima 'one of the most impressive lefties I've ever seen, with stuff I've never seen before from anybody.' Former Yankees manager Joe Torre called Okajima 'unhittable.'"[131]

In Okajima's first Red Sox appearance, his first pitch was hit out of the park by John Buck of Kansas City, but he went on from there to hold the opposition scoreless over the next seven weeks as the setup man for Boston closer Jonathan Papelbon, and he was selected for the American League All-Star team, although he didn't get to pitch in the game. The six-foot, one-inch, 195-pound southpaw finished the season with a 3–2 mark in 66 games with an excellent 2.22 ERA. He was also a standout in post-season play, throwing 11 innings in eight games in the three post-season series, with a 2.45 ERA.

He had his ups and downs during the 2008 season, but he came on strong in the second half to finish with a 3–2 won-lost mark, pitching 62 innings in 64 games with one save and a 2.61 ERA. He was one of Boston's bright spots in the post-season playoffs, pitching 2⅔ innings in three games against the Los Angeles Angels in the ALDS and 7⅓ innings in five games against the Tampa Bay Rays in the ALCS, with a combined ERA of 1.80. In 2009, he appeared in 68 games with a perfect 6–0 won-lost record and a 3.32 ERA. The 34-year-old southpaw had an off-season in 2010 posting a 4–4 won-lost record in 56 games with a hefty 4.50 ERA, and in 2011 he pitched in only seven games for Boston, going 1–0 in eight innings before being sent to the Pawtucket Red Sox of the International League, possibly ending his major league career.

O'Leary, Troy

It took Troy Franklin O'Leary seven years to navigate the Milwaukee Brewers' minor league system, but once he left it in his wake, he fashioned a successful 11-year major league career for himself. The handsome Californian was born in Compton on August 4, 1969, and began his long trek to the top of the baseball world after signing a free agent contract with the Milwaukee Brewers in 1987. He spent seven years in the Brewers' minor league system, with two short trials in Milwaukee in 1993 and 1994, but his erratic batting statistics in the minors, with averages bouncing up and down between .263 and .334, established a pattern that would haunt him throughout his major league career.

The Boston Red Sox claimed O'Leary off the waiver list on April 14, 1995, and the six-foot-tall, 190-pound, left-handed hitter was immediately assigned to patrol the unique right field garden in Fenway Park, but after struggling with the idiosyncrasies of that part of the ballpark for three years he was shifted to left field, where he became one of the better left fielders in the American League and an expert at playing the Green Monster. The 25-year-old Californian played in 112 games for Kevin Kennedy's crew in 1995, stinging the ball at a .308 clip with 31 doubles, 10 home runs, 49 RBI, and 60 runs scored, in 399 at-bats. O'Leary's batting average tailed off to .260 in 1996, but he still contributed 28 doubles, 15 home runs, and 81 RBI to the Boston offense. In keeping with his minor league pattern, he bounced back the following year to hit .309 with 32 doubles, 15 homers, and 80 runs batted in, in 499 at-bats. His batting average slipped again to .270 in 1998, but he slammed 36 doubles, 23 home runs, and 83 RBI, all high-water marks in his Boston career thus far.

Troy O'Leary had his best season in a Red Sox uniform in 1999. In addition to doing a competent job defensively, he batted a hard .280 with 36 doubles, career-highs of 28 home runs and 103 runs batted in, and a .495 slugging average. Boston's 94–68 won-lost record during the season brought them home in second place in the American League's Eastern Division, four games behind the New York Yankees, but it qualified them for a wild-card spot in the post-season. In the ALDS, won by Boston over Cleveland in five games, O'Leary hit just .200 but he came through in the clutch in the deciding fifth game. Twice with men on base, Cleveland walked Nomar Garciaparra to pitch to O'Leary, and both times O'Leary drove the ball out of the park, driving in seven runs and pacing Jimy Williams' team to a 12–8 triumph. In the AL Championship Series, a five-game loss to Joe Torre's Bronx Bombers, Boston's new slugger hit a hefty .350 with three doubles. Troy O'Leary played with the Red Sox two more years, but his best years with the bat were behind him. He batted .261 and .240 in 2000 and 2001 respectively, and was not offered a contract for 2002, subsequently joining Montreal as a free agent.

Oliver, Tom

Thomas Noble "Rebel" Oliver was born in Montgomery, Alabama, on January 15, 1903. His first recorded entry in the baseball archives was his season with Minot in the North Dakota League in 1923. The 19-year-old outfielder batted a lowly .207 that year, but as he advanced through the minor league cauldron, he improved his hitting to the point where he stroked the ball at a .321 clip with a league-leading 218 base hits for the Little Rock Travelers in the Southern Association in 1928, and .338 with the same team the following year.

The 27-year-old Oliver joined the Boston Red Sox in 1930 and played his entire four-year major league career in Boston. On defense he was called "a graceful centerfielder whose defensive ability, sportswriter Fred Lieb likened to that of Tris Speaker and Joe DiMaggio. Oliver thrilled Boston fans with his speed and strong arm."[132] He played 154 games in center field for Heinie Wagner's team in his rookie season, covering the vast reaches of Fenway Park seemingly like a cheetah in full flight, compiling a sensational 2.92 6 range factor, 55 points higher than the league average of 2.37, and posting a glossy .982 fielding average, 17 points above the league average. At the plate, the six-foot-tall, 168-pound, right-handed hitter put together a .293 season with 86 runs scored and just 25 strikeouts in a league-leading 646 at-bats. The following year, he essentially duplicated his defensive play, but he displayed more power with the bat, crushing 35 doubles and driving in 70 runners with a .276 batting average in 586 at-bats. His offensive numbers declined in 1933 and 1934, as he batted .264 in 1933 with 37 RBI in 122 games, and .258 with 23 RBI in 90 games the following season.

When owner Tom Yawkey began to restock his Boston franchise in hopes of claiming an American League pennant through the purchase of high priced talent like the Ferrell brothers, Lefty Grove, and Jimmie Foxx, Oliver became expendable, and he was sold to the Baltimore Orioles of the International League on October 31, 1933, beginning a nine-year minor league fade-out for the Alabama native. Tom Oliver was a good hitter with an exceptional batting eye who struck out only 17 times a year for Boston, but he had little power, with just 29 doubles and three triples for every 550 at-bats, hit no home runs in 1,931 major league at-bats, and he walked only 26 times a year, giving him a disappointing .31v6 OBP and .346 slugging average.

Ortiz, David

David "Big Papi" Ortiz is one of the greatest clutch hitters in the annals of Boston Red Sox baseball, if not THE BEST. The big, six-foot, four-inch, 230-pound, happy-go-lucky native of Santo Domingo, Dominican Republic, was plucked off the streets of his hometown by the Seattle Mariners at the age of 17 and began his professional baseball career in the Dominican League in 1993. After way-stops in such minor league hamlets as Phoenix, New Britain, and Fort Myers, and with a change of owners from Seattle to Minnesota as well, David Ortiz arrived in the Twin Cities in September, 1997, to begin his assault on major league pitchers.

Ortiz played 15 games for the Twins in 1997, batting .327 in 49 at-bats, with one homer and six runs batted in. He split the following season between Minnesota and their Triple-A farm team in Salt Lake City, hitting .243 in 11 games for Salt Lake and .277 with 20 doubles, nine homers, and 46 RBI for the Twins in 278 at-bats over 86 games. For some reason, Big Papi's offensive production was never enough to satisfy Minnesota management and he continued to commute between the Twin Cities and the minor leagues for another three years before settling down to a more comfortable major league existence. In 2002, the hulking left-handed slugger played 125 games for the Twins, most of them as a designated hitter or pinch-hitter, with just 15 games at first base. His slugging prowess that included 20 home runs and 75 RBI in 417 at-bats was not enough to convince Minnesota management to retain the rights to the smiling Dominican. He was released by the Twins on December 16, 2002, and was subsequently signed by the Boston Red Sox on January 22, 2003. It was probably one of the worst decisions in Minnesota Twins history.

David Ortiz took to Boston like a fish to water, and the Red Sox welcomed his smiling countenance immediately. In his baptism of fire in The Hub in 2003, he ripped the ball at a solid .288 clip with 35 doubles, 31 homers, and 101 runs batted in. His .592 slugging average was third-best in the American League and he finished fifth in the MVP voting. In the ALCS, a losing effort against the New York Yankees, he slugged two home runs and drove in six runs in seven games. It was a sign of things to come.

The 2004 season was one of the most memorable seasons in Boston baseball history as the self-proclaimed "Bunch of Idiots" finally ended "The Curse of the Bambino" forever with their electrifying triumphs in the ALCS and the World Series. Ortiz was one of their most dangerous weapons. He played 150 games during the season, with 115 of them as the designated hitter, and amassed 47 doubles, 41 home runs, and 139 runs batted in, to go along with a .301 batting average. Big Papi became an instant Boston legend with his game-winning hits in post-season play, most notably in the ALDS and the ALCS. His walk-off home run, a towering drive into Fenway Park's Monster Seats in left field, in the bottom of the tenth inning in Game 3 of the American League Division Series sent the California Angels home by an 8–6 score. As exciting as that was, his feats in the ALCS were even more breathtaking. In the bottom of the 12th inning of Game 4 with Boston down three games to none to their hated rivals from the Bronx, he revitalized the team by launching one of his patented high fly balls over the 380-foot mark and into the morgue-like atmosphere of the Yankees bullpen, to bring the Sox back from the brink of defeat to a 6–4 victory. He followed up that bit of heroism with another miracle finish to rescue his team once again in Game 5. In the eighth inning, with New York up, 4–2, he launched a blast into the seats beyond the Green Monster to cut New York's lead to one run at 4–3. Six innings later, with the game tied at 4–4, he brought the Fenway Park faithful to their feet screaming when he stroked a dying quail into short center field to send Johnny Damon racing across the plate with the game-winner. Boston went on to sweep the final four games of that series to advance to the World Series against the National League Champion St. Louis Cardinals. In all, Big Papi tormented New York pitching for 12 base hits, three homers, six runs scored, 11 RBI, and a .387 batting average. The proud Redbirds were no match for Terry Francona's warriors either, and they bowed out quietly in four games, with Ortiz hammering a double and a home run with four RBI and a .308 batting average.

Not only did David Ortiz produce world-class slugging numbers in 2004, his off-field contributions were just as important. As Albert Chen in *Sports Illustrated* noted, "Ortiz's sunny demeanor has helped to keep the Sox afloat this season. 'This team has been so up and down all year,' says first baseman Kevin Millar. 'One constant has been David's hitting. He has saved us.' 'Beyond his numbers, David is a huge club-

David Ortiz

house presence,' says outfielder Gabe Kapler. 'He knows exactly the right thing to say or do at the right time to fire us up and get us going again.' Ortiz is often seen flashing his wide, gap-toothed smile, but don't be fooled, he is a fiery competitor."[133]

Big Papi continued his cannonading in 2005 and 2006 with two of the most prodigious offensive performances in Boston Red Sox history. In 2005, the big lefty scorched American League pitchers for a .300 batting average in 159 games, with 40 doubles, 47 home runs, and a league-leading 148 RBI, and the following year he rattled the fences for a .287 average in 151 games, with 115 runs scored, while leading the league with 54 home runs, a Boston record, and 137 runs batted in. The Red Sox family entered 2007 eager for another World Championship to prove their achievement of three years earlier was no fluke. Their enthusiasm paid off as they won again and this time in more impressive style. Unlike 2004, when they were the wild-card entry in the post-season, Terry Francona's charges went into the post-season as the American League's Eastern Division Champions, unseating the powerful New York Yankees by two games. One constant, however, was the big-bat production of its designated hitter, David Ortiz, who pummeled opposing pitchers for a career-high .332 batting average, with 52 doubles, 35 home runs, 116 runs scored, 117 RBI, 111 bases on balls, a .445 on-base percentage, and a .621 slugging average. He kept his bat singing throughout the playoffs. In the ALDS against Mike Scioscia's Los Angeles Angels, a three-game sweep for Boston, Ortiz was 5-for-7 for a .714 batting average, with two homers and three RBI, plus six bases on balls including four in Game 2 as Scioscia tried to keep Big Papi's firepower under control. Boston's seven-game triumph over the Cleveland Indians in the ALCS was a team effort with Ortiz chipping in with three doubles, a homer, three RBI, and a .292 batting average. Francona's Back Bay Bombers closed out their unforgettable season by disposing of the National League Champion Colorado Rockies in four straight. Once again, the victory was a team effort, and Big Papi's contribution was a .333 batting average with three doubles, four runs scored, and four RBI. In the 13–1 rout of the Rockies in Game 1 that set the tone for the entire series, Boston's designated hitter ripped three base hits in five at-bats, with two doubles, two RBI, and two runs scored.

The 2008 and 2009 seasons were years that David Ortiz would just as soon forget. Hampered by a partially torn tendon sheath in his left wrist in 2008, Boston's answer to Paul Bunyan made two trips to the disabled list during the season, and suffered through 109 painful games when he forced himself to play hurt. His numbers, all lows for him since joining the Red Sox in 2003, included a .264 batting average, 23 home runs, and 89 RBI, in 416 at-bats. Big Papi's troubles continued into 2009, when he batted just .238 with 28 homers in 541 at-bats. But he had more serious problems than just his hitting in 2009. His season got off to a bad start when a rumor circulated to the effect that he was one of the 103 players who tested positive for steroids in 2003. That rumor was never confirmed, however, and the individual making the accusation didn't have the courage to identify himself, so it can be discounted as sheer nonsense. Additionally, Ortiz, whose credibility is unquestioned, denied ever taking steroids. In fact, he took and passed more than 15 official drug tests between 2004 and 2009, further establishing his innocence while at the same time leading Boston to two World Championships. David Ortiz rebounded in magnificent fashion in 2010. After struggling through a difficult April where he hit just .143 with one home run, the big slugger pounded the ball at a torrid .363 pace in May, en route to a .270 season with 32 home runs and 102 RBI. The 34-year-old Dominican native sidestepped Father Time one more time in 2011 when he put together one of his better seasons, stinging the ball at a .309 clip while crushing 29 home runs and driving in 96 teammates.

Big Papi has been a member of the Boston Red Sox for nine years, and he is arguably the greatest clutch hitter in the annals of Boston baseball, with 17 game-winning base hits including 11 home runs. His amazing achievements have made him a cult favorite in Boston, and his "popularity with fans is based as much on his gentle-giant reputation as on his hitting, both as the affable 'Papi' who helped keep fellow Dominican star, Manny Ramirez, and the rest of the clubhouse on an even keel, and as the 'Cookie Monster,' the nickname his three-year-old daughter gave him that stuck."[134]

Papelbon, Jonathan

The high-strung closer for the Boston Red Sox has been baseballs "Mr. Automatic" over the past five years with a save percentage of 88 percent. He has also been Mr. Automatic in post-season play with seven saves in his first seven save opportunities, including three for three in the 2007 World Series. At just 30 years of age, the tall, lanky right-hander has his future ahead of him, and a potential Hall of Fame plaque waiting to be unveiled in the year 2026. "Called a free spirit by some people, he is an exhibitionist of the first order, but on the mound, he is all business."[135]

Jonathan Robert Papelbon was drafted by the Boston Red Sox in the fourth round of the 2003 amateur draft and assigned to their Lowell Spinners farm team in the New York-Pennsylvania League, where he received a rough introduction to the professional ranks, going 1–2 in 13 games with a hefty 6.34 earned run average. Two years later, on July 31, 2005, he made his major league debut in Fenway Park, starting against the Minnesota Twins and pitching 5⅓ innings, yielding three runs, two earned, striking out seven and walking five in a no-decision, won by Boston, 4–3. After two more starts, he was assigned to the bullpen, where he made 14 appearances down the stretch. In his second relief appearance, he was charged with a 12–8 loss to the Detroit Tigers, yielding two runs in one inning of work. His first major league victory came on September 12, in his tenth appearance, as he tossed three scoreless innings at the Toronto Blue Jays in the Rogers Centre, with David Ortiz's home run in the 11th inning making the difference. Over his last 11 appearances, all in relief, Pap put together a 3–0 record, with ten base hits allowed in 14 innings pitched, with 15 strikeouts, five bases on balls, and a sparkling 1.29 ERA. In the American League Division Series against the eventual World Series Champion Chicago White Sox, he pitched four scoreless innings in two games.

The six-foot, four-inch, 230-pound flamethrower was scheduled to be a starter in 2006, but when Keith Foulke floundered during spring training, Francona sent Papelbon back to the bullpen as the closer and, as they say, the rest is history. Boston's free spirit has not started another major league game while making 316 relief appearances through 2010. Armed with an explosive fastball that tops out at 98 miles per hour, and a devastating splitter, with an occasional changeup and curve thrown in, and sending his pitches plate-ward from a deceptive three-quarter delivery, he has been deadly coming out of the pen in the ninth inning. On April 5, 2006, he recorded his first major league save. Entering the game in the ninth inning in Ameriquest Field in Arlington, Texas, he fanned two men to preserve a 2–1 victory for Josh Beckett. Twenty-four days later, he set a major league rookie record when he recorded his tenth save in April, but took it matter-of-factly. "I set my goals high. If you had told me I would have had ten saves and not given up a run, I would have believed it. That's just the way I go about it. It's not cocky. It's just confidence." Papelbon continued to shine

Jonathan Papelbon

in his new role, pitching 68⅓ innings in 59 games with four wins, two losses, a Red Sox rookie-record 35 saves, and a brilliant 0.92 ERA. He developed a sore shoulder in August, and as soon as the Red Sox were out of contention for post-season play, Francona shut him down for the rest of the season. The 2006 season determined his future path. He had found a home in the bullpen, noting, "I like the competition, the fact that you have to go out there and be successful every day. You've got to get outs right then and there — the pressure is on. I get a lot of satisfaction out of closing. Whenever Tito gives me the ball, I just go out there and pitch my heart out. I don't ever want to start another game."

The 2007 season was a satisfying one for the 26-year-old Louisiana native. He recorded his 30th save of the season on August 21 to become the first Red Sox pitcher to have two 30-save seasons. He came in from the bullpen 59 times, pitched 58 innings with one victory, three losses, and 37 saves, yielding just 30 base hits, with 84 strikeouts, 15 bases on balls, and a 1.85 ERA. Boston, with Mike Lowell, David Ortiz, and rookie Dustin Pedroia leading the way, won the Eastern Division title by two games over the New York Yankees. Papelbon, clad only in a red T-Shirt, Spandex shorts, and swim goggles, celebrated the victory in style, doing an Irish step-dance on the Fenway Park mound while the crowd howled and screamed with delight. In the ALDS, Terry Francona's troops swept the Anaheim Angels out of the playoffs in three straight. Boston's closer had an easy series, pitching 1⅓ scoreless innings and recording one victory. In the ALCS, a hard-fought, seven-game triumph over the Cleveland Indians, the Red Sox had to come back from a three-games-to-one deficit to sweep the last three games but, once again, they made Pap's job easy by routing the Indians by scores of 7–1, 12–2, and 11–2 to close out the series, with their closer pitching in three games with one save. By the time the World Series came around, he was well rested and ready to go. When Boston demolished the Colorado Rockies in four games, Papelbon appeared in three of the games, pitching a total of four-and-a-third innings, yielding just two base hits with one strikeout, no walks, and three saves. In game two, the last game to be played in Boston, Pap came on with two men out and no one on base in the eighth inning, with the Red Sox nursing a 2–1 lead. He walked Matt Holliday, but then picked off the Colorado outfielder to end the inning. He finished up with a one-two-three ninth, fanning Seth Smith for the final out, and the celebration began. Boston's man of the hour proceeded to put on another show for the crowd, this time in uniform, with an impromptu Irish stepdance on the Fenway infield to Dropkick Murphy's song, "I'm Shipping Up To Boston." He repeated the act a few days later on the back of a flatbed truck during the "Rolling Rally" World Championship parade through the streets of Boston, to the cheers and screams of thousands of frantic Red Sox fans. A week or two later, when reporters inquired about the location of the historic baseball that had recorded the final out of the Series, Papelbon confided to them that he had taken the ball back to Hattiesburg, Mississippi, with him and his dog "Boss," a playful Boston Terrier, ate it. "He plays with balls like they're his toys. He jumped up one day on the counter and snatched it. He likes rawhide. He tore that thing to pieces."

Papelbon, like Okajima, had his ups and downs during the 2008 season, blowing two consecutive saves in early May, noting philosophically, "I let my team down today, but tomorrow I'll be ready to go. There's a long way to go and I have a lot of innings to pitch." And go he did. He finished strong with 41 saves in 46 save opportunities for an outstanding 89 percent success rate, and he recorded his 100th major league save on July 13. He appeared in 67 games during the season, pitching 69⅓ innings with a 5–4 won-lost record and a 2.34 ERA. Somewhere along the way, he discovered that he could improve his chances of winning if he slowed the game down. That tactic didn't go over too well with the big brass, however, and he was cited on at least five occasions and fined more than $10,000. He jokingly told the *Boston Herald*, "I think they're going to call my parole officer and put me away."[136] In the postseason he was perfect, pitching a combined 10⅓ innings in seven games in the ALDS and ALCS, with three saves and a 0.00 ERA.

He continued to dominate opposing batters

in 2009, appearing in 66 games with 38 saves in 41 save opportunities, a sparkling 93 percent success rate. Unfortunately for Papelbon and the rest of his Red Sox teammates, they were dismissed from the ALDS by the Anaheim Angels, three games to none. Pap was saddled with the loss in Game 3. He entered the game in the eighth inning with two men out, two men on base, and the Red Sox holding a comfortable 5–2 lead. But this time the Boston closer was not up to the task. The first batter he faced, Juan Rivera, rapped a two-run single, cutting the Boston lead to a single run. In the ninth inning, with Red Sox Nation looking on in disbelief, he was raked over the coals after retiring the first two batters. Two singles, two walks, and a double gave Mike Scioscia's club three runs and a 7–6 victory. Pap left the mound to a torrent of boos from the Fenway Faithful, but he understood what that meant. "The fans don't expect any more out of me than I do out of myself. You know I think they got so accustomed to seeing me do what I do, I think it's kind of like 'Well, why didn't he do that'?" Overall, Jonathan Papelbon's four-year post-season totals are impressive, 27 innings pitched in 18 games, with two wins, one loss, seven saves, one blown save, 14 base hits allowed, 23 strikeouts, eight bases on balls, and a barely visible 1.00 earned run average. He holds the major league record for the most consecutive scoreless innings to start a post-season career, with 26.

Unfortunately, there was no post-season for Papelbon and his teammates in 2010 as an avalanche of injuries to key players decimated the Red Sox roster and several other players, Pap included, struggled through disappointing seasons. The Boston closer appeared in 65 games with a 4–4 won-loss record and 37 saves but he also had eight blown saves and a horrible 3.90 ERA, the first time in his six-year career that he had an ERA higher than 2.65. After compiling a 4–1 record with 31 saves and a 2.94 ERA in 63 appearances in 2011, Pap filed for free agency, eventually signing with the Philadelphia Phillies.

Parent, Freddy

Freddy Parent, a five-foot, five-inch, 148-pound mighty-mite from Biddeford, Maine, held down the shortstop position for Jimmy Collins' Boston Pilgrims from 1901 through 1907, giving the fans the type of game they would expect from a team leader. Alfred Joseph Parent was born on November 25, 1875, and he quit school at the age of 14 to help his family by working in the "Laconia Mill harness shop for sixty-five cents a day. When not working, he enjoyed playing 'scrub' ball in the city's back lots, captain of a team he helped organize."[137] He continued playing town ball into his twenties, now with a wife to support, until in 1898 he joined the New Haven Blues in the Connecticut League, his first professional affiliation. The man everyone said was too small to play professional baseball proved everyone wrong by ripping the ball at a .326 clip to finish in the upper echelon of league batters. One year later, the St. Louis Perfectos of the National League gained the rights to the pint-sized shortstop, but he played only two games before spraining his ankle and drawing his release from the team. In 1900, he was back in the minors, playing for the Providence Grays, and he earned his keep with Providence by hitting .287 with 21 doubles, six triples, four home runs, and 23 stolen bases. That performance, coupled with his strong defensive prowess, brought him to the attention of the Boston Pilgrims, who signed him to a contract in March, 1901.

Parent immediately became the sparkplug of Jimmy Collins' team, stroking line drives with regularity, running the bases like a frightened fawn, stealing bases, and covering the left side of the infield with distinction. The right-handed-hitting Parent "was a wrist-hitter, slapping balls to all fields. He hovered over the plate with an exaggerated piece of lumber, a wagon tongue, but of suspicious weight. Known as an excellent bunter, Parent also showed some power."[138] In his rookie season in the American League in 1901, the league's first year as a major league, the Biddeford native batted a tough .306 with 36 extra-base hits and 87 runs scored in 517 at-bats. The next season, he batted .275 with 42 extra-base hits and 91 runs scored. The scrappy infielder also took his share of punishment for crowding the plate, being hit by a pitch nine times in 1901 and six times each in 1903–04–05. That didn't deter him, however, and he produced a .304 average in 1903 with career highs in doubles (31) and triples (17), while driving in 80 runs and scoring 83. His efforts helped the Pilgrims carry home the American League pennant by a comfortable margin over the Philadelphia Athletics. They crossed swords with the National League Champion Pittsburgh Pirates in the first-ever World Series, and they came away victorious, five games to three in the best-of-nine confrontation. Parent not only batted a hard .281 with three triples, eight runs scored, and four RBI, he also out-fielded the great Honus Wagner, making 28 assists in all, several of them of the spectacular variety.

Boston won the pennant again in 1904, beating the New York Highlanders by one-and-a-half games, but there was no World Series as the two leagues squabbled. Freddy Parent continued his solid defensive play that year and stroked the ball at a .291 clip, but that was, for all intents and purposes, the great shortstop's swan song. His batting average plummeted to .234 in 1905 and .235 the following year. He recovered to .276 in 1907, but he lost his shortstop job to Heinie Wagner after a salary dispute with Red Sox owner John Taylor. Parent was traded to the Chicago White Sox in 1908, giving them four years of service before retiring in 1911. As a member of the White Sox, he had one more memorable day, September 20, 1908. "His pitcher, Frank Smith, had thrown nine innings of no-hit ball, but the game was still scoreless in the bottom of the ninth, until Frank Isbell came to bat. Chicago's first baseman led off with a single to right field, advanced to second base on an out, and took third on a passed ball. Eddie Plank, pitching for Philadelphia, walked George Davis intentionally and intended to walk Freddy Parent as well to load the bases. But the aggressive Parent had other ideas. With the count 2–0, Plank lobbed the next pitch plateward, but it never reached the catcher's mitt. The shortstopper suddenly hunched himself up to the plate, grasped the bat as near the tip of its handle as he dare, and reached for that ball."[139] He hit a dying quail to right field, the ball falling in front of Scotty Barr as Davis raced home with the winning run, and Smith had his no-hitter.

Parnell, Mel

The stylish left-handed pitcher spent his entire ten-year major league career with the Boston Red Sox, outlasting four managers along the way. He pitched in 289 games for Boston, with 232 starts, 113 complete games, and 20 shutouts, winning 123 games against 75 losses for an excellent .621 winning percentage. He won more than 20 games twice and 18 games twice. Debunking the old adage that left-handers can't win in Fenway Park, the bellwether of the Red Sox staff from 1948 through 1953 posted a 71–30 won-loss record at home. Melvin Lloyd Parnell was born in New Orleans, Louisiana, on June 13, 1922. He spent all his free time playing baseball as a youngster, encouraged by his father, who was a former semi-pro player. Standing six feet tall and topping the scales at 130 pounds, he played first base in high school, but he intimidated his teammates with his live fastball when he pitched batting practice. One day the coach asked him if he would like to pitch a game and, after striking out 17 opposing batters, he became a permanent member of the pitching staff. He was also

Mel Parnell

dubbed "Dusty" by his coach because he threw the ball in the dirt so often.

Boston Red Sox scout Herb Pennock signed the 19-year-old southpaw to a free-agent contract in 1941, giving him a $5,000 bonus and a salary of $125 a month. Parnell began his professional baseball career with the Centreville Red Sox in the Eastern Shore League, going 4–4 in nine games with a 4.13 earned run average. The following year, with the Canton Terriers in the Middle Atlantic League, he came into his own, compiling a won-lost record of 16–9 with a league-leading 1.59 ERA in 204 innings. His march to the major leagues was sidetracked for three years beginning in 1943 as Uncle Sam beckoned him to military service in World War II. He spent his service time in the Air Force and like many professional baseball players he played baseball during the war, one year leading his team to the Eastern Flying Command Championship.

The 24-year-old southpaw, now a solid 180 pounds, returned to the baseball wars in 1946, and was assigned to Scranton in the Eastern League where, pitching for one of the greatest minor league teams of all time, a team that finished the year with an 18½ game lead over the second-place team, he ran up a 13–4 record with a still-standing Eastern League record ERA of 1.30. The following year, he began the season in Boston, making his major league debut on April 20, a losing effort against Walt Masterson of the Washington Senators. He pitched well in the game but took a 3–1 loss. Not long after that, he won his first game, a decision over "Prince Hal" Newhouser in Briggs Stadium, Detroit. Overall, he posted a 2–3 record that season with a lofty 6.39 earned run average in 15 games, but with Boston struggling to stay alive in the American League pennant race, he was sent to Louisville in the American Association to get more work. His sojourn with the Colonels lasted only four games as he injured his pitching hand fielding a ground ball and was sidelined for the rest of the season.

He was back with Boston to stay in 1948, quickly becoming one of the key members of the Boston pitching corps. The secret to his success in Fenway Park was that he was a low-ball pitcher. He pitched straight over the top and threw to the bottom half of the strike zone, making it especially difficult to pick up his pitches. His repertoire included a slider, a fastball, a curve, and a sinker. As he noted, "What I would do was use the slider to back a right-handed hitter off the plate a bit, then come back with a sinker outside. If he moved up again, I'd return to the slider, so I kept working in and out, always giving the hitters a lot of movement and changing speeds."[140] He pitched in 35 games in 1948, with 27 starts and 16 complete games, winning 15 games and losing eight with an outstanding 3.14 ERA, a full 1.15 runs below the league average. Joe McCarthy's cohorts battled the Cleveland Indians and New York Yankees down the stretch, eventually ending the season in a flat-footed tie with Cleveland. A one-game playoff was scheduled for Fenway Park on October 4, and Mel Parnell, expecting to start the game, was rested and ready to go. The day dawned cool with a brisk wind blowing out to left field, and manager Joe McCarthy made a last-minute change in his starting pitcher, deciding to go with 36-year-old Denny Galehouse, saying he thought the right-hander would fare better in the Fenway wind. It turned out to be a bad decision. Lou Boudreau's Indians jumped on the Red Sox righty early, with Boudreau slashing a first-inning home run, and Cleveland adding a four-spot in the fourth inning, en route to an 8–3 victory.

The year 1949 was a career season for Mel Parnell, but the year ended just as badly as the previous one. Joe McCarthy's team battled the Yankees tooth and nail all through the summer, finally coming down to the last two games, with Boston and New York playing each other in Yankee Stadium. Boston held a one-game lead over New York and needed only one more victory to clinch the pennant. They are still waiting. Parnell started the first game for Boston and was staked to a 4–0 lead after three innings but he was unable to hold it. Casey Stengel's troops nicked him for two runs in the fourth inning, two more in the fifth, and the winning run in the bottom of the eighth. When Boston dropped the finale by a 5–3 score, their season was over. Individually, however, Mel Parnell was never better. He led the American League with 25 victories (against seven losses), 27 complete games, and 295⅓ innings pitched. He was selected for the All-Star team, and finished fourth in the MVP voting. There was no Cy Young Award in those days, but if there had been one, he would have won it easily.

The graceful left-hander won 18 games in 1950 and another 18 games in 1951 as the ace of the Red Sox staff. He had an off year in 1952, winning only 12 games against 12 losses, but he bounced back emphatically the following year, going 21–8 with a .724 winning percentage and a 3.06 ERA. His 100th major league victory came on July 1, a 4–0 shutout of the New York Yankees. Injuries caught up with Parnell after 1953, and his career tapered off until his retirement after the 1956 season. Pitching against his old friend, Mickey McDermott, in 1954, the Boston ace suffered a broken wrist after being hit by one of McDermott's heaters and, when he tried to come back too soon, he injured his elbow. He finished the season with a 3–7 record in 92⅓ innings, and looked forward to the new season ahead. But the new season wasn't any better than the old one. The bad elbow never got better and he pitched in pain the rest of his career. He appeared in only 13 games in 1995, winning two and losing three, and the following year he pitched in 21 games with a 7–6 won-loss record and a decent 3.77 ERA. He did have one more moment of glory before he hung up his glove for good, however. He tossed a no-hitter at the Chicago White Sox in Fenway Park on July 14 before a small but enthusiastic gathering of 14,542 sun worshippers. It was the first no-hitter in Fenway Park in 33 years, since Howard Ehmke no-hit Philadelphia in 1923. Parnell won the game by a 4–0 score, striking out four men and walking two. He was aided by two double plays and a fine running catch of a line drive by Jim Piersall in right-center field. Reminiscing about the game years later, he said, "I was really on that day. My sinker was working and my slider was very sharp. I wasn't nervous because I didn't believe that it could possibly happen."[141] Mel Parnell was elected to the Boston Red Sox Hall of Fame in 1997.

Pedroia, Dustin

Dustin Luis Pedroia was born in Woodland, California, on August 17, 1983 and developed a strong work ethic as a youngster working in his parents tire shop and witnessing their 15-hour work days. The 2001 graduate of Woodland High School batted .450 over his three-year high school career and followed that with a sensational college career at Arizona State University. In his freshman year, he punished the ball to the tune of a .347 average and made only four errors in 223 chances for a .982 fielding percentage. As a sophomore, the five-foot, eight-inch shortstop was selected as a first-team All-American after batting a torrid .404 '.478 with runners in scoring position.' Another All-American season followed in 2004, when he hit .393 overall and .453 with runners in scoring position. He also fielded brilliantly at shortstop, being selected as the NCAA defensive player of the year for the second consecutive year. His three-year batting average at ASU was .384 with 298 base hits in 777 at-bats, including 71 doubles, six triples, 14 home runs, 146 runs batted in, 108 bases on balls, and just 47 strikeouts. The undersized overachiever finished his collegiate career as a three-time first-team All-Pac-

Dustin Pedroia

10 selection and a finalist for the 2004 Golden Spikes Award as the NCAA's most valuable player. One coach called the down-and-dirty infielder the Pete Rose of college baseball. Other sources referred to him as a feisty, trash-talking pit bull.

Pedroia was signed by the Boston Red Sox in the 2004 amateur draft and split the season between Sarasota in the Single-A Florida State League and Augusta in the Single-A South Atlantic League. He batted .307 in 30 games for Sarasota and an even .400 for Augusta, giving him a combined average for the year of .357 in 157 at-bats. His hits included 13 doubles, three triples, and three home runs but, more importantly, he demonstrated his keen batting eye, walking 19 times and striking out just seven times. In the field, he displayed his defensive strengths, playing 42 games at shortstop without an error. Pedroia was converted to a second baseman in 2005, splitting the season between Double-A Portland, where he hit .324, and Triple-A Pawtucket, where he hit .255. The next year, he stung the ball at a crisp .305 pace for Pawtucket with 30 doubles in 111 games, bringing him an end-of-season promotion to the parent Boston Red Sox, where he managed a .191 batting average in 31 games.

The year 2007 was a coming-of-age year for the 23-year-old second baseman. Manager Terry Francona named Pedroia his second baseman in spring training, and even after the rookie fell into a dreadful slump, his patient skipper hung in there with him, and was rewarded in the end. After a slow start that saw him hitting a microscopic .172 after games of May 2, Pedroia came on strong the rest of the season, finishing with a .317 batting average, with 39 doubles and eight home runs in 520 at-bats, and winning the American League's Rookie of the Year Award. In post-season play he hit just .154 in the ALDS, but bounced back in the ALCS, scorching the ball at a .345 clip with ten base hits and eight runs scored in seven games. In the Game 7 finale against the Cleveland Indians, Pedroia went 3-for-5 with a two-run homer into the Monster Seats in the bottom of the seventh inning and a bases-clearing double in the eighth. He ended his outstanding year by hitting .278 with four RBI in four games in the World Series as Boston swept the Colorado Rockies. He set the tone for the Series in the opening game by ripping a Jeff Francis slider over the left field wall in Coors Field in a 13–1 Boston massacre. In Game 3, another Red Sox romp, this one by a 10–5 score, he went 3-for-5 with two RBI. The west coast firebrand beat out a bunt single in the third inning, later scoring, as Francona's Back Bay Bombers scored six big runs to open, what turned out to be, an insurmountable lead. Pedroia continued his assault on American League pitchers in 2008, finishing second in the American League batting race with an average of .326, with 17 home runs, 83 RBI, and 20 stolen bases, while leading the league with 118 runs scored, 54 doubles, and 213 base hits. After a flameout in the ALDS, where he batted just .059, he hit a torrid .467 in the ALCS with two home runs in 15 at-bats. In recognition of his sensational season, Dustin Pedroia was selected as the American League's Most Valuable Player.

The 25-year-old second baseman hit .296 in 2009 with 48 doubles, 15 home runs, 72 RBI, and a league-leading 115 runs scored. He bolted from the gate like a thoroughbred, putting James Shields' heater into orbit with one out in the first inning on opening day, causing the Fenway crowd of 37,057 to leave their seats in unison and sparking Boston to a 5–3 triumph over the Tampa Bay Rays. His biggest day of the year was probably September 9, again in Fenway Park against the Baltimore Orioles, with another sellout crowd in attendance. In the first inning, after Jacoby Ellsbury had walked, Pedroia unloaded a tremendous home run over the Green Monster Seats, off the top of the billboard, and completely out of the park. He then led off the bottom of the third with another blast in support of Clay Buchholz, who pitched a sensational seven scoreless innings en route to a 10–0 blowout.

The California native, like several of his Boston teammates, had an injury-filled year in 2010. Playing in Coors Field on June 24, Pedroia sparked Terry Francona's crew to a thrilling 13–11 triumph over the Colorado Rockies, going 5-for-5 with three home runs. He hit a ground ball double in the first inning, slammed a leadoff home run to left field in the fourth, walked in the fifth, cracked a line drive single to center in the seventh, launched a two-run shot to left field in the eighth, and hit a two-run homer to left in the tenth inning, breaking an 11-all tie and giving Boston its final margin of victory. The next night, he fouled a ball off his instep, breaking a bone in his left foot, essentially ending his season. An attempted comeback in late August lasted two games and he went back to the bench for the rest of the season, having played in 75 games with a .288 batting average and 12 home runs. He had a successful comeback season in 2011, scorching the ball at a .307 clip with 21 homers, 91 RBI, and 26 stolen bases in 159 games played.

Dustin Pedroia has shown himself to be an outstanding all-around second baseman during his six years with Boston, with sure hands, decent range, and a measure of athleticism that permits him to make sensational stops and throws from all over the right side of the infield. And the 170-pound, right-handed hitter never gets cheated out of his at-bats. He swings from the heels on every pitch, peppering Fenway Park's famous Green Monster with a constant barrage of singles and doubles.

Pena, Tony

The long-time Pittsburgh Pirates catcher had a distinctive crouch with his right leg extended straight out from his body. He was one of baseball's greatest defensive catchers, number six all-time in one recent study. A product of the Dominican Republic baseball factory in San Pedro de Macoris, Tony Pena signed a professional baseball contract with Pittsburgh in 1976 and began his career with the Bradenton Pirates in the Rookie Gulf Coast League, playing catcher, first base, third base, and outfield. By his second year in organized baseball, he had settled in to the catching position, where he excelled. He broke into the major leagues with Pittsburgh on September 1, 1980, batting .429 over eight games. He took over the full-time catching duties for Chuck Tanner's team the following year and responded with a .300 batting average in 66 games, one of two times he hit .300 in his major league career. During his six-year tenure in Pittsburgh, the six-foot, 185-pound, right-handed hitter displayed a decent bat with a .286 average, 12 home runs for every 550 at-bats, and a .411 slugging average. The four-time Gold Glove winner was traded to St. Louis in 1987 and helped the Cardinals win the World Championship, hitting .381 in the NLCS and a torrid .409 in the World Series. Three years later, the 32-year-old backstop filed for free agency and joined Joe Morgan's Back Bay Bombers in Boston. Once again, he helped his team reach the post-season, but this time they were dispatched in four straight games by the Oakland Athletics by a combined score of 20–4 in the American League Championship Series.

Tony Pena spent four years with the Red Sox, giving them superb defensive play. As noted in *The Red Sox Fan Handbook*, he "was credited with helping stabilize the Sox pitching staff."[142] He also kept baserunners honest with his snap throws to first base and his cannon-like shots to second base to cut down would-be base stealers. His 33 percent caught-stealing success rate was three percent better than the league average. Unfortunately, his bat couldn't keep up with his glove, and his batting average plummeted over his Boston sojourn, falling from a high of .263 in 143 games in 1990 to .181 in 126 games in 1993. Tony Pena moved on after the 1993 season, joining Cleveland for three years and the White Sox for one year before retiring in 1997, closing out a brilliant 18-year major league career that included 1,950 games caught, the fourth-highest total in baseball history. He is also number five in double plays with 156. During his career, "he was a clubhouse leader and true baseball gamer, falling to the disabled list just once in his tenure with six teams. Admired in the league for his love of the game, the adept catcher became a master at calling a game. 'They can throw what they want out there. It's when they're having trouble, then it's up to me to know how to help them.'"[143]

Pennock, Herb

Herbert Jefferis Pennock was signed to a professional baseball contract by Connie Mack of the Philadelphia Athletics in 1912 and made his major league debut on May 14 in Shibe Park, pitching four scoreless innings of one-hit ball in a 7–0 loss to the Chicago White Sox. Four days later, the 18-year-old southpaw pitched three scoreless innings in the famous 24–2 Detroit massacre, a game where the Tigers used replacement players because the regulars were on strike, a protest strike that lasted only one day. Pennock was used sparingly his first two years in Philadelphia, going 1–2 in 17 games in 1912 and 2–1 in 14 games the following year. Finally, in 1914, he saw action in 28 games, pitching 151⅔ innings and compiling a sparkling 11–4 won-lost record with a 2.79 ERA. When he got off to a slow start in 1915 however, posting a 3–6 record in 11 games, he was waived to the Boston Red Sox, who sent him to Providence to fine-tune his repertoire.

Pennock spent most of 1916 with Buffalo, winning seven games and losing six in 15 games pitched, and he went 0–2 with Boston in eight games. By 1917, Herb Pennock was back in the Big Show for good, but he still saw little action, pitching 100⅔ innings in 24 games with a 5–5 won-lost mark. Frustrated with his limited major league action, the six-foot, 160-pound pitcher enlisted in the United States Navy in 1918 to help the war effort in World War I. He returned to the Red Sox the following year only after manager Ed Barrow promised to use him regularly. The 25-year-old Pennsylvanian finally matured as a pitcher in 1919, winning 16 games against eight losses, and pitching 219 innings in 32 games with a 2.71 ERA. Pennock, whose arm was described as being as skinny as a high school girl's from shoulder to wrist, was never a power pitcher. "He pitched with grace, economy, and style. Nothing he did was overpowering. Everything he did was tantalizingly effective."[144] He threw with an effortless motion, mixing an average fastball with a curve and a change of pace, constantly changing arm angles and speeds to keep batters off-balance. He himself said, "I think curve pitching is on the whole the most effective delivery. Of course, you cannot use curves exclusively. No pitcher's arm would stand that. You must mix them up with something else, so I have learned to depend very greatly on a change of pace. This, mixed up with my curves, is the secret of my delivery, such as it is."[145]

Unfortunately for Pennock, the Boston Red Sox were entering a prolonged period of mediocrity, finishing sixth, fifth, fifth, and eighth in an eight-team league, from 1919 to 1922. Pennock went 16–13 in 1920, but fell to 13–14 and 10–17 the next two years as his defense and his offense failed him repeatedly. But to his good fortune, he was traded to the New York Yankees on January 30, 1923, and developed into a world-class pitcher. "Relaxed, humble, and with a quirky sense of humor that kept Babe Ruth and Lou Gehrig loose, Herb Pennock came into his own in Yankee Stadium."[146] He won 20 games twice with the Yankees, and helped them win five American League pennants and four World Championships, going 5–0 in ten World Series games.

He won 241 games in his 22-year major league career against 162 losses, including a 62–59 won-loss record with Boston. Bill Werber had the last word on "The Knight of Kennett Square": "Pennock was a fine gentleman. He gave me a lot of sound advice one day which I will never forget. 'In this game, be nice to everyone on your way up, because you're going to meet a lot of them on your way down.'"[147] Herb Pennock was elected to the Baseball Hall of Fame in 1948.

Perez, Tony

Atanasio Rigal "Tony" Perez, one of the key members of Cincinnati's Big Red Machine of the 1970s, was one of baseball's foremost clutch hitters, with an average of 93 runs batted in for every 550 at-bats over a memorable 23-year major league career. The six-foot, two-inch, 205 pound, right-handed slugger joined professional baseball with Geneva in the New York-Pennsylvania League as a fuzzy-cheeked 17-year-old infielder-outfielder in 1960, batting a respectable .279. Four years later, he made his debut in Crosley Field on July 26, 1964, going 0-for-2 with a walk in the Reds' 7–2 win over the Pittsburgh Pirates. Overall, he finished the year with a .080 batting average in 12 games.

Tony Perez suffered the usual growing pains during his next two years in the National League, but in 1967, at the age of 25, he blossomed into the slugger the baseball world remembers. In the 1967 All-Star Game in Anaheim Stadium, Perez presented the National League with a 2–1, 15-inning victory by putting a Catfish Hunter delivery into orbit over Anaheim. He drove in over 90 runs every year for the next 11 years, with six years over 100 RBI. His best year with the Reds was 1970 when he scorched the ball at a .317 clip with 40 homers, 129 RBI, and a .589 slugging average. As Pittsburgh Pirates slugger Willie Stargell noted, "With men in scoring position, and the game on the line, Tony's the last guy an opponent wanted to see."

Perez spent three years in Montreal after leaving Cincinnati, and was subsequently signed by the Boston Red Sox in the re-entry draft on November 20, 1979, at the age of 37. He played in Boston for three years before spending a year in Philadelphia and finishing his career with a three-year stint back in Cincinnati. He had one strong year in Boston, and two less-than-successful seasons there. In 1980, he batted a solid .275 for Don Zimmer's team with a team-high 25 homers and 105 RBI, but his heroics could not offset the discord that reportedly permeated the Boston clubhouse as the team finished a disappointing fourth, 19 games behind the New York Yankees.

Pesky, Johnny

John Michael Paveskovich was born in Portland, Oregon, on September 27, 1919. As a youngster, Johnny played in city leagues and worked as the clubhouse boy for the Pacific Coast League Portland Beavers. Fortunately for baseball fans, sports writers around the city decided that Paveskovich was too long a name for box scores so they shortened it to Pesky. "Since he was a pesky hitter, a little guy who slapped the ball around, the new name seemed especially appropriate. His name started going into sports stories as Pesky, and then people started using it all the time."[148] He had it changed to Pesky legally in 1947, much to the chagrin of his mother, who thought he was ashamed of his real name. By 1938, several major league scouts were buzzing around Pesky, including scouts from the St. Louis Cardinals, New York Yankees, Cleveland Indians, and Boston Red Sox. Pesky decided to go with Boston, even though St. Louis offered a bigger bonus, because his mother liked the Red Sox scout better. He played his first professional baseball season across the country, in Rocky Mount, NC in the Piedmont League, and he showed the skill with the bat that would stay with him throughout his career. He stung the ball for a .325 batting average, scored 114 runs, hit 28 doubles, and led the league with 187 base hits and 16 triples. The next year, he repeated his .325 average with Louisville in the Double-A American Association, leading the league in hits with 195 and in putouts with 308. His outstanding all-around play earned him recognition as the league's Most Valuable Player.

The year 1942 found 22-year-old Johnny Pesky, who was considered to be a tough out and a slick fielder, in Boston, holding down the regular shortstop position, and the five-foot, nine-inch, 168-pound, left-handed hitter didn't disappoint manager Joe Cronin. He hit his first major league home run, a two-run shot off St. Louis Browns pitcher Bob Moncrief, in the top of the third inning in Sportsman's Park on July 24, helping the Red Sox to a 5–3 victory in the first game of a doubleheader. For the season he hit a crisp .331 with 105 runs scored, while leading the league with 205 base hits and 465 assists in the field. Unfortunately, that was the end of Pesky's major league career for awhile, as he spent the next three seasons in the United States Navy during World War II. When he returned to the Red Sox in 1946, he picked right up

Johnny Pesky

where he had left off in 1942. The slash-and-burn, line-drive hitter tattooed the ball at a .335 clip with 115 runs scored and a league-leading 208 base hits, including a run of eleven base hits in a row, and he found the right field corner or the power alleys in Fenway Park often enough to accumulate 43 doubles. His best day at the plate was May 8, when he set an American League record for the most runs scored in a game with six. With all the Red Sox stars back from the war, including Williams, Doerr, DiMaggio, Hughson, and Ferriss, Boston raced to the American League pennant by 12 games over the defending World Champion Detroit Tigers.

The Boston Red Sox were favored to defeat their National League opponents, the St. Louis Cardinals, in the World Series, but Eddie Dyer's team obviously didn't read the script. The Redbirds captured the World Championship in seven games, thanks to Enos "Country" Slaughter's daring baserunning that saw him score all the way from first base on a double by Harry "The Hat" Walker in the eighth inning of Game 7. Johnny Pesky was unjustly branded the goat of the Fall Classic for hesitating to throw the ball home on Slaughter's mad dash around the bases but, in retrospect, Pesky's play was not at fault. Slaughter made a great play, for which he should be congratulated. He ran with abandon at the crack of the bat, and he had the throw beaten in any case.

Johnny Pesky played another five-plus years in Boston, batting over .300 four times with a high of .324 in 1947 when he scored 106 runs, led the league with 207 base hits and ran off a 27-game hitting streak. In 1949, the Oregon native, now playing third base after having been displaced at shortstop by slugging Vern Stephens, batted .306 with 111 runs scored and led the league's third basemen with 184 putouts and 333 assists. The 32-year-old infielder hit .312 with 112 runs scored in 1950, and .313 with 93 runs scored the following year, but was traded to Detroit for third baseman George Kell after playing just 25 games in 1952.

Johnny Pesky was one of the greatest shortstops ever to wear a Boston Red Sox uniform, and he may have missed his opportunity to gain admittance into the National Baseball Hall Of Fame through no fault of his own. World War II deprived him of three years of baseball service during the prime of his career, from ages 22 to 24. Still, the sweet-swinging, left-handed contact hitter posted a solid .313 average with Boston in 4,085 at-bats with a superb .398 on-base percentage. He had only 17 home runs in his career and only six of them came in Fenway Park, modest hits of slightly more than 300 feet that curved around the right field foul pole. Mel Parnell dubbed the pole the "Pesky Pole," a designation that has endured. Johnny Pesky batted ahead of Ted Williams during his Red Sox career, which was a hindrance to him as well as a blessing. It helped his run-scoring average immeasurably but it also deprived him of numerous extra-base hits. He was discouraged from trying to stretch singles into doubles because that would leave first base open, giving the opposing team the opportunity to take the bat out of Williams' hands by walking him.

Petrocelli, Rico

Americo Peter "Rico" Petrocelli began his professional baseball career in the Boston Red Sox organization, with their Winston-Salem farm club in the Class-B Carolina League in 1962, hitting .277 and slugging 30 doubles and 17 home runs in 487 at-bats. The following season, with the Reading Red Sox in the Double-A Eastern League, the 20-year-old shortstop hit .239 with 19 homers and 78 RBI. He moved to the west coast in 1964, hitting .231 for the Seattle Rainiers in the Triple-A Pacific Coast League. Petrocelli was promoted to the Boston club for the 1965 season to replace Eddie Bressoud at shortstop, in spite of his mediocre batting average, to take advantage of his superior defensive skills. For the first few years, he gave them just what they expected, solid defensive play and an undistinguished bat that exhibited occasional power. From 1965 through 1968, the six-foot-tall, 185-pound, right-handed hitter batted .242 with 19 home runs for every 550 at-bats. His offensive contributions to the team effort were adversely affected by a sore elbow that bothered him off and on during his career. "To add insult to injury, Petrocelli was not a favorite of (Billy) Herman. The 'Old School' manager had little patience for his brooding and insecurities, and made life miserable for the young shortstop."[149] The Boston clubhouse was tense during the summer of 1966, but it became

Rico Petrocelli

more relaxed after Herman was fired in September. The following year, the year of the "Impossible Dream," Petrocelli raised his batting average 21 points, socked 17 home runs, and was his old self on defense, ranging far and wide to glove would-be hits and gun down frustrated hitters. The defining game in the season was played in Yankee Stadium on June 21, when a verbal joust between old friends Joe Pepitone and Rico Petrocelli turned physical, igniting a bench-clearing brawl that took a dozen New York security guards to separate the warring factions and restore order. Boston, which was positioned in fourth place when the game was played, went 60–39 down the stretch to grab the brass ring.

Petrocelli missed 39 games in 1968 when his elbow flared up again, but in 1969, he had a breakout season, ripping the ball at a .297 clip, with 98 bases on balls, and a .403 on-base percentage. After refining his "Fenway Stroke" and learning to pull the ball, he set an American League record for the most home runs by a shortstop with 40. On defense, he committed only 14 while leading the American League in fielding average for the second straight year and setting a record for Red Sox shortstops with a fielding average of .981. The following year he slammed 29 homers and drove in a career-high 103 runs.

The Brooklyn native moved to third base in 1971 to make room for future Hall Of Famer Luis Aparacio, and he excelled at that position also, leading the league's third basemen with a .976 fielding average his first year at the hot corner. He also provided good power with the bat, hitting .251 with 28 homers, 89 RBI, and a .354 OBP. Petrocelli's power, and his playing time, gradually declined over the next five years, partly the result of injuries such as a strained hamstring and a sore elbow, and aggravated by being felled by a Jim Slaton fastball that left him with an inner ear problem that affected his balance. He finally hung up his glove after relinquishing his third base job to Butch Hobson in 1976. He was just 33 years old.

He played in two losing World Series during his 13 years with the Red Sox. In the 1967 Series, he slugged two home runs in Game 6 as Boston tied the Series at three games apiece, before dropping Game 7 to the St. Louis Cardinals, 7–2. In 1975, his home run off Oakland closer Rollie Fingers in the seventh inning of Game 2 helped Boston to a three-game sweep of the A's in the American League Championship Series. He stung the ball at a .308 clip in the Fall Classic with four RBI and fielded flawlessly, but once again the Red Sox fell in seven, this time to the Cincinnati Reds. He went 1-for-3 in the final game and his bases-loaded walk in the third inning drove in a run as Boston raced to a 3–0 lead after five innings.

Rico Petrocelli was an exceptional all-around shortstop and third baseman for the Boston Red Sox from 1965 to 1976. He led the league in fielding average three times, twice at shortstop where he finished his career with a .969 fielding average, and his range was far superior to his peers. At the plate he hit a modest .251 in 5,390 at-bats, but his hits included 237 doubles and 210 home runs.

Piersall, Jimmy

He was one of the most colorful characters in Boston Red Sox history, an outstanding defensive center fielder who survived a nervous breakdown in his rookie season to go on to a successful 16-year career in the major leagues. He came into this world in Waterbury, Connecticut, on November 14, 1929, the year of the great stock market crash. The only child of a baseball fanatic father, he learned to, as he said, "catch and throw a ball before I learned the alphabet."[150] By the age of 14, he was well known around Naugatuck Valley where he excelled in both baseball and basketball. He was signed to a baseball contract by the Boston Red Sox after his graduation from Leavenworth High School, and spent his first year in professional baseball with Scranton in the Single-A Eastern League, hitting a respectable .281 and leading the league with 27 doubles and 92 RBI in 141 games. He played with Louisville in the American Association in 1949 and 1950, with a six-game cup of coffee in Boston at the end of the 1950 season, split the 1951 season between Louisville and Birmingham in the Southern Association where he tortured opposing pitchers to the tune of a .346 average, and then joined the Red Sox the following year as the regular shortstop.

Unfortunately, the 1952 season turned into a nightmare for the 22-year-old baseball phenom. His bizarre behavior was well noted in the local press and made him a crowd favorite as fans waited to see what he would do next. "Piersall, who much to his dismay had opened the season at shortstop, became a one-man, three-ring circus. He took deep bows after his every catch, flapped his arms like a seal, shook his fist at the crowd, and loudly berated the umpires every chance he got. After moving to right field, his natural habitat, he shadowed center fielder Dom DiMaggio all the way to the dugout between innings, mimicking his Groucho Marx lope as the fans hooted and howled."[151] On May 24, before a game against the New York Yankees in Fenway Park, Piersall and Yankees second baseman Billy Martin got into a verbal altercation on the field that culminated in a celebrated fist fight in the tunnel under the stands. Later he had a confrontation with teammate Mickey McDermott in the Red Sox clubhouse and reportedly broke down crying when he was benched. After spanking the four-year-old son of Red Sox shortstop Vern Stephens, Piersall was banished to the minors, but within a matter of weeks, after being ejected from games four times, he finally had to be hospitalized for psychiatric treatment, ending his season.

Jimmy Piersall was back in uniform the following spring, recovered from his illness, and ready to make his mark on the baseball world. He went on from there to have a long and notable career, but his zany behavior continued unabated on the advice of his doctors, who told him not to keep his feelings bottled up. He readily admitted his problem, noting, "Probably the best thing that ever happened to me was going nuts. Whoever heard of Jimmy Piersall until that happened?" One time, protesting playing a game in the rain, he walked up to the plate wearing a rubber raincoat and a fisherman's rain hat. Another time, in Yankee Stadium, the umpires held up play when they could only count eight Red Sox players on the field. Piersall was eventually found hiding behind one of the monuments in center field. Still another time, he squirted an umpire with a water pistol. Still, he played a brilliant center field over the next ten years, six of them in Boston. He led the American League in fielding

Jim Piersall

average five times, twice with Boston, twice with Cleveland, and once with Washington. He won Gold Gloves in 1958, and 1961, and led the league in putouts three times and assists once with Boston. His .990 career fielding average was six points higher than the league average, and he exhibited exceptional range in center field. At the plate, he hit between .272 and .293 during his first four years with the Red Sox. His best years with Boston were 1956, when he hit .293 with a league-leading 40 doubles, 14 homers, and 87 RBI, and 1957, when he batted .261 with 27 doubles, 19 homers, and 103 runs scored.[152] His batting average declined to .237 in 1958, after which he was traded to the Cleveland Indians.

Pratt, Del

Del Pratt was one of the best all-around second basemen of his era, had outstanding range, led the league in total chances five times, and was a dangerous hitter.[153] The hard-nosed infielder was an All-American running back at the University of Alabama, as well as captain of the baseball team, but after graduation he gravitated toward baseball and began his career with Montgomery in the Single-A Southern Association. Two years later, still with Montgomery, the five-foot, 11-inch, 175-pound second baseman hit .316 in 139 games with 32 doubles, 10 triples, eight home runs, 84 RBI, and 36 stolen bases, and led the league with 96 runs scored and 167 base hits. That brought him to the attention of the St. Louis Browns, who added him to their roster for the 1912 season, and the aggressive right-handed batter hit the ground running, stinging American League pitchers to the tune of a .302 average with 26 doubles, 15 triples, and 24 stolen bases for a team that finished in seventh place with a record of 53–101, a full 53 games behind the front-running Boston Red Sox. Pratt demonstrated his skills for the St. Louis fans for the next five years, leading the league with 103 RBI in 1916, but the Browns could never rise above fifth place. The durable infielder played in 360 consecutive games between 1914 and 1917, and if he hadn't been thrown out of a game on September 2, 1914, the streak would have passed the 700 mark. In 1918, he was traded to the New York Yankees, who were on the verge of league dominance but still had a few years to go before they reached the Promised Land. Miller Huggins' team finished fourth in 1918 and third the next two seasons, but by 1921, when they captured their first American League pennant, Del Pratt was gone. He had given the Yankees three superb seasons covering the right side of the infield while hitting between .275 and .314, and missing only one game in three years, but he was high-strung and outspoken, and had been at odds with Yankees management for more than a year, so when the opportunity arose, he was unceremoniously traded to the Boston Red Sox as part of the Waite Hoyt deal.

Another of Del Pratt's problems was his timing, which was just awful. He left the Yankees one year before they won the pennant and he joined the Red Sox three years after the last of Boston's five American League pennants. In 1921, Del Pratt had his usual outstanding defensive season with Boston, fielding .961 and participating in a career-high 90 double plays. At the plate, the bad-ball hitter batted a crisp .324 with 36 doubles, 10 triples, 102 runs batted in, and a .461 slugging average, but Hugh Duffy's team limped home in fifth place, 23½ games behind New York. Pratt had several big games for Boston in 1921 such as the game of June 22, when his bases-loaded triple in the eighth inning snapped a 1–1 tie and paced the Red Sox to a 5–1 Fenway Park victory over the Yankees. On August 5, Boston's cleanup hitter went 4-for-5 with a double and five RBI, leading his team to a 10–1 win over the Chicago White Sox and giving Joe Bush his ninth win against seven losses, as the home fans voiced their approval. Eighteen days later, he ripped two doubles and two singles as Boston routed the St. Louis Browns by a 15–2 score in Sportsman's Park. The next day, Hugh Duffy's big man had another four-hit day, but the team fell to the Browns by a 12–11 score. Pratt rose to the occasion again on September 28 in Shibe Park. His two-run homer in the first inning gave the Red Sox a lead they never relinquished. They won the game, 5–4, behind his four-hit barrage, giving Herb Pennock his 12th victory of the season against 13 losses. Overall, he had 15 games with three or more base hits in 1921 and 11 games with three or more RBI. The next year, his last year in a Boston uniform, he batted .301 with 44 doubles, 86 RBI, and a .427 slugging average.

Pratt was traded to Detroit in October, 1922, played two more years with decreasing defensive skills, then left the major leagues at the age of 35, in spite of having hit over .300 his last five years in the American League. His two-year totals in Boston included a .312 batting average in 1,128 at-bats.

Radatz, Dick

Richard Raymond Radatz, better known as "The Monster" in baseball circles, reached his full height of six-foot, six-inches, topping the scales at a muscular 260 pounds, in 1959. Joining the Boston Red Sox organization that summer, the right-handed power pitcher unleashed his heater with Raleigh in the Carolina League, striking out 76 batters in 77 innings in 13 games as a starter, while compiling a 4–6 record. The following year, with the same team, he won nine games against four losses and fanned 133 batters, an average of 11 strikeouts for every nine innings pitched. Radatz was gradually converted to a relief pitcher over the next two years, pitching 54 innings in 13 games after a promotion to Minneapolis in the American Association in 1960, and 71 innings in 54 games with Seattle in the Pacific Coast League the following year, bringing about his promotion to the Boston Red Sox.

Dick Radatz burst on the American League scene in 1962 and immediately became the Boston Red Sox fireman, appearing in a league-leading 62 games, saving a league-leading 24 games, striking out 144 batters in 124⅔ innings, and posting a 9–6 won-lost record with a 2.24 ERA. Unlike today's closers, the big flamethrower averaged two innings per appearance. His performance that year brought him the American League Fireman of the Year award. The following year, he pitched in 66 games, going 15–6 with 162 strikeouts in 132⅓ innings, a microscopic 1.97 ERA, and 25 saves. At the All-Star Game, Radatz fanned five men in two innings, including Willie Mays, Duke Snider, Dick Groat, Willie McCovey, and Julian Javier, causing Yankees manager Ralph Houk to say, "He's the greatest relief pitcher I've ever seen." The year 1964 was more of the same. The Monster came on in relief in 79 games, winning 16 games, losing nine, saving a league-leading 29 games, and winning another Fireman of the Year Award. He fanned 181 men in 157 innings with a 2.29 ERA. Sadly, by 1965, the flame was beginning to fade from his heater. He was still Boston's fireman, appearing in 63 games with 22 saves, but his won-lost record was just 9–11, his strikeouts were down to 121 in 124⅓ innings, and his ERA ballooned to 3.91.

The following year he was traded to the Cleveland Indians on June 2 after appearing in 16 games with Boston and saving four. He pitched for three more years in the major leagues, winning just three games and saving 18, before retiring after the 1969 season at the age of 32. Dick Radatz responded to the media's concerns about his brief career by saying, "No, I didn't burn myself out as a pitcher. Pitching so often isn't what ended my career. I was a power pitcher, a one-pitch pitcher. And my specialty — the fastball — is the most perishable. I wish I'd been able to develop another pitch because the day comes when the fast one disappears. I tried to develop another pitch but I couldn't do it and retain my fastball. I worked

Dick Radatz

hard to develop a sinker. I came up with a pretty good one and fell in love with it. The only trouble was that in doing so I lost my fastball. I'd developed a different motion for the sinker, and my fastball wasn't effective out of that motion. That was the beginning of the end. I couldn't regain my good control, and it got to be a mental thing."[154]

Dick Radatz pitched for the Red Sox for just over four years, but The Monster of legend will live forever. The image of a six-foot, six-inch, 260-pound behemoth peering down at them from a 15-inch-high pitching mound, just 60 feet, six inches away and preparing to throw a baseball in their direction at speeds approaching 100 miles an hour, struck fear into the hearts of most enemy batsmen. Radatz appeared in 286 games for Boston, all in relief, compiling a 49–34 won-lost record, with 104 saves. The husky right-hander fanned 627 batters in 557⅓ innings, an average of 10.1 strikeouts for every nine innings pitched. Amazingly he averaged 1.95 innings per appearance, occasionally pitching as many as four or five innings and one time going nine innings to beat the Yankees.

Ramirez, Manny

Manny Ramirez was one of the greatest hitters, and also one of the most engaging yet aggravating characters, ever to don a Red Sox uniform. His tremendous batting skills and charismatic personality were somewhat offset by his defensive deficiencies and his often lackadaisical efforts on the field, at the plate, and on the bases. According to one source, Ramirez may have been the zaniest character ever to play for the Red Sox, who also employed the likes of Bill "Spaceman" Lee, Steve Lyons, and Jimmy Piersall. "Among Ramirez's more notable eccentricities was his penchant for disappearing inside the Green Monster at Fenway Park when the Sox brought in a reliever in mid-inning. He reportedly has multiple social security numbers and more than one driver's license."[155]

The native of Santo Domingo, Dominican Republic, emigrated to the United States as a child and began his climb to the top of the baseball ladder as a 19-year-old in 1991. His first taste of professional baseball was with the Burlington Indians in the short-season Appalachian League, and the six-foot-tall, 200-

Manny Ramirez

pound, right-handed slugger put his enormous talents on display immediately, much to the enjoyment of the rookie league fans. He hit a resounding .326 while leading the league in home runs (19) and runs batted in (63) in 59 games, as the Indians won the pennant by four games. After two more seasons in the Cleveland farm system, Manny found his way to the big club at the end of the 1993 season. He was in the majors to stay. He debuted in 22 games at the end of the 1993 season, hitting just .170, but the following year, playing in 91 games, he increased his batting average to .269 while hitting 17 home runs and driving in 60 runs in 290 at-bats. From 1995 through 2000, Manny Ramirez tortured American League pitchers to the tune of a .319 average, with 38 doubles, 38 home runs, and 130 runs batted in, for every 550 at-bats. But, as he was to display several times in Boston, the superstar grew disenchanted with the Cleveland organization, and he declared free agency after the 2000 season, eventually signing with the Boston Red Sox on December 13.

Manny quickly won the support and admiration of the Red Sox faithful, batting .306 in 2001 with 41 homers and 125 RBI in 529 at-bats. The next year, he won the American League batting title with a sizzling .349 average, with 31 doubles, 33 home runs, and 107 RBI, in 436 at-bats. He hit .325 with 36 doubles, 37 home runs, and 104 runs batted in, in 2003, as the Red Sox moved to within six games of the division-winning New York Yankees while capturing the wild card slot in the post-season playoffs. In the American League Division Series, Boston defeated Oakland three games to two, and Manny contributed a homer and three RBI. In the ALCS, manager Grady Little's charges lost a seven-game series to the Yankees as Manny hit .310 with two homers and four RBI.

General Manager Theo Epstein and new manager Terry Francona felt the Red Sox were ready to challenge for the brass ring in 2004 and they quickly secured the services of fireballing Curt Schilling and closer Keith Foulke. Manny Ramirez had a great season in 2004, batting .308 with 108 runs scored, 130 runs batted in, 44 doubles, and a league-leading 43 home runs. The Red Sox set the pace in the American League most of the season, but they faded down the stretch, finishing second to New York once again. Still, they managed to win another wild-card berth in post-season play, and this time they were armed and ready. After sweeping the Anaheim Angels in three games, with Manny ripping the ball at a .385 pace with seven RBI, they rallied from a three-games-to-none deficit against New York to sweep the last four games and claim the American League pennant. In the World Series, they routed the St. Louis Cardinals four straight, ending an 86 year jinx and, along with it, the "Curse of the Bambino." Manny chipped in with a .412 average with one home run and four RBI.

Manny, and his slugging sidekick, David Ortiz, had outstanding seasons in 2005 and 2006, but Boston could do no better than second- and third-place finishes respectively. As Palmer and Gillette noted, Ramirez "alternated saying he wanted a trade and then saying he was happy playing for the Red Sox. This led one teammate to opine that it was just 'Manny being Manny.'"[156] In 2007 history repeated itself as the Red Sox won their second World Championship in four years. This time they even won the American League Eastern Division title, finishing two games ahead of the hated New York Yankees, and Manny was a big contributor to the victory, although it was a sub-par season for him, with a .296 batting average, 20 home runs and 88 RBI. He came to life in the post-season, however, slugging the ball at a .375 pace with two homers and four RBI in the ALDS as Boston swept the Anaheim Angels three straight, outscoring them, 19–4. Manny wore the hero's mantle in Game 2, hitting a three-run, walk-off homer in the bottom of the ninth inning to give Terry Francona's boys a 6–3 victory. In the ALCS, Boston bounced back from a three-games-to-one deficit to capture the American League pennant in seven games, with Manny pounding the ball at a .409 clip with two homers and 10 RBI. He took a back seat to Mike Lowell and Jacoby Ellsbury in the World Series, batting .250 as Boston swept the Colorado Rockies in four games.

There were periodic grumblings from the man-child in 2006 and 2007, asking to be traded because he wasn't appreciated or respected by management, but always the furor subsided and Manny was happy again. He even impressed people with his defense in 2007, leading the league with a .990 fielding average and finishing sixth in range factor and fifth in assists. Shortly after the 2008 season got under way, on May 14, Ramirez made one of the most exciting yet entertaining and bizarre plays ever witnessed in a major league park. In the bottom of the fourth inning in Camden Yards, with Boston leading the O's by a 1–0 score, Baltimore put a runner on first base with one out. The batter, Kevin Millar, sent a rocket to deep left field, sending Boston's man-child in hot pursuit. He reached up at the last instant and made a sensational over-the-shoulder catch on the warning track going at full speed. He took three steps before leaping and putting one foot on the wall to brace himself, high-fived a fan in the front row while in the air, turned and threw the ball to shortstop Julio Lugo, who relayed it to Kevin Youklis at first base to double-up Aubrey Huff. Red Sox coach Brad Mills said, "You see something new with Manny all the time. It was a great catch." Two weeks later, on the 31st, he slammed the 500th home run of his illustrious career against six-foot, five-inch right-hander Chad Bradford. He jumped on the first pitch from Bradford and sent it 410 feet to section 94, row P, in Camden Yards. Shortly after this, his off-field behavior became too much of a distraction for Red Sox officials to tolerate, and he was traded to the Los Angeles Dodgers on July 31. At the time of his departure, he was hitting .299 with 20 home runs and 68 RBI in 365 at-bats.

During his Red Sox career, from 2001 into 2008, the future Hall Of Famer was generally recognized as one of the greatest clutch hitters in the game and a particularly dangerous hitter after he had two strikes on him. He was also one of the primary antagonists of Joe Torre's New York Yankees. Overall, he rattled the fences to the tune of a .312 average with Boston in 3,953 at-bats. He is a 12-time all-star, and the winner of nine Silver Slugger awards. He also has 29 career post-season home runs, the most in baseball history, and 21 career grand slams, the most of any active player and two behind Lou Gehrig. Manny Ramirez is gone but he won't soon be forgotten in Beantown.

Reardon, Jeff

Jeffrey James Reardon was born in Pittsfield, Massachusetts, on October 1, 1955. The six-foot, one-inch, 200-pound, right-handed pitcher was signed to a baseball contract by the New York Mets in 1977 and sent to their Single-A farm team in Lynchburg in the Carolina League, where he posted a record of 8–3 as a starting pitcher. The following year, with the Jackson Mets in the Double-A Texas League, he led the league with 17 victories and an .810 winning percentage, pitching 163 innings in 28 games with a 2.53 earned run average. When he joined Tidewater in the International League in 1979, he was converted to a relief pitcher, going 5–2 with five saves in 30 games covering 69 innings. He was promoted to the New York Mets in late summer, making his major league debut on August 25. Over the last month of the season, the hard-throwing rookie pitched 20⅔ innings in 18 games with a 1–2 won-lost record and an impressive 1.74 ERA.

Reardon worked out of the bullpen for the Mets over the next year and a half, pitching 139 innings in 79 games, with a 9–7 won-loss record and eight saves. On May 29, 1981, the big fireballer was traded to the Montreal Expos and helped them reach post-season play, pitching in 25 games with two wins, no losses, six saves, and a minuscule 1.30 ERA. He recorded two saves against Philadelphia in the National League Division Series, won by the Expos in five games, but he appeared in only one game, with no record, in the NLCS loss to the Los Angeles Dodgers. The Massachusetts native spent five more years as Montreal's closer, with 146 saves, including a league-leading 41 saves in 1985, followed by three years in Minnesota where he saved another 104 games and was a key factor in the Twins' 1987 World Championship. He appeared in 63 games that year, pitching 80⅓ innings with an 8–8 record and 31 saves as Tom Kelly's team nosed out the Kansas City Royals by two games to win the American League West Division. "The Terminator," as he was called by then, was 1–1 with one save in the ALCS and 0–0 with two saves in the World Series against Whitey Herzog's St. Louis Cardinals. Fittingly, he was on the mound when the last out was recorded in Minnesota's exciting 4–2 victory in Game 7.

The bearded closer filed for free agency after the 1989 season and signed with his home-state Boston Red Sox on December 6. He pitched for Boston over the next three years, helping his new team win the American League East title in his first season, but also struggling through a so-so season two years later. Reardon pitched 51⅓ innings in 47 games in 1990, compiling a 5–3 record with 21 saves, before he was sidelined from July 30 to September 12 after having back surgery. He pitched in just one game in the ALCS, with no record, as Joe Morgan's cohorts were blown away by the Oakland Athletics in four straight. The following year, he pitched 59⅓ innings in 57 games, winning one, losing four, and saving 40, becoming the first closer in baseball history to save 40 games with three different teams. Reardon's heroics couldn't prevent Boston from slipping into third place, however, and the 1992 season was even worse as the team plummeted into the American League cellar. Rookie manager Butch Hobson couldn't stem the bleeding as Boston won just 73 games against 89 losses, finishing 23 games behind the high-flying Toronto Blue Jays. Reardon had a so-so season in 1992, pitching in 46 games with a 2–2 won-loss record and 27 saves, but his ERA ballooned to 4.25

and he blew eight saves for a modest 77 percent save percentage. He was traded to the Atlanta Braves on August 31, closing the Boston chapter of his baseball career. One highlight of his 1992 season was breaking Rollie Fingers' major league career saves record of 341. Jeff Reardon pitched two more years in the major leagues, increasing his saves record to 367, before retiring.

Reed, Jody

Jody Eric Reed was born in Tampa, Florida, on July 26, 1962, and attended Florida State University, where he blossomed into an outstanding defensive shortstop. In his junior year at FSU, the scrappy infielder led the team with 97 runs scored, 23 doubles, 68 bases on balls, and 31 stolen bases, and was selected to the All-South Regional team. The following year he was the MVP of the Metro Conference. The Boston Red Sox signed Reed to a baseball contract in 1984 and sent him to Winter Haven in the Single-A Florida State League, where he hit .271 in 77 games.

After three more years of minor league preparation, the five-foot, nine-inch, 165-pound infielder made his Boston debut in Fenway Park on September 12, 1987, as a pinch-runner in Boston's 4–3 win over the Baltimore Orioles. Six days later, he made his first start, batting leadoff and going 3-for-6 with two RBI and a stolen base in the second game of a doubleheader in Baltimore's Memorial Stadium, pacing the Red Sox to a 10–7 victory. He rapped four base hits in five at-bats, with a double and three RBI in Boston's 9–6 loss to the Milwaukee Brewers on September 27, and the next night, in Yankee Stadium, he slugged a bases-loaded triple in the first inning, giving John McNamara's team a quick 5–0 lead, but the Boston bullpen self-destructed in the bottom of the ninth inning as New York pushed over six runs for a 9–7 victory. Reed finished the season with a .300 batting average in 30 at-bats. The following year, he earned his major league stripes, as manager Joe Morgan, after replacing McNamara, installed him as the regular shortstop replacing Spike Owen, and the move was a major factor in Boston's race to the division title. Reed batted .293 during the season with 23 doubles and just 21 strikeouts in 338 at-bats, and gave Morgan solid defense. In post season play, he chipped in with a .273 average in a losing effort against Oakland in the ALCS.

In the off-season between the 1988 and 1989 seasons, the baby-faced infielder went on a weight-lifting regimen in hopes of finding Fenway's left field wall more frequently and driving more balls into the gaps for extra bases. The move paid immediate dividends as

Reed added 13 pounds of muscle to his slight frame and went on to almost double his two-base production from the previous year, from 23 to 42. The Florida native was shifted to second base in 1990, giving Boston tight defense on the right side to go along with his timely offense. He averaged from .283 to .293 during his first four years in Boston, and put together three consecutive seasons of more than 40 doubles, including a league-leading 45 doubles in 1990. On the flip side, on July 17, 1990, Jody Reed became a part of baseball history he would rather forget. In the bottom of the fourth inning of a game between the Red Sox and the Minnesota Twins in Fenway Park, Boston had the bases loaded with no outs and Tom Brunansky at bat. The Red Sox right fielder hit a bullet toward third base but Gary Gaetti was perfectly positioned and he gloved the ball, stepped on third for one out and started an around-the-horn triple play. Four innings later, as Yogi Berra would say, "It was déjà vu all over again." Boston had men on first and second with no outs and Jody Reed at the plate. Reed pulled the ball down the third base line where Gaetti picked it up while standing on the base and started another 5-4-3 triple play, the first time in major league history that one team hit into two triple plays in the same game. The bright spot in the fiasco was that Boston won the game by a 1–0 count behind rangy southpaw Tom Bolton, and Tim Naehring drove in the only run with his first major league base hit. After the game, Gaetti said he was expecting a ground ball from Brunansky because Scott Erickson, a noted sinker ball artist, was on the mound, and he said to Wade Boggs, the Red Sox runner on third, "Watch this, a triple play," to which Boggs just shook his head and made a face. After falling to .247 in 1992, Reed was left unprotected in the expansion draft and was selected by the Colorado Rockies, subsequently playing for four different teams over the next five years. Jody Reed played for the Red Sox for five full seasons, batting .280 and posting a brilliant .988 fielding average. He had few equals as he patrolled the inner garden, with quick reflexes, exceptional range, and a magnet for a glove.

Regan, Bill

William Wright Regan was born in Pittsburgh, Pennsylvania, on January 23, 1899. He spent a year in the U.S. Army during World War I, and played semi-pro baseball for four years before giving the professional game a try. He began his career in organized baseball with the Columbus Senators in the Double-A American Association in 1925, at the advanced baseball age of 26, batting a hard .297 with 33 doubles, 10 triples, and 12 home runs in 548 at-bats. The following season, he completed his minor league schooling, splitting his time between the Senators and the Portsmouth Truckers of the Class-B Virginia League, hitting .332 with the Truckers in 563 at-bats and .318 with the Senators in 148 at-bats, before moving up in class to the Boston Red Sox, beginning a five-year tenure as the team's regular second baseman.

Bill Regan came to the Red Sox with a reputation as a smart base runner and a dependable line-drive hitter who was adept at finding gaps in the outfield for two and three bases. He made his major league debut with Boston on June 2, 1926, going hitless as a pinch-hitter. After one more pinch hitting chore, he made his first start at second base on June 8, fielding flawlessly but going 0-for-4 at the plate as Boston dropped a 6-5 decision to the St. Louis Browns in Sportsman's Park. The next day he got his first major league base hit, going 2-for-4 as Boston once again fell to the Browns by a 6-4 score. Regan had one of his biggest days at the plate on June 13, ripping four base hits in five at-bats with two RBI as the Red Sox brought the Detroit Tigers to their knees, 7 to 3, in Navin Field. He also handled 11 chances in the field flawlessly and was the middle-man on two double plays. On July 24, the slightly built second baseman went 2-for-5 with three RBI and two runs scored as Boston battered the St. Louis Browns, 14-9. On September 26, as the Red Sox season was winding down to another last place finish, Regan slammed a three-run homer in the first inning, giving his team a temporary 3-0 lead over Detroit, but it was not enough as the Tigers fought back with three runs in the eighth and another run in the bottom of the ninth to pull out a 5-4 victory. Overall, the five-foot, ten-inch, 155-pound infielder had a decent rookie season in the Hub, posting a .263 batting average with 28 extra-base hits in 403 at-bats.

Regan's sophomore year was one of his better years as he hit .274 with 37 doubles, 10 triples, and 66 RBI in 468 at-bats. He increased his run production in 1928, playing in 138 games, a career high, and batting .264 in 511 at-bats, with 30 doubles, six triples, seven home runs, and 75 runs batted in. He also had his biggest day at the plate as a major leaguer that year. On June 16, he had a once-in-a-lifetime thrill as he blasted two home runs in the fourth inning, one of them an inside-the-park job, against the Chicago White Sox, tying a major league record, as Boston rallied from a 3-0 deficit to put eight big runs on the board en route to a 10-5 triumph. Boston's second baseman also had a single and a double in five at-bats and drove in three runs. In the field, he handled six chances flawlessly. The Pittsburgh native played two more years in Boston, batting .288 in 1929, and .266 in 1930 with 35 doubles and 10 triples in 507 at-bats. He was waived to his hometown Pittsburgh Pirates in January, 1931, played one year with the Pirates and then retired. Bill Regan had the misfortune of playing for the Boston Red Sox during the worst period in the team's history. They finished in last place in each of Regan's five years with the club. Still, he posted a strong .270 batting average and was a solid defensive.

Remy, Jerry

The five-foot, nine-inch, 160-pound infielder was known as a hard-nosed, gritty, all-around second baseman. He was smart, had good range, and a reliable glove. At the plate, he was an excellent bunter, a tough out, and a dangerous clutch hitter. On the bases, he had speed to burn, constantly tormenting opposing pitchers. As Hugh McGovern reported, "Remy does everything right. He sprays hits. He covers ground. He steals bases. Above all, he hustles."

Remy himself confirmed that. "No one has ever seen me loaf in a game. It's not my style."[157]

Gerald Peter Remy was drafted by the Washington Senators out of high school in 1971, but entered college for a semester instead. The California Angels drafted Remy out of the Senators' system the following January, and he joined the west coast contingent as their regular second baseman four years later, after hitting .338 with El Paso in the Texas League and .292 with Salt Lake City in the Pacific Coast League. He made his major league debut against Kansas City on April 7, 1975, going 1-for-3 with an RBI. In the second inning, with two on and two out, Remy lined a single to left field, driving in a run, but he was so excited after getting his first major league base hit that he was immediately picked off first base by Steve Busby to kill the rally. Fortunately, the Angels went on to defeat the Royals, 3–2. He played 147 games for California in his rookie season, batting a respectable .258 with 82 runs scored and 34 stolen bases, and he was rewarded with a spot on the Topps All-Rookie team. Remy played two more years on the west coast, hitting .263 and .252 respectively, stealing 35 and 41 bases, and winning "the Angels Owners Trophy, voted by his teammates for his leadership, sportsmanship, and professional ability during the 1976 campaign."[158] When the Angels signed the fancy-fielding Bobby Grich to a free-agent contract, Remy's days in California were numbered. The Red Sox acquired him in a trade for Don Aase on December 8, 1977, and California's loss was Boston's gain.

The Massachusetts native was thrilled to be a member of the Boston Red Sox, having followed the team as a youngster. He remembered his first view of Fenway Park. It's a sight that most people, including the author, never forget. As he walked up the ramp toward the field for a night game, he was mesmerized first by the bright lights, then by the enormous green left field wall that hovered over the brilliant green outfield. Jerry Remy was happy to be home. He played the last seven years of his major league career with Boston, but injuries severely restricted his playing time. In fact, he had only three years where he played in more than 100 games.

His first year in Boston, in 1978, was one of his best. He hit a solid .278 in 148 games with 87 runs scored and 30 stolen bases. The year ended in a disappointing manner for the Red Sox, however, as Bucky Dent knocked them out of the pennant race with his now famous home run into the screen over the Green Monster in the one-game playoff to decide the American League Eastern Division Champion. Remy went 2-for-4 with a double in a losing cause. He ripped a two-base hit down the right field line leading off the eighth inning and eventually came around to score a run to cut the New York lead to 5–3. In the ninth, with one on and one out in a one-run game, he lined a single to right field, putting runners on first and second, but that was all the Sox could get. Goose Gossage, who had already been nicked for two runs in two innings, settled down, took a deep breath and retired Jim Rice on a fly ball to right field and Carl Yastrzemski on a popup to third base, ending Boston's season. The next year, he injured his knee sliding home against the New York Yankees and spent 53 days on the disabled list. He put together seasons of .297, .313, and .307 over the next three years, but he played in only 231 of 462 scheduled games because of his knee problems. One game he will remember was played on September 3, 1981, in Fenway Park against the Seattle Mariners. The game lasted 20 innings before Seattle pushed over the eighth and deciding run in the six-

Jerry Remy

hour, one-minute marathon. Remy went 6-for-10 in the game including a leadoff infield single in the ninth inning that keyed a three-run, game-tying rally. The scrappy infielder returned to full-time action in 1982, batting .280, beating out 19 bunt singles, sacrificing 18 times in 21 attempts, and swiping 16 bases. The following year he hit .275 but played with pain much of the time. Still, he tied for the league lead with a .990 fielding percentage. He played in just 30 games in 1984, finally retiring when the pain became too severe. In all, Remy had suffered through ten knee operations in six years before throwing in the sponge.

During his Boston career, the little left-handed hitter scorched the ball at a .286 clip in 2,809 at-bats with 98 stolen bases. Defensively, he led the league in double plays once and triple plays twice. His .981 career fielding average was two points higher than the league average and his range was outstanding. Remy explained the secret to his success in "The 1978 Red Sox Magazine": "I'm not blessed with tremendous talent and skill. But I try to make the most of my ability. I give 100 percent and I push as hard as I can every day."[159] Jerry Remy became a sportscaster after his baseball career ended, and in 1978 he joined the New England Sports Network, doing color commentary for the Boston Red Sox. The man that Red Sox Nation calls "RemDawg," brought his work ethic with him into the broadcasting booth, and now he and his sidekick, Don Orsillo, are two of the most popular sportscasters in Red Sox history. Remy was inducted into the Red Sox Hall of Fame in 2006.

Rhyne, Hal

Harold J. "Hal" Rhyne was a solid Triple-A player, both offensively and defensively, in the Pacific Coast League, but his bat failed him frequently during his seven-year major league career. The five-foot, eight-and-a-half-inch, 163-pound, right-handed hitter was born in Paso Robles, California, on March 30, 1899. He joined the San Francisco club in the Pacific Coast League in 1922 and showed great promise of future major league stardom. He hit between .285 and .315 for the Seals from 1922 through 1925, slamming 147 doubles and driving in 347 runs in 2235 at-bats, and he led all PCL shortstops in fielding the last two years. He was sold to the Pittsburgh Pirates, along with Paul Waner, for $100,000 in 1925, but he was converted to a second baseman by manager Bill McKechnie, who already had the sensational Glenn Wright at shortstop. Hal Rhyne made his major league debut in Redland Field, Cincinnati, on April 18, 1926, as the Pirates were downing the Reds by a 3–1 score. The new Pittsburgh second baseman hit in the number seven slot in the batting order and was hitless in four trips to the plate, but he distinguished himself in the field, handling six chances cleanly. He got his first base hit four days later in a 5–3 loss to the St. Louis Cardinals. Rhyne hit .251 in 109 games for Pittsburgh in his rookie season but, in 1927, an illness kept him on the sidelines much of the season, limiting his activity to 62 games during which he hit .274. George Grantham, his replacement at second base, batted a solid .305 as the Bucs raced to the National League pennant by one-and-a-half games over the St. Louis Cardinals, and suddenly Rhyne was expendable.

He was traded to the Boston Red Sox over the winter and spent the next four years in the Hub as their regular shortstop. He performed admirably in the field for the Sox and led the American League in fielding average (.963) and assists (502) in 1931, but he was erratic at the plate, posting season averages of .251, .203, .273, and .227. His best offensive year with the Red Sox was 1931, when he stroked the ball at a respectable .273 pace with 34 doubles and 75 runs scored. On August 30 of that year, the Red Sox moved their Sunday game with the New York Yankees to Braves Field in order to handle the anticipated large turnout. There, before 23,000 noisy Red Sox fans, Rhyne, hitting out of the number two slot, ripped four base hits in five at-bats with an RBI in a 14–4 loss to Ruth, Gehrig, and company. He also had two putouts and five assists in the field and started a 6-4-3 double play. The home plate umpire for the game was the hero of Boston's first World Series triumph in 1903, Bill Dinneen. After playing in just 71 games in 1932 and hitting a weak .227, the smooth-fielding shortstop was traded to the Chicago White Sox on December 15. He saw action in 39 games with the

White Sox in 1933 and then returned to the Pacific Coast League, playing another four years with the Seals before retiring in 1938.

Rice, Jim

James Edward Rice was born in Anderson, South Carolina, on March 8, 1953. He attended Westside and Hanna High Schools in the city, winning ten letters in baseball, track, football, and basketball. He signed a professional baseball contract with Boston on June 10, 1971, and was sent to the Williamsport Red Sox in the Single-A New York-Pennyslvania League, where he hit .256 in 60 games, with five homers and 27 RBI. The following year, with Winter Haven in the Florida State League, he hit .291 with 17 homers in 491 at-bats, leading the league in runs scored (80) and base hits (143), and earning a place on the league's All-Star team. He hit a league-leading .317 with 27 homers and 93 RBI for Bristol in the Double-A Eastern League in 1973 and followed that up with a banner season with the Pawtucket Red Sox in the Triple-A International League, where he won the Triple Crown, batting .337 with 25 home runs and 93 runs batted in, in 117 games. He was called up to Boston after the IL season ended, making his major league debut on August 19, going 0-for-2 as the designated hitter in Boston's 6–1 win over the Chicago White Sox. Two days later, he went 2-for-4 with two RBI to support Roger Moret's one-hit, 12-strikeout, 4–0 gem. He appeared in 24 games over the last seven weeks of the season, batting .269 in 67 at-bats.

The six-foot, two-inch, 200-pound, right-handed slugger had an excellent rookie season with Boston in 1975, stinging the ball at a .309 clip with 22 homers and 102 RBI. On July 18, Rice, whose short, compact swing allowed him to wait until the last second to commit to a swing, hit a tremendous home run over the center field wall to the right of the flagpole in Fenway Park that Red Sox owner Tom Yawkey called the longest homer he ever saw hit in the old park. The Boston left fielder, who was noted for his strong wrists, regularly sent balls on a high arc over the screen above the Green Monster and out of the park. Rice's strength was legendary. Once he snapped his bat in half on a checked swing without ever making contact with the ball. One source on baseballlibrary.com said he had golf clubs bend in his hands on his downswing. Unfortunately for Rice and the Red Sox, his season came to an abrupt end on September 21 when he was hit by a pitch thrown by Vern Ruhle, breaking his left hand. The injury kept him out of post-season play and perhaps cost the Red Sox a World Championship.

Jim Rice was not only a slugger. He was also a capable defensive left fielder who was a worthy successor to Ted Williams and Carl Yastrzemski. "Rice was never blessed with great speed or agility in left field, but he mastered the intricacies of Fenway Park's left field wall. He was particularly adept at decoying opposing base runners, who would often be surprised to slide into outs at second base after ripping line drives high off The Wall."[160] During his career, he led the league in fielding average, double plays, and putouts twice each.

The South Carolina native hit .282 in 1976 and .320 the following year, with 104 runs scored and 114 RBI, while leading the league in

Jim Rice

both home runs (39) and slugging average (.593). He reached his peak as a player in 1978 when he was named the American League's Most Valuable Player after rattling the fences to the tune of a .315 average with 121 runs scored and 25 doubles, and leading the league with 213 base hits, 15 triples, 46 home runs, 139 RBI, 406 total bases, and a .600 slugging average. He was, according to the Red Sox Fan Handbook, "the first player in 37 years to amass 400 total bases in a season." From 1977 to 1986, James Edward Rice was the most feared slugger in the American League, batting .305 and averaging 28 home runs and 101 RBI for every 550 at-bats. In 1986, he hit .324 with 39 doubles, 20 home runs, and 110 runs batted in, as Boston won the Eastern Division title by five-and-a-half games over the New York Yankees. He hit just .161 in the ALCS but he made his hits count as he ripped two home runs and drove in six runs in the seven-game series. In the Game 7 finale he stepped to the plate in the fourth inning with two men on base and two out and promptly brought 33,001 wild Fenway fanatics to their feet with a blast to left. It made the score 7–0 and just about iced the game. He hit .333 with a double, a triple, and six runs scored in the seven-game World Series loss to the New York Mets.

Rice missed 54 games during the 1987 season with various elbow and knee problems, finally having arthroscopic surgery on both knees in October. He struggled through two more painful seasons, aggravated by recurring eye problems, before retiring after the 1989 season. Jim Rice spent his entire 16-year major league career with the Boston Red Sox, hitting .298 in 8,225 at-bats with 382 home runs and 1451 RBI. He was elected to the National Baseball Hall of Fame in 2009.

Rivera, Luis

Luis Antonio Rivera, a five-foot, nine-inch, 170-pound shortstop, was signed to a minor league contract by the Montreal Expos in 1982 at the age of 18 and was shipped all the way to California, to the Expos' San Jose farm club in the California League, where he batted .258 with 26 extra-base hits in 130 games. He made his way through the Montreal farm system over the next three years, in such way-stops as West Palm Beach, Jacksonville, and Indianapolis, always struggling with the bat, but earning his stripes with his glove. Four years later, he joined the Expos, hitting .205 in 55 games. In 1988, he replaced Hubie Brooks, an offensive weapon but a defensive liability at shortstop. Unfortunately, Rivera's smooth defense couldn't offset his .224 batting average and he was shipped off to the Boston Red Sox for slick-fielding Spike Owen on December 8, 1990. He was Boston's regular shortstop for five years before giving way to John Valentin in 1993. During his Boston years, the right-handed hitter posted averages of .257, .225, .258, .215, and .208. He filed for free agency on October 25, 1993, eventually signing with the New York Mets.

Roberts, Dave

Dave Roberts played for the Boston Red Sox for just one year, appearing in 46 games with 86 at-bats, but one play in the 2004 American League Championship Series elevated the five-foot, ten-inch, 180-pound speedster to legendary status in Boston. His name will be remembered in the Hub as long as baseball is played there. The year 2004 was a magical season in Boston as Terry Francona's cohorts erased the "Curse of the Bambino" forever by powering their way through the post-season to win the team's first World Championship in 86 years. The key game of the post-season was the fourth game of the American League Championship Series against the New York Yankees. Joe Torre's troops had raced to a three-games-to-none lead over the Fenway Flock, including a 19–8 thrashing in Game 3, and they held a 4–3 lead in the bottom of the ninth inning of Game 4 with their all-world closer, Mariano Rivera, on the mound. When Kevin Millar drew a base on balls from Rivera to open the inning, Francona wasted no time in inserting Dave Roberts into the game as a pinch-runner. Roberts said when he looked at Francona from his perch on first base, Terry winked at him, and he knew what that meant. The Boston speedster took off on the first pitch and slid into second base safely, his head-first slide just beating an accurate throw from Jorge Posada, putting the tying run in scoring position. Minutes later, Roberts carried Boston's biggest run of the season across the plate on a single by Bill

Mueller. Three innings later, Big Papi sent the Fenway crowd home happy with a walk-off home run. From there, the Red Sox swept the last eight post-season games, taking the Yankees to task, four games to three, and sweeping the Colorado Rockies in the World Series, four games to none. Dave Roberts, in his only year in a Boston uniform, batted .256 with 22 base hits in 86 at-bats, with ten doubles, five stolen bases, and 14 RBI. He appeared in three games in the post-season with no at-bats, two runs scored, and one historic stolen base.

Rothrock, Jack

He played for the Boston Red Sox during their darkest days. From 1925 through 1932, Boston's American League franchise finished in last place in seven of the eight years he played for them. They finished sixth in 1931. John Houston Rothrock began his professional baseball career as a shortstop with the Class-D Arkansas City Osages in the Southwest League in 1924, batting .314 with 28 extra-base hits in 449 at-bats. The following year, with the same team, he hit .337 with 20 doubles, seven triples, and seven home runs in 329 at-bats, before being sold to the Boston Red Sox, where he made his major league debut on July 28, 1925. He was a late-inning replacement in a 16–7 loss to the Cleveland Indians, and he hit a weak ground ball back to the pitcher in his only at-bat. He finally got a base hit in his third game, slamming a double as a pinch-hitter. His best game of the year took place in Fenway Park on October 2 against the Washington Senators, when he had three hits in five at-bats, including a bases-loaded triple in the first inning that sent the Red Sox off to a quick 4–0 lead. The final score was 10–2 as Howard Ehmke won his ninth game of the year against 20 losses. The big right-hander labored tirelessly for the Sox, pitching 260⅔ innings, but he was the victim of poor run support as Boston was dead last in runs scored and dead last in the league, finishing with a record of 47–105, 49½ games behind the pennant-winning Senators. Rothrock, who was considered to be the fastest man in the major leagues, and who once said, "I'd rather play ball than eat," played 22 games at shortstop for Boston over the last half of the season, scorching the ball at a .345 clip with three doubles, three triples, and seven RBI in 55 at-bats. In the 1926 opener, he slammed a pinch-hit double, driving in a run in Boston's 12–11 loss to the New York Yankees in the Fens, but he was soon farmed out to Rochester in the Double-A International League, where he played 84 games at second base and batted .302 in 315 at-bats. His Red Sox season totaled 15 games where he batted .294 in 17 at-bats.

The five-foot, 11-and-a-half-inch, 165-pound switch hitter was back in the big show to stay in 1927, primarily as a utility player, playing 40 games at shortstop, 36 games at second base, 20 games at third base, and 13 games at first base, and he hit .259 in 428 at-bats. Boston's Jack-of-all-trades was back on the job in 1928, playing all nine positions at one time or another. He played ten or more games at six different positions, including 53 games in the

Dave Roberts

outfield, plus two games at second base, and one game each at catcher and pitcher, before being given the center field job on a permanent basis to take advantage of his speed and his strong arm. His best year with Boston was 1929 when he covered the expansive terrain in Fenway Park as if he were born to play that position. At the plate, he hit an even .300 with 32 extra-base hits, 59 RBI, a .361 on-base percentage, and 24 stolen bases. Rothrock broke his leg sliding into second base in the fourth game of the 1930 season and missed three months. When he returned, he was used primarily as a pinch-hitter the rest of the year, batting .277 in 65 at-bats. He bounced back to play 133 games the following season, hitting .278 with 32 doubles, but saw action in only 12 games in 1933 before being traded to Chicago in a five-player deal on April 29. He went on to play another three years with the St. Louis Cardinals and the Philadelphia Athletics before returning to the minor leagues in 1938. He played for the Cardinals' 1934 World Championship team, batting a crisp .284 with 35 doubles, 11 home runs, 72 runs batted in, and 106 runs scored. He had a team-high six RBI in their World Series victory over the Detroit Tigers. Rothrock ended his professional baseball career with the Los Angeles Angels in the Pacific Coast League in 1940.

Ruffing, Red

Charles Herbert "Red" Ruffing, a 1967 inductee into the National Baseball Hall of Fame in Cooperstown, New York, is the perfect example of a pitcher whose place in baseball history is determined as much by his team's success as by his pitching skills. Unlike position players, whose statistics are more individual accomplishments, pitchers have to play for a winning team if they hope to get recognized for their skills. For the first five years of his 22-year major league career, Red Ruffing pitched for the hapless Boston Red Sox, whose incompetence kept them more than 43 games out of first place every year from 1925 through 1929. That period was one of the darkest chapters in the history of the Boston franchise, with five consecutive last-place finishes, a total of 259 victories against 507 losses, and a .338 winning percentage. Fortunately for Ruffing, he was traded to the New York Yankees on May 6, 1930, and went on to win 231 games for the Bronx Bombers over the next 15 years, helping them capture seven American League pennants and six World championships.

Ruffing began his professional baseball career as an 18-year-old right-handed pitcher with Danville of the Three-I League in 1923, where he fashioned a 12–16 record in 239 innings pitched over 39 games. The next year, he won four games against seven losses for Dover in the Eastern Shore League before being purchased by the Boston Red Sox. He pitched in eight games for Lee Fohl's team at the end of the season with no record, and quickly evolved into one of the top pitchers in Boston's starting rotation, behind Howard Ehmke and Hal Wiltse. The six-foot, one-and-a-half-inch, 205-pound flamethrower pitched 217⅓ innings in 37 games in 1925, with 27 starts, 13 complete games, and three shutouts, while struggling through a 9–18 campaign. He compiled won-lost records of 6–15, 5–13, 10–25, and 9–22 for Boston over the next four years, while perfecting his pitching repertoire that included a sharp curve and a slider in addition to his blazer. "I pitch three or four fastballs for every curve. I have a pretty good curve, pretty good control, pretty good everything except luck," he noted.[161]

The big right-hander was rescued from the scrap heap on May 6, 1930, when he was traded to the New York Yankees for Cedric Durst and $50,000. He went on to enjoy four consecutive 20-win seasons with Joe McCarthy's Bronx Bombers between 1936 and 1939, and the Yankees captured the World Championship in each of those years. He pitched in a total of ten World Series games for New York, with eight complete games, a 7–2 won-lost record, and 61 strikeouts in 85⅔ innings. He was also one of the game's best-hitting pitchers, compiling a .269 career batting average with 36 home runs, the third highest home run total for pitchers. He had a day to remember on Saturday August 18, 1932, in Griffith Stadium, with 10,000 fans looking on. He tossed a ten-inning, 1–0 shutout at the Senators, striking out 12 men along the way, and winning his own game with a home run, becoming one of just three pitchers to win a 1–0 ten-inning game with a home run while striking out ten or more batters. Ruffing finished the 1932 season with a record of 18–7 and a batting average of .306.

Red Ruffing's five-year career totals with the Red Sox show a mediocre 39–96 won-lost record. He led the American League with 25 complete games in 1928. At the plate, he averaged .263 with the Red Sox with 118 base hits in 438 at-bats, with 32 doubles, five triples, and five home runs. He hit .314 in 1928 and .307 in 1929.

Runnels, Pete

James Edward Runnels, who was born in Lufkin, Texas, on January 28, 1928, was called scrappy, competitive, tough, and energetic. He was also known as a sportsman and a team player, and he was all of those things. He was also a dangerous singles hitter, a contact hitter, and a versatile defensive player with good hands and decent range who played all the infield positions at one time or another. Runnels attended Lufkin High School, where he played quarterback on the football team and guard on the basketball team. His baseball education was limited to playing sandlot ball as baseball was not popular in Lufkin. He became addicted to the game after serving as the batboy for his brother's team, but playing it wasn't easy, as he remembered. "We used to have trouble rounding up nine guys to play on the team. In those days, most people there didn't even know what baseball was."[162] Runnels enlisted in the U.S. Marines after graduation from high school, and he was able to play baseball during his three years of military service. He was discharged in 1948 and started his professional baseball career one year later, signing a contract for the 1949 season with Chickasha in the Sooner League, and he tattooed the Class-D pitchers to the tune a of .372 average. The following year, he joined the Texarkana Bears in the Class-B Big State League, where he posted a fine .330 average, persuading the Washington Senators to purchase his contract for $12,500. He played half a season with the Chattanooga Lookouts of the Southern Association in 1951, hitting a crisp .356 and earning himself a trip to the Big Show in July.

Pete Runnels made his major league debut on July 1, and he went on to compile a respectable .278 batting average in 78 games over the last two months of the American League season while doing a workmanlike job at shortstop. He was Washington's regular shortstop for the next four years before showing his versatility by shifting to second base and first base when needs arose. The six-foot, 170-pound, left-handed hitter struggled with the bat early in his career with averages ranging from .230 to .310. But that would all change when he was traded to the Boston Red Sox on January 23, 1958. He gave the Red Sox five outstanding seasons, both offensively and defensively, but his first year may have been his best. He found himself in a race with teammate Ted Williams for the American League batting title. Williams had been tutoring Runnels in batting, teaching him to be more patient at the plate, and now the two men were battling it out, head to head, tied for the highest batting average in the league with two games remaining in the season. In the next-to-last game, Runnels ripped a single, a triple, and a home run, but the Splendid Splinter kept pace with a single, a home run, and a walk. Runnels went hitless in the season finale, however, while Williams picked up two more hits to win the batting title, .328 to .322. The hard-nosed second baseman earned a measure of satisfaction by being named the American League's Comeback Player of the Year. A tough competitor and a true sportsman, Runnels would comment years later on losing the 1958 batting title to Ted Williams, "I enjoyed his catching me on the last day of the season more than my titles in 1960 and 1962 because of the great competition. Wasn't he capable?"

The Texas native, now Boston's regular second baseman, batted .314 in 1959 with 33 doubles, 95 bases on balls, and a superb .415 on-base percentage, the second-best OBP in the American League. He also did an outstanding job at second base, covering the right side of the infield like a blanket and posting a .982 fielding average. The following year he outshone all other second basemen, stinging the ball at a .320 clip to capture the batting championship, and leading the league with a .986 fielding average. On August 30, he tied a major league record for the most hits in a doubleheader with nine. He was 6-for-7 in the opener, including a game-winning double in the 15th inning, and he added three base hits in four at-bats in the nightcap. In 1961, now playing first base, he put together another sterling season, batting .317 and leading all American League first basemen with a .995 fielding average. His last season in Boston was 1962 and he won another batting title, stroking the ball at a .326 pace with 33 doubles, a career-high ten home runs, 79 RBI, and 80 runs scored. After the season was over, Runnels asked to be traded to the expansion Houston Colt 45's so he could end his career in his home state, and Tom Yawkey granted his request, dealing him to Houston on November 26, 1962. Runnels played two years with the Colt 45's, batting .253 and .196 in 22 games before calling it a day at the age of 36.

Pete Runnels spent five productive years in Boston, batting over .300 every year while playing in 732 games with a glittering .320 batting average and an outstanding .408 on-base percentage. He gave the team solid defense wherever he played, including 407 games at first base, 343 games at second base, ten games at shortstop, and 14 games at third base. Pete Runnels was the ultimate team player.

Ruth, Babe

Former teammate Waite Hoyt was quoted in *The Baseball Page* as saying, "I stopped telling people stories about how great (Babe Ruth) was because no one believed me." Lefty Gomez, a long-time teammate, added, "He was a circus, a play and a movie all rolled into one. Kids adored him. Men idolized him. Women loved him. There was something about him that made him great." His tremendous achievements and larger than life personality changed the face of the sport forever. There will never be another Babe Ruth.[163] He was quite simply the greatest all-around baseball player that ever lived. During his first six years in the American League, he was the league's best southpaw pitcher. Later, after he had been converted to an outfielder, he became the most devastating slugger the game has ever known.

George Herman Ruth, Jr., was born in Baltimore, Maryland on February 6, 1895, one of eight children of George Ruth, Sr., and Kate Ruth. His father owned a tavern in the Ridgely's Delight section of the city near the docks, and he and his wife were kept busy 16

Babe Ruth

hours a day working in the tavern, leaving young George to fend for himself. As a result, George ran wild with other unsupervised boys, drinking and smoking, harassing the street prostitutes, stealing fruit from the pushcart peddlers, and rolling drunken sailors on the docks. His life of crime came to an end when, at the age of seven, his father sent him to St. Mary's Industrial School, a combination orphanage and reform school, as an incorrigible. While at St. Mary's, he met Brother Matthias, a hulking six-foot, five-inch, 250-pound behemoth, who was the Head of Discipline at the school. George, who disliked authority of any kind, crossed swords with Brother Matthias many times over the years, but slowly Brother Matthias came to be a father figure to the young delinquent, and the good priest introduced the seven-year-old boy to the game of baseball, channeling his energy in a constructive direction.

Over the 12 years Ruth spent at St. Mary's, he spent all his free time playing baseball, being taught how to hit, how to field, and even how to pitch by Brother Matthias. He, like the other players, rotated positions from game to game, so he learned to play outfield, catcher, shortstop, and pitcher. But most of all, George loved to hit, and he was launching mammoth blasts even as a young teenager. By the time he was 19 years of age, his reputation as a baseball player was well known around the Baltimore area, and he soon came to the attention of Jack Dunn, the owner and manager of the Baltimore Orioles of the International League, who signed him to a professional baseball contract on February 14, 1914, for $250 a month after watching him pitch in the schoolyard.

George Ruth traveled to Florida with the Orioles that spring for his first spring training camp, where he was greeted with indifference by the other players who called him "Jack's Babe," a nickname he would carry with him the rest of his life. The six-foot, two-inch, 190-pound, southpaw pitcher was crude, dirty, and unkempt, with no knowledge of hygiene, but his pitching skills soon earned him the respect of his teammates. Young Babe Ruth helped pitch his team into first place, winning 14 games by early July, but financial considerations forced Dunn to sell his star pitcher, along with two other players, to the Boston Red Sox for $30,000 on July 9, 1914.

Two days later, just five months after leaving St. Mary's Industrial School, Ruth made his major league debut in Fenway Park, pitching a complete-game 4–3 victory over the Cleveland Indians before a raucous Saturday afternoon crowd. He pitched again five days later, dropping a 5–2 decision to the Detroit Tigers at home. At that point in the season, Bill Carrigan's crew was in fifth place, just three-and-a-half games behind the front running Philadelphia Athletics, so Babe Ruth languished on the bench while Carrigan went with experienced players in his chase of Connie Mack's A's. After pitching just one more game over the next month, the teenage southpaw was optioned to the Providence Grays of the International League, who were in a pennant chase of their own. Ruth joined the Grays on August 18 and won nine games down the stretch, helping them capture the league pennant. Along the way, he hit the first home run of his professional baseball career, a towering blast in Toronto on September 5, while he was in the process of pitching a one-hitter. Ruth was recalled to Boston at the end of the International League season, and was called upon to pitch one more time. Since Boston had been eliminated from the pennant race, he took the mound in Fenway Park on October 2 to face the New York Yankees, and he came away with an 11–5 victory. Overall, Babe Ruth posted an excellent 25–9 record in his first season in organized baseball, 23–8 with Baltimore and Providence and 2–1 with Boston.

The year 1915 was the Babe's first full season in the major leagues and he made it a good one. He won 18 games against eight losses for the Red Sox, making 28 starts in 36 games pitched, with 16 complete games and a fine 2.44 ERA over 217⅔ innings. He also swung a mean bat, hitting .315 with ten doubles and four home runs in 92 at-bats. Boston won the American League pennant by two-and-a-half games over the Detroit Tigers that year and met the Philadelphia Phillies in the World Series. Carrigan's crew won the Series in five games, but Ruth's only appearance was as a pinch-hitter in Game 1. The following year, the big lefty unleashed his fastball and his crackling curve with a new energy as he gradually assumed the position of the team's ace. He posted a sensational 23–12 won-loss record with league-leading totals in games started (41), shutouts (9), and ERA (a minuscule 1.75). He pitched 323⅔ innings in 44 games with 170 strikeouts and 118 bases on balls. Thanks to the Babe, the Red Sox took the measure of the Chicago White Sox by two games in the American League pennant race and met the National League Champion Brooklyn Robins in the World Series. Ruth started Game 2 and was touched up for an inside-the-park home run to deep right-center field by Robins outfielder Hy Myers in the first inning. He drove in the tying run himself with an infield out in the bottom of the third inning and then threw goose eggs at the Robins for another 11 innings until Boston pushed over the game-winner in the 14th inning. That game is still the longest complete-game victory in World Series history. Ruth did not have another opportunity to pitch in the Series as Boston closed it out in five games.

In 1917, the Boston Red Sox engaged in another knock-down, drag-out battle for the American League pennant, but this time they came up short, finishing nine games behind the Chicago White Sox. Babe Ruth held up his end of the pitching rotation, going 24–13 with a league leading 35 complete games in 38 starts. He pitched 326⅓ innings in 41 games with six shutouts, 128 strikeouts, and a 2.01 ERA. The young, 22-year-old southpaw was already being recognized as the best left-handed pitcher in the American League, and perhaps the major leagues. He was earning an even bigger reputation as a slugger. He crushed the ball at a .325 clip in 1917 with six doubles, three triples, and two home runs in 123 at-bats over 52 games. His best game of the season, and one he called his greatest thrill, was a Wednesday afternoon game in Briggs Stadium, Detroit, on July 11. He threw a one-hitter at Hughie Jennings' team, holding them hitless until the eighth inning, when Donie Bush hit a hard ground ball that deflected off Ruth's glove to shortstop Deacon Scott, whose throw to first just failed to nip the fleet-footed Detroit infielder. Boston pushed over the winning run in the ninth inning on a triple by Chuck Shorten, and Ruth finished off the Tigers with a flourish, fanning the heart of the Detroit batting order, Bobby Veach, Sam Crawford, and Ty Cobb, in order.

The 1918 season was the turning point in Babe Ruth's career. He loved hitting the baseball and told Red Sox management that he wanted to play the outfield instead of pitching, so manager Bill Carrigan accommodated him. There was a shortage of players in 1918 due to military service in World War I, so Ruth was pressed into service in the outfield or at first base as needed. On May 6, batting sixth and playing first base, the big left-handed slugger went 2-for-4 with a home run in a 10–3 loss to the New York Yankees. Three days later, he pitched and batted cleanup against the Washington Senators in Griffith Stadium, going 5-for-5 with the lumber, including three doubles and a triple, before dropping a ten-inning, 4–3 decision. Over the last half of the season, Ruth took his regular turn on the mound, but played the outfield or first base when he wasn't pitching. For the year, he played 59 games in the outfield, 13 games at first base, and 20 games as pitcher. He went 13–7 on the mound, pitching 166⅓ innings in 20 games with a 2.22 ERA. At the plate, he hit an even .300 while leading the league with 11 home runs and a .555 slugging average. He also contributed 26 doubles and 11 triples to the Boston offense, driving in 66 runs in 95 games covering 317 at-bats.

His 1918 season has been called the greatest two-way performance in the history of the game. Ruth's heroics helped Boston nip Cleveland by two-and-a-half games to recapture the American League pennant and face the National League champion Chicago Cubs in the World Series. Babe Ruth started Game 1 and threw a 1–0 shutout at the Cubbies. He came back in Game 4 and pitched another 7⅔ shutout innings before giving up two unearned runs in the eighth en route to a 3–2 victory. Ruth's 29⅔ consecutive scoreless innings in the 1916 and 1918 World Series broke Christy Mathewson's mark of 28 scoreless innings, setting a new major league record that would last 43 years until broken by Whitey Ford. Boston closed out Chicago in six games to capture their fourth World Championship in seven years.

Babe Ruth's pitching career was rapidly drawing to a close as 1919 got under way. Manager Ed Barrow made the man who would soon be known as "The Sultan of Swat" his regular left fielder and spot starter on the mound. Babe pitched in 17 games in 1919, with 15 starts and 12 complete games, posting a 9–5 record with a 2.97 ERA over 133⅓ innings. But it was with a bat in his hands that he did most of the damage. The powerful southpaw swinger absolutely destroyed American League pitching. He batted .322 in 432 at-bats over 130 games while leading the league with 103 runs scored, a new major league record 29 home runs, 114 runs batted in, a .456 on-base percentage, a .656 slugging average, and a .996 fielding average. Babe Ruth could do it all.

During his six-year Boston career, Ruth posted an 89–46 won-lost record on the mound for a scintillating .672 winning percentage, the 11th best career winning percentage of all time. His statistics included 144 starts in 158 games pitched, with 107 complete games, an outstanding 74 percent completion record, 17 shutouts, and a 2.09 ERA, the fifth best career ERA for any pitcher with at least 1190 innings pitched since 1900. He and the great Walter Johnson met on the field of battle ten times during their careers, with Ruth winning six games and losing two. The Babe's pitching career, for all intents and purposes, ended after

1919, when he was traded to the New York Yankees and became a full-time outfielder. He did pitch five more games for New York over the next 14 years, but that was just for show. Ruth's batting statistics in Boston showed 342 base hits in 1,110 at bats for a .308 batting average. He had 82 doubles, 30 triples, 49 home runs, and 230 RBI. Babe Ruth was elected into the National Baseball Hall of Fame in 1936 and was selected as the left-handed pitcher on the all-time Red Sox team.

Scott, Deacon

Lewis Everett "Deacon" Scott was born in Bluffton, Indiana, on November 19, 1892. He made his professional baseball debut with Kokomo in the Class D Northern State of Indiana League in 1909 at the tender age of 16, moving to Fairmont in the Class-D Pennsylvania–West Virginia League during the season. The five-foot, eight-inch, 148-pound infielder went on to spend two years with Youngstown in Class-C ball, batting .266 in his second year, and one year with Youngstown in B-ball where he hit .267. The Washington Senators scouted Scott but "determined that (his) body weight of around 120 pounds would not allow him to keep up the strenuous pace demanded in the Big Show, even though he received rave reviews for his speed in the field, his throwing arm and, most importantly, baseball brains."[164] Washington's loss was Boston's gain as the Red Sox obtained his services in 1913, sending him to St. Paul in the American Association, where he batted .269.

The slick-fielding shortstop was brought up to Boston in 1914 and installed in the lineup as their regular shortstop. He hit only .239 in his rookie season but gave the Sox spectacular defense, fielding .949, 12 points higher than the league average. He dazzled the fans with his quickness and his dependable glove, and "he showed an uncanny knack for playing balls correctly in the field and his throws from any part of the infield were accurate."[165] The next year, he posted a .961 fielding average as the Red Sox swept to the American League pennant by two-and-a-half games over the Detroit Tigers. Boston's finest easily outdistanced the Philadelphia Phillies in five games in the World Series and Scott earned his keep with his glove, fielding flawlessly although hitting a barely visible .056. The next year, Bill Carrigan's club repeated their American League championship, edging the Chicago White Sox by two games after a season-long heated battle. They repeated as World Champions as well, taking the measure of the Brooklyn Robins in five games. The slender shortstop batted only .125, but he led both teams with 24 assists. His fielding average for 16 games in three World Series was .978. As noted in *Red Sox Nation Guide to the Players*, Deacon Scott "was the glue that held the Boston Red Sox infield together for eight years, from 1914 through 1921. A defensive wizard, he led American League shortstops in fielding average for eight straight years,"[166] setting a major league record that has been tied by Lou Boudreau and Ozzie Smith but has never been broken. Along the way, he also set a major league record for consecutive games played at 1,307, a record broken by Lou Gehrig 14 years later.

Boston's Red Sox, now under the tutelage of Ed Barrow, outlasted the Cleveland Indians by a scant two-and-a-half games in the 1918 pennant chase, and went on to take the measure of the Chicago Cubs in six games in the World Series. Once again, Scott was perfect in the field and led all infielders with 26 assists, while hitting just .100. Sadly, Deacon Scott's days in Boston were numbered. Three years later, owner Harry Frazee traded his ace shortstop to the New York Yankees.

Scott, George "Boomer"

George Charles "Boomer" Scott, from Greenville, Mississippi, was signed as an amateur free agent by the Boston Red Sox on May 28, 1962, at the age of 18 and received his baptism of fire with Olean in the Class-D New York–Pennsylvania League, where he batted a lukewarm .238 with five homers in 223 at-bats. Three years later, the six-foot, two-inch, 226-pound, right-handed hitter had a breakout season as a member of the Pittsfield Red Sox in the Double-A Eastern League. The man now known as Boomer because of his booming home runs won the Triple Crown, batting .319 with 25 home runs, and 94 RBI. He also led the league in base hits (167) and doubles (30).

George "Boomer" Scott won Boston's first base job in 1966 and he became an immediate fan favorite with his gap-toothed smile, his col-

George Scott

orful personality, and the long home runs he called "taters." The Greenville native made his major league debut in Fenway Park on April 12, and he had a memorable first game, slamming a triple in four at-bats as well as drawing a base on balls and getting hit by a pitch. His bases-loaded walk in the third inning gave his team a temporary 3–2 lead but Baltimore came back to tie the game going into the eighth inning. Then Boomer unleashed his lumber, crushing a 410-foot triple to center field and carrying the tie-breaking run across the plate minutes later. But the O's were not to be denied and they wiped out that lead with a run of their own in the ninth inning before delivering the coup de grace four innings later. On May 4, in Tiger Stadium, Detroit, he went 2-for-4 at the plate with two home runs and five RBI as Boston slammed the Tigers, 7–0. Boomer, who was selected to start the All-Star Game, went on to hit 27 home runs with 90 RBI in his rookie season, offsetting a .245 batting average. The following season, playing for "The Impossible Dream" team, the big first baseman tattooed opposing pitchers to the tune of a .303 average with 19 homers and 82 RBI, teaming with Carl Yastrzemski and Tony Conigliaro to bring the Boston fans an American League pennant by one game over the Detroit Tigers. A Game 7 loss to the St. Louis Cardinals in the World Series couldn't put a damper on the sensational season that saw the team rebound from a seventh-place finish the previous year.

George Scott played for the Red Sox for another four years and posted strong, but not outstanding, numbers. One of his better days occurred on September 27, 1970, in Robert F. Kennedy Stadium, where he went 2-for-5 with two home runs and five RBI as the Red Sox routed the Washington Senators by a 10–1 count. Boomer's three-run homer in the top of the fourth inning gave Eddie Kasko's team a 3–0 lead they never relinquished. The next year was probably his best year of the four, as he hit 24 home runs and drove in 78 runs. He was traded to Milwaukee on October 10, 1971, and played with the Brewers for five years before returning to Boston for another two-and-a-half year tour of duty. He batted .269 for the Red Sox in 1977, slugging 33 "taters" and driving in 95 runs, but his career wound down after that and he retired in 1979, ending a noteworthy 14-year major league career. George Scott, a big man with a big smile and a buoyant personality, was not only a dangerous long-ball hitter, he was also one of the slickest fielding first basemen of all-time. The eight-time Gold Glove recipient, who named his favorite glove "Black Beauty," led American League first basemen in fielding average once, and in putouts, assists, and double plays three times each. In addition, he gave Boston two years of outstanding defensive play at third base.

Shore, Ernie

Ernie Shore pitched one of the more interesting games in baseball history, the first game of a Saturday doubleheader against the Washington Senators in Fenway Park on June 23, 1917. Babe Ruth started the game but after walking the leadoff batter he got into a heated argument with the umpire and was given the heave-ho. Ernie Shore was rushed into the game to relieve the embattled Ruth, and the baserunner was thrown out trying to steal on the first pitch. The six-foot, four-inch, 220-pound fireballer then retired the next 26 batters in order to earn his place in baseball history. Unfortunately, he didn't receive credit for a perfect game because he didn't start the game, and he only got credit for a combined no-hitter.

Ernest Grady Shore was born in East Bend, NC on March 24, 1891. He was signed off the campus of Guilford College by the New York Giants in 1912, but left the team after a disastrous major league debut in which he was raked for ten runs in one inning of relief. The following year he bounced around between the Utica club in the New York State League and Greensboro in the North Carolina League, with Greensboro subsequently selling him to the Baltimore Orioles in the International League. He went 5-3 in ten games with the Orioles, who then sold him, along with a pitcher named Babe Ruth, to the Boston Red Sox for $25,000 on July 9, 1914.

The big right-hander immediately began to carve out a niche for himself in the Boston pitching rotation. He defeated Cleveland by a 2-1 score on July 14, tossing a two-hitter at the hapless Indians in his American League debut. He won ten games and lost five for Bill Carrigan's crew over the last two-and-a-half months of the season, as Boston improved their position from fourth place to second place. In 1915, Boston captured the American League pennant by two-and-a-half games over the Detroit Tigers, and Shore put the last nail in the Tigers coffin when he tossed a 12 inning, 1-0 shutout at them down the stretch. The Red Sox were led by their strong starting pitching of Shore, Ruth, Rube Foster, Smoky Joe Wood, and Dutch Leonard, all of whom won at least 15 games, with Shore going 19-8 with a 1.64 ERA. The man with the devastating sinker continued his domination in the World Series against the Philadelphia Phillies. After losing the opener of the Series to Grover Cleveland Alexander by a score of 3-1, he beat the Phillies 2-1 in Game 4, and Boston wrapped up the championship the next day. In 1916, Carrigan's charges repeated as the American League champions with Shore going 16-10, and they went on to down the Brooklyn Robins in the World Series in five games. The East Bend native won the opener 6-5, but was not around at the finish as the Robins rallied for four runs in the top of the ninth to make it close. Carl Mays recorded the last out with the bases loaded. Shore got his revenge five days later when he won the deciding game of the Series by a 4-1 count in Fenway Park before 43,620 enthusiastic Red Sox rooters.

Shore went 13-10 in 1917 as Boston slipped to second place behind the Chicago White Sox, but he left his mark on the game with his brilliant relief appearance on June 23, as noted above. He lost the 1918 season to military service in World War I, and was traded to the New York Yankees in December 1918 after his discharge from the service, one of the first victims of the Frazee fire sale that decimated the Boston Red Sox for decades. Shore lasted only two years with the Yankees, going 5-8 in 1919 and 2-2 the following year. For some strange reason, he could no longer control his pitches after the war, with his walks increasing from two walks a game to over four walks a game. He retired after the 1920 season at the age of 29. Before his departure, however, he may have saved Babe Ruth from serious injury during a game in Yankee Stadium. Ruth, who was being heckled unmercifully by a disgruntled fan, leaped into the stands to confront the man and found himself staring at a mean-looking knife. Shore quickly got between the two men, preventing the escalation of a potentially dangerous situation that could have led to serious injury to his teammate. During Ernie Shore's four-

Ernie Shore

year tenure in Boston, he pitched in 125 games with 103 starts, 51 complete games, and nine shutouts. He won 58 games against 33 losses, with a glittering 2.22 ERA.

Smith, Reggie

Reggie Smith was a five-tool player according to Jeff Angus of SABR's The *Baseball Biography Project*, who noted that Smith "batted with power from both sides of the plate, was a fine center fielder, had superior base-running speed, and had a legendary throwing arm that may have been the best of his era."[167] Carl Reginald Smith, an all-state high school football and baseball player in Louisiana, was scouted by major league scouts even before graduation. He was drafted by the Minnesota Twins on June 21, 1963, but was lost to the Boston Red Sox, who plucked him from the Dallas–Fort Worth roster on December 2, 1963. Three years later, the 21-year-old outfielder led the International League in batting with a .320 average, with 30 doubles, 18 home runs, 13 stolen bases, 86 runs scored, and 80 RBI. He was recalled to Boston after the International League season ended, and made his major league debut in Fenway Park on September 18, going 0-for-5 in a 5–3 loss to the California Angels.

Boston manager Dick Williams installed Reggie Smith at second base as the 1967 season got under way, explaining, "I want his bat and speed in the lineup and right now we have a set outfield."[168] That experiment lasted only ten games and by the end of April the young phenom was holding down center field on a regular basis. He was instrumental in their pennant-winning season, giving Dick Williams outstanding defense and chipping in with 15 homers and 61 RBI at the plate. On August 20, the switch-hitter homered from each side of the plate as Boston thumped the California Angels, 12–2. His first-inning, three-run homer into the left field screen from the right side of the plate gave Boston a quick lead, and his sixth inning two-run homer from the left side of the plate put the game on ice. In the World Series loss to the St. Louis Cardinals, Smith hit two homers and drove in three runs. Bobby Doerr, a Boston coach, noted, "There goes one of our soundest insurance policies for a successful future. There's no telling how good that boy can

Reggie Smith

be."[169] Manager Williams added, "Smith has only one weakness as an outfielder — coming in for fly balls. That failing which has kept Smith from being rated as one of the super fielders, has been to some degree overcome, as has his tendency to throw wildly with one of the strongest arms in the majors."[170]

Reggie Smith went on to play seven full seasons in Boston, giving the Red Sox a potent bat and stellar outer garden defense in both center field and right field, where his powerful throwing arm kept baserunners honest. The Louisiana native hit over .300 three times in Boston, hit more than 20 home runs in a season five times, and hit more than 22 doubles in a season seven times, including leading the league in doubles in 1968 (37) and 1971 (33). He also led the league in putouts (390) and won a Gold Glove in 1968. But all was not peaches and cream during Reggie's tenure in Boston. There were also confrontations with fans and with teammates. One day in Milwaukee, after Brewers pitchers had hit several Boston batters, Bill Lee failed to respond, bringing a venomous response from Smith. Reggie called Lee gutless and accused him of not protecting his players. After leaving the game and heading upstairs to the clubhouse, he was followed by Lee and the two were soon wrestling, but the altercation was broken up by teammates. Later, in the clubhouse, the two went at it again, but this time it was short-lived as Smith KO'd Lee with one punch.

After hitting .303 with 21 homers for Boston in 1973, the 28-year-old Smith was traded to the St. Louis Cardinals on October 26, and played another nine years in the majors before retiring. When he did put his glove away in 1982 after a memorable 17-year major league career, he was recognized as one of the best switch-hitters ever to play major league baseball. He was the first switch-hitter to have more than 100 home runs in both the American League and the National League, and he was the only player to homer from both sides of the plate in the same game twice in each league.

Speaker, Tris

The man known as "The Grey Eagle," is arguably the greatest center fielder ever to play the game of baseball. Tris Speaker, who was noted for his shallow positioning, his quick reflexes, and his blazing speed, earned the number one spot in a recent study to identify baseball's greatest all-around center fielder.[171] "Spoke" finished in sixth place behind Mickey Mantle, Joe DiMaggio, etc., in the offensive competition, but easily outdistanced all competitors in the defensive competition to capture the title of baseball's greatest all-around center fielder. Joe DiMaggio finished in second place, followed by Willie Mays and Mickey Mantle in that order.

Tristram E. Speaker of Hubbard City, Texas, attended Texas Wesleyan College before embarking on a professional baseball career in 1906. The 18-year-old left-hander pitched and played outfield for the Cleburne Railroaders of the Class-D Texas League, going 2–7 on the mound and batting .268. The following season, playing outfield exclusively, he led the same league in batting with an average of .314 while playing for the Houston Buffaloes. He was sold to the Boston Red Sox for $750 at the end of the season and made his major league debut on September 12. He batted an unimpressive .150 for Boston in seven games that year and was farmed out to the Little Rock Travelers of the Single-A Southern Association in 1908, where he proceeded to be a one-man wrecking crew, dominating the league both offensively and defensively. The five-foot, eleven-and-a-half-inch, 193-pound dynamo led the league in batting average (.350), runs (81), base hits (165), putouts (330), and assists (37). That performance brought about his quick return to Boston, where he hit .224 in 31 games over the last two months of the season.

The 21-year-old rookie hit his stride in 1909, batting .309 for Fred Lake's third-place Red Sox, ripping 26 doubles and 13 triples in 143 games. He also led American League outfielders with 319 putouts and 35 assists, and thrilled the Huntington Avenue Baseball Grounds faithful with his shallow position in center field. Playing what seemed to be more like a deep second base, the fleet-footed Grey Eagle, who possessed exceptional reflexes and instincts, was able to run down most balls hit over his head. But it was all the result of hard work, according to Speaker. "When I was a rookie Cy Young used to hit me flies to sharpen my abilities to judge in advance the direction and distance of an outfield-hit ball." His outfield partner Duffy

Tris Speaker

Lewis added, "Speaker was the king of the outfield it was always 'Take it' or 'I got it.' In all the years, we never bumped into each other."[172]

Tris Speaker batted .340 in 1910 and led the league in putouts (337) once again. He came back with a .334 batting average the following year and, in 1912, he sparked Jake Stahl's team to the pennant by scorching the ball at a .383 clip with 136 runs scored, 222 base hits, 12 triples, and 98 RBI. He led the league with 53 doubles, 10 home runs, 372 putouts, 35 assists, and nine double plays. In recognition of his outstanding season, he was the recipient of the Chalmers American League Award, the precursor of the Most Valuable Player award. In the World Series, an eight-game victory over the New York Giants, he hit .300 with a double, two triples, four runs scored, and two RBI. Spoke had the key hit in the eighth and deciding game, the famous "$30,000 muff" game. In the bottom of the tenth inning, with New York leading 2–1, after Fred Snodgrass had dropped Clyde Engle's easy fly ball and Yerkes had walked, Speaker lined a single to right field, scoring Engle and sending Steve Yerkes, the potential World Championship run, around to third, where Larry Gardner's fly ball scored him. Three years later, he and his Red Sox teammates captured another American League pennant, nipping the Detroit Tigers by two-and-a-half games. His .322 batting average paced Boston's offense, and his 378 putouts and eight double plays led all outfielders. He hit .294 in the World Series, a five-game conquest of the Philadelphia Phillies.

Boston's all-world center fielder was traded to the Cleveland Indians for pitcher Sam Jones on April 12, 1916, after a salary dispute with Red Sox President Joe Lannin, who wanted to cut his salary because his batting average had been in decline over the previous three years, even though it was still a healthy .322. Lannin's error in judgment was reflected in the fact that Speaker, who was still only 27 years old, stung the ball at a .354 clip over the next 11 years. During his memorable 22-year major league career, Tris Speaker legged out 792 doubles, a major league record. He led the league in doubles eight times with a high of 59 in 1923, in runs scored twice, home runs once, batting average once, on-base percentage four times, slugging average once, fielding average twice, putouts eight times, assists four times, and double plays five times. He is number one all-time in career outfield assists with 449 and double plays with 139, number two in putouts with 6,788, number five in base hits with 3,514, number six in triples with 222, and number ten in runs scored with 1,882. Tris Speaker was elected into the National Baseball Hall of Fame in Cooperstown, New York, in 1937. He was in the second class of electees. Grantland Rice said of Speaker, "He was a model of ball-playing grace. He never wasted a motion or gave you any sign of extra effort. He played with the smoothness of a summer wind." "At the crack of the bat he'd be off with his back to the infield," said teammate Joe Wood, "and he'd turn and glance over his shoulder at the last minute and catch the ball so easy it looked like there was nothing to it, nothing at all."[173]

Stahl, Chick

Charles Sylvester "Chick" Stahl was a handsome, charming free spirit with a magnetic personality. He was born in Avilla, Indiana, on January 10, 1873, and, according to Dennis H. Auger, Stahl "attended Catholic schools and developed his baseball skills on Fort Wayne's vacant lots and diamonds south of the railroads." He played "for Brunswick, a local amateur team in 1889 (and) pitched for the Pilsener Club in the City League."[174] The five-foot, ten-inch, 150-pound left-hander pitched and played the outfield as a teenager. Finally, in 1895, at the age of 22, he signed a professional baseball contract with Roanoke in the Virginia League, where he hit .311 and led the league with 13 triples while playing a sensational outfield. The following year, playing with Buffalo in the top-rated Eastern League, he hit .340 with a league-leading 23 triples, 34 stolen bases, and 130 runs scored. That performance convinced the Boston Beaneaters of the National League that he was major league material, and they purchased his contract at the end of the season.

Chick Stahl, who would have won the National League Rookie of the Year Award if such an award was given in 1897, scorched opposing pitchers for a .354 average in 114 games covering 469 at-bats. On May 31, during a 25–5 rout of the St. Louis Browns in Boston's South End Grounds, Stahl hammered six hits in six at-bats, "five of which were very long drives" according to one report. The Beaneaters, who captured the National League pennant by three-and-a-half games over the Baltimore Orioles, were defeated by the same team in the post-season Temple Cup Series, four games to one, despite Stahl's .381 average and six RBI. He had a career season two years later, batting .351 with 202 base hits, 122 runs scored, 23 doubles, 19 triples, and 33 stolen bases.

In 1901, the American League was formed and Jimmy Collins jumped from the Beaneaters to the Boston Somersets as player-manager, taking Chick Stahl with him. The fleet-footed Hoosier covered center field for Collins, giving the Somersets superb defense as well as timely offense. He batted .303 in 1901 but had to survive a brush with death in the off-season. "On the evening of Jan. 26, 1902, while he was walking with a friend in Fort Wayne, Louise 'Lulu' Ortman, a 22-year-old stenographer, a lover he had reportedly jilted, reached for a revolver concealed in the folds of her dress. A police officer, who had been tipped off that the infuriated woman was stalking Stahl, arrived just in time to disarm and arrest her."[175] Stahl tattooed the ball at a .323 clip in 1902 but he suffered a leg injury sliding into a base the following year and missed half the season. Fortunately for the team, now known as the Pilgrims, he returned for the stretch run and hit .274 over the last 77 games as Boston raced to the league pennant by a comfortable margin. They went on to defeat the Pittsburgh Pirates in the major leagues' first World Series, five games to three, in the best-of-nine competition, as Chick Stahl led the team with ten base hits and tied for the lead in triples with three. His long triple to center field in the first inning of Game 7 drove in the first run of the game, and he carried the second run across the plate minutes later as the Pilgrims cruised to a 7–3 victory. They wrapped up the World Championship the next day as Bill Dinneen tossed a 3–0 shutout at Fred Clarke's team.

The pride of Avilla, fully healed, batted a hard .290 in 1904 with 27 doubles, a league-leading 19 triples, 67 RBI, and 83 runs scored. The Pilgrims edged the New York Highlanders by one-and-a-half games for their second consecutive American League pennant, but no World Series was played because the two leagues were squabbling. Chick slumped to .258 in 1905 but came back to hit .286 in 1906, and was named interim manager late in the season after Jimmy Collins was suspended. Stahl's Pilgrims could do no better than 14 wins against 26 losses down the stretch, giving them a season record of 49–102 and a last-place finish. The following spring, on March 28, Stahl, who had suffered from depression with thoughts of suicide since 1889, took a fatal dose of carbolic acid, dying at the age of 34. One source said he committed suicide because he couldn't stand the pressure of managing. Baseball fans everywhere were devastated by his death. Boston catcher Lou Criger was overcome with grief. "Stahl was a king among men," said Criger. "He was the squarest man I ever knew. He had only one fault — he was too generous. I never saw him go back on a friend or a deserving acquaintance. In fact, he was often bunkoed because he believed in the goodness of man."[176] Chick Stahl was a .290 hitter during his six-year Red Sox career. He was also one of the best center fielders of his day, with exceptional hands and blazing speed. His career fielding average was a full 16 points above the league average.

Stahl, Jake

"Big, powerful, and deceptively fast, Jake Stahl parlayed the skills he first demonstrated as a college football star at the turn of the century, into an even more successful career on the baseball field."[177] The Elkhart, Indiana, native, at six foot, two inches tall and weighing a muscular 195 pounds, towered over the average player who stood about five feet, seven inches tall and tipped the scales at about 155 pounds. Garland "Jake" Stahl, who first saw the light of day on April 13, 1879, worked in his father's general store after graduating from high school, but his education was foremost in his mind and in 1899 he entered the University of Illinois, where he played football and baseball for three years. He was a hard-hitting catcher on the baseball team, and his powerful bat produced a .441 batting average one year.

After graduating from Illinois with a law degree in 1903, he decided to give professional baseball a try, and signed a contract to play for the Boston Pilgrims that year, seeing action in 40 games as a catcher and batting .239. Since the Pilgrims already had a world-class catcher in Lou Criger, Jake Stahl was traded to the Washington Senators, where he toiled for three years as a first baseman, and for the last two years as player-manager. He compiled a mediocre .245 batting average as a player and had two seventh-place finishes to show for his managing efforts. John Stahl quoted his ancestor as saying in 1906, "If I'd been able to hit .300 this year (instead of .222) as many of my friends predicted, we'd have been up in the first division, but I was a frost."[178]

Disgusted with his performance, both at the plate and on the bench, Stahl, who had been traded to the Chicago White Sox over the winter, sat out the 1907 season, playing semi-pro ball in Chicago. He returned to the game in 1908 after the White Sox traded him to the New York Highlanders. With "Prince Hal" Chase firmly entrenched at first base, Jake was sent to left field, but his play was less than acceptable and he was shipped off to Boston after 75 games. He played 78 games at first base for the Red Sox over the last half of the season and batted .244 with 11 triples in 262 at-bats. The right-handed hitter followed with two good seasons in Boston, hitting .294 with 19 doubles and 12 triples in 1909, and compiling a .271 batting average with 19 doubles, 16 triples, a league-leading ten home runs, and 77 RBI in 531 at-bats the following season. Then, to everyone's surprise, the independently wealthy, 31-year-old first baseman announced his retirement and went to work in his father-in-law's bank.

His first retirement lasted just one year and he returned to the baseball wars in 1912 as Boston's player-manager. This time everything went smoothly. He played 95 games at first base, caressing the ball at a .301 pace with 21 doubles and 60 RBI in 326 at-bats, and he brought his team home in first place by a whopping 14 games over the Washington Senators. He also directed them to the World Championship by defeating John McGraw's New York Giants in eight games. He singled in the bottom of the seventh inning of the finale with his team trailing, 1–0, and carried home the tying run on a double by Olaf Henriksen. Boston won the game, 3–2, in ten innings, the beneficiary of the famous "Snodgrass Muff." Jake Stahl broke his foot before the 1913 season got under way and, when his team plummeted to fifth place midway through the season, he was replaced by Bill Carrigan.

Stanley, Bob

Bob Stanley was the workhorse of the Boston Red Sox pitching staff for more than a dozen years, ready and willing to do whatever the team asked of him. He pitched in 637 games during his 13 years in a Red Sox uniform, starting 85 games and relieving in 552 games. The six-foot, four-inch, 215-pound right hander was not a power pitcher, but more of a finesse pitcher whose devastating palm ball induced opposing batters to drive the ball into the ground, the ideal result for a bullpen specialist. Stanley's repertoire also included a slider and a sinker.

Robert William Stanley was Boston's first pick in the January 1974 amateur draft, and was sent to Elmira in the Single-A New York-Pennsylvania League that summer, going 6–6 with a 4.60 ERA as a starter. After one year in Winter Haven in the Florida State League, where he struggled through a 5–17 season, and one year with Bristol in the Double-A Eastern

Bob Stanley

League, where he went 15–9 with a 2.66 ERA, he joined the Red Sox in 1977 as a swing man in the rotation, starting 13 games and relieving in 28 others, while compiling an 8–7 won-loss record in 151 innings pitched, with a 3.99 ERA.

The stocky right-hander pitched in 49 games as a long reliever in 1978, winning 15 games against just two losses, with all but two of the wins in relief. He averaged almost 2½ innings per game out of the bullpen that year, posting an excellent 2.60 earned run average. He was a two-way pitcher for Don Zimmer his first four years in Boston, but when Johnny Pesky and then Ralph Houk took the reins, he was gradually given a full-time job in the bullpen. In 1981, he pitched 98⅔ innings in 35 games, an average of 2.8 innings per appearance. He compiled a won-lost record of 10–8 with a 3.83 ERA. The following year, he pitched middle relief, appearing in 48 games with a 12–7 won-loss record and 14 saves, and pitching 168⅓ innings, an average of three-and-a-half innings per appearance. He was given the job as the team's fireman in 1983, being asked to pitch up to ten innings in one game. The position of closer, a reliever who pitched one inning or less at the end of the game, was not yet in vogue. Stanley pitched 145⅓ innings in 64 games in 1983, an average of 2.3 innings per game, with a 2.85 ERA, and he set a Boston Red Sox record of 33 saves for the season. According to *The Red Sox Fan Handbook*, "Stanley was known for his palm ball which he threw almost every pitch; it was slow and looked very hittable, but its crazy action made the ball seem to dart and flutter like a butterfly. He never struck out very many batters but he had good control and threw a lot of double play balls."[179] The pride of Portland, Maine, saved 22 games in 1984, breaking Ellis Kinder's Franchise record of 365 games pitched on July 16. He saved 10 games in 1985 and 16 games in 1986. He both started and relieved in 1987, starting 20 games and relieving in 14. During his last two years in the major leagues, he was strictly a bullpen specialist, appearing in 57 games in 1988 and 43 games in 1989. Lee Smith had assumed the key role of closer in the bullpen in 1988, averaging 1.1 innings per game, a far cry from Bob Stanley's tenure as the fireman when he averaged more than three innings per game.

Unfortunately for Stanley, his legacy is closely tied to the Red Sox collapse in the 1986 World Series when they were within one out of the World Championship in Game 6, only to see it slip away in a nightmare of miscues. With Boston leading the New York Mets three games to two in the Series and 5–4 in the last half of the tenth inning of Game 6, Stanley came on in relief with runners on first and third and two out. The big right-hander almost immediately uncorked a wild pitch, allowing the runner on third to scamper across the plate with the tying run and the runner on first to move into scoring position, from where he eventually scored the winning run on Bill Buckner's error. The Mets went on to capture Game 7 and win the World Championship when the Red Sox bullpen blew another lead.

Stanley pitched in 50 or more games six times in 13 years with a high of 66 games in 1986. He won ten or more games five times early in his career with a high of 16 victories in 1979. He led the major leagues in relief innings pitched in two straight years, 1982 and 1983, with 168⅓, and 145⅓ innings pitched respectively. He also pitched 106⅔ innings in relief in 1984. He was voted the Red Sox Most Valuable Pitcher in both 1982 and 1983. His career statistics, all with Boston, included 115 victories, 97 losses, and 132 saves. When he retired he held the Red Sox records for most games pitched (637), most saves (132), and most relief wins (85).

Stanley, Mike

Robert Michael Stanley, a six-foot, one-inch, 185-pound, right-handed hitter, began his professional baseball career in 1985 as a first baseman-catcher for the Salem Redbirds, a farm team of the Texas Rangers in the Single-A Carolina League. After just four games with Salem, he was sent to Burlington in the Midwest League, where he hit .310 in 13 games, then was moved again, this time to Tulsa in the Double-A Texas League, where he batted .309 in 46 games. The following year, still with the Drillers, he hit .294 in 67 games and was promoted to the Texas Rangers, where he played in 15 games, batting .333 with one home run in 30 at-bats. He also played with Oklahoma City in the American Association that year, stinging the ball at a .366 clip with 49 RBI in 202 at-bats. He started 1987 with the 89ers, now as a full-time catcher, and he responded with a .335 batting average, 13 home runs, and 54 RBI in 182 at-bats. He was brought back up to Texas in mid-season, beginning a 14-year career in the major leagues. Stanley played for the Texas Rangers for six years, but when he refused a minor league assignment, he became a free agent, eventually signing with the New York Yankees on January 21, 1992. He played four years for Buck Showalter's team, primarily as a catcher, and he led the league with a .996 fielding average in 1993. He also provided the Yankees with some unexpected power, slugging 26 homers in 1993, 17 homers the following year, and 18 homers in 1995. Stanley filed for free agency on November 4, 1995, signing with the Boston Red Sox on December 14.

Mike Stanley was Boston's regular catcher in 1996, catching 105 games and banging the ball at a .270 clip with 24 home runs and 69 RBI in 397 at-bats. With the arrival of Scott Hatteberg in 1997, Stanley became the designated hitter and the backup first baseman. He still gave Jimy Williams' team a powerful bat, hitting an even .300 with 13 homers and 53 RBI in 260 at-bats, but he was traded to the Yankees on August 13 for two pitchers, neither of whom ever appeared in a game for Boston. After spending part of 1997 in New York, and part of 1998 in Toronto, he returned to the Red Sox in a trade on July 30 and was Boston's designated hitter the rest of the year, rapping the ball to the tune of a .288 average with 12 doubles, seven homers, and 32 RBI in 156 at-bats. The following year, the 36-year-old Florida native played in 136 games as Boston's first baseman, and he hit .281 with 19 homers and 72 RBI in 427 at-bats. Stanley slumped to .222 in 58 games in 2000, and was traded to Oakland in mid-season, ending his Boston career.

Stephens, Gene

Gene Stephens was a reserve outfielder for the Boston Red Sox from 1952 to 1960. He was usually called in as a late-inning replacement for the aging Ted Williams and, as noted in *The Ballplayers*, he was often referred to as Williams' caddy. He played in an average of 112 games a year from 1955 to 1959, but had fewer than two at-bats per game. Being a reserve was less than satisfactory for a young man who always believed he was short-changed when it came to playing regularly. "I knew I could hit, run, throw, and field. I didn't have any weaknesses. I regret that I didn't get to play as a regular."

Glen Eugene Stephens, who hailed from Gravette, Arkansas, worked his way through the Red Sox minor league maze on the fast track, arriving in Boston in 1952 at the age of 19. He started that season with the Red Sox but, after hitting just .226 in 21 games, he was sent back down to the minors for more experience. After posting a .177 average with Albany in the Double-A Eastern League and .282 with Louisville in the Triple-A American Association in 1952, Stephens returned to Boston the following spring, hoping to improve on his offensive contributions, but it was not to be. He played in 78 games for Lou Boudreau's club, hitting a barely visible .204 in 221 at-bats, resulting in another demotion. He did, however, have a career day for Boston before he was sent down. On June 18, the Red Sox raked the Detroit Tigers over the coals for 17 runs in the bottom of the seventh inning in Fenway Park, before a sparse weekday crowd of 3,108, breaking open what had been a competitive 5–3 struggle, and the rookie outfielder punched out three base hits in the inning, a double and two singles, tying a major league record. After the game, won by Boston 23–3, he was on cloud nine. "I was the youngest ballplayer in the major leagues at the time. I was 19 years old and I probably shouldn't have even been in the major leagues at the time." Stephens continued with his erratic batting in the minor leagues, hitting .214 for Louisville in 1953 and .286 for the same club the following year. He was back in the major leagues to stay in 1955, spending the next five-and-a-half years with the Red Sox, but he was unable to break into an outfield that included Williams, Jimmy Piersall, and Jackie Jensen, serving, as noted above, as a late-inning defensive replacement. He had one memorable game in Fenway Park against the New York Yankees on June 13, 1959. He went into the game as a pinch-runner for Ted Williams in the sixth inning and, when the team batted around, he came up with the bases loaded and sent the crowd into a frenzy by hammering a grand slam homer to pace the Sox to a 13–3 win, completing a five-game sweep of the mighty Bronx Bombers.

The lanky left-handed hitter was finally traded to the Baltimore Orioles midway through the 1960 season and played another four years with the O's, the Kansas City Athletics, and the Chicago White Sox, before retiring. His eight-year Boston statistics showed a .247 batting average. Gene Stephens was known as a neatnik during his career. An article in "Baseball Digest" noted that "he wears three pairs of shoes during a game — and if it's a night game with wet grass, he wears four pairs. 'That way, he explained, 'the leather doesn't get sweat-soaked.'"

Stephens, Vern

Vern Stephens, aka "Junior" or "Buster," was a long-ball-hitting shortstop in the American League for 12 years. The stocky, right-handed slugger, whose powerful upper body was developed by swimming, signed an amateur free agent contract with the St. Louis Browns for a $500 bonus at the age of 17. He began his organized baseball career with Johnstown in the Class-C Middle Atlantic League in 1938, batting a mediocre .257, but the following year, the New Mexico native impressed St. Louis upper management when he launched 30 home runs for Mayfield in the Class-D Kitty League, leading the league in batting (.361), doubles (44), and runs batted in (123). He made the jump to the Big Show two years later, playing three games with St. Louis at the end of the season. The following year, Browns shortstop Johnny Berardino left the club to serve in the U.S. Army during World War II, and the 21-year-old Stephens inherited the shortstop job by default. Junior had injured his knee in the minors and was classified 4F in the draft, meaning he was not physically fit to serve in the military. As a result, during the lean war years, he was one of the best players in the major leagues.

Junior Stephens was an outstanding shortstop for the Browns for the next five years, both offensively and defensively. He was solid in the field with a strong throwing arm, and he was dangerous at the plate. He led the American League in RBI in 1944 with 109 while leading Luke Sewell's team to the American League pennant, but he hit just .227 with two RBI in the World Series, a losing effort against the cross-town St. Louis Cardinals. He led the American League in both home runs (24) and fielding average (.961) in 1945, but during the off-season, the husky slugger signed a five-year, $175,000 contract to play baseball in Mexico for the Pasqual brothers, who were raiding the major leagues to improve the quality of play in the Mexican League. When baseball commissioner Happy Chandler threatened to suspend any player who went to Mexico from organized baseball for life, Stephens returned to the U.S. after playing just two games for Veracruz and going 1-for-8. The four-time All-Star was traded to the Boston Red Sox in time for the 1948 season, and he had his best years in Beantown, as well as two monumental disappointments.

When Junior Stephens joined the Red Sox, he had to battle Johnny Pesky, the incumbent, for the shortstop job, and according to Harold Kaese, he "won the battle for the position because he was one of the best fielding shortstops in baseball. Stephens' defensive statistics were generally better than Pesky's and (manager Joe) McCarthy was undoubtedly aware of Stephens' great range and arm." Junior's second base partner, Bobby Doerr, said, "Perhaps the best thing that impresses me about Vern is the speed with which he gets across the bag on double plays." Johnny Pesky, who was moved to third base after Stephens arrival, added, "I always believed McCarthy did it because Stevie had such a great arm."[180]

The new Boston shortstop joined a powerful Red Sox lineup that included Ted Williams, Bobby Doerr, Dom DiMaggio, and Johnny Pesky, and routinely led the league in runs scored. He dazzled the Fenway faithful with his all-around play in 1948, rapping the ball at a respectable .269 clip with 25 doubles, 29 home runs, 137 runs batted in, and 114 runs scored. His RBI totals were helped by the fact that he hit behind Ted Williams. Sadly for Stephens and the Red Sox, they lost the American League pennant to the Cleveland Indians in a one-game playoff after the regular season ended in a deadlock. Cleveland player-manager Lou Boudreau led his team to a convincing 8–3 triumph with a two-home-run day. Stephens singled in one run for Boston but it was not enough. The next year, disaster struck again. Boston held a one-game lead over the New York Yankees with two games left to play in the season, needing just one win against Casey Stengel's crew in Yankee Stadium to clinch the pennant. That win never came as they were beaten by scores of 5–4 and 5–3. Vern Stephens' disappointment was assuaged somewhat by his personal accomplishments that included an all-time major league record of 159 RBI by a shortstop. The five-foot, ten-inch, 185-pound, right-handed slugger posted a .290 batting average in 1949 with 31 doubles, 39 home runs, 101 bases on balls, and 113 runs scored, in addition to his RBI record. He followed that offensive outburst by hitting .295 with 34 doubles, 30 home runs, a league-leading 144 RBI, and 125 runs scored in 1950. His career began to decline the next year as he was slowed down by an old knee injury that limited his playing time to 109 games in 1951 and 92 games in 1952. He was traded to the Chicago White Sox after the '52 season, retiring three years later.

Junior Stephens was one of the top shortstops of his era, as well as the most powerful. In addition to his slugging prowess that included a career .460 slugging average, he was an outstanding defensive shortstop, leading the league in fielding average and double plays once each and in assists three times. He was an eight-time All-Star, four times each with St. Louis and Boston. His five-year Boston tenure established him as one of the most popular players on the team, with fellow teammates, with the press, and with the fans. He was inducted into the Boston Red Sox Hall of Fame in 2006.

Stuart, Dick

Dick Stuart was a powerful, right-handed, slugging first baseman who stood six-foot, four-inches tall and topped the scales at 210 pounds. He hit prodigious home runs wherever he played, including a record 66 homers for Lincoln in the Western League in 1956, but he also had a proclivity for striking out, fanning 132 times for every 550 at-bats during his major league career. Perhaps, even worse, he had other problems with the ball — he couldn't catch it — a fact that resulted in his nickname, "Dr. Strangeglove."

Richard Lee Stuart began his professional baseball career in 1951 as an 18-year-old outfielder with Modesto in the Class C California League, batting a mediocre .229 with four homers in 201 at-bats. The next year he flexed his muscles with Billings in the Class-C Pioneer League, stinging the ball at a .313 clip in 515 at-bats, and leading the league in runs scored (115), base hits (161), home runs (31), and RBI (121). His march to the top of the baseball world was interrupted by two years of military service, but when he returned to the baseball wars in 1955, he picked right up where he left off, hitting .309 with Billings and leading the league with 32 home runs. That brought him a promotion to Single-A Lincoln, where he exploded as noted previously. In addition to his 66 home runs, he also led the league with 158 RBI in 141 games. He split the 1957 season with three teams, eventually finishing the season with Hollywood in the Triple-A Pacific Coast League, where he cranked out six homers in 23 games. The next year, with Salt Lake City in the PCL, he hit .311 with 31 homers in 80 games before being purchased by the Pittsburgh Pirates, where he debuted on July 10. He played 67 games for Pittsburgh that year, hitting a respectable .268 with 16 homers and 48 runs batted in, in 254 at-bats covering 67 games.

Dick Stuart was in the major leagues to stay, and he stayed for ten years, including five years with Pittsburgh and two years with the Boston Red Sox. "Stuart was one of a crop of big bangers that operated in the late fifties and early sixties. Big guys (Stuart was 6'4") can't field much maybe, can't run much, strike out a lot, but when they got hold of one — forget it. Downtown."[18] The right-handed hitter had the misfortune of playing five years in mammoth Forbes Field, where the left field wall was 360 feet from home plate and the left-center field power alley was a distant 406 feet away. Still, during his tenure in Pittsburgh, he hit as many as 35 home runs in a season, but overall he hit 44 percent more home runs on the road than he did in Forbes Field. He had his best year in the Steel City in 1961 when he batted .301 with 35 homers and 117 RBI.

The big first baseman was traded to Boston in the fall of 1962 and spent two years displaying his skills in Fenway Park, a much more inviting target for a right-handed slugger of Stuart's ilk. He had two decent seasons there. In 1963, he hit .261 in 157 games with 42 home runs and a league-leading 118 runs batted in, and the following year he scorched the ball at a .279 clip with 33 homers and 114 RBI. But his defense was still atrocious. As noted by John Sayles, "The awfulness of Stuart's fielding has not been exaggerated. In his first seven seasons, he led the league's first basemen in errors five times outright and was co-leader the other two years despite playing just 64 and 101 games in the field. His 29 errors in 1963 almost tripled that of his nearest competitor."[182] Dr. Strangeglove was traded to the Philadelphia Phillies after the 1964 season, replaced by Lee Thomas and then George "Boomer" Scott. He hit a respectable .270 in 1215 at-bats during his two years in Boston, with 75 home runs and 232 RBI. His epitaph can be summed up thusly: "He couldn't field. He couldn't run. But every couple days, boy, runners on base and Dick Stuart at bat, and WHAM! Forget it. Downtown."[183]

Sullivan, Frank

A fastball pitcher who also threw a curve and a hesitation pitch, big, six-foot, five-inch, 215-pound Frank Sullivan was the ace of the Boston Red Sox pitching staff and the team workhorse during the mid–1950s. Unfortunately, the Red Sox were a mediocre team during Sullivan's tenure, never finishing higher than third place and never finishing closer than 12 games from the top. One year they were 42 games behind the league leaders, and another year they were 32 games behind. Yet, in spite of that overall futility, Sullivan posted a winning record for Boston. He always maintained a good sense of humor. Returning to Logan Airport after one particularly disastrous road trip, Sullivan advised his teammates, "Spread out, men, so they can't get us all with one burst."

Franklin Leal Sullivan was born in Hollywood, California, on January 23, 1930, and attended Burbank High School. He signed an amateur free agent contract with the Boston Red Sox in 1948 and began his trek through the Boston Red Sox farm system with short stints with Oroville in the Class-D Far West League and San Jose in the Class-C California League, where he compiled an overall record of 1–4 in 27 innings. He returned to San Jose in 1949, winning 12 games against 10 losses with a 2.83 ERA in 172 innings pitched. The following year, he went 3–6 with Scranton in the Eastern League, and then left for military service during the Korean War. He spent two years with the U.S. Army in Korea and was awarded the Combat Infantry Badge.

On his discharge from military service in 1953, Sullivan joined the Boston Red Sox and made his major league debut in relief in Fenway Park during a 5–3 loss to the Detroit Tigers on July 31. He pitched in 14 games out of the bullpen over the last two months of the season, compiling a record of 1–1 with a 5.61 ERA in 25⅔ innings. The 24-year-old Californian made his first start in a Red Sox uniform in Yankee Stadium on May 21, 1954, before 30,119 partisan New York fans, throwing a complete-game, 6–3 victory at the Bronx Bombers and beating Whitey Ford in the process. Boston scored all its run in a big sixth inning uprising that included a three-run homer by the ill-fated Harry Agganis.

Frank Sullivan almost immediately inherited the ace mantle as Mel Parnell came down with arm miseries and Mickey McDermott was traded to Washington. The tall right-hander, who said he didn't possess an overpowering fastball, added, "It'd be a miracle if I could break an eight-inch curve. As far as I'm concerned, I pitch now with my head. It's my mental state that matters when I pitch."[184] But Sullivan responded like an ace should, going 15–12 in 36 games, with 26 starts, 11 complete games, 206⅓ innings pitched, and a fine 3.14 earned run average, this for a fourth-place team that posted a sorry 69–85 won-lost record and finished a full 42 games behind the pennant-winning Cleveland Indians. After the season ended, he reflected on his success. "I certainly don't have exceptional speed or stuff. I don't even have a set delivery. I work on batters carefully, and trust to luck that they'll try to hit my best pitches. I think that I fool them mostly with my motion — I try to make the ball come out of nowhere and up to the plate before they can get set. Above all, I pitch to spots, and try to make the batters hit rather than striking them out."[185]

The next year, Frank Sullivan went 18–13 in

35 games, all starts, with 16 complete games, 260 innings pitched, and a 2.91 ERA, a full 1.05 runs better than the league average, and he led the American League in victories, games started, and innings pitched. He put together three more excellent seasons for Pinky Higgins' club before his arm gave out. He posted records of 14–7, 14–11, and 13–9 from 1956 to 1958, bringing his innings pitched totals to 1,148⅓ innings over a five-year period, an average of 230 innings a year. He was only 29 years old in 1959, but his arm was tired, his fastball had lost its zip, and his efficiency had declined. He went 9–11 for Boston in 1959 with just five complete games in 26 starts, covering 177⅔ innings, with a 3.95 ERA. The following year, he won six games against 16 losses, with 22 starts, four complete games, 153⅔ innings pitched, and a 5.10 ERA, 1.23 runs above the league average. He was traded to the Philadelphia Phillies on December 15, 1960. Three years later, after compiling an overall record of 7–20 with Philadelphia and Minnesota, he retired at the age of 33.

Tabor, Jim

James Reuben Tabor attended the University of Alabama in 1935 and 1936 and played baseball on their 1936 Southeastern Conference Championship team. The Boston Red Sox signed him off the Alabama campus as an amateur free agent later that year and sent him to Little Rock in the Class-A1 Southern Association in 1937, where he held down third base for the Travelers, batting .295. The next year, playing with the Minneapolis Millers in the Double-A American Association, he rattled the fences for a .330 batting average with 30 doubles, five triples, 13 home runs, and 72 runs batted in, in 437 at-bats. That was enough to bring about his promotion to the Boston club in late July, and he made his major league debut in Cleveland on August 4 in a 7–4 loss to the Indians. He played 19 games for the Red Sox at the end of the season, splitting his time between third base and shortstop, and hitting a hard .316 in 57 at-bats.

Tabor was joined by former Minneapolis teammate Ted Williams in Boston, and the two sluggers gave American League pitchers headaches throughout the 1939 season. On July 4, the second-place Red Sox hammered Connie Mack's seventh-place Philadelphia Athletics for 35 runs in a doubleheader, winning by scores of 17–7 and 18–12, and Jim Tabor was the number one sharpshooter. He homered and drove in two runs in the opener, then put on a one-man power display in the nightcap, slamming three home runs including two grand slams, one of which was an inside-the-park job. The second grand slam, in the sixth inning, broke an 11–11 tie. Home run number three, a solo shot in the eighth inning, gave him nine RBI for the game and a total of 11 RBI for the day. Overall, his rookie season was a huge success as he batted .289 in 149 games with 167 base hits in 577 at-bats, including 33 doubles, eight triples, 14 homers, 95 runs batted in, and 16 stolen bases. His defense, however, was a different story as he posted a .923 fielding average with a league-leading 40 errors. Tabor had above-average speed that allowed him to run down more than his share of ground balls, but he also had a shotgun arm that sent first basemen diving for cover. His accuracy didn't improve over time as he ran up seasonal totals of 33, 30, 33, 26, and 20 errors, from 1940 through 1944.

Still, the man they called "Rawhide," because of his prickly personality and combative nature might have had an outstanding major league career if he had been able to control himself off the field, but he was unable to do that. He had a strong verbal exchange with Ted Williams when they both played for the Millers, and he had an equally vicious confrontation with Lefty Grove in Boston. And Rawhide had even bigger problems. *The Red Sox Fan Handbook* reported that, "Tabor had a reputation for hard drinking. He once stretched out to field a ball hit down the third base line and failed to get up. Everyone rushed over, thinking he'd been hurt. He was drunk. He'd just passed out."[186] He was suspended twice during the 1939 season for being drunk in public. The second time, on June 26, he was, according to reports, drunk as a skunk in the hotel lounge, but the media tactfully reported the suspension as being for a training infraction.

Jim Tabor had another big year with the bat in 1940, posting a fine .285 batting average with 28 doubles, 21 home runs, 81 RBI, and 14 stolen bases. The six-foot, one-inch, 175-pound, right-handed slugger joined his Red Sox teammates in a display of power seldom seen on a ball field on Tuesday, September 24, in the first game of a doubleheader against hapless Philadelphia in Shibe Park. He was one of four Boston players to homer in the same inning. Ted Williams, Jimmie Foxx, and Joe Cronin homered in succession in the sixth inning and, after Bobby Doerr cracked a triple, Tabor put number four over the left field wall, pacing Cronin's team to a 16–8 thrashing of the A's. They also won game two by a 4–3 score. The Hope, Alabama, native had his best season with the bat in 1941, hitting .279 with 29 doubles, 16 home runs, 101 runs batted in, and 17 stolen bases. That same year, Ted Williams became the last of the .400 hitters, posting a memorable .406 batting average, but Boston, with a fine 84–70 won-loss record, still finished 17 games behind the mighty New York Yankees.

Rawhide Jim played three more seasons in Boston, contributing some important long balls to the Boston offense, but in October, 1944, with World War II heating up, he entered the U.S. Army and served his country for more than a year, being discharged in December, 1945. Boston management wasted no time in selling him to the Philadelphia Phillies on January 22, 1946, ending his Red Sox career. Tabor had been Boston's regular third baseman for six years, displaying good power and above-average speed, but his glove was leaky as noted above. He led the American League in errors five times.

Tebbetts, Birdie

George Robert Tebbetts was born in Burlington, Vermont on November 10, 1912, and grew up in Nashua, New Hampshire. As Tom Simon noted, "his round, freckled face and flaming red hair reflected his mother's Irish heritage."[187] He acquired his nickname as a young boy when an aunt, commenting on his high-pitched voice, said he sounded like a bird chirping. Tebbetts played football, basketball, and baseball at Nashua High School and signed a baseball contract with the Detroit Tigers after graduation when Detroit management agreed to give him a bonus so his mother could pay off the family debts, and offered to pay for his college education. He attended Providence College from 1931 to 1934, earning a Bachelor of Science degree in Philosophy, then reported to the Tigers, who sent him to the New Bedford Whalers in the Northeastern League, where he handled his defensive responsibilities with the poise of a veteran and hit a respectable .277 in 46 games covering 166 at-bats. The 22-year-old backstop split the following year between the Springfield Senators in the Class-B Triple-I League and the Beaumont Exporters in the Class-A1 Texas League, where he hit .263 and .219 respectively and excelled defensively in both leagues. He returned to Beaumont in 1936 and raised his batting average to .292 with 74 RBI in 472 at-bats, prompting the Tigers to recall him in September.

Birdie Tebbetts made his major league debut in Briggs Stadium on September 16 as the Tigers took the Philadelphia Athletics to task by a 6–2 score. Over the last two weeks of the season, the young catcher appeared in ten games, batting .303 with a home run in 33 at-bats. The following two years, he served as the backup catcher to Rudy York in Detroit, catching 50 games and 53 games respectively. He hit a meager .191 in 162 at-bats in 1937, but when he brought his average up to .294 the next year, he was promoted to Detroit's regular catcher and York was moved to first base, a good move for both men. Tebbetts caught 100 games in 1939 and batted .261 in 341 at-bats. He had his peak years in Detroit from 1939 to 1941, batting .296 in 1940 and .284 the next year, and being selected for the American League All-Star team both years. The Vermont native played 99 games for Detroit in 1942, but entered military service with the United States Air Force before the season ended and was away from the game for the next three years. He spent his military career playing and managing baseball in such places as Texas, Hawaii, the Mariana Islands, and Saipan. He was discharged from the Air Force as a Captain in February, 1946, and returned to Detroit to find Bob Swift entrenched behind the plate. After catching 87 games that year and 20 games early in 1947, he was traded to the Boston Red Sox on May 20 for catcher Hal Wagner. The 34-year-old backstop blossomed in Boston, doing his usual superlative job behind the plate and hitting the ball with authority.

Birdie Tebbetts batted .299 in 90 games for Boston in 1947, followed by seasons of .267,

.280, .270, and .310. He drove in 62 runs in 446 at-bats in 1948 and 62 runs in 403 at-bats the following year, and was selected for the American League All-Star team both years. He, like the rest of the team, suffered through the two painful pennant losses, to the Indians in the 1948 playoff and to the Yankees in the 1949 collapse in Yankee Stadium in the last two games of the season. The outspoken catcher batted a career-high .310 in 1950 but, after making disparaging remarks about some members of the pitching staff in the off-season, calling them juvenile delinquents and moronic malcontents, he was traded to the Cleveland Indians on December 13, 1950. He played for Cleveland for two years before retiring in 1952 at the age of 39.

The five-foot, 11-inch, 170-pound, right-handed hitter had a respectable .270 career batting average, but not much power. His forte, however, was defense. He was recognized as one of the top defensive catchers in the American League, leading the league in putouts and double plays once each, and in assists and total chances per game three times each. He possessed a strong throwing arm, shooting down 44 percent of all baserunners attempting to steal, two percentage points above the league average. Birdie Tebbetts was one of Boston's finest catchers even though he played only three-and-a-half seasons in the Hub.

Tiant, Luis

The man known as "El Tiante," one of Boston's all-time favorite players, was born in the hotbed of Cuban baseball, Marianaro, on November 23, 1940, the son of the great Cuban League and Negro League pitcher, Luis "Lefty" Tiant, Sr., often called the "Cuban Carl Hubbell" because of his herky-jerky motion and his devastating screwball. Luis Jr. followed in his father's footsteps, pitching professionally from the time he was 18. Imitating his father's pitching motion, which included turning his back to the plate before delivering the ball, pitching from a variety of angles, and feeding the batter four or five different pitches at different speeds, young Tiant was signed by Bobby Avila to play baseball with the Mexico City Tigers in the Double-A Mexican League in 1959, and he struggled to a 5–19 record with a

Luis Tiant

5.92 ERA in his rookie season. The following year, he went 17–7, leading the league in victories, winning percentage (.708), and bases on balls, (124 in 180 innings), as the Tigers made the big jump from the cellar to first place. After a 12–9 year with the same team in 1961, Tiant signed a contract with the Cleveland Indians, who sent him to their Charleston farm club in the Single-A Eastern League. In 1964, after cruising to a 15–1 record in his first 17 starts with the Portland Beavers in the Triple-A Pacific Coast League, the cagey Cuban, who stood five feet, 11-nches tall and weighed 195 pounds, was rewarded with a promotion to the Cleveland Indians, and he brought his mesmerizing assortment of pitches and deliveries with him, driving American League batters crazy. According to *The Ballplayers*, "He baffled hitters with a rocking, twisting windup and an assortment of release points that ranged from over-the-top to almost underhand. Or, as announcer Curt Gowdy noted, 'He comes from everywhere except between his legs.'"[188] He was an immediate success in Cleveland, going 10–

4 in 19 games after his promotion, followed by seasons of 11–11, 12–11, 12–9, and 21–9. The year after his 21-victory season was a humbling experience, however, as he won just nine games against a league-high 20 losses in the Indians' fall from third place all the way to the basement. That was enough for Cleveland management and they passed the big right-hander on to the Minnesota Twins where he immediately went on the Disabled List with a hairline fracture of his shoulder. When he returned to the pitching rotation after being inactive for two months, Tiant couldn't find his rhythm, even though he posted a 7–3 won-loss record, and the Twins released the 29-year-old pitcher, fearing he might be over the hill. He was subsequently signed and released by the Atlanta Braves in 1971, before being rescued by the Boston Red Sox, who sent him to their Louisville farm team. Boston manager Eddie Kasko recalled him in July, but the best Tiant could do was a 1–7 record with the third-place Sox. As time would prove, it was one of the best deals ever made by the Red Sox in their history.

Boston stuck with the 31-year-old Cuban and, in 1972, with his shoulder fully recovered, he joined Bill Lee at the top of the Red Sox pitching rotation. He compiled a sparkling 15–6 mark that year, with 12 complete games, six shutouts, and a league-leading 1.91 ERA, earning him the American League Comeback Player of the Year Award. El Tiante, armed with an exploding fastball, a curve, and a slider, became an imposing figure in Boston, with his Fu Manchu mustache, his chunky build, and his back-to-the-batter delivery. He was an immediate fan favorite, and he fed off the adulation of the crowd, being not only a pitcher, but a celebrity and an entertainer as well. In 1973, he enjoyed his second 20-victory season, his first with Boston, going 20–13 with 23 complete games in 35 starts and a 3.34 ERA. Another 20-win season followed, as El Tiante compiled a 22–13 record with 25 complete games in 311 innings pitched, a league-leading seven shutouts, and a 2.92 ERA.

Darrell Johnson's powerful contingent finally put it all together in 1975, winning the American League East title with a 95–65 won-loss record, leaving the Baltimore Orioles four-and-a-half games in arrears. The team was an offensive powerhouse with Rice, Lynn, Yastrzemski, and Evans spearheading an attack that led the league with 796 runs scored, 284 doubles, and a .714 slugging average. The pitching was adequate with Rick Wise (19–12), Tiant (18–14), and Bill Lee (17–9) anchoring the starting rotation. Boston pounded the Oakland Athletics into submission in three straight games in the ALCS, outscoring their west coast adversaries, 18–7. Luis Tiant pitched the opener of the series, tossing a three-hit, 7–1 victory at Alvin Dark's crew. The ensuing World Series pitted Boston against the Big Red Machine of Cincinnati, and El Tiante got the Red Sox off and running in the opener, blanking the mighty Reds, 6–0. He came back in Game 4 to earn a 5–4 victory, and put the brakes on a two-game Boston slide, and he took the mound again in Game 6, pitching seven innings in Boston's thrilling, 7–6, 11-inning victory, but that only delayed the inevitable as Cincinnati took Game 7, 4–3, scoring the championship run in the top of the ninth inning.

Luis Tiant won 21 games against 12 losses in 1976, with 19 complete games in 38 starts, pitching 279 innings with a 3.06 earned run average, but Boston could do no better than third place in the American League Eastern Division, 15½ games behind Billy Martin's high-flying Yankees. Carl Yastrzemski once said of Tiant, "As great as Palmer and Catfish Hunter were, if you had to win one game in the seventies, you'd have to have Tiant. He was the best pitcher with a lead that I ever saw. Get him a 1–0 lead and he defended it as if it were his family. He'd refuse to lose."[189] El Tiante's star began to wane after the 1976 season. He won 12 games in 1977, 13 games the following year, and then filed for free agency, signing with the New York Yankees. He won 13 games for George Steinbrenner's crew in 1979 and then fell off to eight wins with New York, and two wins each with Pittsburgh and California, before retiring in 1982. Over his 19-year major league career, Luis Tiant led the American League in shutouts three times and ERA twice, with a 1.60 ERA in 1968 and a 1.91 ERA in 1972. During his eight-year Boston tenure, he won 122 games and lost 81 for an excellent .601 winning percentage.

Tillman, Bob

John Robert Tillman, a six-foot, four-inch, 205-pound catcher-outfielder, was signed to a professional baseball contract by the Boston Red Sox out of Middle Tennessee State College on January 18, 1958, and sent to their farm club in Raleigh, North Carolina, in the Class-B Carolina League for his first taste of organized baseball. The big, right-handed hitter had an excellent rookie season, stroking the ball at a .282 clip with 18 home runs and 76 runs batted in. He split his time in the field between the outfield and catcher that year, but concentrated on catching the rest of his career. He moved up the minor league ladder over the next three years, passing through Allentown, Minneapolis, and Seattle, coming to rest in Boston.

In spite of his futile offense with Seattle, Tillman stayed with Boston in 1962, serving as backup to Jim Pagliaroni. He made his first major league start on May 19 at home before a small crowd of 6,590, and tied a major league record by slamming a home run in his first official at-bat as the Red Sox lost to the Los Angeles Angels by a 6–5 score. His homer, a two-out solo shot in the fourth, gave the Sox a 1–1 tie, and he drove in another run in the sixth inning as Boston took a 5–3 lead, but the bullpen couldn't hold it as the Angels scored two runs in the eighth and pushed over the game-winner against Chet Nichols in the tenth. That home run was enough to impress manager Pinky Higgins, however, and Tillman caught most of the games over the next six weeks. On May 29, in Metropolitan Stadium, the Nashville native rang up a 3-for-3 day with two home runs, three RBI, and three runs scored. He walked in the sixth inning and scored the eventual game-winning run as Boston nipped the Twins, 6–5. One month later, on June 26, he was behind the plate when Earl Wilson tossed a no-hitter at the Los Angeles Angels, winning 2–0 and hitting the game-winning home run in the third inning. The season passed much too quickly for Bob Tillman; his batting average cooled off after his fast start, and he finished with a .229 average in 249 at-bats, although he did launch 14 homers and drive in 38 runs. He spent the off-season working out diligently at Tufts University to build up his strength and stamina. He also admitted during a local radio interview that he couldn't hit a curve ball with an oar. Unfortunately, the Tufts regimen didn't help him hit a curve ball, and he wasn't allowed to carry an oar to the plate, so he struggled through another frustrating season with the bat in 1963, hitting .225 with 64 strikeouts in 307 at-bats. In spite of his off-season conditioning program, his home run total fell to eight and his RBI leveled off at 32. Once again, however, he did enjoy one big day at the plate. On August 14, the husky catcher posted a 4-for-4 day in the Fenway ballpark, smashing three singles and a double in a 14–7 trouncing of the New York Yankees. Tillman singled and scored in the Red Sox seven-run fifth inning that brought the Bostonians back from a 5–2 deficit to a healthy 9–5 lead.

Tillman caught 131 games in 1964 and responded with a career-high .278 batting average with 18 doubles, 17 homers, and 61 RBI. It was the only time in his nine-year major league career that he hit over .238. On April 16, he stroked four base hits in five at-bats as Boston whipped the New Yorkers, 4–3, in 11 innings in Yankee Stadium. The Red Sox backstop tripled leading off the 11th inning and Roman Mejias, running for him, carried the winning run across the plate. He had another game to remember on July 18 when he had a two-home run day with six RBI. He sent the Fenway Park faithful into a frenzy in the sixth inning when he drove a ball over the Green Monster with the bases loaded, giving his team an insurmountable 9–2 lead. Two innings later, he hit a two-run shot, upping the Boston lead to its final score, 12–6. Tillman caught 106 games the following season, including Dave Morehead's no-hitter, but when his average bottomed out at .215 he lost his regular job to Mike Ryan. He spent most of 1967 in manager Dick Williams' doghouse after his error cost the Sox a victory, and he was unloaded to the New York Yankees for cash on August 8, after seeing action in just 30 games. Bob Tillman was a decent receiver in most respects except for his 24 percent caught-stealing percentage that was well below the league average. He had good power at the plate but he was a low-average hitter who struck out in about 22 percent of his at-bats.

Timlin, Mike

Mike Timlin was one of the premier middle-relief men and setup men of his time. As manager Terry Francona said in 2004, "I know Foulkey's our closer, but this has been Timlin's bullpen. He kind of leads the bullpen. He'll take the ball every day you give it to him, even when he shouldn't. You have to be careful of that, but it's also a real compliment for a guy when I say that."[190]

Michael August Timlin was born in Midland, Texas on March 10, 1966. He attended Southwestern University in Georgetown, Texas, where he pitched for the Pirates from 1985 to 1988. The Toronto Blue Jays selected him in the fifth round of the 1987 free agent draft and signed him on June 6. His first stop in organized baseball was with Medicine Hat in the Rookie Pioneer League, where he started 12 games for the Blue Jays, compiling a 4–8 won-loss record with a 5.14 earned run average. He turned it around the next year, going 10–6 with the Myrtle Beach Blue Jays in the Single-A South Atlantic League, with a 2.86 ERA covering 35 games with 22 starts and 151 innings pitched. Timlin stayed in "A" ball in 1989, pitching out of the bullpen for Dunedin in the Florida State League, appearing in 33 games with just seven starts, and going 5–8 in 88⅔ innings with a 3.25 ERA. He was back with Dunedin in 1990 to fine-tune his middle relief approach, but after winning seven games against two losses with a minuscule 1.43 ERA, he was promoted to Knoxville in the Double-A Southern League, where he continued to dominate as a relief pitcher, throwing 26 innings in 18 games with a 1–2 record and a 1.73 ERA.

That completed Mike Timlin's minor league education, and he spent the 1991 season with Toronto, pitching middle relief and handling the heavy workload like a veteran. He appeared in 63 games, including three starts, working 108⅓ innings, an average of 1.7 innings per game, with an 11–6 won-loss record and a 3.16 ERA. The big right-hander was not primarily a strikeout pitcher although he did average 6.8 strikeouts a game during his career. He possessed a mid–90s fastball, but he also owned a slider and a heavy sinker that had batters driving the ball into the dirt, resulting in a lot of ground ball outs. Cito Gaston's team won the first of three straight American League Eastern Division titles in 1991, but they were eliminated by the Minnesota Twins in the ALCS. Timlin pitched in four of the five games, posting a 0–1 record with a fine 3.18 ERA. The following year, he spent three months on the DL, but came back to pitch in 26 games down the stretch as Toronto won another division title, and this time they defeated the Oakland Athletics four games to two in the ALCS. The Blue Jays met the Atlanta Braves in the World Series and disposed of Bobby Cox's contingent in six games, with Timlin pitching in two games with one save. He was on the mound when the Series ended, and he threw out Otis Nixon on an attempted bunt to clinch the championship. Toronto won the World Series again the next year, defeating Philadelphia in six games, and Timlin, who had pitched in 54 games during the season, pitched in two Series games with no record. The hard-nosed veteran pitched for five teams over the next nine years, appearing in from 31 to 72 games a season and serving as the closer for Toronto, Seattle, and Baltimore between 1996 and 1999, with 99 saves. In 2002, he was granted free agency and signed with the Boston Red Sox on January 6, 2003.

Mike Timlin's first year in Beantown saw him march in from the bullpen on 72 occasions, pitching 83⅔ innings and posting a 6–4 record with two saves and a 3.55 ERA. He struck out 65 men and walked only nine, the fewest walks per nine innings for any major league pitcher. A Red Sox source noted that Timlin "wears his red socks knee high, and looks a lot like a player straight out of baseball's World War II Golden Age, staring down batters with a steely-eyed scowl and a cheek full of chaw."[191] The big Texan appeared in eight games in the ALDS and ALCS, pitching 9⅔ innings of one-hit ball with 11 strikeouts, two bases on balls, and a perfect 0.00 ERA. The following year, he pitched 76⅓ innings in 76 games with a 5–4 record, 56 strikeouts, and a 4.13 ERA, and on September 3 he appeared in his 80th game, the 29th pitcher to reach that impressive level. The 2004 post season, that saw Boston come back from a three-games-to-none deficit to the New York Yankees to defeat Joe Torre's cocky contingent in seven games, and then saw them demolish the St. Louis Cardinals in four straight games in the World Series to once and for all destroy the "Curse of the Bambino," gave Timlin, who appeared in 11 games in the post-season, his third World Series ring. The man from Midland enjoyed his best season in a Red Sox uniform in 2005, leading the American League with 81 games pitched, fanning 59 men in 80⅓ innings, posting a 7–3 record with 13 saves, and compiling a 2.24 ERA. The next year, he appeared in 68 games, going 6–6 with nine saves and, in 2007, he helped Boston capture another World Championship, coming back from a mid-season injury to pitch 55⅓ innings in 50 games, with a 2–1 record, one save, and a 3.42 ERA. He reached another personal milestone along the way. On August 31, he pitched in his 1,000th major league game, just the 11th pitcher in major league history to reach that exalted number. He threw 3⅓ scoreless innings at the Cleveland Indians over three games in the ALCS as Terry Francona's troops fought their way into another World Series, this one against the Colorado Rockies, and they polished off the National League upstarts in four games. The 42-year-old workhorse went 4–4 with one save and a hefty 5.66 earned run average in 2008 and was granted free agency at the end of the season, ending a notable 18-year major league career. Mike Timlin's memorable six-year Boston sojourn totaled 394 games with no starts, 409 innings pitched, a 30–22 won-loss record and 27 saves.

Todt, Phil

Philip Julius "Hook" Todt began his minor league career with the Tulsa Oilers in the Single-A Western League in 1921, playing outfield and punishing opposing pitchers to the tune of a .308 average with 42 doubles and 28 home runs in 611 at-bats. The following year found him with Columbus in the Double-A American Association, but his playing time was limited to 85 games and he hit a modest .273 with the Senators, with ten doubles and 12 homers. The line-drive hitter was back in "A" ball in 1923, playing with San Antonio of the Texas League, and he unleashed a dangerous bat once again, hammering the ball at a .333 clip with 36 doubles, 11 triples, and seven home runs. That display brought him to the attention of the Boston Red Sox, who purchased him from the Bears prior to the 1924 season.

Hook Todt made his major league debut with the Red Sox in Yankee Stadium on April 25, 1924, going 0-for-1 as a pinch-hitter during Boston's 5–2 loss to the Yankees. The six-foot, 175-pound, left-handed hitter was hitless in his next four pinch-hit assignments before smashing a two-run single in the middle of a seven-run, fifth-inning Boston rally that overcame an early 5–0 Cleveland lead and paved the way for an eventual 10–9 Red Sox victory before a small mid-week Fenway Park gathering. Todt made his first start in Dunn Field, Cleveland, on June 12, playing first base and batting fifth, and he chipped in with a double and an RBI in four trips to the plate, as Boston edged the Indians by a 4–3 score. On June 22, he cracked a single, a double, and his first major league home run in a 6–2 win over the Yankees before 30,000 quiet New Yorkers in their spacious stadium. He played a total of 52 games in his rookie season, batting .262 with eight doubles, two triples, and one home run in 103 at-bats.

Unfortunately for the smooth-swinging lefty, his power was compromised by Fenway Park's distant right-center field and center field fences that lurked 403 feet and 488 feet from home plate respectively. He hit just 13 of his 57 career home runs at Fenway. The New York Yankees reportedly offered to send their new first baseman, Lou Gehrig, to Boston in exchange for Phil Todt prior to the 1925 season, but Boston owner Bob Quinn turned down the offer. The Boston first baseman hit with authority in 1925, batting .278 with 29 doubles, 13 triples, 11 home runs, and 75 runs batted in. Gehrig hit .295 with 20 homers in his rookie season with New York, but went on to carve out a legendary career for himself over the next 14 years. The 25-year-old Missouri native slumped to .255 in 1926, with 69 RBI, but he showed the Boston fans some fancy fielding at first base as he posted a .988 fielding average and a 12.21 range factor, the third highest range factor for first basemen in baseball history. His good hands and quick reflexes permitted him to run down balls that other first basemen couldn't reach.

Phil Todt's batting averages were mediocre during his last five years with the Red Sox, ranging from .236 to .269, but the likable infielder gave Bill Carrigan's perennial cellar-dwellers consistent defense year-in and year-out, leading the American League with a .997 fielding average in 1928, and leading the league in putouts, assists, and triple plays, once each. His career 10.73 range factor is still the 17th-best range factor for first basemen in baseball history.

Torrez, Mike

Michael Augustine Torrez won 185 games in his 18-year major league career, 60 of them in a five-year sojourn with the Boston Red Sox, but from a Boston standpoint his legacy is identified by one tragic pitch he made to Bucky Dent that the Yankees shortstop rode into history during a playoff game in Fenway Park on Tuesday, October 2, 1978. Torrez, who was born in Topeka, Kansas, on August 28, 1946, began his professional baseball journey in 1965 with the Raleigh Cardinals in the Single-A Carolina League, where he posted a 4–8 won-loss record in 20 games. Two years later, on September 10, 1967, he made his major league debut with St. Louis, the first of five major league teams he would play for over the next ten years. He won 20 games against nine defeats with a league-leading .690 winning percentage for Earl Weaver's Baltimore Orioles in 1975, and two years later, he went 14–12 with the New York Yankees and pitched two complete-game victories against the Los Angeles Dodgers in the World Series. That winter, he played out his option and signed with the Boston Red Sox on November 23, 1977.

The year 1978 was a year Mike Torrez would rather forget. The Boston Red Sox held a commanding 14-game lead over Billy Martin's fourth-place New York Yankees on July 18. Five days later Bob Lemon replaced Martin at the Yankees helm and the team began to jell. Boston still held a comfortable seven-game lead on August 30, when their season suddenly unraveled. They dropped 13 of their next 16 games including a four-game Yankees sweep in Fenway Park where the Bronx Bombers outscored the pride of Boston, 42–9. The following week, New York won two of three in Yankee Stadium, giving them a two-and-a-half game lead over Boston. The Red Sox finally turned things around in the nick of time, winning their last eight games to tie the Yankees for first place. A one-game playoff was scheduled for Fenway Park on October 2, and manager Don Zimmer named Torrez, a 16–13 pitcher for Boston during the season, to face "Louisiana Lightning" Ron Guidry, Lemon's 24-game winner. The Boston starter was coming off a disastrous stretch run where he went 1–7 after August 18, including two losses to the Yankees, following a dazzling 15–6 start to the season. He felt the full fury of the Yankees bats on September 7 when he was touched up for five runs in one-plus innings of work during a 15–3 massacre at the hands of the New Yorkers. A second-inning home run by Carl Yastrzemski gave the Red Sox a 1–0 lead in the playoff, but Torrez was unable to protect it. In the top of the seventh, with Boston nursing a 2–0 lead, the Yankees put two men on base with two outs, bringing shortstop Bucky Dent, a .243 hitter during the season with five home runs to his credit, to the plate. With a count of 0–2, "Torrez and catcher Carlton 'Pudge' Fisk agreed on a fastball on the inside part of the plate as a setup pitch. But Torrez got too much of the plate, and Dent put it in the air. His high fly ball carried barely 320 feet, just enough to clear the Green Monster in left field for a three-run homer that gave the Yankees a lead they would never relinquish."[192] The eventual 5–4 victory sent New York to the World Series and Boston home.

Mike Torrez went 16–13 again in 1979, but the Red Sox could do no better than third place in the American League East, eleven-and-a-half games behind the Baltimore Orioles. The six-foot, five-inch, 210-pound right-hander played three more years with Boston, going 9–16, 10–3, and 9–9, before moving to the New York Mets and the Oakland Athletics, where he retired after the 1984 season.

Valentin, John

John Valentin was a key member of Boston's powerful Red Sox contingent during the 1990s. Born John William Valentin in Mineola, New York, on February 18, 1967. He was educated in St. Anthony's High School in Jersey City and Seton Hall University in South Orange, NJ, where he played baseball on the 1987 Big East Championship team, along with his roommate and future Boston teammate, Mo Vaughn. Boston drafted the six-foot, 180-pound infielder in the fifth round of the amateur entry draft in 1988, and sent him to Elmira in the New York–Pennsylvania League, where he played shortstop for the Pioneers and hit a weak .217 in 207 at-bats. The following year, he played for two teams, hitting a combined .257 and, in 1990, he moved up to New Britain in the Double-A Eastern League, but he was still unable to get his bat untracked, hitting a barely visible .218. The 24-year-old right-handed hitter was slow to mature in organized baseball, but he finally showed some life at the plate in 1991 when he posted a .264 average while shuttling back and forth between Double-A and Triple-A teams.

He hit .260 with Pawtucket the following year and was called up to the big club in July, making his major league debut on the July 27 in a night game against the Texas Rangers in Fenway Park. He went 1-for-4 on the night with an RBI single in the eighth inning as Boston took the measure of the Rangers by a 7–5 count. Valentin stayed with the Sox the rest of the year, seeing action in 58 games at shortstop after taking over from the good-field, no-hit Luis Rivera. He gave manager Butch Hobson an additional bonus by spanking the ball at a .276 clip with five homers in 185 at-bats. Valentin was the regular shortstop for the next four years, playing solid defense and contributing big base hits at the plate. He hit .278 in 1993 with 11 homers and 66 RBI, but was put out of action for an extended period of time the following year with an injury to his right knee that required arthroscopic surgery. He did manage to play in 84 games and batted a career-high .316 with nine homers and 49 RBI in 301 at-bats. On July 8, he accomplished one of baseball's rarities, pulling off an unassisted triple play, a feat made by only 14 other players in baseball history. In a Fenway Park night game against the Seattle Mariners, with the Mariners leading by a 2–0 score in the top of the sixth inning, and two men on base, "he caught a line drive off the bat of Marc Newfield, stepped on second base to retire Mike Blowers, then tagged runner Keith Mitchell who was heading (slowly!) for second."[193] As often happens, the man making the big defensive play

John Valentin

leads off the next inning, and Valentin led off the bottom of the sixth with a screamer over the left field wall, leading to a four-run Boston rally and a 4–3 victory. He had his best year in the major leagues in 1995, ripping the ball at a .298 clip with 37 doubles, 27 home runs, 102 RBI, 108 runs scored, a .399 on-base percentage, and a .533 slugging average. On June 2, he enjoyed a 5-for-5 day with three home runs and three RBI in a 6–5 win over Seattle in the Fenway ballyard. On August 1, he went 3-for-5 with a two-run home run and six RBI in a 13–3 rout of the Detroit Tigers in Tiger Stadium. He batted .250 with a homer and two RBI in the ALDS, but Boston was eliminated by Cleveland Indians in three straight.

John Valentin batted .296 the following year, but his 13 homers and 59 RBI in 527 at-bats were a far cry from his 1995 production. His biggest day of the year was June 6, when he hit for the cycle against the Chicago White Sox in friendly Fenway Park before 24,382 appreciative Red Sox rooters. The six-foot, 180-pound, right-handed hitter smashed a two-run home run over the Green Monster in the first inning, giving Boston a 2–1 lead, and his triple to center field in the third inning led to another Red Sox run. A two-run single in the fourth opened up a 5–1 lead, and a two-out double in the sixth completed the cycle and led to another

Boston run, making the final score 7–4. He tattooed the ball at a .306 clip in 1997 with a league-leading 47 doubles, 18 homers, and 77 RBI, but Jimy Williams' team could do no better than fourth place, their 78–84 won-loss record leaving them a distant 20 games behind the Baltimore Orioles.

Williams brought his team back in 1998 and 1999, finishing second both years and qualifying for post-season play. Valentin had a decent season in 1998 but it was his last good year. He batted a career-low .247 but he contributed 44 doubles, 23 homers, and 73 RBI to the Boston offense. In the ALDS, another loss to the Cleveland Indians, he was Jimy Williams' go-to guy, ripping Cleveland pitching for a .467 average with a double and five runs scored.

His career was winding down rapidly in 1999, as he played just 113 games after getting hit by a pitch in a game against the Chicago White Sox on June 25. He finished the season with a modest .253 batting average, with 12 homers and 70 RBI, but he rose to the occasion one more time in the post-season, leading the Red Sox offense in the ALDS, with a .318 batting average, two doubles, three home runs, and 12 RBI, as Boston defeated Cleveland in a tough five-game series. The Sox lost the first two games of the series, before bouncing back to capture the final three by scores of 9–3, 23–7, and 12–8. John Valentin went 2-for-5 with a double, a home run, and three RBI in Game 3, posted a 4-for-5 day with a double, two home runs, and seven RBI in the Game 4 massacre, and went 1-for-4 with two RBI in Game 5. Unfortunately, the Beantown boys could not maintain their momentum, and they fell to the Yankees in five games in the ALCS, although Valentin hit New York pitching for a .348 average with two doubles, a homer, and five RBI. In Game 3, with Boston down two games to none, Jose Offerman led off the first inning with a triple, bringing Valentin to the plate. He caught the ball flush on the sweet spot and "the roar could be heard in Mineola as he lifted a majestic two-run blast over the Monster in left to give the Sox a 2–0 lead en route to a dramatic 13–1 win."[194] That was the last shot in the Boston cannon as Joe Torre's troops closed the Sox out in the next game by a 6–1 score.

Injuries spelled finis to John Valentin's career after 1999. He played only ten games in 2000 before rupturing the tendon in his left knee, requiring surgery, and he went down with another knee injury the following year after just 20 games. He tried a comeback with the New York Mets in 2002 and managed to play 114 games, batting .240 in 208 at-bats, but his knees wouldn't allow him to continue playing.

Varitek, Jason

Jason Varitek, the latest captain of the Red Sox, has spent his entire 14-year career with Boston, beginning in 1997. The six-foot, two-inch, 230-pound catcher came into this world much smaller and much lighter, first seeing the light of day in Rochester, Minnesota, on April 11, 1972. The switch-hitter, who was arguably the best catcher in NCAA history, caught for Georgia Tech from 1991 through 1994, and was a three-time All-American. He was Baseball America's 1993 Player of the Year, and led his team to the 1994 College World Series, where they were the runners-up. The legendary college catcher remains the only player to have his number retired by Georgia Tech. He was drafted by the Minnesota Twins after he received his degree in management, but the two sides couldn't agree on a contract, and he waited another year before he was drafted by the Seattle Mariners. After another year-long negotiation, Varitek finally began his organized baseball career with the Port City Roosters in the Double-A Southern League in 1995, where he struggled with the bat after missing two years of competition, hitting just .224 in 104 games. He upped his average to .262 with Port City the following year while splitting his time between catcher, third base, and the outfield. In 1997, he started the season with the Tacoma Raniers in the Triple-A Pacific Coast League, where he hit .254 in 87 games before he was traded to the Boston Red Sox on July 31. Boston sent him to their Pawtucket farm team in the Triple-A International League, but he struggled once again, batting below the Mendoza line at .197. He was recalled to Boston after the International League season ended, and he made his major league debut on September 24, stroking a single as a pinch-hitter in his only plate appearance of the year.

Jason Varitek

The next year, he joined Boston as the backup to Scott Hatteberg, catching 86 games and hitting a respectable .253. On September 15, in Yankee Stadium, Varitek had a 2-for-4 day with two home runs and five RBI as Boston routed the Bronx Bombers 9–4. Tek's three-run homer in the second inning gave the Red Sox a lead they never relinquished. In 1999, Jason Varitek took over the regular catching duties, playing 144 games and slugging 39 doubles and 20 home runs, with 76 RBI and a .269 batting average in 483 at-bats. The big switch-hitter, who was still a work in progress both offensively and defensively, slumped to .248 in 2000, and then missed all but 51 games the following year because of injuries, finishing the year with a .293 batting average.

From 2001 through 2008, he caught at least 125 games each season except for 2006, when injuries limited him to just 103 games. His batting average over that period fluctuated between .220 and .296, his home runs ranged from ten to 25, and his RBI went from 43 to 85, but his defense got measurably better every year and he was generally considered to be one of the best all-around catchers in the American League. On May 20, 2001, a Sunday afternoon game in Kauffman Stadium in Kansas City, Varitek had one of his best days as a major leaguer. He went 4-for-4 at the plate with three home runs and seven runs batted in as Jimy Williams' cohorts humbled the last-place Royals by a 10–3 count. One year later, on May 8, 2002, on his way to a .266 season, Varitek led the Red Sox to a 12–6 hammering of the Oakland Athletics, with a double, a home run, and five RBI, in four trips to the plate. His three-run homer in the second inning gave Boston a 3–0 lead and the Sox added another seven runs in the third to ice the game. He batted .273 in 2003 with 25 homers and 85 runs batted in, and the team appeared ready to grab the brass ring in the post-season, but they self-destructed instead. In the ALCS against the New York Yankees, they held a commanding 5–2 lead after seven-and-a-half innings in Game 7, with their ace, Pedro Martinez, on the mound, but New York routed Pedro with three runs in the eighth, and then sent Boston home early compliments of Aaron Boone's 11th inning home run. That debacle cost manager Grady Little his job.

The Red Sox, with new manager Terry Francona at the helm, were determined to reclaim their rightful place in the World Series in 2004, but they stumbled along during the first half of the season, and were firmly entrenched in second place on July 23, falling a full nine-and-a-half games behind the Yankees after losing the opener of a series against the New Yorkers by an 8–7 score. The Fenway Faithful jammed the little park along Yawkey Way in a nationally televised contest on Saturday the 24th, hoping against hope that their heroes could awake from their season-long slumber. In the third inning, their wish was granted. With New York leading 3–0, Bronson Arroyo hit Alex Rodriguez in the ribs with a pitch and A-Rod went berserk. He screamed at Arroyo, and when Varitek went to his pitcher's defense, A-Rod challenged him — a big mistake. Varitek shoved his glove in A-Rod's face, a sign that Boston would not be intimidated by the big boys from the Bronx. Varitek and Rodriguez were ejected, and the game continued, but the bench-clearing fracas finally brought Francona's troops to life. They scored two runs in the third, two more in the fourth, and four in the sixth, but they still trailed by a 10–8 score entering the bottom of the ninth inning with Yankees legend Mariano Rivera on the mound. That scenario didn't deter them, however, and a double by Garciaparra, a single by Millar, and a three-run homer by Bill Mueller off baseball's greatest closer sent the crowd home happy. That game has been called the turning point of the Red Sox season. From that game through the end of the season, Boston posted the division's best won-lost record. They still finished second to the Yankees but, as everyone knows, they polished off the Anaheim Angels in the ALDS, roared back to dethrone the New Yorkers in the ALCS, and swept the St. Louis Cardinals in the World Series to claim their first World Championship in 86 years.

Jason Varitek filed for free agency at the end of the season, but re-signed with Boston on December 24 and was later named the official Captain of the team because of his leadership qualities, an honor he carried with distinction. As general manager Theo Epstein noted, "It's not every day that you're lucky enough to find a player who embodies everything you want a franchise to be. When you're lucky enough to have that player, you don't let him get away. You lock him up for as long as you can and you make him the rock of your franchise."[195] Boston won another World Championship in 2007 and the Captain was one of the heroes. After hitting .255 during the season with 17 homers and 68 RBI, he concentrated on his defense during the ALDS, but against Cleveland in the ALCS, he had three doubles, a home run, and four RBI, and in the World Series sweep of the Colorado Rockies, he batted .333 with five runs batted in. Varitek's career began to wind down after the 2007 championship season, his batting average slipping to .220 and .209 over the next two years. In 2010 the 38-year-old catcher was relegated to a backup role behind Victor Martinez, but he stepped in whenever needed, did his usual yeoman job behind the plate, and slammed seven home runs in 112 at-bats while batting .232. He played in 68 games in 2011 batting a .221 with 11 home runs in 222 at-bats.

Tek has been a dangerous offensive weapon for the Sox over the years, averaging 33 doubles, two triples, 21 home runs, and 81 RBI, for every 550 at-bats. But his greatest strength is his defense. He has excellent leadership qualities, both on the field and in the clubhouse. He excels at calling a game and at handling a pitching staff. As he noted, "You've got to find out who you can push, who you can pat on the back, who you need to say nothing to."[196] The Captain is also a force to be reckoned with at blocking the plate, and at preventing passed balls. In his first three seasons, he had an embarrassing passed ball record, averaging 26 passed balls for every 154 games played, but through hard work he reduced his passed balls to just 6.9 passed balls for every 154 games played since 2001, one of the best percentages in the American League.

Vaughn, Moe

Maurice Samuel "Mo" Vaughn, who first saw the light of day in Norwalk, Connecticut, on December 15, 1967, was one of the most likable, kind, and humble players ever to wear a Red Sox uniform, but he was also confident, dedicated, and upbeat. Off the field he was involved in community service and various charitable organizations such as the Jimmy Fund, the Food Bank, and the Boys and Girls Clubs. The man who grew to six-foot, one-inch tall, with a muscular 240 pound frame, was always big for his age, and he always played baseball with older boys because of his size and his skills. One source noted that by the age of 12, he hit as many as 30 home runs in a 13-game Little League season. He received his nickname from his high school athletic director, who thought Maurice was too long a name so he shortened it to Mo. He attended Seton Hall University in South Orange, NJ and, in his first year with the Pirates, he broke the school's career home run record by sending 28 balls into orbit. He played three years of college ball and was selected to the All-American Team each year. By the time he left school, Vaughn, who was called "Hit Dog," by his fraternity brothers, had posted a career batting average of .417 with 57 home runs and 218 runs batted in, and had been chosen as "The Player of the Decade" by the Big East Conference.

Mo Vaughn

The Boston Red Sox selected Mo Vaughn in the first round of the free agent draft on June 5, 1989, and sent him to their farm team in New Britain, Connecticut, in the Double-A Eastern League, where he took some time getting adjusted to professional baseball, but wound up hitting .278 with eight homers and 38 runs batted in, in 245 at-bats. He moved up to Pawtucket in the Triple-A International League in 1990, batting .295 with 26 doubles, 22 home runs, and 72 RBI in 386 at-bats over 108 games. He was back in Pawtucket to start the 1991 season, but after 69 games where he hit .274 with 14 homers and 50 RBI in 234 at-bats, he was recalled to Boston.

Mo Vaughn made his major league debut with the Red Sox in a night game in Fenway Park on June 27, 1991, going 0-for-2 with a walk as Joe Morgan's team was blanked by the New York Yankees, 8–0. He batted .260 in 74 games the remainder of the season, with 12 doubles, four home runs, and 32 RBI in 219 at-bats. The Hit Dog won the starting first base job by default in 1992 after the incumbent, Carlos Quintana, was seriously injured in a car accident in Venezuela and was lost for the season. The pressure seemed to get to Mo early and he hit a mediocre .185 in 23 games before being shuttled off to Pawtucket to rediscover his swing and his confidence. After 39 games back in the bushes, his .282 average, six home runs, and 28 RBI in 149 at-bats was enough for Boston to recall him. The big, left-handed slugger hit better the second time around and, although he couldn't erase his poor start completely, he did bring his average up to .234 by the end of the season with 16 doubles, 13 homers, and 57 RBI. The 25-year-old slugger felt more comfortable in his new environment in 1993, and he unleashed his big lumber, stinging the ball to the tune of a .297 average with 34 doubles, 29 homers, and 101 RBI. He hit over .300 for the first time the following season, batting a cool .310, with 26 homers and 82 RBI, setting the stage for his career season. The 1995 Red Sox, under new manager Kevin Kennedy, rebounded from three straight losing seasons and a fourth-place finish the previous year, to a division title and a seven-game bulge over the New York Yankees. Mo Vaughn was the leader of the Boston juggernaut, crushing the ball at a .300 clip with 28 doubles, 39 home runs, and a league-leading 126 runs batted in, a performance that earned him the American League's MVP award. On July 3, in Kauffman Stadium in Kansas City, the Norwalk native tattooed Royals pitching for three base hits including a triple and two home runs, driving in six runs in a 12–5 Red Sox victory. Sadly, Vaughn and the rest of the Sox brigade cooled off in the ALDS against the powerful Cleveland Indians, who had led the league in runs scored, home runs, and ERA, and they were eliminated in three straight games.

Boston did not qualify for post-season play the next two years, finishing third and fourth respectively, but Vaughn continued to punish the opposition, batting .326 in 1996 with 44 homers, 118 runs scored, and a career-high 144 RBI. On September 24, in Fenway Park, the Hit Dog kept the Red Sox fans screaming from the first inning to the ninth inning, as he hammered Baltimore pitching for three home runs and a single in five at-bats, good for five RBI, in a 13–8 Boston victory. The following year, he hit .315 with 35 homers and 96 RBI. His biggest day of the year was April 16 in Fenway Park, when he sent two three-run homers into the Boston night sky as the Red Sox defeated the Cleveland Indians in a slugfest, 11–6. Six weeks later, on May 30, he had a three-homer night against the hated New York Yankees, sending the 32,341 Fenway Faithful into a wild celebration. After singling in the first inning, he homered in the third to give the Sox a 2–0 lead, added another round-tripper in the fourth upping the score to 8–0, and then, after walking in the fifth, he hit a leadoff homer in the eighth, making the final score 10–4.

In 1998, Jimy Williams' team qualified for the ALDS even though their second-place finish in the Eastern Division left them 22 games off the pace of Joe Torre's high-flying Yankees. The Sox were led by third-year shortstop Nomar Garciaparra, Mo Vaughn, and a powerful pitching staff that included Tim Wakefield, Pedro Martinez, and closer Tom Gordon, who led the league with 46 saves in 47 opportunities. Mo's contribution was a career-high .337 batting average, 40 home runs, 115 RBI, and 107 runs scored. The big first baseman got the Red Sox off on the right foot on opening day against the Seattle Mariners in Fenway Park before 32,805 early-season party animals. Boston drew first blood when Damon Buford cracked a two-run homer off a Randy Johnson heater in the fourth inning, but that lead was short-lived as the Mariners scored three in the sixth and entered the bottom of the ninth with a comfortable 7–2 lead. Johnson had pitched the first eight innings, holding Boston to two scattered hits and sending 15 of them back to the bench shaking their heads, but after 131 pitches manager Lou Pinella turned the pitching duty over to the bullpen. It was the wrong decision as Seattle relievers couldn't retire a single Boston batter. Before the Seattle manager knew what was happening, two walks, three base hits, and a hit batter gave the Red Sox three runs, and they still had the bases loaded with no one out and The Hit Dog, Mo Vaughn, coming to the plate. Vaughn, who had fanned three times against Randy Johnson, was happy to see southpaw Paul Spoljaric on the mound, and he jumped all over an 0–1 pitch and hammered it 392 feet into the right field seats for a walk-off grand slam as Red Sox Nation exploded, giving their hero a standing ovation.

Vaughn's contributions carried over into the ALDS as he drove in seven runs in the opener of the series in Jacobs Field, Cleveland. His three hits in five at-bats included a double and two home runs as Boston routed the home team by an 11–3 score. But that was the highlight of the Boston season as they succumbed to the underdog Indians in the next three games by scores of 9–5, 4–3, and 2–1. Mo Vaughn, whose relationship with Boston management had soured over the years, filed for free agency after the 1998 season, signing with the Anaheim Angels on December 11, 1998. He played major league ball four more years before retiring at the age of 35.

Vosmik, Joe

Joseph Franklin Vosmik was a local neighborhood hero as a Cleveland teenager for his tremendous baseball feats in the city sandlot leagues. On August 26, 1928, he played in a single-A All-Star Game in League Park, the home of the major league Indians. During the pre-game warm-ups, as noted in *The Ballplayers*, "Vosmik caught the eye of the wife of the Indians general manager, Billy Evans. Needing to sign one more local boy, Evans asked his wife's opinion," and she pointed to Vosmik and said, "take the good looking blond boy."[197] Cleveland eventually did sign the local hero and sent him to their farm club in Frederick, Maryland in the Class D Blue Ridge League for the 1929 season. The Warriors 19-year-old outfielder was too much for Class-D pitching and he punished opposing pitchers to the tune of a .381 average while leading the league with 39 doubles and 24 triples in 407 at-bats. The following year, the powerful hitting machine played for the Terre Haute Tots in the Class-B Three-I League, where he went on another rampage, leading the league with an astronomical .397 batting average, while ripping 25 doubles, 15 triples, and 13 homers, with 116 runs batted in, in 458 at-bats. That was the end of Joe Vosmik's minor league apprenticeship. He spent the next 11 years in the major leagues.

The six-foot, 185-pound, right-handed hitter was recalled to Cleveland in September, 1930, and made his major league debut in League Park on September 15 in a 9–2 whipping at the hands of the American League champion Philadelphia Athletics. The next year, he was a regular in the Indians lineup and, in League Park on April 18 against the Chicago White Sox, he enjoyed a 5-for-5 day, sending three doubles ricocheting off the inviting right field wall, just 290 feet from home plate. The 21-year-old outfielder's bat sizzled during his rookie season and he tortured American League pitchers to the tune of .320, with 36 doubles, 14 triples, seven homers, and 117 RBI. He was not a home run threat but he consistently found the alleys to accumulate a basket-full of doubles and triples. And he had a good eye at the plate, drawing 52 bases on balls for every 550 at-bats, while striking out just 27 times. He would have been a shoo-in for the Rookie of the Year Award if that award had been given out in 1931. Vosmik had five more productive years in Cleveland, including 1935 when he batted a career-high .348 with ten home runs, 110 RBI, 93 runs scored, a .408 on-base percentage, and a .537 slugging average, while leading the league with 216 base hits, 47 doubles, and 20 triples. He went into the last day of the season leading Buddy Myer by three percentage points in the batting race so he chose to sit out the final game to protect his lead. Unfortunately Myer stroked four base hits in five at-bats to claim the batting title, .349 to .348. After a .287 season the following year, the 28-year-old slugger was traded to the St. Louis Browns, who shipped him off to Boston at the end of the 1937 season.

Joe Vosmik played for Joe Cronin's powerful team for two years, joining such superstars as Lefty Grove, Jimmie Foxx, Bobby Doerr, and Cronin. In his first year with the Red Sox, he batted .324 with 37 doubles, 86 RBI, 121 runs scored, and a league-leading 201 base hits, but the team could do no better than second place, nine-and-a-half games behind New York. In 1939, the 29-year-old slugger's average fell off to .276 and he was sold to the Brooklyn Dodgers in the off-season. He retired after the 1941 season, came back to play 14 games for Washington during the war year of 1944, and then hung up his glove except for two brief minor-league stints.

Wagner, Heinie

Heinie Wagner was a wide-ranging shortstop who used his exceptionally big feet to block baserunners sliding into second base and to trip baserunners between second and third. He was often called one of the finest defensive shortstops of his era. Charles F. Wagner played sandlot baseball in New York City from an early age and "as a boy Wagner mastered the inside game in gritty fashion, playing barefoot on the rough-and-tumble side streets and vacant sandlots of Harlem."[198] Later, as a teenager, he played sandlot ball in Hell's Kitchen and was considered one of the most talented ballplayers in New York. He received his nickname about this time because of his German heritage.

After he graduated from high school in 1898, he began to play semi-pro ball around the island, bringing him to the attention of professional baseball scouts. The Columbus Senators of the independent American Association liked what they saw, and signed the 21-year-old infielder to a contract in 1902. He handled the shortstop chores for the Senators early in the season, batting a light .191 in 29 games with just one double to show for his effort, but his defensive play was enough for the last-place New York Giants to purchase him from Columbus on July 1, and he made his major league debut the same day, suffering through an 8–3 loss to the Boston Beaneaters in the Polo Grounds. Manager John McGraw was less than impressed with his new shortstop so he gave the job to Joe Bean and released Wagner. The talented New Yorker caught on with the Newark Sailors of the Single-A Eastern League, where he spent four years, with his batting average fluctuating between .209 and .241, but good hands and a strong throwing arm kept him in the lineup. The Boston Pilgrims, seeking a replacement for their 30-year-old shortstop, Freddy Parent, who had lost a step in the field, selected Wagner in the major league draft in September, 1906.

Heinie Wagner played nine games with Boston at the end of the season, fielding well and hitting .281 in 32 at-bats. His first game with the team was September 26 in South Side Park in Chicago, and he had two base hits in a 2–0 loss to the White Sox. The batting and fielding skills he demonstrated during his nine-game trial earned him the plaudits of the Boston press and the fans. The *Boston Globe* even said Wagner had all the earmarks of a real find. The five-foot, nine-inch, 183-pound, right-handed hitter couldn't sustain the high batting average in 1907, however, and he slipped back to .213, but he provided his usual strong defense for the team, now called the Red Sox. After a last-place finish in 1906, Boston gradually worked its way up the American League standings over the next six years and Wagner was one of the keys to its success. According to Foster and Hulbert, "On and off the field, his quiet leadership, dogged loyalty, and wry humor, earned him the respect of teammates, adversaries, and fans in Boston for over two decades."[199] The New York City boy batted .247 in 1908, but brought that up to .256 the following year, and then hit a solid .273 in 1910, with 26 doubles, seven triples, 61 runs scored, 52 RBI, and a career-high 26 stolen bases. He suffered an injury at the end of spring training in 1911, but came back to play 80 games, although his batting average was a modest .257.

The year 1912 was a big year for the Boston Red Sox and an even bigger year for their 31-year-old shortstop. Manager Jake Stahl had his team in top physical condition coming out of spring training, and they were ready to take on all comers. The home opener on April 20, after a series of disappointing rainouts, was a satisfying 7–6 victory over the New York Highlanders. The Chicago White Sox raced to the front of the pack early but faded after a 9–15 month in June, when Boston overtook Nixey Callahan's charges on June 11 and never looked back. Smoky Joe Wood, en route to a spectacular 34–5 season, had a perfect 7–0 record in June to pace the Red Sox surge. They continued to increase their lead down the stretch until it stood at 14 games when the curtain came down. Heinie Wagner had career highs in batting average (.274), runs scored (75), RBI (68), bases on balls (62), and on-base percentage (.358). He also stole 21 bases.

The World Series matched Boston against the National League champion New York Giants under the direction of feisty John McGraw. It was a grueling eight-game series won by Boston, but it wasn't decided until the last batter. Heinie Wagner's contribution was primarily defensive in the Series, as he and his second base partner gave Stahl's team a tight inner defense. He was involved in one key play in Game 1. With Boston trailing 2–1 in the top of the seventh inning, Wagner ripped a one-out single to center field and carried home the tying run on Harry Hooper's double to right. Boston added two more runs in the frame and won the game by a 4–3 score.

Heinie Wagner played four more years in Boston but his best days were behind him. He batted .227 in 1913, but then suffered an attack of rheumatism as well as a weak throwing arm over the winter that forced him to sit out the 1914 season and restricted his playing time to just 84 games the following year. He played six games in 1916 and three games in 1918, bringing his career to a close.

Wakefield, Tim

He was a slugging first baseman in college, setting a career home run record at the school and being voted the team's MVP. His dream of major league fame died quickly when he entered organized baseball and batted a mediocre .189 in his Single-A debut and .235 the following season. He also had defensive problems at both first base and third base. Fortunately, he was a resourceful individual and developed a knuckleball that catapulted him into the major leagues as a pitcher in less than four years. Timothy Stephen Wakefield, from Melbourne, Florida, attended Florida Institute of Technology from 1985 to 1989. As a sophomore, he set a school single-season home run record with 22 homers and 71 RBI. The following year, he was voted the team's Most Valuable Player and, by the time he graduated, he owned Florida Tech's career home run record with 40 round-trippers. He was drafted by the Pittsburgh Pirates in the eighth round of the 1988 free-agent draft and was assigned to their Single-A farm club in Watertown, NY in the New York–Pennsylvania League. His professional baseball debut was very disappointing as he committed eight errors in 44 games at first base and hit an embarrassing .189. The following year, playing third base for the Augusta Pirates in the Single-A South Atlantic League, he made three errors in six games and hit .235. When one of the coaches told him he would never make it above Double-A ball as a position player, he began experimenting with a knuckleball and reinvented himself as a pitcher. He went to the mound 18 times for Welland in the NY–Penn League in 1989, pitching 39⅔ innings and posting a 1–1 record with a 3.40

ERA. Over the next three years, he perfected his butterfly pitch and, after racking up a 10–3 record with the Buffalo Bisons in the Triple-A American Association in 1992, he was recalled to Pittsburgh.

He made his major league debut in Three Rivers Stadium against the St. Louis Cardinals on July 31 and he came away a winner, stopping the Redbirds by a 3–2 score with a ten-strikeout, 146-pitch-complete-game effort. He went 8–1 down the stretch for the Bucs and was voted the National League's Rookie Pitcher of the Year by *The Sporting News*. In the NLCS against the Atlantic Braves, he pitched and won two complete games, but the Braves prevailed in seven games. He struggled through a rough sophomore season in which he couldn't find the strike zone, posting a 6–11 won-loss record with a 5.61 ERA. After two failed minor league assignments, he was released by the Pirates on April 20, 1995, subsequently signing with the Boston Red Sox one week later. It turned out to be one of the best transactions in Red Sox history.

Tim Wakefield joined Boston armed with a frustrating knuckleball, a mediocre fastball, and a decent curve ball. He started the season with Pawtucket in the Triple-A International League but after just four games in which he went 2–1 he was called up to Boston. He made his first start in Anaheim Stadium on May 27 and coasted to a 12–1 win over the Angels, pitching seven innings of five-hit ball. He was pressed into action again three days later, pitching 7⅓ innings in a 1–0 victory over the Oakland Athletics and, on June 4, a bright, sunny Sunday in Boston, he defeated the Seattle Mariners in another pitching duel by a 2–1 score in ten innings. Troy O'Leary's home run in the bottom of the tenth was the game-winner. He stopped the A's 4–1 on June 9, and ran his record to 7–1 on July 9 with a 7–0 complete game effort against the Minnesota Twins. The 28-year-old right-hander finished the season as Boston's top pitcher with a spectacular 16–8 won-lost record, and a 2.95 ERA in 195⅓ innings pitched. One source, noting Wakefield's success with the knuckleball, claimed the pitch screws everybody up. The batter can't hit it, the catcher can't catch it, and the umpire can't call it.

The Florida native has won ten or more

Tim Wakefield

games 11 times for Boston with highs of 17 games in both 1998, when he went 17–8, and 2007, when he went 17–12. He has been a valuable innings-eater for Red Sox managers over the years. He is always ready to pitch, either starting or in relief. He started 121 games between 1995 and 1998, but when Tom Gordon, Boston's closer, went down with an injury on June 12, 1999, manager Jimy Williams called upon his versatile knuckleball artist to take over the closer's job for the rest of the season. Wakefield appeared in 32 games out of the bullpen and, according to Leigh Grossman, "He was effective in that role, saving 15 games, although he frequently terrified fans by giving up walks and long fly balls in late innings of close games."[200] He was a two-way pitcher over the next three years, starting 49 times and relieving 92 times, but since 2002 he has been primarily a starting pitcher, winning 88 games and losing 78. On September 23, 2008, he won the pennant-clinching game against the Cleveland Indians, going six innings in a 5–4 Sox victory. He went 11–5 for the Sox in 2009, 4–10 in 2010, and 7–8 in 33 games in 2011.

As successful as he has been for the Red Sox during the regular season over the past 15 years however, he has been spectacularly unsuccessful in post-season play, posting an overall 3–7 record with an ERA of well over 8.00. That could be due to the fact that his knuckleball doesn't move as well in cold weather as it does in warm weather. As all baseball fans know, a knuckleball is almost unhittable when it sinks or sails on its way to the plate, but when it doesn't move it often leaves the ballpark in fair territory. Tim Wakefield's regular season Boston Red Sox statistics through 2011 show a 186–168 won-lost record and 22 saves in 590 games pitched.

Webb, Earl

Earl Webb had a relatively short major league career, totaling just seven years, but he made the most of it, setting a record for doubles in one season that still stands, and leaving behind a career batting average of .306. The six-foot, one-inch, 185-pound, left-handed hitter joined the professional baseball ranks with Clarksdale in the Class-D Mississippi State League in 1921, where he hit a respectable .282 in 92 games while pitching and playing the outfield. After a brief stay with Memphis as a pitcher in 1922, Webb moved up the minor league ladder through Memphis, Pittsfield (Massachusetts), and Toledo over the next three years, batting between .323 and .343, and putting away his pitcher's toe-plate for good. His four-year record as a pitcher was a mediocre 37–47 in 118 games pitched. In 1925, after hitting a crisp .329 with the Toledo Mud Hens in the American Association, Earl Webb was traded to the New York Giants, where he played in four games at the end of the season. He spent the next five years bouncing around the major leagues and minor leagues from team to team, without ever finding a home. During two trials with the Chicago Cubs in 1927 and 1928, he hit a combined .286 in 472 at-bats, but his lack of speed and his mediocre defense kept him on the move.

The Boston Red Sox, coming off a span where they finished last in seven of eight years, and seventh the other year, obtained the services of the left-handed slugger from the Washington Senators in April 1930, after he had destroyed Pacific Coast League pitching to the tune of a .357 average with 56 doubles, 37 home runs, and 164 RBI in 658 at-bats with the Los Angeles Angels. Webb played in 127 games for the last-place Red Sox his first year in Boston, stroking the ball at a .323 clip with 30 doubles, 16 homers, and 66 runs batted in, in 449 at-bats. But his defense was atrocious. "He looked the worst of all the bad right fielders who have been tried out at Fenway Park.... Webb dropped them, misjudged them, and almost had his head knocked off by fly balls." Webb himself confessed, "I have seen some mighty bad outfielders but none of them had anything on me."[201]

The following year, he set a major league record with 67 doubles, to go along with 14 homers, 103 RBI, and a .333 batting average. On September 17, during a doubleheader in Fenway Park, Boston's hitting machine went 4-for-9 with a double in each game to break George Burns' record of 64 doubles in a season. He hit number 66 the following day and then went seven games without a double before hammering number 67 on the last day of the season. His manager, Shano Collins, explained Webb's success. "The reason he hits so many doubles is that he's hitting a long, hard ball this year and he's too darned slow on the bases to get to third."[202] His offensive contributions helped pull the Red Sox up to sixth place in the American League. However, in 1932, with Boston slipping back into the cellar again, and Webb's batting average dipping to .281 after 52 games, he was traded to the Detroit Tigers on June 12. He left the major leagues for good after the 1933 season, playing four more years in the minor leagues before retiring. Earl Webb played in 330 games with the Boston Red Sox between 1930 and 1932, batting .321. If the designated hitter rule had been in vogue during Webb's time, he might still be playing.

Werber, Billy

Billy Werber was, as he said, a cocky young man and an aggressive ballplayer who was ready to fight at the drop of a hat. He was a fine defensive third baseman with good hands and quick reflexes, a capable batter who sported a .271 career batting average and a .364 on-base percentage, and a daring baserunner who led the league in stolen bases three times during his career. William Murray Werber was born in Berwyn, Maryland, on June 20, 1908, and grew up to become an All-American basketball player at Duke University. He was also an outstanding baseball player who New York Yankees scout Paul Krichell said had "the best baseball legs I ever saw including Cobb."²⁰³ Werber signed an agreement with the Yankees after his freshman year at Duke, with New York paying for his last three years of college. According to the five-foot, 11-and-a-half-inch, 172 pound infielder, he played "four more-than-decent years at shortstop for Duke's baseball team, hitting around .400 each year."²⁰⁴ He continued his baseball education and supplemented his income by playing semi-pro baseball during the summer months.

Werber received a bonus from New York and signed a contract with them following his graduation from college in 1930, and joined the Yankees on a hot, muggy day in St. Louis where he made his major league debut at shortstop in the second game of a doubleheader on June 25. He walked in his first at-bat, just ahead of a Babe Ruth home run. The brash 22-year-old, wanting to impress the crowd with his speed, raced around the bases as fast as he could, arriving in the dugout well ahead of the Babe. When Ruth finally appeared, he patted the rookie on the head and said, "Son, you don't have to run when the Babe hits one." Werber finished the day with two base hits and three bases on balls in five trips to the plate, and he handled ten chances in the field without an error. He was farmed out to Albany in the Eastern League shortly thereafter, and he dazzled the New York state fans, stroking the ball at a .339 clip in 316 at-bats covering 84 games, and capturing the league's Most Valuable Player trophy. He split the 1931 season between Toledo in the American Association and Newark in the International League, holding down the shortstop job for both teams while hitting .276 for the Mud Hens and a disappointing .211 for the Bears in 52 games. After rebounding with a .289 batting average for Buffalo in the International League the following year, Billy Werber joined the Bronx Bombers for spring training in 1933. Unfortunately for him, the Yankees had obtained the much-touted shortstop Frankie Crosetti from the Pacific Coast League the previous year, so Werber found himself without a job. That was rectified on May 12 when New York sold the young infielder to the Boston Red Sox.

Billy Werber joined a Boston team that was still struggling to find its identity after spending most of the previous decade in the American League basement. The new arrival shared the shortstop job with Rabbit Warstler in 1933, batting .259 with 15 stolen bases in 108 games for Marty McManus's seventh-place team. He had his biggest day of the year on August 31 when the Sox invaded Yankee Stadium and humiliated Joe McCarthy's proud Bronx Bombers, 15–2. Werber, batting leadoff, cracked a double and a triple off Yankees southpaw Herb Pennock, driving in five runs. After being moved to third base in 1934, the right-handed hitter put together his best overall season in the major leagues. He scorched the ball to the tune of a .321 average with 200 base hits, 41 doubles, ten triples, 11 home runs, 67 RBI, and 129 runs scored, while leading the league with 40 stolen bases and 323 assists. He also struck out just 37 times in 623 at-bats and drew 77 bases on balls for an excellent .397 on-base percentage.

Boston had moved into fourth place in 1934 and, with the addition of Wes Ferrell, Lefty Grove, and Joe Cronin to support Werber, Rick Ferrell, and Bob Johnson, they had hoped to challenge for the pennant in 1935, but their hopes were dashed as they finished fourth again behind new manager Cronin. Werber's batting average tailed off to .251 but he still put together 30 doubles and 14 home runs, driving in 67 runs and scoring 84 runs himself. He once again led the league in stolen bases with 29 and in total chances per game with 3.9. On July 17, he tied a major league record by hammering four doubles in one game. The following year, the Red Sox added Jimmie Foxx to the mix, but in spite of his 41 homers and 143 RBI, the team slipped back to sixth place with a 74–80 won-loss mark. Werber, who batted .275 with 29 doubles, 10 home runs, 67 RBI, 89 runs scored, and 23 stolen bases, was traded to the Philadelphia Athletics on December 9, 1936, for Pinky Higgins, a better hitter but an erratic defensive third baseman. He played another six years in the major leagues before retiring in 1942.

Wertz, Vic

The husky, left-handed slugger was one of the most feared hitters in the American League from 1949 to 1960. He had more than 100 RBI five times and hit more than 20 home runs six times with a high of 32 homers in 1956. He was also the victim of Willie Mays' miraculous catch in the 1954 World Series. Victor Woodrow Wertz signed an amateur free agent contract with the Detroit Tigers in 1942 and began his professional baseball career with Winston-Salem in the Class-B Piedmont League, where he batted .239 for the Twins in 63 games. The following year he was inducted into military service with the U.S. Army on June 30 and spent the next two-and-a-half years in the U.S. Army, serving in the Pacific Theatre of Operations, although he got to play baseball at several military posts. After he was discharged from the Army in December, 1945, he joined the Buffalo Bisons and began tormenting International League pitchers, batting .301 with 19 homers and 91 RBI in 478 at-bats.

The 22-year-old outfielder became a major leaguer in 1947, patrolling right field for Steve O'Neill's Tigers, and batting a respectable .288 in 333 at-bats. The balding, well-liked, six-foot, 186-pound slugger added 15 pounds of muscle over the next year and emerged as a power to be reckoned with. He hit .304 in 1949, rapping 20 homers and driving in 133 runs for the fourth-place Tigers. He repeated his offensive pyrotechnics the following year, scorching the ball at a .308 clip with 37 doubles, 27 home runs, and 123 runs batted in. After short sojourns in St. Louis and Baltimore, Wertz landed in Cleveland in 1954 and helped the Indians capture the American League pennant by eight games over the New York Yankees, hitting .275 in 295 at-bats with 14 homers and 48 RBI. Al Lopez's Indians lost the World Series to the New York Giants in four games, but not through any fault of Wertz, who batted a torrid .500 with a double, triple, home run, and three RBI. The turning point of the Series may have come as early as the first game when, in the top of the eighth inning, with the score deadlocked at two runs apiece, Cleveland put the first two men on base, bringing Vic Wertz to the plate. The big first baseman, who had slugged a two-run triple off the right field wall in the first inning, jumped all over a 2–1 pitch from Don Liddle and drove it to dead center field, causing one wag to note that it would have been a home run in any other park, including Yellowstone. But not in this park, and not on this day. Willie Mays took off at the crack of the bat, with his back to the infield, raced to the deepest part of the Polo Grounds, 440 feet from home plate and, with the center field wall looming before him, made a miraculous over-the-shoulder catch to short-circuit the rally. The Indians never recovered. New York won the game, 5–2, in ten innings and swept the next three games to claim the World Championship.

The 34-year-old slugger, now a permanent first baseman after being diagnosed with non-paralytic polio and having to wear a knee brace the rest of his career, was traded to the Boston Red Sox on December 2, 1958, for Jimmy Piersall. Vic Wertz provided the Sox with some valuable offense over the next three years, although his damaged knees required frequent rest. He played in 94 games in 1959, batting .275 with seven homers and 49 RBI in 247 at-bats. On April 24, batting cleanup, he went 2-for-5 with a double, a homer, and five RBI in Boston's 7–2 win over Washington before 7,387 fans in Griffith Stadium. On August 14, his pinch-hit grand slam home run off Ryne Duren in the eighth inning in Yankee Stadium set the stage for a nine run Boston rally, pacing them to an 11–6 victory. The following year, he played 131 games as the regular first baseman for the seventh-place Red Sox, batting .282 with 19 homers and 103 RBI, and he had several memorable days along the way. On July 9, he stroked a single, double, and home run, driving in four runs in Boston's 6–5 win over the hated Yankees. Two weeks later, his three-run homer and four RBI gave his team a 6–4 win over Cleveland. On the 31st, before a lively crowd of 30,334 in Fenway Park, he sparked the Red Sox to an 8–4 victory over Detroit by slamming two home runs good for six RBI. He was limited to 99 games in 1961 but still hit .262 with 11 homers and 60 runs batted in, in 317 at-bats. He was claimed on waivers by the Detroit Tigers on September 8, ending his Boston career.

White, Sammy

Sammy White was one of the finest defensive catchers ever to don Red Sox red, white, and blue. He was an excellent handler of pitchers, called a great game, had no equals in framing pitches, and owned a shotgun for an arm. Regarding his pitch-framing ability, Casey Stengel once said, "He steals more pitches from umpires than anyone else. I'm not being critical. I'm just bowing to his skill."[205] His arm strength is reflected in his 47 percent caught-stealing percentage, the highest caught-stealing percentage by a Red Sox catcher in their history.

Charles Samuel White was born in Wenatchee, Washington, on July 7, 1927. He starred in athletics at Lincoln High School in Seattle and led the Lynx to the 1945 State Basketball Championship. He went on to star in baseball and basketball at the University of Washington, where he won All-American honors in basketball. He played varsity baseball in 1947 and 1948 and led the team in batting both years. He was drafted by the Boston Red Sox following graduation and was sent to their Oneonta farm club in the Class-C Canadian-American League, where he received his baptism of fire in professional baseball. He hit a respectable .256 in 30 games for Oneonta, then was shipped to Seattle in the Triple-A Pacific Coast League, where he hammered PCL pitchers to the tune of a .301 average in 60 games, before finishing the season with Louisville in the American Association, where he hit .143 in eight games. He spent the entire 1950 season with Roanoke in the Class-B Piedmont League, refining his defensive skills and hitting .258 in 409 at-bats over 111 games. The following year, he caught for Scranton in the Class-A Eastern League and responded with a .267 average with 12 home runs in 120 games. He made his major league debut on September 26, 1951, in Griffith Stadium in a 7–3 loss to the Washington Senators. He played four games for Steve O'Neil's team at the end of the season, hitting .182 with two base hits in 11 at-bats.

The six-foot, three-inch, 195-pound, right-handed hitter won the regular catcher's job for Boston in 1952, replacing Les Moss, who had been traded to St. Louis the previous November. He surprised everyone in the organization by tattooing the ball at a .281 clip with 20 doubles and 10 home runs in 381 at-bats over 115 games. On June 11, White hit a grand-slam home run off Satchel Paige in the ninth inning to defeat the St. Louis Browns. He celebrated the feat by crawling from third base to home plate on his hands and knees and kissing the plate. In his sophomore season he batted .273 with 34 doubles, 13 homers, and 64 runs batted in, in 476 at-bats covering 136 games. He became the only player in the twentieth century to score three runs in one inning on June 18 during a 17-run Red Sox rally in the eighth inning that contributed to a 23–3 victory over the visiting Detroit Tigers. He was selected for the 1953 All-Star Game in Cincinnati in July but did not see any action as the National League came away a 5–1 winner.

Sammy White played for the Red Sox for another six years, but the wear and tear of catching gradually caught up with him, affecting his offensive production, and his batting average decreased year after year. He hit .282 in 1954 followed by .261, .245, and .215. He picked it up somewhat in 1958 and 1959, batting .259 and .284 respectively, but the power was gone from his stroke and his RBI totals plummeted into the low 20s. On defense he was as strong as ever as far as calling a game was concerned, and his caught-stealing percentages actually increased, to 52 percent in 1956 and 57 percent in 1958, but he caught fewer games each year as his body did not recover from the bumps and bruises as quickly as it did in his younger days. Finally, on March 16, 1960, the 32-year-old backstop was traded to the Cleveland Indians. His nine-year Boston career produced a .264 batting average. On defense his 47 percent caught-stealing percentage was three percentage points higher than the league average, and he led the American League in putouts and double plays once each, in caught-stealing percentage twice, and in assists four times.

Williams, Ted

Theodore Samuel Williams was unquestionably the greatest player in Boston Red Sox history, and the greatest hitter ever to step on a ball field in the lively ball era beginning in 1920. As he said more than once, his goal was to walk down the street and have people say, "There goes the greatest hitter that ever lived." Williams, who was born in San Diego, California, on August 30, 1918, joined the hometown San Diego Padres as a gangly 17-year-old outfielder in 1936, and hit .271 in 42 games. He hit .291 for the Padres the following year, and was quickly signed by the Boston Red Sox, who recognized the unlimited potential in the six-foot, four-inch, 165-pound, left-handed hitter with the smooth, compact stroke. Boston sent the teenager to Minneapolis in the American Association, where he destroyed opposing pitchers, leading the league in batting (.366), runs scored (130), home runs (43), and RBI (142), in 528 at-bats.

Williams joined the Red Sox in 1939 and was immediately dubbed "The Kid" by Johnny Orlando, the clubhouse boy, a nickname that stayed with him throughout his career. He was also called "The Splendid Splinter." The youngster had an outstanding rookie season, powdering the ball to the tune of a .327 average with 44 doubles, 11 triples, 31 home runs, 131 runs scored, a league-leading 145 runs batted in, and a league-leading 344 total bases. But the brash, cocky slugger also drew the ire of the fans, his teammates, and the sportswriters for his disdain of defense, as evidenced by his league-leading 19 errors. His attitude quickly became the basis for the love-hate relationship that existed between The Kid and his public

over his 19-year major league career. There was no questioning his offensive capabilities, however, as he performed brilliantly with a bat in his hand, year after year.

Ted Williams hit .344 in 1940, and the following year, he had a season for the ages. He slugged the ball at a better-than-.400 clip most of the summer, but as the season reached its final Sunday, his average stood at .39955, with a doubleheader scheduled in Philadelphia's Shibe Park. Manager Joe Cronin offered to let Williams sit out the final two games to protect his batting average that would be rounded off to an even .400. But Williams refused, saying, much to his credit, that the average had to be won or lost on the field. In the first game, "Teddy Ballgame," as he liked to call himself, singled in his first at-bat and slugged a long home run over the right field fence in his second at-bat. He singled again his next time up. That raised his average to .404 and practically guaranteed he would bat over .400. He would have had to go hitless in his next five at-bats for his average to fall below that mark. Everyone seemed aware of that fact and the Red Sox players in the dugout were cheering as vigorously as was the crowd. "His teammates don't consider him a necessary evil any more," wrote a Boston Sportswriter.[206] Williams finished the first game with four hits in five at-bats, and he continued his cannonading in game two, ripping a single and a double in three at-bats to finish the year at .406, the last major leaguer to reach the magic .400 mark. He also starred in the All-Star Game in Briggs Stadium, Detroit, that year, going 2-for-4 with a home run and four RBI, as the American League outscored the National League by a 7–5 count. When he came to bat in the bottom of the ninth inning, the National League held a 5–4 lead with Chicago's Claude Passeau on the mound, two runners on base, and two men out. The 22-year-old Splendid Splinter wasted no time, jumping on a Passeau fastball and sending it on a line into the upper right field stands for a game-winning homer. As 54,674 American League fans roared their approval, Williams clapped his hands and jogged around the bases, hopping and jumping with joy as he went.

The San Diego native had another sensational season the following year, winning the

Ted Williams

Triple Crown by leading the league in batting (.356), home runs (36), and RBI (137). He won his second Triple Crown five years later with a batting average of .343, 32 home runs, and 114 runs batted in. Only nine other major league players have won Triple Crowns since 1900, and Rogers Hornsby was the only other player to win two. After the 1942 season ended, with World War II in full bloom, Ted enlisted in naval aviation and spent the next three years training to be a pilot, then serving as a flight instructor at naval air stations in Kokomo, Indiana, and Pensacola and Jacksonville, Florida. In 1945, he was in San Francisco waiting for a boat to carry him to the Pacific theatre when the war ended.

It was hard to believe, but the three years Williams spent in the U.S. Navy didn't affect his hand-eye coordination one iota. He led the Red Sox to the American League pennant in 1946 by stinging the ball at a crisp .342 clip, slugging 38 homers, driving in 123 runs, and leading the league with 142 runs scored, 156 bases on balls, a .497 on-base percentage, and a .667 slugging average. The All-Star Game that was played in friendly Fenway Park on July 9 was one of the most memorable days in Ted Williams' career. As the eighth inning approached, the American League held a comfortable 8–0 lead over their National League adversaries and Williams already had a home run, two singles, and two RBI to his credit. Rip Sewell, noted for his "eephus" pitch, a blooper pitch that occasionally reached a height of 25 feet before returning to earth and settling into the catcher's mitt, took the mound for the Senior Circuit. Two outs later, with another run across the plate and two men on base, Ted Williams stepped to the plate and yelled out to Sewell, "You're not going to throw me that damn pitch of yours, are you?" to which Sewell replied, "I might." The Pittsburgh righty not only threw Williams the pitch, he threw him four of them. Ted took the first eephus pitch for a ball and then swung and missed the second pitch, looking bad doing it. He fouled off the third one. But just before Sewell threw the fourth eephus pitch, he yelled to Williams, "Here it comes again." This time Ted was ready. He took two quick steps toward the pitcher, actually stepping out of the batter's box, which was illegal, and sent the ball on a high arc to right field where it came to rest in the visitor's bullpen. As Williams loped around the bases, laughing all the way, the Fenway Faithful let loose with a barrage of screams and yells that could be heard as far away as the State House. Ten days later, manager Lou Boudreau of the Cleveland Indians initiated the "Boudreau Shift" where he stacked the right side of the infield and outfield with players in an attempt to stop Ted Williams' from hitting safely. Williams responded by hitting three home runs and driving in eight runs in the game. On July 21, he hit for the cycle.

Boston won the pennant by a healthy 12 games over the Detroit Tigers and met the National League Champion St. Louis Cardinals in the World Series. The Series was the biggest disappointment in Ted Williams' life. The Red Sox were defeated by St. Louis in seven games and Williams batted a lowly .200 with just five singles in 25 times at-bat. He fanned five times, drove in one run, and scored two. His wounded ego was soothed somewhat when he was recognized as the American League's Most Valuable Player, an award he would win again three years later when he batted .343 and led the league in home runs (43) and RBI (159).

A fractured elbow limited Williams to 89 games in 1950, but the following year, back at full strength, he hit .318 in 148 games, with 30 home runs and 126 RBI. Two weeks into the 1952 season, fate entered his life again and dealt him a dismal hand. He was recalled to active duty as a Marine fighter pilot and was soon flying jets in Korea, where he became an authentic war hero, flying 39 combat missions and one time crash-landing his flaming F-9F Panther after being hit by ground fire. Shortly after that, he was hospitalized with pneumonia and was finally shipped back to the States, where he was discharged in July 1953. The aging slugger managed to play 37 games at the end of the season and hit a surprising .407. He followed that by hitting .345 league in 1954 and .356 the following year.

The year 1957 was an historic year for Ted Williams. In September, he set the major league record for the most consecutive times reaching base safely with 16. His streak included two singles, four home runs, nine bases on balls, and one hit-by-pitcher.

He also became the oldest major league player to win a batting title when he scorched opposing pitchers to the tune of a .388 average at the age of 39. He won another batting title the following year with a .328 average. Barry Bonds was one month older when he won a batting title in 2004, but Williams still owns the American League record.

Teddy Ballgame finally retired from the game after the 1960 season. Fittingly, in his last time at-bat on September 26, the lanky slugger took a 1–1 pitch downtown against Jack Fisher of the Baltimore Orioles in the bottom of the eighth inning in Fenway Park, sending the ball into the bullpen in right center field, bringing the Red Sox within one run of the Orioles at 4–3, as 10,454 fans lifted the rafters off the old park. True to his demeanor for all his 19 years in Boston, Ted did not tip his hat to recognize the cheers of the crowd, nor did he come out of the dugout to take a bow afterward. Boston won the game with two runs in the bottom of the ninth inning.

Ted Williams hit 17 grand-slam home runs during his career, an all-time Boston Red Sox record. He led the league in batting and runs scored six times each, doubles twice, home runs and runs batted in four times each, bases on balls eight times, on-base percentage (OBP) 11 times, and slugging average eight times, even though he lost almost five years to military service. He is the all-time leader in career on-base percentage (.482), number two in slugging average (.634), and number four in bases on balls (2,021). His .344 batting average is number seven all-time, and the highest major league career batting average since 1937. If he had not lost five years to military service, he would probably have finished as number one in career bases on balls, runs scored, extra-base hits, and runs batted in, as well as hitting more than 700 home runs. He was elected to the National Baseball Hall of Fame on the first ballot in 1966.

But more important to Williams than individual records or even his election to the Hall of Fame, was his vigorous support of the Jimmy Fund, a fundraising organization associated with the Dana-Farber Cancer Institute in Boston. The Kid was on call 24 hours a day to visit any child that needed him. His only request was that the media never be told about his association with the children of Dana-Farber. As far as he was concerned, it was a private matter between him, the hospital, and the children. Williams loved children and went out of his way to befriend them. After his death, his eulogies rightly noted that he was a great ballplayer, a great patriot, and a great humanitarian.

Wilson, Earl

He was the first black player signed by the Boston Red Sox, but he had to wait six years to make his major league debut because the Red Sox converted him from a catcher to a pitcher when he joined the organization in 1953. Robert Earl Wilson was a six-foot, three-inch, 215-pound right-hander who threw smoke. His best pitch was a high fastball, and he used it almost exclusively until the years caught up with him and he lost the zip on his heater.

The converted pitcher was born in Ponchatoula, Louisiana, on October 2, 1934, and he began his professional baseball career with Bisbee-Douglas in the Class-C Arizona-Texas League in 1953, where he went 4–5 in 14 games. Wilson's biggest problem with Bisbee-Douglas was his lack of control that resulted in 61 bases on balls in 85⅓ innings. It was a problem that would hinder his progress throughout his entire six-and-a-half year stay with the Red Sox. The big fireballer moved up the minor league ladder gradually over the following three years, eventually producing a 13–9 record with Albany in the Single-A Eastern League in 1956 but, at that point, his career was interrupted by two years of military service in the U.S. Marine Corps. Upon his return in 1959, Wilson alternated his time between Minneapolis in the Triple-A American Association and the home club in Boston. He pitched well for the Millers, going 10–2, but he was still hampered by wildness, and it followed him to Boston where, in his first major league stunt, against the Detroit Tigers on July 28, he lasted just 3⅔ innings, tossing no-hit ball but walking nine batters before departing with a 4–0 lead. For the season, he went 1–1 in nine games for the Red Sox with a 6.08 ERA. In 1960, he again split his time between Minneapolis and Boston, going 6–6 with the Millers and 3–2 with the Red Sox, with 48 walks in 65 innings. He spent the entire 1961 season with the Seattle Rainiers, trying to overcome his lack of control, but it was to no avail as he walked 113 batters in 166 innings and led the PCL in losses.

Earl Wilson returned to the Boston Red Sox roster in 1962 and was in the major leagues to stay. His most unforgettable day in the major leagues occurred on June 26, when he threw a 2–0 no-hitter at the Los Angeles Angels, and hit the game-winning home run in the third inning. According to Rich Coberly, the 26-year-old right-hander "had a good fastball that he mixed with a quick-breaking slider and a soft curve. He walked four and struck out five." Wilson added, "I never had any idea anything like that would ever happen to me. The Good Man was with me tonight."[207] The Louisiana native finished the year with a 12–8 record and a 3.91 ERA in spite of issuing 111 walks in 191⅓ innings pitched. The next year, he posted an 11–16 mark with a league-leading 105 bases on balls and an American League-record 21 wild pitches in 210⅔ innings with a 3.76 ERA. By 1964, his control was vastly improved, with his bases on balls decreasing from 5.2 walks per nine innings in 1962 to 3.3 walks per nine innings. The improvement was not immediately noticeable, however, as he went 11–12 with a 4.49 ERA. He still had a losing record in 1965, winning 13 games against 14 losses, but he was the ace of a ninth-place team that won only 62 games against 100 losses.

In 1966, Earl Wilson engaged in a pitched battle with Red Sox management over his treatment, and he was subsequently traded to the Detroit Tigers on June 12. He went 13–6 for the Tigers after going 5–5 with Boston to finish the year with an admirable 18–11 won-lost record. The next year, he led the American League in victories with 22, against 11 losses, but that was his swan song. He pitched three more years in the major leagues before retiring. In addition to compiling a noteworthy 121–109 won-lost record, Wilson was also one of the greatest sluggers ever to toe the rubber. Unlike Wes Ferrell, he wasn't a high-average hitter, compiling a .195 career batting average, but he hit with exceptional power, sending 35 balls into orbit in 740 at-bats, second only to Ferrell, who hit 38 home runs in 1,176 at-bats. His average of 26 home runs for every 550 at-bats is number one all-time for a pitcher.

Wood, Joe

He, like Tony Conigliaro, streaked across the heavens like a brilliant meteor. For one brief moment his dazzling brilliance illuminated the baseball world. Then he was gone and only a memory remained. He might have been one of the greatest pitchers in the history of the game if things had turned out differently, but as one baseball expert said, "He had everything but luck." Howard Ellsworth Wood was born in Kansas City, Missouri, on October 25, 1889. He grew up playing baseball on town teams in Ouray, Colorado, and Ness City, Kansas. He was pitching for the Ness City team in 1906 when he was recruited by a traveling team of girls. The Bloomer Girls paid him $20 to play for them for three weeks. The next year he joined the professional ranks in earnest, with the Hutchinson White Sox in the Western Association. He pitched in 29 games and compiled a record of 18–11 with 224 strikeouts in 196 innings. He moved up to Kansas City in the Triple-A American Association in 1908, but struggled with a 7–12 record, before Red Sox owner John I. Taylor, impressed by his speed, purchased his contract and brought him to Boston.

The 18-year-old flamethrower pitched in six games at the end of the season, going 1–1 and acquiring a nickname along the way. Wood remembered, "I think it was around 1908 when I was warming up on the sidelines and a sports

Smoky Joe Wood

reporter for the Boston Post named Paul Shannon was watching me. He turned to somebody and said, 'That kid sure throws smoke.'"[208] From then on, it was Smoky Joe. The kid from Ness City went through a learning process over the next two years while he put together won-lost records of 11–7 and 12–13. In 1911 the five-foot, 11-inch, 180-pound right-hander came of age, pitching in 44 games with 33 starts, 25 complete games, and five shutouts. He racked up 23 victories against 17 losses and fanned 231 men in 275⅔ innings with a 2.02 ERA. His biggest day of the season was Saturday, July 29, when he no-hit the St. Louis Browns at the Huntington Avenue Baseball Grounds, winning 5–0. Smoky Joe struck out 12 men, walked two, and hit one in his masterpiece. Two errors and a single by Bill Carrigan gave Boston a 1–0 lead in the second inning. The Sox added a run in the fifth and two in the sixth, and Tris Speaker ended the scoring by hitting a home run into the left field bleachers in the eighth.

The 1912 season was one for the ages. Smoky Joe Wood dominated the league's pitching statistics, winning 34 games against just five losses with a 1.91 ERA. He pitched in 43 games with 38 starts, and he led the league in complete games (35), shutouts (10), and winning percentage (.872). Another pitching legend, Walter Johnson, went 33–12 that season and ran off a 16-game winning streak. As summer drew to a close, Smoky Joe was in the midst of a winning streak of his own, running off 13 straight victories when Washington visited Fenway Park. The date was September 6, and the baseball world was clamoring for a matchup between Johnson and Wood, so Smoky Joe's manager juggled the rotation so the game's two greatest pitchers could face each other. It was an epic pitching duel in a circus atmosphere, before a sellout crowd of 35,000 Royal Rooters that overflowed the grandstands and circled the infield and outfield. As the words of the Red Sox anthem, "Tessie," echoed around the ballpark, the Sox gave Wood a one-run lead in the bottom of the sixth inning on back-to-back doubles into the overflow crowd by Tris Speaker and Duffy Lewis, and he made it stand up for a 1–0 victory. As noted in *Red Sox Nation Guide to the Players*, "In response to a question directed at him in 1912, Walter Johnson said, 'Can I throw harder than Joe Wood? Listen, my friend. There's no man alive that can throw harder than Smoky Joe Wood.'"[209] The Red Sox ace won two more games to bring his consecutive game winning streak to 16, tying Johnson, before he lost one. In the World Series against the New York Giants that year, Smoky Joe won three games against a single loss, and Boston won the Series in eight games.

Joe Wood's world came crashing down the following spring when he slipped on wet grass in Detroit on July 18 and broke his right thumb. He noted, "The thumb on my pitching hand was in a cast for two or three weeks. I don't know if I tried to pitch too soon after that, or whether maybe something happened to my shoulder at the same time. But whatever it was, I never pitched again without a terrific amount of pain in my right shoulder. Never again."[210] Smoky Joe pitched only one inning the rest of the season, finishing with a decent 11–5 record and a 2.29 ERA. He struggled through the 1914 season, pitching every two weeks or so to let the pain subside before he could pitch again, but the zip was gone from his fastball and the pain got worse with each passing day. He went 10–3 in 1914 and 15–5 the following year, pitching ten complete games in 16 starts with a league-leading 1.49 ERA. But that was it. He consulted dozens of doctors but to no avail. His pitching days were behind him. He sat out the 1916 season, played briefly in 1917, and then made a comeback as an outfielder the following year. He played in the outfield for Cleveland for five years, batting .296 in 1918, and a high of .366 in 66 games in 1921. He retired after the 1922 season, leaving behind a .297 career batting average as an outfielder.

Yastrzemski, Carl

Carl Michael Yastrzemski was given the unenviable task of replacing the legend that was Ted Williams in left field for the Boston Red Sox. The pressure associated with that heavy responsibility took its toll on the man from Long Island, and the joy of playing the game was replaced by the drudgery of a job that needed to be done, but he persevered and by the time he retired, he was a legend in his own right. He left behind numerous Red Sox career records that are still intact, including most at-bats (11,988), most base hits (3,419), most extra-base hits (1,157), most doubles (646), most total bases (5,539), most runs batted in (1,844), and most runs scored (1,816).

Yastrzemski was born in Southampton, New York, on August 22, 1939, to Carl Sr., a potato farmer, and his wife Hattie. His father was a talented semi-pro baseball player who had been recruited by several major league teams, and Carl learned the game from him from the time he could walk. He pitched for his father's team, the Bridgetown Eagles, when he was 14 years old and he continued to play with them during his high school years. He attended Bridgehampton High School, where he set numerous records in football, basketball, and baseball, setting the all-time basketball conference record for career points with 628, and compiling a career baseball batting average of .512. His athletic prowess brought him a scholarship to the University of Notre Dame but the lure of the diamond got the better of him and he left school after two semesters to try his hand at professional baseball. He signed an amateur free agent contract with the Boston Red Sox on November 29, 1959, and left school in the spring to join the Raleigh Capitals in the Class-B Carolina League. He proceeded to tear the league apart, batting a torrid .377, 64 points higher than the runner-up, with 34 doubles, 15 home runs, and 100 RBI. He was selected as both the league's Rookie of the Year and its Most Valuable Player, and the Capitals rode his coat-tails to the pennant with a 78–52 won-loss record. The following year, the sweet-swinging left-hander rpounded American Association hurlers for a .339 average with 36 doubles and 84 RBI in 148 games. His dominance in the minors brought the 20-year-old slugger to the major leagues, where he would stay for 23 years, all with the Red Sox.

Being in Boston, a hotbed of major league baseball, and being the successor to Ted Williams, put tremendous pressure to succeed on the husky left fielder. Carl Yastrzemski was more than up to the challenge. He was an intense player who, as one teammate said, lived, breathed, ate, and slept baseball. He had a better-than-expected rookie season in 1961, playing in 148 games, with a .266 batting average, 31 dou-

Carl Yastrzemski

bles, 11 home runs, and 80 RBI, but Pinky Higgins' team was a disappointment, finishing in sixth place with a 76–86 record, 33 games behind the New York Yankees. The following year, the five-foot, 11-inch, 182-pound slugger stepped up his production, slamming 43 doubles and 19 home runs, good for 94 RBI and 99 runs scored. It took him two years to get adjusted to major league baseball, but in his third year he won the first of his three batting championships, with a .321 average, while leading the American League with 183 base hits, 40 doubles, 95 bases on balls, and a .418 on-base percentage. He led the American League in doubles twice more, in 1965 with 45 and in 1966 with 39.

The year 1967 has gone down in Boston lore as the year of "The Impossible Dream." The beloved Red Sox had finished in seventh place in 1966, their 72–90 record leaving them 26 games behind the pennant-winning Baltimore Orioles. But with new players like Mike Andrews and Reggie Smith on board, and Carl Yastrzemski and Jim Lonborg heading into their greatest seasons, the feeling in Boston land was upbeat in spring training. Still, the team got off to a modest start that season. They won the opening game, 5–4, before a noisy Fenway Park audience. Lonborg was the winning pitcher and Rico Petrocelli provided the fireworks for Dick Williams' team, going 3-for-3 with a three-run homer and four RBI. Yaz went 0-for-4. At month's end, the Red Sox found themselves in third place with an 8–6 record. Boston's left fielder had one of his first big days of the year on May 17 when he cracked two home runs and drove in four runs for the home crowd in a 12–8 loss to the Baltimore Orioles. Two weeks later, he had another two-homer game, plus a single, and two RBI as Boston edged the Minnesota Twins, 3–2. The team made a major trade on June 4 when they acquired hard-throwing Gary Bell from Cleveland for two players. The big right-hander got off to a fast start in Beantown, defeating the Chicago White Sox 7–3 on the June 8, and racking up four more victories against a single loss by the end of the month. Yaz had another two-homer day on the ninth to pace the Red Sox to an 8–7 win over the Washington Senators.

It took Boston awhile to smooth out all the wrinkles, but Williams had the team in high gear by the beginning of July. They won 19 games against 10 losses that month and moved into second place, two games behind the Chicago White Sox. In August, they went 20–15 and slipped into first place in the American League, with Minnesota, Detroit, and Chicago all breathing down their necks, within one-and-a-half games of the summit. The dogfight continued into September with all four teams jockeying for position. On the 17th of the month, the Twins held down the top spot with Chicago one-half game behind, and Boston and Minnesota both one game off the top. There were 12 games remaining in the season when Carl Yastrzemski hoisted the team on his husky back and single-handedly carried them to the Promised Land. On the 18th, he went 3-for-4 with a double and a game-tying home run in the top of the ninth inning, as Boston beat the Detroit Tigers 6–5 in ten innings. Two days later, he had four hits with a home run, an RBI and two runs scored in a 5–4 win over Cleveland. He finished the season with a ten-game hitting streak, pacing Boston to a 6–4 record.

The four teams were still within one-and-a-half games of each other on September 27 and the Red Sox had two games remaining with the first-place Twins, needing to win both games for the pennant. On September 30, behind Jose Santiago's 12th victory and Gary Bell's strong relief, the Sox defeated Minnesota by a 6–4 score before a wild crowd of 32,909 in the Fens. Yastrzemski was the big gun for Boston, pounding out three hits including a home run and driving in four runs. His two-run single in the sixth tied the game at 2–2 and his three-run homer in the seventh iced the issue. The next day, the Red Sox clinched the pennant as big Jim Lonborg threw a complete game at Cal Ermer's crew, winning 5–3, and once again Yaz carried the big bat. He went 4-for-4 with a double and two RBI. Overall, down the stretch, the kid from Long Island had 23 base hits in 44 at-bats for a sensational .523 batting average. He slugged four doubles and five home runs in 12 games, driving in 16 runs and scoring 14. His teammate, George Scott, said, "Yaz hit 44 homers and 43 of them meant something big for the team. It seemed like every time we needed a big play, the man stepped up and got it done."[211]

In the World Series, a heartbreaking seven-game loss to the St. Louis Cardinals, Yastrzemski was solid, batting a torrid .400 with ten base hits, including two doubles and three home runs, with five RBI. In Game 2, he went 3-for-4 with two home runs and three RBI as Boston won 4–0. And in game six, he went three-for-four with a homer as the Red Sox won again, 8–4. Captain Carl's disappointment over the Series loss was assuaged somewhat by his winning the American League's Triple Crown with a .326 batting average, 44 home runs, and 121 RBI. He is the last major league player to win the Triple Crown. He was also selected as the American League's Most Valuable Player, *Sports Illustrated*'s Sportsman of the Year, and the winner of the Hickok Belt as the top Professional Athlete of the Year. The following year, Boston finished in fourth place, but Yastrzemski captured another batting title, with a .301 average, the lowest batting average ever to win a major league batting title. He was the only player in the American League to finish with a .300 or higher average and, in fact, only four players hit above .284. He hit just .255 in 1969 but slugged 40 home runs and drove in 111 runs. In 1970, he hit another 40 home runs with 102 RBI.

The 30-year-old outfielder's career began to decline after the 1970 season with his home run totals falling into the teens with corresponding drops in his RBI and runs scored totals. The Red Sox were generally in the thick of the pennant races over the next four years but always seemed to fade down the stretch. Such was not the case in 1975 when Darrell Johnson brought them home a winner behind the hitting of Fred Lynn and Jim Rice and the pitching of Rick Wise, Louis Tiant, and Bill Lee. Yaz, who was now a fifteen-year veteran and "the old man" on the team, batted .269 with 14 homers and 60 RBI, but he rose to the occasion one more time in the postseason, batting .455 against the Oakland Athletics in the American League Championship Series and .310 with four RBI and seven runs scored against the Cincinnati Reds in the World Series. In Game 6 of the Series, the 12-inning thriller that has been called one of the best World Series games ever played, Yaz went 3-for-6 with a run scored before Carlton Fisk's dramatic game-ending, foul pole homer gave Boston a 7–6 victory. Unfortunately, the Reds won Game 7 and the World championship by a 4–3 score. Three years later, the Red Sox, now led by Don Zimmer, found themselves in a knockdown, dragout, brawl with the New York Yankees that resulted in a one-game playoff to decide the American League pennant winner. And once again, Boston drew the short straw as Bucky Dent's three-run homer in the seventh inning gave the Bronx Bombers the game and the pennant by a 5–4 score. Yaz went 2-for-5 in the game with a homer and two RBI but made the final out of the game with the tying and winning runs on base. He played for the Red Sox five more years, finally retiring after the 1983 season.

Carl Yastrzemski was an outstanding all-around outfielder and one of the game's most underrated and unappreciated players. His major league accomplishments would fill a book. He led the American League in batting average, runs scored, doubles, and slugging average three times each, on-base percentage five times, and home runs and RBI once each. He holds the American League record for intentional bases on balls with 190. He was the first American League player to hit 400 home runs and amass 3,000 base hits, and he was the first player to get 100 base hits his first 20 years in the major leagues. On defense, he was an expert at playing balls off the Green Monster in Fenway Park and, with his powerful throwing arm, he led American League outfielders in assists a record seven times. He tied the major league record for fielding percentage for a season with 1.000 in 1977 and won seven Gold Gloves as the American League's best defensive left-fielder. He is in the top-ten all-time for career games played, plate appearances, at-bats, base hits, doubles, extra-base hits, total bases, and bases on balls. He is also number 16 in runs scored and number 12 in runs batted in. He spent his entire 23-year career with the Boston Red Sox, tying a major league record for years played with one team. He played 3,308 games with Boston, with 3,419 base hits in 11,988 at-bats for a .285 batting average.

Yerkes, Steve

Stephen Douglas Yerkes attended the Wharton School of Business at the University of Pennsylvania in 1905 and 1906 and played shortstop on the Quakers baseball team both years, before leaving school to concentrate on a baseball career. The five-foot, nine-inch, 165-pound infielder played on semi-pro teams in Millville, New Jersey, and Altoona, Pennsylvania, before joining Wilson in the Class-D Eastern Carolina League in 1909. He was only with Wilson a short time when he was sold to the Boston Red Sox for $1,200 on July 17. The 21-year-old shortstop made his major league debut in the Huntington Avenue Baseball Grounds on September 29 in an 8–3 loss to the Detroit Tigers, and played five games with Boston at the end of the season, batting .286 in seven at-bats. He spent the 1910 season with the Chattanooga Lookouts of the Single-A Southern Association, batting .279 in 459 at-bats, returning to the Red Sox for the 1911 season. He was Boston's regular shortstop in 1911, hitting .279 with 28 extra-base hits in 502 at-bats. He moved to second base the following year when Boston's regular shortstop came off the injured list, and he proved to be one of the better defensive second basemen in the American League while stroking the ball at a decent .252 pace in 523 at-bats. Jake Stahl's team led the league in runs scored while racing to 105 victories and a 14-game bulge over the Washington Senators. They met and conquered John McGraw's New York Giants in a tough eight-game World Series, famous for Fred Snodgrass's "$30,000 muff." Steve Yerkes' sensational play in the clutch paced the Red Sox to the title. In the opening game of the Series, the little right-handed hitter drove in the winning run with a two-run single in the top of the seventh inning, Boston winning 5–4. In the third inning of Game 5, Yerkes tripled Harry Hooper home and later scored himself as Boston came away a 2–1 winner. In the Game 8 finale, he walked and scored the championship run on a single by Tris Speaker and a sacrifice fly by Larry Gardner. In addition to his offensive displays, his spectacular defensive play in Game 4 broke the Giants' back. In the seventh inning, with Boston up two games to one with one tie, and protecting a 2–1 lead in the game, Art Fletcher of New York reached second base with one out. Then, as reported in *Sporting Life*, "McCormick, who had been selected to bat for Tesreau, drove a grass-cutter over second base. Nine times out of ten nothing could have prevented the ball from continuing on to center field. But here, Yerkes, making a desperate stab, speared the ball with his bare hand and with absolutely no chance of getting McCormick at first, drove the sphere to Cady in plenty of time to retire Fletcher who was trying to score."[212] Yerkes hit .267 for Boston in 1913 and was hitting a lowly .218 midway through 1914 when he jumped to the Pittsburgh Rebels of the outlaw Federal League. He returned to the major leagues in 1916, hitting .263 for the Chicago Cubs in 44 games, before retiring.

Youkilis, Kevin

Kevin Edmund Youkilis is an intense performer on the playing field. He is known for his scrappiness, grittiness, dirt-stained jerseys, and home plate collisions. According to sportswriter Jackie MacMullan, his stocky frame has been compared to "a refrigerator repairman, a butcher, the man selling hammers behind the counter at the True Value hardware store." The native of Cincinnati, Ohio, graduated from the University of Cincinnati in 2001 and was signed by the Boston Red Sox for a bonus of $12,000 although his father claimed he would have signed for a six-pack of beer.[213] Youkilis spent his first season in professional baseball with Lowell in the Single-A New York-Pennsylvania League, where he held down third base and scorched the ball at a .314 clip in 59 games. He played for three teams in three different leagues in 2002 as he made his way up the minor league ladder, ending the season at Trenton in the Double-A Eastern League, where he posted a healthy .344 average in 44 games. He joined the Portland Sea Dogs in the same league the following year, where he batted .327 with a league-leading .487 on-base percentage in 94 games. He was promoted to Pawtucket on July 29, but he forgot to bring his bat to Rhode Island with him, hitting a minuscule .165 in 32 games. He did reach base in 71 straight games that summer, however, including nine with Pawtucket. He split the 2004 and 2005 seasons between Pawtucket and Boston, where he made a distinct impression on Red Sox management

Kevin Youkilis

with his versatility, playing first base, second base, and third base. He would later add the outfield to his repertoire. He demonstrated his hitting ability by batting .260 and .278 in his two temporary tours of duty in Boston, one for 72 games and the other for 44 games. His major league debut on May 15, 2004, in the Sky Dome in Toronto was a memorable day, as he recalled, "I got in there, and man, I was just amped up and excited." He popped up to shortstop in his first at-bat, and then slammed a home run in his second at-bat, finishing with a 2-for-4 day as Bronson Arroyo blanked the Blue Jays, 4–0.

Youkilis became a permanent member of the Boston Red Sox in 2006. He was given the first base job, but he also played occasionally at third base or in left field as the situation warranted. He responded in his typical professional manner, hitting a solid .279 with 42 doubles, 13 homers, and 72 runs batted in, in 569 at-bats over 147 games. The man known as "The Hitting Machine" also drew 91 bases on balls for a .381 on-base percentage. One of the coaches at the University of Cincinnati had said of Youkilis, "He has a great batting eye and very seldom swings at a bad pitch. He hardly ever strikes out looking. When he does, you knew the ump missed the call. He works the count and outthinks the pitcher. He makes solid contact against both fastballs and breaking pitches."[214] When he does strike out, whether it's a swinging strike or a called strike, he returns to the dugout in a rage. At times like these, it's best to just keep out of his way and leave him alone as he's not fit to live with.

As his career progressed, he developed into one of Boston's best clutch hitters. In 2007, he hit .288 with 35 doubles, 16 homers, and 83 RBI in 528 at-bats over 145 games. In one of his outstanding post-season performances, he punished Cleveland pitching in the 2007 ALCS to the tune of a .500 average with 14 base hits in 28 at-bats in seven games, with a double, a triple, three homers, ten runs scored, and seven RBI. The following year, with Manny Ramirez just a distant memory, Kevin Youkilis, the ultimate team player, was inserted into the cleanup spot in the lineup and produced on schedule. He enjoyed a career-year as the team's clutch hitter, spanking the ball at a .312 clip with 43 doubles, 29 homers, and 115 runs batted in. His .569 slugging average was the best on the club.

Youkilis continued his offensive pyrotechnics in 2009, batting .305 with 36 doubles, 27 homers, and 94 RBI. On April 24, he hit a walk-off home run in the 11th inning to defeat Mariano Rivera and the New York Yankees by a 5–4 score. On August 11, the big first baseman's intensity precipitated a bench-clearing brawl in the Fens. It was a Tuesday night game with 38,013 rabid Red Sox fans in the stands, and Detroit pitcher Rick Porcello hit Youkilis in the upper back leading off the second inning. An infuriated Youkilis charged the mound, slung his batting helmet at the backtracking Porcello, and tackled him, sending them both sprawling to the ground, as both benches and the bullpens emptied. Order was quickly restored and both Youkilis and Porcello were ejected from the game and subsequently suspended for five games. Terry Francona's charges, who were trailing 3–0 at the time of the fracas, came back to win the game by a 7–5 score.

Kevin Youklis was pounding the ball to the tune of .307 in 2010 with 26 doubles, 19 home runs and 62 RBI, but his season came to an abrupt halt on August 3 when he tore a muscle in his right thumb swinging at a pitch. The 2011 season was more of the same. The 220-pound slugger arrived in Fort Myers in February bulked up but with too little flexiblilty, and he paid the price during the season. He was hobbled by a variety of injuries including a sports hernia, a sore hip, a pulled hamstring, and back problems. He played through the pain for four months, stinging the ball at a .273 clip with 15 home runs and 65 RBI in 352 at-bats through July, but his infirmities caught up with him down the stretch. He hit a barely visible .190 in August and September with just two home runs and six RBI in 79 at-bats before calling it a day. He played his last game on September 15.

Young, Cy

Denton True Young was arguably the greatest pitcher in major league history. He holds numerous records that will probably never be broken, including most career victories (511), most losses (316), most games started (815), most complete games (749), and most innings pitched (7,356). He is also number three in shutouts with 76. The six-foot, two-inch, 210-pound, right-handed pitcher towered over the average player of his day, who stood about five-foot, seven-inches tall and weighed a wispy 155 pounds. He used his size to great advantage as he whipped balls to the plate at speeds unheard of in those days. His sensational fastball, that he called his whistler, gave rise to his nickname, Cyclone, that was shortened to Cy over time. Honus Wagner, the National League's greatest hitter, noted, "Walter Johnson was fast but no faster than Rusie. And Rusie was no faster than Johnson. But Young was faster than both of 'em."[215] According to Young, however, control, not speed, was the most important weapon in his arsenal. "I had good control. I didn't try to strike out every batter. I aimed to make the batter hit the ball, and I threw as few pitches as possible. That's why I was able to work every other day."[216] He attributed his success as a pitcher to the strength and stamina he gained while working on his father's farm, doing heavy lifting and splitting wood. He had another baseball philosophy that he passed on. "I had a good arm and good legs. When I went to spring training, I wouldn't touch a ball for three weeks. I would just do a lot of walking and running. I never did any unnecessary throwing. I figured the old arm had just so many throws in it, and there wasn't any use wasting them."[217]

Cy Young was born in the small farming community of Gilmore, Ohio, on March 29, 1867, the oldest of five children of McKinzie and Nancy Young. Life on the farm gave Cy Young the strength and stamina that would be his forte throughout his baseball career. He quit school in the sixth grade to work on the farm, but that didn't keep him from playing baseball. He played every chance he got, even throwing the ball around during lunch time. He played sandlot baseball around Newcomerstown where he was raised, and soon discovered he was a better pitcher than a hitter. By the time he was 17, he was playing semi-pro ball around southern Ohio in places like Carrollton, Cadiz, and Urhichsville, pitching and playing second base, but it was his pitching, especially his whistler, that drew rave notices from spectators. In 1890, he signed a baseball contract to play for Canton in the Tri-State League at a salary of $60 a month. The muscular, 170-pound flamethrower proved to be worth the money as he compiled a respectable 15–15 record with 201 strikeouts and just 33 bases on balls for the cellar-dwelling Canton club that finished the season with a record of 27–47, 22 games behind Mansfield. His performance on the afternoon of July 25 made baseball scouts sit up and take notice as he set McKeesport down without a hit, winning 4–1 and fanning 18 batters in the process. The Cleveland Spiders quickly purchased his contract from Canton for $500, and signed the 23-year-old pitcher for the lucrative sum of $200 a month..

The raw-boned farm boy made his major league debut in the first game of a doubleheader on August 6 against the second place Chicago White Stockings, and he tossed a three-hitter at Cap Anson's team, winning 8–1. His repertoire included a fastball, curve, a sidearm curve, a screwball, a changeup, and he "occasionally even threw submarine style to upset the batters' timing."[218] Cy Young finished his rookie season

Cy Young

in the major leagues with a 9–7 won-loss record in 16 starts, all complete games. On October 4, the last day of the season, he pitched both ends of a doubleheader against the Philadelphia Athletics, winning by scores of 5–1 and 7–3. The following season, already the ace of the Cleveland staff, he went 27–20 in 55 games with 46 starts and 43 complete games, pitching 423⅔ innings with an excellent 2.85 earned run average. He posted a record of 36–12 in 1892 and, in 1893, the year they moved the mound back from 55 feet to 60 feet, six inches, he didn't miss a beat, winning 34 games against 16 losses and posting a fine 3.36 ERA. He enjoyed his best season in major league baseball in 1895 when he won 35 games against ten losses, with a 3.26 ERA, pitching 369⅔ innings in 47 games with 40 starts and 36 complete games. In 1897, he went 21–18 in 46 games and 335⅔ innings pitched. In the first game of a doubleheader at League Park in Cleveland on September 18, the Canton Cyclone stymied the Cincinnati Reds, 6–0, with a no-hitter. The only baserunner reached on an error. Cy Young pitched for Cleveland one more year, and then was sold to the St. Louis Perfectos, where he pitched in 1899 and 1900, going 26–16 and 19–19 respectively.

The 34-year-old fireballer jumped to the Boston Americans, also known as the Somersets and Pilgrims, in the newly organized American League in 1901 and immediately took the new league by storm, leading the league in victories his first three years with Boston, going 33–10, 32–11, and 28–9. He won the pitcher's Triple Crown in his first year with Boston, with 33 victories as noted, 158 strikeouts, and a 1.62 ERA. He also led the league with five shutouts. Two years later, he led the league with a .757 winning percentage, 34 complete games, 341⅓ innings pitched, and seven shutouts. His contributions paid huge dividends as Boston raced to the American League pennant by 14½ games over Connie Mack's Philadelphia Athletics. They went on to meet the National League champion Pittsburgh Pirates in the game's first modern World Series and, with Cy Young and Bill Dinneen pitching lights-out baseball, they captured the first World Championship in eight games. Young pitched the opener of the Series and absorbed a 7–3 drubbing at the hands of the visiting Bucs. Fred Clarke's team pushed across four runs in the first inning, three of them unearned, and added single runs in the third, fourth, and seventh. Young pitched seven innings in relief in Game 3 in a 4–2 Boston loss, then came back to win Game 5 by an 11–2 score, with both runs being unearned. After Bill Dinneen won Game 6 to even the Series at three-all, the Canton Cyclone took the measure of the Pirates again in Game 7, winning handily by a 7–3 score. Three days later, Dinneen wrapped up the best-of-nine series, tossing a 3–0 shutout at the pride of Pittsburgh.

The Boston Americans repeated as American League Champions in 1904 but there was no World Series that year due to a disagreement between the two leagues. Still, it was a big year for Cy Young. On May 5, he threw his second career no-hitter, this one a perfect game, blanking Rube Waddell and the Philadelphia Athletics, 3–0, before 10,267 wildly enthusiastic Huntington Avenue Baseball Grounds fans who whooped and hollered from the first pitch to the last. The runs were batted in by Criger, Freeman, and Young himself. Waddell, the A's zany southpaw, had taunted Young before the game started, so when the Boston right-hander retired his mound opponent on a fly ball to end the game, he yelled, "How do you like that, you hayseed?" According to A's manager, Connie Mack, there was not one ball hit hard by the A's the entire day. Young, who had pitched eight no-hit innings prior to his perfecto, added another six no-hit innings in his next outing, giving him a major league record 23 consecutive no-hit innings. He also completed a then-record 45 consecutive scoreless innings before yielding a run. Boston won the pennant by one-and-a-half games over the New York Highlanders and Young finished the season with a record of 26–16, with 40 complete games in 41 starts and a brilliant 1.97 ERA in 380 innings pitched. When it was suggested that he was able to pitch so many innings because he paced himself by easing up on batters when he had a big lead, he said that was ridiculous because that would put the game "on the level with lawn tennis, tiddle-de-winks, or some other school girl frivolity."[219]

The aging flamethrower, now 38 years old, began to slow down in 1905, but he could still show the youngsters a thing or two. Even though his record in 1905 was just 18–19, he completed 31 of 33 starts, pitching 320⅔ innings and posting a 1.82 ERA, the third-best ERA in the league. His record fell off to 13–21 in 1906 but he bounced back the following year to post a 21–15 won-lost record with a 1.99 ERA in 343⅓ innings. He repeated his success in 1908 with his 16th 20-win season, going 21–11 with a 1.26 ERA, 30 complete games in 33 starts, and 299 innings pitched. It was only the second time in 16 years that Cy Young failed to pitch at least 300 innings in a season. He added to his legend, however, by tossing his third no-hitter at the New York Highlanders in Hilltop Park, New York, on June 30. He faced only 27 batters in the game as the one man he walked was thrown out attempting to steal. He was traded to the Cleveland Naps on February 16, 1909, retiring two years later.

Zarilla, Al

Allen Lee "Zeke" Zarilla began his long march to the major leagues at the age of 19 when he signed a free-agent contract with the St. Louis Browns and joined their farm team in Batesville in the Class-D Northeast Arkansas League. He hit a lusty .329 for the White Sox in 1938 with 37 doubles and 10 home runs while leading the league with 100 runs scored. Moving up the minor league ladder, the five-foot, 11-inch, 180-pound, left-handed hitter joined the parent St. Louis Browns in 1943, where he made his major league debut on June 30 in Sportsman's Park as the Brownies nipped the last-place Philadelphia Athletics, 3–1. He played in 70 games for the sixth-place Brownies over the final three months of the season and batted a respectable .254 in 228 at-bats. The next year, manager Luke Sewell's contingent scaled the heights, winning the American League pennant by one game over the Detroit Tigers, and Al Zarilla, the team's fourth outfielder, played a big part in their success, appearing in 100 games, scorching the ball to the tune of a .299 average, and driving in 45 runs in 288 at-bats with 13 doubles, six triples, and six home runs. The Browns met their cross-town rivals, the St. Louis Cardinals, in the World Series and came out on the short end of a six-game Series. Zarilla saw action in four games, going 1-for-10 with one RBI. The 26-year-old outfielder lost the 1945 season to military service, but returned in 1946, hitting .259, and followed that with a .224 season the following year. By 1948, he had fully recovered from his service time and went on to have a career year, batting .329 with 39 doubles, 12 home runs, 74 RBI, and 77 runs scored in 529 at-bats. He was also selected for the American League All-Star team, going 0-for-2 as the American League defeated its National League rivals by a 5–2 score in Sportsman's Park.

After playing 15 games with the Browns in 1949, Al Zarilla was traded to the Boston Red Sox for Stan Spence on May 5, and he gave Joe McCarthy's team excellent defensive play plus a dangerous bat. The line-drive-hitting outfielder hit a solid .281 in 124 games for the Red Sox in 1949 with 32 doubles, nine home runs, and 71 RBI in 474 at-bats. Boston held a one-game lead over the New York Yankees with just two games left to play in Yankee Stadium at the end of the season, but they dropped both encounters to Casey Stengel's crew, losing the pennant by a single game. The next year, Zarilla batted .325 with 32 doubles, 10 triples, nine homers, 74 RBI, 92 runs scored, and a career-high .493 slugging average. He was a member of Boston's .300-hitting outfield that included Ted Williams (.317) and Dom DiMaggio (.328), but their efforts were not good enough to keep the Red Sox from slipping into third place behind New York and Detroit. Still, Zarilla tied a major league record on June 8 by denting the Green Monster for four doubles in one game as Joe McCarthy's finest manhandled the St. Louis Browns by a 29–4 score. Boston traded their right fielder to the Chicago White Sox over the winter, but after bouncing between Chicago and St. Louis, he was sold back to Boston on August 31, 1952. He hit just .183 in 60 at-bats over the last month of the season, and batted .194 in 67 at-bats the following year before being released by the Red Sox.

APPENDIX

Batting with Boston

Name	G	AB	R	H	D	T	HR	RBI	SB	BA
Agganis, H.	157	517	65	135	23	9	11	67	8	.261
Almada, M.	316	1171	160	319	51	16	6	102	28	.272
Andrews, M.	566	2101	327	563	96	4	47	209	13	.268
Aparicio, L.	367	1426	159	361	66	4	7	133	22	.253
Armas, T.	525	2023	274	510	90	16	113	352	1	.252
Barrett, M.	941	3378	418	938	163	9	18	314	57	.278
Baylor, D.	268	924	157	220	31	1	47	151	8	.238
Bellhorn, M.	223	806	134	199	57	3	24	110	9	.247
Berry, C.	366	1043	109	280	47	15	14	130	9	.268
Boggs, W.	1625	6213	1067	2098	422	47	85	687	16	.338
Boone, I.	266	978	152	325	65	10	22	168	3	.332
Bragg, D.	340	1144	154	302	78	6	20	136	21	.264
Bressoud, E.	558	1958	255	528	115	19	57	208	4	.270
Brunansky, T.	457	1555	184	392	89	10	56	249	8	.252
Buckner, B.	526	2070	240	577	112	8	48	324	27	.279
Buddin, D.	640	2126	318	519	116	11	39	211	14	.244
Burks, E.	733	2827	446	791	160	27	94	388	95	.280
Burleson, R.	1031	4064	514	1114	203	21	38	360	67	.274
Burns, G.	293	1109	162	352	79	10	19	155	17	.317
Carbo, B.	344	986	152	257	54	4	45	157	9	.261
Carrigan, B.	709	1970	194	506	67	14	6	235	37	.257
Chapman, B.	240	903	168	293	63	19	13	137	40	.324
Clinton, L.	412	1427	190	359	70	26	49	198	7	.252
Collins, J.	741	2972	448	881	171	65	25	385	102	.296
Collins, S.	464	1599	175	433	80	29	5	168	33	.271
Conigliaro, T.	802	2955	441	790	121	23	162	501	17	.267
Cooke, D.	404	1257	229	357	81	24	15	161	24	.284
Cramer, R.	722	3111	509	940	146	44	1	270	22	.302
Criger, L.	628	1943	190	405	54	33	6	193	29	.208
Crisp, C.	368	1300	198	352	68	12	21	137	70	.271
Cronin, J.	1134	3892	645	1168	270	44	119	737	31	.300
Damon, J.	597	2476	452	730	136	29	56	299	98	.295
Daubach, B.	541	1802	241	477	125	10	86	306	4	.265
Di Maggio, D.	1399	5640	1046	1680	308	57	87	618	100	.298

Appendix (Batting)

Name	G	AB	R	H	D	T	HR	RBI	SB	BA
Doerr, B.	1865	7093	1094	2042	381	89	223	1247	54	.288
Dougherty, P.	296	1223	217	398	36	22	4	97	65	.325
Doyle, D.	343	1197	155	313	49	13	6	111	15	.261
Drew, J.D.	606	2122	339	532	113	15	80	286	13	.264
Dropo, W.	283	1092	154	307	51	7	51	229	0	.281
Easler, M.	311	1169	158	337	60	9	43	165	1	.288
Ellsbury, J.	507	2032	341	611	106	23	52	235	175	.301
Engle, C.	512	1680	238	445	55	25	6	177	80	.265
Evans, D.	2505	8726	1435	2373	474	72	379	1346	76	.272
Ferrell, R.	522	1791	221	541	111	17	16	240	7	.302
Ferris, H.	991	3689	383	876	148	77	34	418	72	.237
Finney, L.	535	1930	294	580	100	37	13	265	13	.301
Fisk, C.	1078	3860	627	1097	207	33	162	568	61	.284
Flagstead, I.	789	2941	466	867	196	32	27	299	51	.295
Foster, E.	285	907	110	240	38	12	0	79	24	.265
Fox, P.	464	1717	225	496	92	23	6	201	51	.289
Foxx, J.	887	3288	721	1051	181	45	222	788	38	.320
Foy, J.	431	1515	232	373	63	14	41	172	36	.246
Freeman, B.	937	3077	461	879	177	103	54	569	69	.286
Frye, J.	342	1176	179	347	79	4	9	117	40	.295
Garciaparra, N.	966	3968	709	1281	279	50	178	690	84	.323
Gardner, L.	1123	3919	496	1106	151	87	16	481	134	.282
Gedman, R.	903	2856	315	741	164	12	83	356	3	.259
Geiger, G.	618	2002	324	507	78	23	71	246	57	.253
Gernert, D.	706	2255	337	568	96	8	101	377	9	.252
Goodman, B.	1177	4399	688	1344	248	34	14	464	33	.306
Greenwell, M.	1269	4623	657	1400	275	38	130	726	80	.303
Griffin, D.	614	2081	207	517	69	12	7	161	33	.248
Harper, T.	409	1565	250	405	67	8	36	144	107	.259
Hatteberg, S.	454	1310	163	350	86	2	34	159	1	.267
Higgins, P.	356	1294	183	386	73	11	16	240	12	.298
Hillenbrand, S.	344	1287	166	365	80	6	33	170	8	.284
Hoblitzell, D.	468	1534	195	413	62	23	3	184	46	.269
Hobson, B.	623	2230	285	561	98	19	94	358	10	.252
Hoffman, G.	678	1927	228	473	98	9	22	197	5	.245
Hooper, H.	1647	6270	988	1707	246	130	30	497	300	.272
Janvrin, H.	512	1548	179	357	47	12	4	148	62	.231
Jefferson, R.	449	1398	207	442	100	7	50	215	1	.316
Jensen, J.	1039	3857	597	1089	187	28	170	733	95	.282
Johnson, B.	287	1054	177	318	67	15	29	180	7	.302
Johnson, R.	515	1954	313	611	130	30	31	327	48	.313
Jones, D.	656	1842	210	447	77	19	26	186	17	.243
Klaus, B.	458	1626	255	428	77	11	25	168	9	.263
Lepcio, T.	532	1622	181	401	73	10	53	200	8	.247
Lewis, Da.	469	1489	220	381	60	10	13	132	60	.256
Lewis, Du.	1184	4325	500	1248	254	62	27	629	102	.289
Lord, H.	368	1420	179	391	33	18	3	103	77	.275
Lowell, M.	612	2244	293	650	153	4	80	374	9	.290
Lugo, J.	266	940	114	236	53	3	10	103	48	.251
Lynn, F.	828	3062	523	944	217	29	124	521	43	.308
Malzone, F.	1359	5273	641	1454	234	21	131	716	14	.276
Mantilla, F.	349	1137	156	326	45	3	54	171	9	.287

Appendix (Batting)

Name	G	AB	R	H	D	T	HR	RBI	SB	BA
McInnis, S.	537	2006	194	594	75	23	3	261	26	.296
McNair, E.	300	1045	137	289	66	7	16	157	13	.277
Menosky, M.	484	1601	240	459	66	23	9	166	47	.286
Metkovich, G.	436	1690	235	440	87	17	23	173	41	.260
Miller, R.	1101	2573	374	683	107	23	23	266	63	.265
Mirabelli, D.	389	1026	120	244	56	0	48	160	2	.238
Montgomery, B.	387	1185	125	306	50	8	23	156	6	.258
Mueller, B.	406	1442	229	437	106	9	41	204	3	.303
Myer, B.	280	1005	137	303	48	17	3	91	39	.301
Naehring, T.	547	1872	254	527	104	4	49	250	5	.282
Newsome, S.	497	1681	169	437	89	6	4	137	27	.260
Nixon, R.	499	1337	108	358	68	9	13	138	0	.268
Nixon, T.	982	3285	547	912	204	28	133	523	29	.278
Offerman, J.	465	1798	295	482	84	17	30	186	31	.268
O'Leary, T.	962	3456	490	954	209	37	117	516	12	.276
Oliver, T.	514	1931	202	534	101	11	0	176	12	.277
Ortiz, D.	1287	4738	844	1367	348	13	320	1028	6	.289
Parent, F.	986	3846	519	1051	156	63	19	386	129	.273
Pedroia, D.	715	2825	479	862	206	8	75	344	82	.305
Pena, T.	543	1669	166	390	74	4	17	161	20	.234
Perez, T.	304	1087	126	289	56	8	40	175	1	.266
Pesky, J.	1029	4085	776	1277	196	46	13	361	48	.313
Petrocelli, R.	1553	5390	653	1352	237	22	210	773	10	.251
Piersall, J.	931	3369	502	919	158	32	66	366	58	.273
Pratt, D.	289	1128	153	352	80	17	11	188	15	.312
Ramirez, M.	1083	3953	743	1232	256	7	274	868	7	.312
Reed, J.	715	2658	361	743	180	7	17	227	23	.280
Regan, B.	613	2260	228	611	150	36	17	282	36	.270
Remy, J.	710	2809	385	802	90	20	2	211	98	.286
Rhyne, H.	445	1414	176	348	78	18	0	126	11	.246
Rice, J.	2089	8225	1249	2452	373	79	382	1451	58	.298
Rivera, L.	504	1501	167	357	78	6	21	150	15	.238
Roberts, D.	45	86	19	22	10	0	2	14	5	.256
Rothrock, J.	604	1905	280	529	92	26	14	172	57	.278
Runnels, P.	732	2578	407	825	147	21	29	249	20	.320
Scott, D.	1096	3887	355	956	141	41	7	346	61	.246
Scott, G.	1192	4234	527	1088	158	38	154	562	27	.257
Smith, R.	1014	3780	592	1064	204	33	149	536	84	.281
Speaker, T.	1065	3935	704	1327	241	106	39	542	267	.337
Stahl, C.	781	3004	464	871	122	62	17	339	105	.290
Stahl, J.	486	1648	213	456	71	50	21	228	65	.277
Stanley, M.	459	1425	224	391	76	1	73	254	3	.274
Stephens, G.	693	1316	193	325	55	12	24	149	18	.247
Stephens, V.	660	2545	449	721	124	20	122	562	7	.283
Stuart, D.	313	1215	154	328	52	5	75	232	0	.270
Tabor, J.	806	3074	393	838	162	27	90	517	64	.273
Tebbetts, B.	419	1408	151	404	60	3	19	189	16	.287
Tillman, B.	527	1617	131	382	53	10	49	194	0	.236
Todt, P.	895	3218	349	832	169	56	52	409	28	.259
Valentin, J.	991	3709	596	1043	266	17	121	528	47	.281
Varitek, J.	1546	5099	664	1307	306	14	193	757	25	.256
Vaughn, M.	1046	3828	628	1165	199	10	230	752	28	.304

Appendix (Pitching)

Name	G	AB	R	H	D	T	HR	RBI	SB	BA
Vosmik, J.	291	1175	210	354	66	12	16	170	4	.301
Wagner, H.	204	658	65	174	28	6	7	96	4	.264
Webb, E.	330	1230	180	395	106	10	35	196	4	.321
Werber, B.	529	2045	366	575	130	25	38	234	107	.281
Wertz, V.	324	1007	116	276	51	2	37	212	0	.274
White, S.	981	3342	316	881	162	20	63	404	14	.264
Williams, T.	2292	7706	1798	2654	525	71	521	1839	24	.344
Yastrzemski, C.	3308	11988	1816	3419	646	59	452	1844	168	.285
Yerkes, S.	507	1808	233	467	92	17	3	170	34	.258
Youkilis, K.	911	3206	569	927	232	16	129	550	26	.289
Zarilla, A.	332	1072	180	310	66	15	20	157	8	.289

Pitching with Boston

Name	G	GS	CG	IP	W	L	H	SO	BB	SV	ERA
Beckett, J.	173	173	7	1113	84	47	1048	1014	300	0	3.60
Boyd, D.	152	145	39	1016⅔	60	56	1067	571	259	0	4.15
Brewer, T.	241	217	75	1509⅓	91	82	1478	733	669	3	4.00
Cicotte, E.	146	102	66	885⅔	52	46	822	406	289	3	2.69
Clemens, R.	383	382	100	2776	192	111	2359	2590	856	0	3.06
Collins, R.	199	151	90	1336	84	62	1246	511	269	4	2.51
Culp, R.	161	155	51	1092⅓	71	58	958	794	404	0	3.50
DeLock, I.	322	142	32	1207⅔	83	72	1211	661	514	31	4.05
Dinneen, B.	180	174	156	1501	85	85	1372	602	338	3	2.81
Dobson, J.	257	202	90	1544	106	72	1459	689	603	9	3.57
Drago, D.	206	29	9	547⅓	30	29	517	305	184	41	3.55
Eckersley, D.	241	191	64	1371⅔	88	71	1408	771	312	1	3.92
Ferrell, W.	118	110	81	877⅔	62	40	982	314	310	1	4.11
Ferriss, D.	144	103	67	880	65	30	914	296	314	8	3.64
Fornieles, M.	286	28	9	642⅔	39	35	655	342	245	48	4.08
Foster, R.	138	103	60	842⅓	58	33	726	294	305	3	2.36
Foulke, K.	159	0	0	178⅓	13	9	168	149	40	47	3.73
Gaston, M.	100	80	44	635⅔	27	52	674	215	220	4	3.95
Gordon, T.	170	59	6	495⅓	25	25	476	432	220	68	4.45
Grove, L.	214	190	119	1539⅔	105	62	1587	743	447	4	3.34
Hughson, T.	225	156	99	1375⅔	96	54	1270	693	372	17	2.94
Hurst, B.	237	217	54	1459	88	73	1569	1043	479	0	4.23
Jones, S.	157	124	83	1045	64	59	1069	307	338	4	3.39
Kinder, E.	365	89	55	1142⅓	86	52	1086	557	403	91	3.28
Lee, B.	321	167	64	1503⅓	94	68	1627	578	448	13	3.64
Leonard, D.	211	160	96	1361⅓	90	64	1134	771	412	11	2.13
Lester, J.	155	154	6	958	76	34	873	894	362	0	3.53
Lonborg, J.	204	163	38	1099	68	65	1031	784	403	2	3.94
Lowe, D.	384	111	2	1037	70	55	1024	673	312	85	3.72
Martinez, P.	203	201	22	1383⅔	117	37	1044	1683	309	0	2.52
Matsuzaka, D.	106	105	1	623	49	30	569	568	301	0	4.25
Mays, C.	173	112	87	1105	72	51	918	399	290	12	2.21
Monbouquette, B.	254	228	72	1622	96	91	1649	969	408	1	3.69
Okajima, H.	261	0	0	246	17	8	221	215	86	6	3.11
Papelbon, J.	396	3	0	429	23	19	322	509	115	219	2.33

Appendix (Pitching)

Name	G	GS	CG	IP	W	L	H	SO	BB	SV	ERA
Parnell, M.	289	232	113	1752⅔	123	75	1715	732	758	10	3.50
Pennock, H.	201	124	70	1089⅓	62	59	1169	358	299	6	3.67
Radatz, D.	286	0	0	557⅓	49	34	420	627	213	104	2.65
Reardon, J.	150	0	0	153	8	9	146	109	42	88	3.41
Ruffing, R.	189	138	73	1122⅓	39	96	1226	450	459	8	4.61
Ruth, B.	158	144	105	1190⅓	89	46	934	483	425	4	2.19
Shore, E.	125	103	51	839	58	33	732	272	204	3	2.12
Stanley, B.	637	85	21	1707	115	97	1858	693	471	132	3.64
Sullivan, F.	252	201	72	1505⅓	90	80	1455	821	475	6	3.47
Tiant, L.	274	238	113	1774⅔	122	81	1630	1075	501	3	3.36
Timlin, M.	394	0	0	409	30	22	422	273	98	27	3.76
Torrez, M.	161	157	36	1012⅔	60	54	1108	480	420	0	4.51
Wakefield, T.	590	430	26	3006	186	168	3014	2046	1095	22	4.43
Wilson, E.	174	156	30	1024⅓	56	58	951	714	481	0	4.10
Wood, J.	218	157	121	1416	117	56	1117	986	412	8	1.99
Young, C.	327	297	275	2728⅓	192	112	2347	1341	299	9	2.00

NOTES

1. Hugh Wyatt, "Harry Agganis — The Golden Greek," http:www.coachwyatt.com/harryagganis.htm.
2. David Nevard, book review, *Harry Agganis, the Golden Greek*, Buffalo Head Society, 1996, http:webpages.charter.net/joekuras/agganis.htm.
3. "Mel Almada," en.wikipedia.org/wiki/Mel_Almada.
4. William F. McNeil, *Black Baseball Out of Season* (Jefferson, NC: McFarland, 2007), 175.
5. Mike Shatzkin, Editor, *The Ballplayers* (New York: Arbor House, 1990), 27.
6. "Luis Aparicio," www.baseballlibrary.com.
7. William F. McNeil, *Red Sox Nation Guide to the Players* (Lebanon, NH: University Press of New England, 2008), 5.
8. William F. McNeil, *Red Sox Nation Guide to the Players*, 6.
9. Jon Goode, "'Spark Plus' Lights Up Vegas" http//www.Boston.com/sports/baseball/red sox/martybarrett.
10. "Marty Barrett," en.wikipedia.org/wiki/Marty_Barrett.
11. William F. McNeil, *Red Sox Nation Guide to the Players*, 11.
12. "Josh Beckett," www.jockbio.com/Bios/Beckett_bio.html.
13. Ibid., 2.
14. Ibid., 7.
15. Horrigan, Jeff, *Boston Red Sox 2007 World Series Champions*, reprinted from *Boston Herald*, October 4, 2007 (Champaign, IL: Sports Publishing, 2007), 48.
16. "Charlie Berry," en.wikipedia.org/wiki/Charlie_Berry.
17. "Wade Boggs," www.thebaseballpage.com/players/boggswa01.
18. Mike Shatzkin, *The Ballplayers*, 88.
19. "Ellis Burks," www.baseballlibrary.com.
20. "Waiting for the Call," www.Boston.com.
21. "George Burns (First Baseman)," en.wikipedia.org/wiki/George_Burns_(First Baseman).
22. Mike Shatzkin, *The Ballplayers*, 155.
23. William F. McNeil, *Red Sox Nation Guide to the Players*, 33.
24. Bill James and Rob Neyer, *The Neyer/James Guide to Pitchers* (New York: Fireside, 2004), 163.
25. Mike Shatzkin, *The Ballplayers*, 195.
26. Sean Cunningham, "The Wonderful, Despicable World of Roger Clemens," *Esquire*, 2010.
27. Jeff Pearlman, *The Rocket That Fell to Earth* (New York: Harper, 2009).
28. David Jones, Editor, *Deadball Stars of the American League* (Dulles, VA: Potomac Books, 2006), 404.
29. David Jones, *Deadball Stars of the American League*, 446.
30. Tom Simon, "Ray Collins," Baseball Biography Project, bioproj.sabr.org.
31. William F. McNeil, *The Dodgers Encyclopedia* (Jefferson, NC: McFarland, 2003), 96.
32. Nevard, David, "Tony C.," Buffalo Head Society, 1990, http://webpages.charter.net/joekuras/tonyc.htm.
33. Ibid.
34. James Costello and Michael Santa Maria, *In the Shadows of the Diamond* (Dubuque, IA: Elysian Fields Press, 1992), 243.
35. Danny Peary, Editor, *Cult Baseball Players* (New York: Fireside, 1990), 109.
36. David Nevard, "Tony C.," 2–3.
37. James Costello and Michael Santa Maria, *In the Shadows of the Diamond*, 248.

38. Bill Werber and C. Paul Rogers III, *Memories of a Ballplayer* (Cleveland, OH: Society for American Baseball Research, 2001), 21.
39. Mark Feeney, "Former Red Sox Star Dom DiMaggio Dies at 92," *Boston Globe*, 8 May 2009, 1.
40. Ibid.
41. *The Sporting News*, October 16, 1946.
42. Jeff Horrigan, *Boston Red Sox 2007 World Series Champions*, 85.
43. William F. McNeil, *Red Sox Nation Guide to the Players*, 57.
44. Ibid., 59.
45. "Jacoby Ellsbury: Biography," *The Mudville Megaphone,* October 27, 2007.
46. "Jacoby Ellsbury," www.sonsofsamhorn.net.
47. William F. McNeil, *Red Sox Nation Guide to the Players*, 58–59.
48. Ibid., 59.
49. Bill Werber and C. Paul Rogers III, *Memories of a Ballplayer*, 31.
50. Ibid.
51. Dennis H. Auger, in *Deadball Stars of the American League*, 408.
52. Dennis Auger, "Hobe Ferris," The Baseball Biography Project, BIOPROJ.SABR.ORG.
53. Ibid.
54. Ibid.
55. Bill James and Rob Neyer, *The Neyer/James Guide to Pitchers* (New York: Simon & Schuster, 2004), 202.
56. William F. McNeil, *The Evolution of Pitching in Major League Baseball* (Jefferson, NC: McFarland, 2006), 183.
57. William F. McNeil, *Backstop*, 108–109.
58. Ibid., 109.
59. NationMaster.com.
60. W. Harrison Daniel, *Jimmie Foxx* (Jefferson, NC: McFarland, 1996), 1–2.
61. Ibid., 3.
62. Bill Werber and C. Paul Rogers III, *Memories of a Ballplayer*, 75.
63. William F. McNeil, *Red Sox Nation Guide to the Players*, 67.
64. David Jones, Editor, *Deadball Stars of the American League*, 413.
65. Leigh Grossman, Compiled by, *The Red Sox Fan Handbook* (Cambridge, MA: Rounder Books, 2005), 139–140.
66. William F. McNeil, *Red Sox Nation Guide to the Players*, 73.
67. "Geiger Hits the Wall, Taken to Hospital," *Washington Post*, 10 June 1962, C2.
68. Stanley Frank, "Most Versatile Player Ever," *Baseball Digest*, September 1956, 64.
69. Hugh McGovern, *Red Sox 1983 Scorebook Magazine*, 1983, 20.
70. William F. McNeil, *Red Sox Nation Guide to the Players*, 79.
71. Larry Claflin, "Be Patient! Tatum Cautions Hub Fans," *The Sporting News*, January 9, 1971, 52.
72. Larry Claflin, "Red Sox Tout Griffin as King of the Keystoners," *The Sporting News*, April 15, 1972, 10.
73. William F. McNeil, *The Evolution of Pitching in Major League Baseball*, 66.
74. Mike Shatzkin, Editor, *The Ballplayers*, 422.
75. Bill Werber and C. Paul Rogers III, *Memories of a Ballplayer*, 158.
76. "That's What the Man Said! Status Quotes," *Baseball Digest*, May 1968, 24.
77. Ibid., 157.
78. Tom Simon, Editor, *Deadball Stars of the National League* (Washington, DC: Brassey's, 2004), 249.
79. Andrew Blume, "Butch Hobson," Baseball Biography Project, BIOPROJSABR.ORG.
80. Ibid.
81. Lawrence S. Ritter, *The Glory of Their Times* (New York: William Morrow, 1966), 139.
82. Paul J. Zingg, *Harry Hooper* (Champaign, IL: University of Illinois Press, 2004).
83. "Tex Hughson," top100redsox.blogspot.com.
84. Andrew Blume, "Tex Hughson," Baseball Biography Project, BIOPROJ.SABR.ORG.
85. Ibid.
86. Leigh Grossman, *The Red Sox Fan Handbook*, 162.
87. "Jackie Jensen," en.wikipedia.org/wiki/Jackie_Jensen.
88. Ted Williams, *My Turn at Bat* (New York: Fireside, 1988), 74.
89. Ray Fitzgerald, "Pressure Pinches Year Round," *Boston Globe*, August 21, 1967, 23.
90. Ibid.
91. Ty Waterman and Mel Springer, *The Year the Red Sox Won the Series*, 184.
92. Lawrence S. Ritter, *The Glory of Their Times*, 247–248.
93. "Shelby Peace All Time All Star Team — Getting to Know Them," Unioncitygreyhounds.homestead.com.

94. William F. McNeil, *Red Sox Nation Guide to the Players*, 105.
95. Mark Armour, "Ellis Kinder," Baseball Biography Project.
96. Ibid.
97. John F. Steadman, "Portrait of the Average Player," *Baseball Digest*, December-January 1960, 24, 26.
98. Mike Shatzkin, Editor, *The Ballplayers*, 611.
99. Danny Peary, Editor, *Cult Baseball Players* (New York: Fireside, 1990), 167.
100. David Jones, Editor, *Deadball Stars of the American League*, 453.
101. Ibid., 451.
102. Ibid., 451.
103. *Top100RedSox.blogspot.com*.
104. *Baseball-reference.com/bullpen/Harry_Lord*.
105. Ibid.
106. Leigh Grossman, *The Red Sox Fan Handbook*, 175.
107. "Mike Lowell," en.wikipedia.org/wiki/Mike_Lowell.
108. Victor Debs, Jr., *That Was Part of Baseball Then* (Jefferson, NC: McFarland, 2002).
109. Leigh Grossman, *The Red Sox Fan Handbook*, 180.
110. "Pedro Martinez," Jockbio.com/Bios/Pedro/Pedro_bio.html.
111. "Daisuke Matsuzaka," Baseball-reference.com/bullpen/Daisuke_Matsuzaka, pg. 1.
112. Ibid.
113. Bill James and Rob Neyer, *The Neyer/James Guide to Pitchers*, 297.
114. David Jones, Editor, *Deadball Stars of the American League*, 461.
115. Ibid.
116. Ibid., 629.
117. Mike Shatzkin, Editor, *The Ballplayers*, 714.
118. Bill Werber and C. Paul Rogers III, *Memories of a Ballplayer*, 69–70.
119. Ibid., 68.
120. Rich Coberly, "'Lady Luck' Plays a Role in Big League No-hitters," *Baseball Digest*, July 1987, 36.
121. Ibid.
122. Mike Richards, "Rick Miller," Baseball Biography Project, BIOPROJ.SABR.ORG.
123. Ibid.
124. William F. McNeil, *Red Sox Nation Guide to the Players*, 134.
125. Rich Coberly, *The No-Hit Hall of Fame* (Newport Beach, CA: Triple Play Publications, 1985), 120.
126. Chaz Coggins, *Boston Red Sox 1978 Scorebook Magazine*, 1978, 40.
127. Tim Daloisio, "Bill Mueller," Top100redsox.blogspot.com.
128. Bill Werber and C. Paul Rogers III, *Memories of a Ballplayer*, 39.
129. www.thebaseballpage.
130. Bill Mahoney, "Trot Nixon's Hat as Filthy as Ever," *Call of the Green Monster*, 1.
131. Leigh Grossman, *The Red Sox Fan Handbook*, 203.
132. "Hideki Okajima," www.wikipedia.org.
133. Mike Shatzkin, *The Ballplayers*, 824.
134. Albert Chen, "Sunshine Superman," *Sports Illustrated*, November 10, 2004, 28.
135. William F. McNeil, *Red Sox Nation Guide to the Players*, 209.
136. Ibid., 150.
137. "Baseball Fines Papelbon $5000," *www.espn.com*, September 4, 2009.
138. David Jones, Editor, *Deadball Stars of the American League*, 415.
139. Ibid.
140. Rich Coberly, *The No-hit Hall of Fame*, 25.
141. Bill James and Rob Neyer, *The Neyer/James Guide to Pitchers*, 335.
142. Herb Crehan, *Red Sox Heroes of Yesteryear* (Cambridge, MA: Rounder Books, 2005), 76.
143. Leigh Grossman, *The Red Sox Fan Handbook*, 213.
144. "Tony Pena," www.baseballlibrary.com
145. Mike Shatzkin, *The Ballplayers*, 853.
146. Bill James and Rob Neyer, *The Neyer/James Guide to Pitchers*, 339.
147. Frank Vaccaro, "Herb Pennock," Baseball Biography Project.
148. Bill Werber and C. Paul Rogers III, *Memories of a Ballplayer*, 7.
149. David Halberstam, *The Teammates* (New York: Hyperion, 2003, 52.
150. Ron Marshall, "Rico Petrocelli," Baseball Biography Project.
151. Danny Peary, Editor, *Cult Baseball Players*, 278.
152. Ibid., 276

153. William F. McNeil, *Red Sox Nation Guide to the Players*, 157.
154. Ibid., 159.
155. George Sullivan, *The Boston Red Sox 1979 Scorebook Magazine*, 1979, 23.
156. "Manny Ramirez," BullZ-eye.com.
157. Gary Gillette and Pete Palmer, *The ESPN Baseball Encyclopedia, Fourth Edition* (New York: Sterling Publishing, 2007), 11.
158. Hugh McGovern, *Red Sox 1978 Scorebook Magazine*, 1978, 12.
159. Ibid., 19.
160. Ibid., 19.
161. Mike Shatzkin, Editor, *The Ballplayers*, 907.
162. Bill James and Rob Neyer, *The Neyer/James Guide to Pitchers*, 367.
163. Hugh Poland, "Pete Runnels," Baseball Biography Project, SABR, BIOPROJECT.SABR.ORG.
164. Thebaseballpage.com/player/ruth.
165. Ray Birch, "Everett Scott," Baseball Biography Project, SABR.
166. Ibid.
167. William F. McNeil, *Red Sox Nation Guide to the Players*, 179.
168. Jeff Angus, "Reggie Smith," Baseball Biography Project, SABR.
169. Ed Rumill, "The Red Sox Insurance Policy," *Baseball Digest*, September 1968, 6.
170. Ibid.
171. Harold Kaese, "Reggie Smith New Leader for the Red Sox," *Baseball Digest*, July 1972, 44–45.
172. William F. McNeil, *All-Stars for All-Time* (Jefferson, NC: McFarland, 2008), 213.
173. "Tris Speaker," baseballlibrary.com.
174. Don Jensen, "Tris Speaker," Baseball Biography Project, SABR.
175. David Jones, Editor, *Deadball Stars of the American League*, 418.
176. Terry Householder, "Baseball Great from Avilla, Chick Stahl, Properly Honored," *Fort Worth Daily News*, April 26 2009.
177. David Jones, Editor, *Deadball Stars of the American League*, 418.
178. Ibid., 428.
179. Ibid., 429.
180. Leigh Grossman, *The Red Sox Fan Handbook*, 245.
181. Harold Kaese, "A Little Slug for the Red Sox," *Sport*, June 1948.
182. John Sayles on Dick Stuart, in *Cult Baseball Players* (New York: Fireside, 1990), 7.
183. Ibid., 8.
184. Ibid., 9.
185. Mark Morgan, "Boston's Head Hurler," *Baseball Digest*, November-December 1955, 69.
186. Ibid., 71.
187. Leigh Grossman, *The Red Sox Fan Handbook*, 250.
188. Tom Simon, "Birdie Tebbetts," Baseball Biography Project, BIOPROJ.SABR.ORG.
189. Mike Shatzkin, Editor, *The Ballplayers*, 284.
190. Danny Peary, Editor, *Cult Baseball Players*, 288.
191. Gordon Edes, "Mike Timlin '88," Southwestern University for Alumni.
192. Mike Miliard, "Mike Timlin," Top100redsox.blogspot.com.
193. James Costello and Michael Santa Maria, *In the Shadows of the Diamond*, 113.
194. Cormac Eklof, "John Valentin," Top100redsox.blogspot.com.
195. Ibid.
196. John Thomase, "Jason Varitek," *Boston Magazine*, August 2005.
197. Ibid.
198. Mike Shatzkin, Editor, *The Ballplayers*, 1125.
199. Mike Foster and Joanne Hulbert, "Heinie Wagner," Baseball Biography Project.
200. Ibid.
201. Leigh Grossman, *The Red Sox Fan Handbook*, 263.
202. "Earl Webb Passed Up by Three Big League Pilots," *Hartford Courant*, March 6, 1932, C5.
203. Iris Webb Glebe, *The Earl of Dublin* (Ann Arbor, MI: McNaughton & Gunn, 1988), 37.
204. Bill Nowlin, "Bill Werber," Baseball Biography Project.
205. Bill Werber and C. Paul Rogers III, *Memories of a Ballplayer*, 240.
206. Mike Shatzkin, *The Ballplayers*, 1166.
207. Robert W. Creamer, *Baseball in '41* (New York: Viking Penguin, 1991), 270.
208. Rich Coberly, *The No-Hit Hall of Fame* (Newport Beach, CA: Triple Play Publications, 1985), 118.
209. Donald Honig, *A Donald Honig Reader* (New York: Simon & Schuster, 1988), 501–502.

210. William F. McNeil, *Red Sox Nation Guide to the Players*, 218.
211. Lawrence S. Ritter, *The Glory of Their Times*, 166.
212. Herb Crehan and Bill Nowlin, "Carl Yastrzemski," Baseball Biography Project.
213. *Sporting Life*, October 19, 1912, 10.
214. "Kevin Youkilis," www.wikipedia.org.
215. Ibid.
216. David Southwick, "Cy Young," Baseball Biography Project.
217. "Cy Young," www.wikipedia.org.
218. "Cy Young obituary," www.baseball-almanac.com.
219. David Southwick, "Cy Young," Baseball Biography Project.
220. Ibid.

BIBLIOGRAPHY

Allen, Maury. *Baseball's 100.* New York: Galahad Books, 1981.
Anderson, Ron. "Doug Griffin." Baseball Biography Project, SABR, BIOPROJ.SABR.ORG.
Angus, Jeff. "Reggie Smith." Baseball Biography Project, SABR, BIOPROJ.SABR.ORG.
Armour, Mark. "Ellis Kinder." Baseball Biography Project, SABR, BIOPROJ.SABR.ORG.
_____. "Vern Stephens." Baseball Biography Project, SABR, BIOPROJ.SABR.ORG.
Auger, Dennis. "Hobe Ferris." Baseball Biography Project, SABR, BIOPROJ.SABR.ORG.
"Baseball Fines Papelbon $5000." ESPN.COM, September 4, 2009.
The Baseball Page. www.thebaseballpage.com/players/chapmbe01.php.
Baseball-reference.com/bullpen/HarryLord.
Birch, Ray. "Everett Scott." Baseball Biography Project, SABR, BIOPROJ.SABR. ORG.
_____. "Joe Foy." Baseball Biography Project, SABR, BIOPROJ.SABR.ORG.
Blume, Andrew. "Butch Hobson." Baseball Biography Project, SABR, BIOPROJ.SABR.ORG.
Boston Red Sox Media Guide. Boston: Boston Red Sox, 2001.
Boston Red Sox 2007 World Series Champions. Tinton Falls, NJ: MMI Sports #03, 2007.
Bouchard, Maurice. "Dalton Jones" Baseball Biography Project, SABR, BIOPROJ.SABR.ORG.
Carter, Craig, ed. *Daguerreotypes, 8th Edition,* St. Louis, MO, *The Sporting News,* 1990.
_____. *The Series.* St. Louis: *The Sporting News,* 1989.
Chen, Albert. "Sunshine Superman." *Sports Illustrated,* November 10, 2004.
Claflin Larry. "Be Patient! Tatum Cautions Hub Fans." *The Sporting News,* January 9, 1971.
_____. "Red Sox Tout Griffin as King of the Keystoners." *The Sporting News,* April 15, 1972.
Coberly, Rich. "'Lady Luck' Plays a Role in Big League No-Hitters." *Baseball Digest,* July 1987.
_____. *The No-Hit Hall of Fame.* Newport Beach, CA: Triple Play Publications, 1985.
Cohen Richard M., and David S. Neft. *The World Series.* New York: Macmillan, 1986.
Cole, Milton. *Baseball's Great Dynasties, the Red Sox.* New York: Gallery Books, 1990.
Costello, James, and Michael Santa Maria. *In the Shadows of the Diamond: Hard Times in the National Pastime.* Dubuque, IA: Elysian Fields Press, 1992.
Crehan, Herb. *Red Sox Heroes of Yesteryear.* Cambridge, MA: Rounder Books, 2005.
_____, and Bill Nowlin. "Carl Yastrzemski." Baseball Biography Project, SABR, BIOPROJ.SABR.ORG.
Cunningham, Sean. "The Wonderful, Despicable Life of Roger Clemens." *Esquire,* January 2008.
"Cy Young." Wikipedia.org, 2009.
Cy Young obituary. baseball-almanac.com/deaths/cy_young_obituary.shtml.
Daisuke Matsuzaka, Baseball-reference.com/bullpen/Daisuke_Matsuzaka.
Daniel, W. Harrison. *Jimmie Foxx.* Jefferson, NC: McFarland, 1996.
Debs, Victor, Jr. *That Was Part of Baseball Then.* Jefferson, NC: McFarland, 2002.
"Dick Radatz." Bullz-eye.com.
"Dick Radatz." Wikipedia.org.
"Earl Webb Passed Up by Three Big League Pilots." *Hartford Courant,* March 6, 1932.
Edes, Gordon. *Mike Timlin '88,* Southwestern University for Alumni, The New York Times Company, 2005.
Edmundson, Larry. "Shelby Peace All Time All Star Team—Getting to Know Them." Unioncitygreyhounds.homestead.com.
Eklof, Cormac. "John Valentin." Top100redsox.blogspot.com.

Bibliography

Feeney, Mark. "Former Red Sox Star Dom DiMaggio Dies at 92." *Boston Globe,* May 8, 2009.
Fitzgerald, Ray. "Pressure Pinches Year Round." *Boston Globe*, August 21, 1967.
Foster, Mike, and Joanne Hulbert. "Heinie Wagner." SABR, Baseball Biography Project, BIOPROJ.SABR.ORG.
Frank, Stanley. "Most Versatile Player Ever." *Baseball Digest*, September 1956.
"Geiger Hits Wall, Taken to Hospital." *Washington Post*, June 10, 1962.
Gilbert, Brother, C.F.X., edited by Harry Rothgerber. *Young Babe Ruth.* Jefferson, NC: McFarland, 1999.
Gillette, Gary, and Pete Palmer, eds., *The ESPN Baseball Encyclopedia, Fourth Edition.* New York: Sterling Publishing, 2007.
Glebe, Iris Webb. *The Earl of Dublin.* Ann Arbor, MI: McNaughton & Gunn, 1988.
Goode, Jon. "Spark Plug Lights Up Vegas." Boston.com/Sports/Baseball/Red Sox/martybarrett.
Grossman, Leigh, comp. *The Red Sox Fan Handbook.* Cambridge, MA: Rounder Books, 2005.
Halberstam, David. *Summer of '49.* New York: HarperPerennial Modern Classics, 2006.
"Harry Agganis." www.bu.edu/agganis/about/arena/harry.html.
"Harry Agganis." en.wikipedia.org/wiki/Harry_Agganis, 2008.
"Herb Pennock." Baseballlibrary.com.
"Hideki Okajima." en.wikipedia.org/wiki/Hideki Okajima, 2007.
Honig, Donald. *A Donald Honig Reader.* New York: Simon & Schuster, 1988.
Hoppel, Joe, editor. *Baseball's Hall of Fame: Cooperstown, Where Legends Live Forever.* New York: Arlington House, 1988.
Horrigan, Jeff. "Blowout Sets Up Game 7." *Boston Herald*, October 21, 2007, in *Boston Red Sox 2007 World Series Champions.* Champaign, IL: Sports Publishing, 2007.
Householder, Terry. "Baseball Great from Avilla, Chick Stahl, Properly Honored." *Fort Wayne Daily News*, April 26, 2009.
"Jackie Jensen." en.wikipedia.org/wiki/Jackie_Jensen.
"Jacoby Ellsbury." www.sonsofsamhorn.com.
James, Bill, and Rob Neyer. *The Neyer/James Guide to Pitchers.* New York: Simon & Schuster, 2004.
Jensen, Don. "Tris Speaker." Baseball Biography Project, SABR, BIOPROJ.SABR.ORG.
"Jody Reed." Top100redsox.blogspot.com.
"Joe Dobson." *The Sporting News*, October 16, 1946.
Johnson, Lloyd, and Miles Wolff. *The Encyclopedia of Minor League Baseball.* Durham, NC: Baseball America, 1993.
Jones, David, ed. *Deadball Stars of the American League.* Dulles, VA: Potomac Books, 2006.
"Josh Beckett." http://www.jockbio.com/Bios/Beckett/Beckett_bio.html.
Kaese, Harold. "Reggie Smith New Leader For the Red Sox." *Baseball Digest*, July 1972.
_____. "A Little Slug for the Red Sox." *Sport*, June 1948.
Kallay, Mike, ed. *Street & Smiths Baseball Yearbook.* Charlotte, NC: 2000 & 2004.
Kaplan, Jim. *Lefty Grove: American Original.* Cleveland, OH: Society for American Baseball Research, 2000.
"Kevin Youkilis." Wikipedia.org.
Levitt, Daniel R., and Mark L. Armour. *Paths to Glory: How Great Baseball Teams Got That Way.* Dulles, VA: Brassey's, 2003.
"Luis Aparicio." www.baseballlibrary.com/ballplayers/player.php?name=LUISAPARICIO-1934-17k.
"Luis Aparicio." en.wikipedia.org/wiki/Luis_Aparicio.
Mahoney, Bill. "Report: Trot Nixon's Hat as Filthy as Ever." *Call of the Green Monster*. N.d.
"Marty Barrett." en.wikipedia.org/wiki/Marty_Barrett.
McDonell, Terry. *Sports Illustrated Presents Boston Red Sox World Champions.* Tampa: Time, 2004.
McNeil, William F. *All-Stars for All-Time.* Jefferson, NC: McFarland, 2008.
_____. *Backstop.* Jefferson, NC: McFarland, 2006.
_____. *Black Baseball Out of Season.* Jefferson, NC: McFarland, 2007.
_____. *The Dodgers Encyclopedia.* Jefferson, NC: McFarland, 2003.
_____. *The Evolution of Pitching in Major League Baseball.* Jefferson, NC: McFarland, 2006.
_____. *Red Sox Nation Guide to the Players.* Lebanon, NH: University Press of New England, 2008.
"Mel Almada." en.wikipedia.org/wiki/Mel_Almada.
"Mike Andrews." thebaseballcube.com/players/A/Mike-Andrews.shtml.
"Mike Andrews." en.wikipedia.org/wiki/Mike_Andrews.
"Mike Lowell." en. Wikipedia.org/wiki/Mike_Lowell.
Miliard, Mike. "Mike Timlin." Top100redsox.blogspot.com.
Minor League Baseball Stars. Cooperstown, NY: Society for American Baseball Research, 1984.
Minor League Baseball Stars, Volume II. Cooperstown, NY: Society for American Baseball Research, 1985.

Minor League Baseball Stars, Volume III. Cleveland, OH: Society for American Baseball Research, 1992.
Morgan, Mark. "Boston's Head Hurler." *Baseball Digest*, November-December 1955.
Nevard, David. "Tony C." The Buffalo Head Society, 1990, http://webpages.charter.net/joekuras/tonyc.htm.
_____. "Harry Agganis, the Golden Greek." The Buffalo Head Society, 1996, http://webpages.charter.net/joekuras/agganis.htm.
Nowlin, Bill. "Earl Webb." Baseball Biography Project, SABR, BIOPROJ.SABR.ORG.
_____. "Joe Dobson." Baseball Biography Project, SABR, BIOPROJ.SABR.ORG.
Oleksak, Michael M., and Mary Adams Oleksak. *Beisbol: Latin Americans and the Great Old Game*. Masters Press, 1996.
Pearlman, Jeff. *The Rocket That Fell to Earth: Roger Clemens and the Rage for Baseball Immortality*. New York: Harper, 2009.
Peary, Danny. *Cult Baseball Players*. New York: Simon & Schuster, 1990.
"Pedro Martinez." Jockbio.com/Bios/Pedro/Pedro_bio.html.
Poland, Hugh, "Pete Runnels." Baseball Biography Project, SABR, BIOPROJ.SABR.ORG.
Powers, Jimmy. *Baseball Personalities*. New York: Rudolph Field, 1949.
Red Sox Scorebook and Magazine. New York City: H.M.S., 1974 to 1979.
Red Sox Scorebook Magazine. Boston, MA: Boston Red Sox, 1983 to 2004.
Redmount, Robert S. *The Red Sox Encyclopedia*. Champaign, IL: Sports Publishing, 1998.
Reichler, Joseph, and Jack Clary. *Baseball's Great Moments*. New York: Galahad Books, 1990.
Reichler, Joseph L., ed. *The Baseball Encyclopedia*. New York: Macmillan, 1979.
Retrosheet, *www.retrosheet.org*.
Richards, Mike. "Rick Miller." Baseball Biography Project. BIOPROJ.SABR.ORG.
Ritter, Lawrence S. *The Glory of Their Times*. New York: William Morrow, 1966.
Rumill, Ed. "The Red Sox Insurance Policy." *Baseball Digest*, September 1968.
Shatzkin, Mike. *The Ballplayers*. New York: William Morrow, 1990.
Simon, Tom. "Birdie Tebbetts." Baseball Biography Project, BIOPROJ.SABR.ORG.
_____. "Ray Collins." Baseball Biography Project, BIOPROJ.SABR.ORG.
_____, ed. *Deadball Stars of the National League*. Washington, DC: Brassey's, 2004.
Skipper, Doug. "Lou Finney." Baseball Biography Project, BIOPROJ.SABR.ORG.
Southwick, David, "Cy Young." Baseball Biography Project, BIOPROJ.SABR.ORG.
"Sports Illustrated" *World Series Commemorative*. New York: Time Inc., 2004.
Steadman, John F. "Portrait of the Average Player." *Baseball Digest*, December-January 1960.
Street & Smith's Baseball. Charlotte, NC: Street & Smith, 2000, 2004, 2008.
"Tex Hughson." Top100redsox.blogspot.com.
"That's What the Man Said! Status Quote." *Baseball Digest*, May 1968.
Thomase, John. "Jason Varitek." *Boston Magazine*, August 2005.
Thorn, John, and Pete Palmer, eds. *Total Baseball*. New York: Warner Books, 1989.
"Tony Pena." baseballlibrary.com.
"Tris Speaker." baseballlibrary.com.
Tsiotis, Nick, and Andy Dabilis. *Harry Agganis, the Golden Greek*. Brookline, MA: Hellenic College Press, 1995.
Vaccaro, Frank. "Herb Pennock." Baseball Biography Project, BIOPROJ.SABR. ORG, pg. 1.
"Wade Boggs." thebaseballpage.com/players/boggswa01.php.
"Waiting for the Call." *http://www.Boston.com/Sports/Baseball/RedSox/rickburleson*.
Waterman, Ty, and Mel Springer. *The Year the Red Sox Won the World Series: A Chronicle of the 1918 Championship Season*. Boston: Northeastern University Press, 1999.
Werber, Bill, and C. Paul Rogers III. *Memories of a Ballplayer*. Cleveland, OH: Society for American Baseball Research, 2001.
Who's Who in Baseball. New York: Who's Who in Baseball Magazine Co., 1916–2007.
Williams, Ted. *My Turn at Bat, the Story of my Life*. New York: Fireside, 1988.
Wyatt, Hugh. "Harry Agganis — The Golden Greek." http://www.coachwyatt.com/harryagganis.htm.
Yastrzemski, Carl, and Gerald Eskenazi. *Yaz*. New York: Doubleday, 1990.
Zingg, Paul J. *Harry Hooper*. Champaign, IL: University of Illinois Press, 2004.

INDEX

Aaron, Hank 29
Aase, Don 154
Abernathy, Brent 105
Adair, Jerry 102
Agganis, Harry 1, 3, 176, 211, 217, 222, 223
Alexander, Grover Cleveland 96, 166
Allen, Maury 109, 221
Allenson, Gary 69, 70
Allison, Bob 103
Almada, Mel 4, 211, 217, 222
Anderson, Ron 221
Andrews, Mike 5, 102, 203, 211, 222
Angus, Jeff 167, 219, 21
Anson, Cap 208
Aparicio, Luis, Jr. 5, 6, 145, 211, 217, 222
Aparicio, Luis, Sr. 5
Armas, Tony 6, 112, 211
Armour, Mark L. 218, 221, 222
Arroyo, Bronson 187, 207
Astroth, Joe 58
Auger, Dennis H. 53, 169, 218, 221
Autry, Gene 16
Avila, Bobby 179
Avila, Ralph 112

Baker, Frank "Home Run" 116
Barr, Scotty 137
Barrett, Marty 6, 7, 211, 217, 222
Barrow, Ed 92, 142, 163, 164
Barry, Jack 116
Baylor, Don 7, 8, 211
Bean, Joe 192
Beckett, Josh 8–11, 47, 106, 134, 214, 217, 222
Bedient, Hugh 68, 96
Belinsky, Bo 91
Bell, Gary 204
Bellhorn, Mark 11, 211
Beltre, Adrian 48, 107
Bench, Johnny 21
Berardino, Johnny 174

Berra, Yogi 152
Berry, Charlie 11, 12, 211, 217
Bevington, Terry 60
Birch, Ray 219, 221
Blair, Paul 82
Blair, Willie 128
Bloodworth, Jimmy 85
Blowers, Mike 185
Blume, Andrew 82, 218, 221
Boggs, Wade 12, 13, 152, 211, 217, 223
Bolling, Milt 94
Bolton, Tom 152
Boone, Aaron 123, 187
Boone, Ike 13, 14
Bosman, Dick 76, 211
Bouchard, Maurice 221
Boudreau, Lou 15, 39, 138, 164, 173, 174, 199
Boyd, Dennis "Oil Can" 14, 86, 214
Brace, George 46
Bradford, Chad 150
Bradley, Phil 24
Bragg, Darren 15, 128, 211
Bransfield, Kitty 53
Bressoud, Eddie 15, 18, 211
Brett, George 75
Brewer, Tom 15, 16, 36, 214
Brooks, Hubie 157
Brown, Charlie 128
Brown, Paul 3
Brunansky, Tom 16, 17, 152, 211
Bryant, Paul "Bear" 81
Buchholz, Clay 140
Buckner, Bill 17, 18, 46, 211
Buddin, Don 15, 71, 95, 211
Buford, Damon 190
Bunyon, Paul 133
Burks, Ellis 18, 19, 211, 217
Burleson, Rick 19, 20, 82, 211
Burns, George 20, 21, 194, 211, 217
Busby, Steve 154
Bush, Donie 163
Bush, George 89
Bush, Joe 147

Cady, Hick 22, 206
Cain, Sugar 117
Callahan, Nixey 192
Callaspo, Alberto 98
Campbell, Paul 41
Canseco, Jose 46
Carbo, Bernie 1, 21, 22, 211
Carmona, Rafael 44, 75
Carrasquel, Chico 5
Carrigan, Bill 22, 28, 59, 60, 69, 81, 96, 101, 116, 125, 162–164, 171, 184, 202, 211
Carroll, Clay 21
Carter, Craig 221
Cerone, Rick 70
Champion, Billy 76
Chance, Dean 92, 102
Chandler, Happy 174
Chapman, Ben 5, 22, 23, 31, 125, 211
Chapman, Ray 115
Charlton, Norm 75
Chase, "Prince Hal" 171
Chen, Albert 132, 219, 221
Cheney, Tom 23
Chesbro, "Happy Jack" 38
Chrisley, Neil 121
Cicotte, Eddie 23, 214
Claflin, Larry 218, 221
Clarke, Fred 42, 65, 170, 209
Clary, Jack 222
Clemens, Roger 1, 17, 23–25, 70, 74, 75, 86, 113, 214, 221
Clinton, Lou 25, 26, 122, 211
Cobb, Ty 12, 20, 57, 97, 163, 195
Coberly, Rich 201, 218–221
Cochrane, Mickey 62, 63
Coggins, Chaz 219
Cohen, Richard M. 221
Cole, Milton 221
Collins, Eddie 40, 116
Collins, Jimmy 26, 27, 32, 38, 42, 136, 170, 211
Collins, Ray 27, 28, 96, 214, 223
Collins, Shano 28, 90, 194, 211
Comiskey, Charles 28

Index

Concepcion, David 5
Conigliaro, Tony 1, 29, 30, 91, 119, 165, 201, 211, 222
Cook, Aaron 107
Cooke, Dusty 30, 31, 211
Cooper, Cecil 82
Cooper, Mort 10
Cooper, Scott 125
Cordeiro, Julie 60
Cordero, Wil 75
Costello, James 30, 217, 219, 221
Cox, Billy 13
Cox, Bobby 182
Cramer, Roger "Doc" 31, 32, 37, 77, 211
Crawford, Sam 163
Creamer, Robert W. 220
Crehan, Herb 219–221
Criger, Lou 32, 170, 171, 209, 211
Crisp, Coco 32, 33, 47, 48, 211
Cronin, Joe 4, 31, 33, 39, 41, 63, 73, 77, 85, 90, 117, 126, 143, 178, 191, 195, 198, 211
Cronin, Margaret (Griffith) 33
Crosetti, Frank 195
Culberson, Leon 37
Culp, Ray 33, 34, 214
Cunningham, Sean 24, 217, 221

Dabilis, Andy 4, 223
Daloisio, Tim 219
Damon, Johnny 32, 34, 35, 105, 124, 132, 211
Daniel, W. Harrison 218
Daubach, Brian 35, 36, 79, 211
Davis, George 137
Davis, Mike 46
Debs, Victor, Jr. 218, 221
Delock, Ike 36, 214
Dent, Bucky 154, 184, 205
Dickey, Bill 125
Didier, Mel 46
DiMaggio, Dominic 36–38, 41, 44, 85, 119, 144, 146, 174, 210, 211, 217, 221
DiMaggio, Joe 36, 37, 127, 168
DiMaggio, Vince 37
Dinneen, Bill 26, 38, 39, 42, 53, 155, 170, 209, 214
Dobson, Joe 39, 40, 41, 214, 222
Doerr, Bobby 37, 40–42, 44, 55, 73, 94, 126, 127, 144, 167, 174, 178, 191, 212
Donovan, Patsy 27, 49, 87, 104
Dougherty, Patsy 26, 42, 212
Doyle, Denny 42, 43, 50, 76, 212
Drabowsky, Moe 29
Drago, Dick 43, 95, 214
Dressen, Charlie 111
Drew, J.D. 9, 43, 44, 47, 212
Dropo, Walt 44, 45, 72, 73, 212
Drysdale, Don 92
Duffy, Hugh 118, 147
Dunn, Jack 77, 162

Duren, Ryne 196
Durocher, Leo 76, 110
Durst, Cedric 159
Dyer, Eddie 85, 144

Easler, Mike 45, 212
Eastwick, Rawley 22, 50
Eckersley, Dennis 17, 45, 46, 214
Edes, Gordon 219, 221
Edmundson, Larry 221
Ehmke, Howard 118, 119, 139, 158, 159
Eklif, Cormac 219, 221
Ellsbury, Jacoby 32, 33, 46–48, 115, 140, 150, 212, 217, 222
Engle, Clyde 48, 49, 68, 81, 104, 169, 212
Epstein, Theo 60, 81, 150, 188
Erickson, Scott 152
Ermer, Cal 204
Eskenazi, Gerald 223
Evans, Billy 190
Evans, Dwight 1, 21, 24, 49–51, 108, 109, 119, 180, 212
Everett, Carl 100

Falk, Bibb 54
Farrell, John 130
Feeney, Mark 36, 217, 221
Feller, Bob 42
Ferrell, George 51
Ferrell, Rick 5, 51, 52, 195, 212
Ferrell, Wes 5, 31, 51, 52, 195, 201, 214
Ferris, Hobe 52–54, 65, 212, 221
Ferriss, Dave 41, 54, 55, 85, 144, 214
Fingers, Rollie 145, 152
Finley, Charlie 5
Finney, Lou 55, 56, 212, 223
Fisher, Jack 200
Fisk, Carlton 1, 20, 22, 50, 56, 57, 122, 184, 205, 212
Fitzgerald, Ray 30, 91, 218, 221
Flagstad, Ira "Pete" 57, 58, 212
Flagstad, Reita 58
Flaherty, John 113
Fletcher, Art 206
Fohl, Lee 159
Ford, Whitey 111, 163, 176
Fornieles, Mike 58, 214
Foster, Eddie "Kid" 58, 59, 212
Foster, George "Rube" 59, 60, 96, 166, 214
Foster, Joanne 192
Foster, Mike 220, 221
Foulke, Keith 35, 60, 61, 67, 134, 150, 182, 214
Fox, Pete 61, 62, 212
Foxx, Del 62
Foxx, Jimmie 1, 55, 56, 62, 63, 80, 178, 191, 195, 212, 218, 221
Foy, Joe 63, 64, 212, 221
Francis, Jeff 10, 140
Francona, Terry 9, 10, 32, 35, 44,

47, 48, 61, 98, 105, 107, 108, 113, 115, 123, 124, 128, 132, 134, 135, 140, 150, 157, 182, 187, 188, 207
Francona, Tito 71
Frank, Stanley 218, 221
Frazee, Harry 84, 93, 101, 118, 164
Freehan, Bill 91
Freeman, Buck 26, 53, 64, 65, 209, 212
Frye, Jeff 65, 66, 212
Fultz, Aaron 123

Gaetti, Gary 152
Galehouse, Denny 138
Garciaparra, Nomar 66, 67, 130, 188, 190, 212
Gardner, Larry 27, 59, 67–69, 87, 97, 169, 206, 212
Garza, Matt 99
Gaston, Cito 182
Gaston, Milt 69, 214
Gedeon, Joe 60
Gedman, Rich 69, 70, 212
Gehrig, Lou 63, 142, 151, 155, 164, 183
Geiger, Gary 70–72, 212, 218, 221
Gernert, Dick 3, 72, 73, 212
Gibson, Bob 103
Gibson, Kirk 46
Gibson, Norwood 53
Gilbert, Brother 221
Gillette, Gary 150, 219, 222
Glebe, Iris Webb 220, 222
Goldberg, Rube 117
Gomez, Lefty 125, 161
Goode, Jon 217, 222
Goodman, Billy 16, 44, 58, 73, 97, 212
Gordon, Tom "Flash" 74, 104, 190, 193, 214
Gossage, Goose 154
Gowdy, Curt 179
Graham, Otto 3
Grantham, George 155
Greenberg, Hank 63
Greenwell, Mike 25, 47, 66, 74–76, 212
Grich, Bobby 154
Griffey, Ken, Jr. 50
Griffin, Doug 5, 42, 76, 212, 218, 221
Griffith, Clark 33, 42, 59, 87, 125
Groat, Dick 15, 148
Grossman, Leigh 59, 218–220, 222
Grove, Lefty 1, 52, 63, 76–78, 84, 111, 177, 191, 195, 214, 222
Guerrero, Vladimir 136
Guidry, Ron 184
Gutierrez, Jackie 82

Halberstam, David 219, 222
Hale, Bob 94
Hall, Irv 127

Hamilton, Jack 30
Hamlet, Stanton 26
Haney, Chris 13
Haney, Fred 111
Harper, Tommy 21, 48, 78, 212
Harrelson, Ken 103
Harris, Bucky 52
Harris, Mickey 41, 55, 84, 85
Harrison, Daniel W. 221
Harriss, Slim 118
Hartsfield, Roy 109
Hatteberg, Scott 78, 79, 187, 212
Hatton, Grady 95
Hayden, Jack 53
Hegan, Jim 127
Heilmann, Harry 57
Henderson, Rickey 105
Hennigan, Phil 119
Henriksen, Olaf 68, 171
Herman, Billy 111, 122, 144, 145
Herzog, Whitey 151
Higgins, Pinky 3, 15, 26, 36, 45, 71, 79, 80, 89, 121, 122, 177, 181, 195, 212
High, Hugh 60
Hillenbrand, Shea 80, 81, 212
Hoblitzel, Dick 81, 87, 96, 97, 212
Hobson, Butch 81, 82, 125, 151, 185, 212, 218, 221
Hodges, Gil 64
Hoffman, Glen 24, 82, 83, 212
Holliday, Matt 135
Honig, Donald 220, 222
Hooper, Harry 27, 28, 49, 68, 83–85, 96, 192, 206, 212, 218, 223
Hoppel, Joe 222
Horlen, Joel 29
Hornsby, Rogers 12
Horrigan, Jeff 44, 217, 222
Houck, Ralph 6, 50, 102, 148, 172
Householder, Terry 219, 222
Howard, Elston 64
Howell, J.P. 107
Hoyt, Waite 92, 147, 161
Hubbell, Carl 179
Huff, Aubrey 150
Huff, David 107
Huggins, Miller 147
Hughes, "Long Tom" 53
Hughson, Tex 41, 55, 84–86, 144, 214, 218, 223
Hulbert, Joanne 220, 221
Hulbert, Mike 192
Hunnefield, Bill 51, 52
Hunter, Catfish 24, 142, 180
Hurst, Bruce 14, 86, 87, 214
Hutchinson, Fred 44
Hyde, Dick 71

Isbell, Frank 137

Jackson, Joe 12
James, Bill 115, 217–219, 222
James, Delvin 105
Janvrin, Hal 87, 88, 212

Javier, Julian 103, 148
Jefferson, Reggie 75, 88, 212
Jennings, Hughie 163
Jensen, Don 219
Jensen, Jackie 16, 19, 49, 88, 89, 173, 212, 218, 222
Jimenez, Ubaldo 44
John, Tommy 74
Johnson, "Indian Bob" 85, 89, 90, 195, 212
Johnson, Darrell 42, 120, 180, 205
Johnson, Davey 86
Johnson, Lloyd 222
Johnson, Randy 111, 190, 212
Johnson, Roy 90
Johnson, Walter 28, 92, 101, 104, 111, 163, 202, 208
Jones, Dalton 90–92, 102, 103, 212, 221
Jones, David 217–219, 222
Jones, Sam 92, 93, 169, 214
Joost, Eddie 15
Judnich, Walt 40
Justice, David 74

Kaat, Jim 91
Kaese, Harold 219, 222
Kaline, Al 102
Kallay, Mike 222
Kaplan, Jim 77, 222
Kapler, Gabe 133
Kasko, Eddie 34, 56, 76, 165, 180
Keane, Cliff 91
Keeler, Willie 26
Kelly, Tom 16, 18, 151
Kennedy, Kevin 6, 6, 88, 126, 130, 189
Kennedy, Robert F. 165
Kennedy, Vern 80
Kerrigan, Joe 74
Kielty, Bobby 44
Killebrew, Harmon 103
Kinder, Ellis 93, 94, 172, 214, 218, 221
Klaus, Billy 94, 95, 212
Konerko, Paul 99
Kotsay, Mark 99
Koufax, Sandy 10
Krentzman, Jackie 123
Krichell, Paul 195

LaChance, Candy 53
Lajoie, Nap 53
Lake, Fred 27, 83, 168
Landis, Kenesaw Mountain 23, 51
Lannin, Joseph 28, 60, 169
Lansford, Carney 20, 82
LaRussa, Tony 46, 105
Lary, Lyn 33
Lasorda, Tommy 112
Lazzeri, Tony 125
Lee, Bill 22, 95, 96, 149, 167, 180, 205, 214
Lee, Derrick 106

Lee, Don 91
Lemon, Bob 184
Leonard, Hubert "Dutch" 60, 96, 97, 166, 214
Lepcio, Ted 97, 212
Lester, Jon 10, 47, 97–99, 214
Levitt, Daniel R. 222
Lewis, Darren 99–100, 212
Lewis, Duffy 68, 83, 96, 97, 100, 101, 168, 169, 202, 212
Liddle, Don 196
Lieb, Fred 119
Liebold, Nemo 28
Little, Grady 35, 105, 113, 150
Lofton, Kenny 74
Lonborg, Jim 34, 64, 91, 92, 101–103, 203, 204, 214
Lopez, Al 122, 196
Lopez, Javier 115
Lord, Harry 103, 104, 212
Lowe, Derek 74, 104–106, 113, 128, 214
Lowell, Mike 9, 44, 99, 106–108, 115, 135, 150, 212, 218, 222
Lugo, Julio 9, 108, 150, 212
Lynn, Fred 20, 108, 109, 119, 180, 205, 212
Lyons, Steve 24, 149

Mack, Connie 26, 38, 63, 77, 79, 89, 116, 117, 126, 141, 162, 177, 209
MacMullan, Jackie 206
Mahoney, Bill 219, 222
Malzone, Frank 95, 109–111, 122, 212
Malzone, Suzanne 110
Mantilla, Felix 111, 212
Mantle, Mickey 168
Manush, Heinie 54
Marcum, Johnny 31
Marion, Marty 6
Maris, Roger 103, 127
Marquard, Rube 97
Marshall, Mike 91
Marshall, Ron 219
Martin, Billy 121, 146, 180, 184
Martin, Pepper 62
Martinez, Leopoldina 111
Martinez, Paolino 111
Martinez, Pedro 1, 35, 111–113, 187, 190, 214, 218, 222
Martinez, Ramon 112
Martinez, Victor 99, 188
Marx, Groucho 146
Masterson, Justin 48
Mathewson, Christy 68, 163
Matsuzaka, Daisuke 9, 10, 44, 107, 113–115, 214, 218, 221
Matthias, Brother 161
Maxwell, Charlie 122
May, Rudy 82
Mays, Carl 60, 92, 115, 116, 166, 214
Mays, Willie 48, 148, 168, 196

Index

McBride, Tom 41
McCarthy, Joe 31, 73, 93, 138, 159, 174, 195, 210
McCormick, Moose 206
McCovey, Willie 148
McDermott, Mickey 89, 139, 146, 176
McDonell, Terry 222
McGovern, Hugh 153, 218, 219
McGowan, Bill 127
McGraw, John 26, 68, 171, 191, 192, 206
McGraw, Tom 72
McInnis, Stuffy 20, 116, 117, 213
McKechnie, Bill 94, 155
McKeon, Jack 8, 106
McLain, Denny 91
McManus, Marty 195
McNair, Eric 40, 41, 117, 118, 213
McNamara, John 6, 7, 14, 17, 24, 70, 75, 152
McNamee, Brian 25
McNeil, William 217- 220, 222
McNutt, Boob 117
Medwick, Joe "Ducky" 62
Mejias, Roman 181
Menosky, Mike 118, 119, 213
Metkovich, George 119, 213
Mientkiewicz, Doug 67
Miliard, Mike 219, 222
Millar, Kevin 35, 132, 150, 157
Miller, Otto 87
Miller, Rick 119, 120, 213, 219, 222
Mills, Brad 150
Mirabelli, Doug 120, 121, 213
Mitchell, Keith 185
Monbouquette, Bill 71, 101, 121, 122, 214
Moncrief, Bob 143
Monday, Rick 17
Montgomery, Bob 122, 123, 213
Moore, Mike 24
Moran, Pat 59
Morehead, Dave 91
Moret, Roger 156
Morgan, Joe 50
Morgan, Joe (mgr) 141, 151, 152, 189
Morgan, Mark 219, 222
Moss, Les 197
Mowrey, Mike 87
Moyer, Jamie 15
Mueller, Bill 35, 81, 123, 124, 158, 188, 213, 219
Munson, Thurman 120
Murphy, Dropkick 135
Murray, Red 68
Myer, Buddy 124, 125, 191, 213
Myers, Hy 87, 97, 162

Naehring, Tim 75, 125, 126, 152, 213
Neft, David S. 221
Nettles, Graig 13
Nevard, David 217, 222

Newfield, Marc 185
Newhouser, "Prince Hal" 138
Newsome, Bobo 5, 55, 213
Newsome, Skeeter 126, 127
Neyer, Rob 115, 217–219, 222
Nichols, Chet 181
Nixon, Otis 182
Nixon, Richard M. 16
Nixon, Russ 127, 213
Nixon, Trot 128, 129, 213, 222
Norman, Bill 121
Nowlin, Bill 220–222
Nunamaker, Leslie 59, 60

O'Brien, Buck 27
Offerman, Jose 129, 186, 213
Okajima, Hideki 9, 10, 47, 115, 129, 130, 135, 214, 219, 222
O'Keefe, Jimmy 93
O'Leary, Troy 75, 130, 131, 193, 213
Oleksak, Mary Adams 222
Oleksak, Michael M. 222
Oliva, Tony 103
Oliver, Tom 131, 213
O'Neil, Steve 94, 196, 197
Orlando, Johnny 198
Ormsby, Red 118
Orsillo, Don 155
Ortega, Phil 91
Ortiz, David 1, 9, 35, 36, 47, 48, 81, 105, 107, 113, 131–135, 150, 158, 213
Ortman, Louise "Lulu" 170
Ott, Mel 62
Owen, Spike 152, 157

Pagliaroni, Jim 122, 127, 181
Paige, Satchel 197
Palmer, Jim 29, 82, 180
Palmer, Pete 150, 219, 222, 223
Papelbon, Jonathan 9, 47, 48, 61, 99, 107, 115, 130, 134–136, 214, 221
Parent, Freddy 53, 136, 137, 191, 213
Parnell, Mel 95, 99, 137–139, 144, 176, 215
Parrott, Mike 50
Partee, Roy 41
Pasqual brothers 174
Passeau, Claude 198
Pavano, Carl 112
Peace, Shelby 218, 221
Pearlman, Jeff 217, 222
Peary, Danny 217–219, 222
Peck, Hal 127
Peckinpaugh, Roger 51
Pedroia, Dustin 1, 9, 10, 47, 99, 107, 135, 139–141, 213
Pena, Tony 70, 141, 213, 219, 223
Pennock, Herb 31, 141, 142, 147, 195, 215, 222, 223
Penny, Brad 106
Pepitone, Joe 145
Perez, Tony 142, 143, 213

Perritt, Pol 118
Perry, Gaylord 76
Pesky, Johnny 26, 29, 41, 44, 72, 73, 85, 91, 111, 126, 127, 143, 144, 172, 174, 213
Petrocelli, Rico 15, 64, 102, 144, 145, 204, 213, 219
Pettitte, Andy 48
Phelps, Ken 24
Philley, Dave 94
Phillippe, Deacon 65
Piazza, Mike 57
Picinich, Val 119
Pierce, Billy 94
Piersall, Jimmy 16, 121, 139, 145–147, 149, 173, 196, 213
Pinella, Lou 190
Plank, Eddie 59, 137
Poland, Hugh 219, 222
Porcello, Rick 207
Posada, Jorge 48, 157
Powell, Jay 123
Powers, Jimmy 222
Pratt, Del 147, 148, 213
Pujols, Albert 105
Pytlak, Frankie 39

Quinn, Bob 183
Quintana, Carlos 189

Radatz, Dick 148, 149, 215, 221
Ramirez, Hanley 9
Ramirez, Manny 1, 9, 35, 47, 48, 105, 113, 133, 149–151, 207, 213, 219
Ramos, Pedro 29
Raschi, Vic 94
Reardon, Jeff 151, 152, 215
Redmount, Robert S. 222
Reed, Jody 152, 153, 213, 222
Reese, Rich 103
Regan, Bill 153, 213
Reichler, Joseph L. 222
Reiser, Pete 76
Remy, Jerry 153–155, 213
Reyes, Carlos 126
Rhyne, Hal 155, 156, 213
Rice, Grantland 169
Rice, Jim 6, 75, 82, 108, 109, 119, 154, 156, 157, 180, 205, 213
Richards, Mike 219, 222
Ritchey, Claude 42
Ritter, Lawrence S. 218, 220, 223
Rivera, Juan 136
Rivera, Luis 157, 185, 213
Rivera, Mariano 35, 80, 113, 124, 157, 188, 207
Roberts, Dave 1, 105, 113, 157, 158, 213
Roberts, Robin 101
Robinson, Bill 64
Robinson, Brooks 13, 71
Robinson, Jackie 22
Rodriguez, Alex 79, 124, 187
Rodriguez, Ivan 57, 106

Rogers, Paul, III 217–220, 223
Rohr, Billy 64
Rose, Pete 22, 140
Rothgerber, Harry 221
Rothrock, Jack 158, 159, 213
Ruffing, Charles "Red" 159, 160, 215
Ruhle, Vern 156
Rumill, Ed 219, 223
Runnels, Pete 97, 122, 160, 161, 213, 219, 222
Rusie, Amos 208
Ruth, Babe 29, 60, 62, 65, 81, 84, 87, 96, 97, 102, 127, 142, 155, 161–166, 183, 215, 221
Ruth, George, Sr. 161
Ruth, Kate 161
Ryan, Mike 181
Ryan, Nolan 76

Sabathia, C.C. 10
Sanchez, Anibal 9
Santa Maria, Michael 30, 217, 219, 221
Santiago, Jose 91, 204
Sayles, John 176, 219
Schilling, Curt 1, 9, 10, 35, 44, 47, 61, 67, 81, 107, 113, 124, 150
Schiraldi, Calvin 17
Schoendienst, Red 103
Scioscia, Mike 133, 136
Scott, Deacon 163, 164, 213
Scott, Everett 96, 219, 221
Scott, George "Boomer" 30, 103, 164, 165, 176, 204, 213
Sele, Aaron 74
Sevada, Packy 46
Severeid, Hank 96
Sewell, Luke 210
Sewell, Rip 199
Shanks, Howard 119
Shatzkin, Mike 217–220, 223
Sheffield, Gary 130
Sheperd, Bert 119
Sheriden, Jack 53
Shields, James 140
Shore, Ernie 59, 60, 69, 165–167, 215
Shorten Chuck 163
Showalter, Buck 173
Simon, Tom 178, 217–219, 223
Simpson, Dick 91
Skipper, Doug 55, 223
Slack, Bill 81
Slaton, Jim 145
Slaughter, Enos "Country" 37, 54, 55, 85, 144
Smith Sherry 87
Smith, Frank 137
Smith, George 5
Smith, Lee 172
Smith, Ozzie 164
Smith, Reggie 21, 30, 102, 119, 167, 168, 203, 213, 221, 222
Snider, Duke 148

Snodgrass, Fred 49, 68, 169, 171, 206
Somers, Charles 1
Southwick, David 220, 223
Speaker, Tris 1, 20, 27, 69, 83, 92, 100, 168, 169, 202, 206, 213, 219, 222, 223
Spence, Stan 210
Spoljaric, Paul 190
Springer, Mel 218, 223
Stafford, Bill 127
Stahl, Chick 27, 169, 170, 213, 219, 222
Stahl, Jake 22, 27, 68, 81, 96, 101, 170, 171, 192, 206, 213
Stallard, Tracy 127
Stanley, Bob 17, 70, 171, 172, 215
Stanley, Mike 78, 172, 173, 213
Stapleton, Dave 17
Stargell, Willie 143
Steadman, John F. 95, 218, 223
Steinbrenner, George 180
Stengel, Casey 40, 119, 138, 197, 210
Stephens, Gene 73, 173, 174, 213
Stephens, Vern 44, 144, 146, 174, 175, 213, 221
Stottlemyre, Mel 64, 102
Stratton, Monty 90
Stuart, Dick 80, 91, 175, 176, 213, 219
Stynes, Chris 79
Sullivan, Frank 36, 176, 177, 215
Sullivan, George 219
Suzuki, Ichiro 114

Tabor, Jim 177, 178, 213
Tanner, Chuck 141
Tatum, Ken 76
Tavarez, Julian 11
Taylor, John I. 42, 137, 201
Tebbetts, Birdie 93, 178, 179, 213, 223
Tessreau, Jeff 206
Thomas, Gorman 24
Thomase, John 219, 220, 223
Thorn, John 223
Tiant, Luis, Jr. 49, 91, 179, 180, 205, 215
Tiant, Luis, Sr. 179
Tillman, Bill 127, 181, 213
Tillotson, Thad 64
Timlin, Mike 182, 183, 215, 219, 221
Todt, Phil 183, 184, 213
Tolan, Bobby 21
Torre, Joe 9–11, 113, 124, 130, 131, 151, 157, 182, 186, 190
Torrealba, Yorvit 107
Torrez, Mike 184, 215
Tovar, Cesar 103
Tsiotis, Nick 4, 223
Tuck, Gary 130
Tudor, John 45

Umphlett, Tom 89
Urbina, Ugueth 105

Vaccaro, Frank 219, 223
Valentin, John 125, 157, 184–186, 213, 219, 221
Varitek, Jason 44, 79, 105, 107, 124, 186–188, 213, 219, 220, 223
Vaughn, Hippo 92
Vaughn, Mo 185, 188–190, 213
Veach, Bobby 57, 97, 163
Veeck, Bill 6
Velarde, Randy 79
Versalles, Zorro 122
Viciedo, Dayan 99
Vizquel, Omar 5, 74
Vosmik, Joe 31, 125, 190, 191, 214

Waddell, Rube 209
Wagner, Hal 41, 178, 214
Wagner, Heinie 137, 191, 192, 220, 221
Wagner, Honus 53, 137, 208
Wakefield, Tim 74, 104, 120, 123, 124, 190, 192–194, 215
Walker, Dixie 125
Walker, Harry "The Hat" 37, 144
Walsh, Ed 100
Waner, Paul 155
Wang, Chien-Ming 10
Warstler, Rabbit 195
Wasdin, John 66
Waterman, Ty 218, 223
Weaver, Jeff 128
Webb, Earl 90, 194, 214, 220–222
Welch, Bob 126
Welch, Frank 118
Werber, Billy 52, 63, 117, 124, 142, 194, 195, 214, 217–220, 223
Wertz, Vic 73, 122, 195, 196, 214
Wheat, Zack 87
White, Sammy 127, 196, 197, 214
Whitehill, Earl 125
Williams, Dick 5, 34, 91, 92, 102, 127, 167, 181, 204
Williams, Jimy 35, 36, 74, 78, 80, 100, 104, 112, 128, 129, 131, 173, 186, 187, 190, 193
Williams, Ted 1, 12, 16, 31, 36–38, 40, 41, 44, 73, 75, 85, 89, 119, 144, 156, 160, 173, 174, 177, 178, 197–200, 202, 203, 210, 214, 218, 223
Wills, Maury 15
Wilson, Earl 101, 181, 200, 201, 215
Wilson, Mookie 70
Wiltse, Hal 159
Wise, Rick 180, 205
Witt, Mike 24
Witt, Whitey 118
Wolff, Miles 222
Wood, "Smoky Joe" 1, 27, 49, 59,

68, 96, 101, 166, 169, 192, 201, 202, 215
Worthington, Al 103
Wright, Glenn 155
Wyatt, Hugh 217, 223
Wyatt, John 102
Wyatt, Whitlow 89
Wynn, Early 122

Yastrzemski, Carl, Jr. 1, 19, 50, 75, 102, 103, 119, 154, 156, 165, 180, 184, 202–205, 214, 220, 221, 223
Yastrzemski, Carl, Sr. 203
Yastrzemski, Hattie 203
Yawkey, Tom A. 50, 156, 161
Yerkes, Steve 68, 169, 205, 206, 214
York, Rudy 41, 85, 178
Youkilis, Kevin 9, 150, 206, 207, 214, 220, 222
Young, Cy 1, 24, 25, 32, 53, 103, 168, 207–210, 215, 220, 221, 223

Zabilis, Andy 4
Zarilla, Al 38, 210, 214
Zauchin, Norm 3
Zeller, Jack 85
Zimmer, Don 3, 50, 96, 113, 143, 172, 184, 205
Zingg, Paul 218, 223

www.ingramcontent.com/pod-product-compliance
Lightning Source LLC
Chambersburg PA
CBHW081552300426
44116CB00015B/2848